Unlawful Occupation

Informal Settlements and Urban Policy in South Africa and Brazil

Marie Huchzermeyer

Africa World Press, Inc.

P.O. Box 1892
Trenton, NJ 08607

P.O. Box 48
Asmara, ERITREA

Africa World Press, Inc.

P.O. Box 1892
Trenton, NJ 08607

P.O. Box 48
Asmara, ERITREA

First Printing 2004

Cover Design: Madonna Davidoff
Book Design: Charlene Bate

Library of Congress Cataloging-in-Publication Data

Huchzermeyer, Marie.
Unlawful occupation : informal settlements and urban policy in South Africa and Brazil / Marie Huchzermeyer.
p. cm.
Includes bibliographical references.
ISBN 1-59221-210-7 (cloth) — ISBN 1-59221-211-5 (pbk.)
1. Squatter settlements—South Africa. 2. Squatter settlements—Government policy—South Africa. 3. Squatter settlements—Brazil. 4. Squatter settlements—Government policy—Brazil. I. Title.

HD7287.96.S68H86 2004
307.3'36—dc22

2004009627

Contents

Part Three

Preface and Acknowledgements

Informal settlements, countless shacks, their residents unlawfully occupying seemingly worthless land – this has become a familiar scene in the South African urban and peri-urban landscape. Many studies have tried to understand this phenomenon and some have asked how it should be dealt with: eviction, demolition, relocation, or legalisation and integration? This book is based on the realisation that these questions have not been researched and debated sufficiently over the past decade. In South Africa, the focus has been the on the delivery of an impressive number of newly laid-out housing developments on the urban periphery, to which informal settlement residents tended to be relocated.

Until early 2003, it appeared unlikely that the national Department of Housing would shift from its mainstream policy of target driven housing delivery. However, Bridget Mbandla, the third Minister of Housing, raised the need for a human rights response to informal settlements in her short term in office which lasted until the third democratic elections in April 2004 (when she was made Minister of Justice). In the spirit of a new term of government, her successor Minister Lindiwe Sisulu (previously Minister of Intelligence) announced that a significant shift in policy was imminent. Minister Sisulu was responding to new commitments made by President Mbeki at the beginning of the ANC's third term in government: to address the persistence of a housing backlog, manifested in part in the constantly growing number of informal settlements; to take bold steps toward closing the gap between the formal and the informal economies; to increase service delivery; and to eradicate poverty.

The development of the new policy has proceeded under enormous time pressure and largely behind closed doors. As a team appointed to undertake background research for a policy to support informal settlements, my colleagues and I were granted the opportunity to be involved in this process. The government task team, which included provincial and municipal officials, debated our proposals and revealed a wide range of interpretations. It was evident that the debate on a suitable policy response to informal settlements had only just begun.

In order for informal settlement upgrading to work outside of the deeply entrenched capital subsidy framework, a fundamental change in mindset will be required across all sectors. This includes the so-called 'class of beneficiaries', which, over the past ten years, had to passively accept governments' housing delivery as an entitlement. While a debate is beginning within the government, a parallel debate is emerging within civil society. The newly formed Coalition of the Urban Poor has brought together various social movements to address the land and housing challenges of the urban poor.

This book had to be updated several times during the publication process. Although it addresses the emerging change in policy, it mainly engages the treatment of informal settlements during the first decade of democracy in South Africa, from 1994 to 2004. By offering a reflection on this period and how it evolved, through a comparison with Brazil, this book hopes to support the new policy's direction and contribute to the debate and change in mindset that has to accompany its implementation. In the hope that the new policy will be periodically evaluated and refined, and shaped in time by civil society, this book encourages a wider paradigm shift inspired by the progressive policy practiced in the cities of Brazil.

On the Brazilian side, the book has also been updated. The victory of the Workers' Party candidate Lula da Silva in the Brazilian federal elections in October 2002 created new prospects for the advancement of social inclusion, particularly in the scaling up of the regularisation of informal settlements. Again, the book does not go beyond acknowledging the spirit of recent change. Instead, it contends that Brazil and South Africa continue to provide challenging material for further comparative studies.

This is by no means the first initiative to recognise the relevance of the Brazilian experience in informal settlement intervention for South Africa. Its origins lie in a Water Research Commission funded project (K5/786) in the Department of Civil Engineering at the University of Cape Town under the leadership of Professor John Abbott, which I was invited to join in 1996. The objective of the project was to transfer a GIS-based approach to informal settlement upgrading from Belo Horizonte in Brazil to South Africa. I am particularly grateful to Professor John Abbott and Ivo Imparato (then from the Settlement Upgrading Programme of UNCHS [Habitat], now Cities Alliance Regional Advisor for Latin America and the Caribbean) for enabling and guiding my initial access to international debates, and for enabling my fieldtrip to Brazil in 1997. My research, which began on this project, led to a PhD in 1999 in the Department of Sociology, University of Cape Town, under the supportive supervision of Dr Owen Crankshaw (from that Department) and Dr Alain Durand-Lasserve (Laboratoire Sociétés en Développement dans l'Espace et le Temps [SEDET] Centre National de la Recherche Scientifique (CNRS)-Université Paris VII). I had the opportunity to deepen and up-date the study through a fellowship at South Bank University in London in 2000, and was able to visit Brazil twice from my new base in the Postgraduate Housing Programme, School of Architecture and Planning, University of the Witwatersrand, once in July/August 2002, and again in November 2003 with a group of our postgraduate students.

Political and legal developments in Brazil between 1997 and 2003, through which the efforts at socio-legal inclusion of the informal settlement population have been advanced significantly, call for an ongoing process of learning from Brazil. The intensity with which Brazilians network, research, debate and campaign on the question of informal settlements is in contrast with the concern that this book addresses, namely the stagnation of thinking on the informal settlement intervention in South Africa that characterised the first decade of democracy. I'm grateful to the Brazilians that have put up with my questions – they are acknowledged in many endnotes to the text. Contact with many relevant Brazilians was enabled through Dr Edesio Fernandes, formerly Director of the Programme to Support Sustainable Land Regularisation in the newly created Ministry of Cities in Brasilia and currently consultant to the Ministry. He coordinates a Brazilian as well as a Latin American network on land regularisation. In South Africa, I am indebted to those that introduced me to, and enabled my access to, the case study settlements: People's Dialogue (in particular Joel Bolnik) for Piesang River and Kanana; Mzwandile Made for Gunguluza; and Steven Poullouras for Weiler's Farm.

This book would not have been possible without the financial assistance of the Water Research Commission (South Africa), the Division of Building Technology of the Council for Scientific and Industrial Research (South Africa), the Centre for Science Development (HSRC, South Africa), the Centre International des Etudiantes et Stagiaires, CIES (France), the Research Office of the University of the Witwatersrand, the City of Johannesburg and the Gauteng Province Department of Housing, at different stages of the research and travels. Opinions expressed in this work, or conclusions arrived at, are those of the author and are not to be attributed to these organisations.

Through the publishing process, I am indebted to Angela Ajayi and Kassahun Checole of Africa World Press, to Stuart Douglas of Boltupright for rigorous editing, and to Charlene Bate for the design and typesetting.

Lastly, I need to acknowledge that parts of the following publications overlap with portions of this book: Huchzermeyer, M. 2001. 'Consent and contradiction: Scholarly responses to the capital subsidy model for informal settlement intervention in South Africa'. *Urban Forum* 21(1):71–106; Huchzermeyer, M. 2001. 'Legalising rights to occupied land: Impediments in the housing process at Weiler's Farm, Johannesburg'. *Trialog*, 69:6–11; Huchzermeyer, M. 2002. 'Production and intervention in twentieth-century Brazil and South Africa'. *Latin American Perspectives*, 29(1):83–105; Huchzermeyer, M. 2002. 'Upgrading through the project-linked capital subsidy: implications for the strategies of informal settlement residents and their community organisations'. *Urban Forum*, 13(2):67–85.

Johannesburg
28 June 2004

List of Figures

Acronymns

ANC	African National Congress (South Africa)
AVSI	*Associazione Voluntari per il Servizio Internazionale* – Association for Voluntary International Service (Italian NGO in Brazil)
BESG	Built Environment Support Group (South Africa)
BLA	Black Local Authority (South Africa)
BNH	*Banco Nacional da Habitação* – National Housing Bank (Brazil)
CAD	computer-aided design
CBO	community-based organisation
CDC	Community Development Council (Sri Lanka)
CDP	*Conselho Democrático Popular* – Popular Democratic Council (Brazil)
CEB	*Comunidade Eclesial de Base* – Ecclesiastic Base Community (Brazil)
CEPAR	Center for Studies, Research Assessment and Consulting on Urban Reform and Citizenship
CUBES	Centre for Urban and Built Environment Studies (South Africa)
DAG	Development Action Group (South Africa)
DBSA	Development Bank of South Africa (South Africa)
DFR	Durban Functional Region (South Africa)
DRI	Development Research Institute (South Africa)
FNRU	*Fórum Nacional de Reforma Urbana* – National Forum for Urban Reform (Brazil)
GEAR	Growth, Employment and Redistribution Strategy (South Africa)
GIS	geographic information system
GRET	Group for Research in Technological Exchange (French NGO in Brazil)
IDT	Independent Development Trust (South Africa)
IFP	Inkatha Freedom Party (South Africa)
iSLP	Integrated Serviced Land Project (South Africa)
KTC	Kakaza Trading Company (informal settlement/site and service area in Cape Town)
LPM	Landless People's Movement (South Africa)
MST	Movimento does Sem Terra – Movement of Rural Workers without Land (Brazil)
NARCO	National Association of Residents and Civic Organisations (South Africa)

NBI	National Business Institute (South Africa)
NGO	non-governmental organisation
NLC	National Land Committee (South Africa)
ODA	Overseas Development Administration (UK)
OPP	Orangi Pilot Programme (Pakistan)
PCB	*Partido Comunista Brasileiro* – Brazilian Communist Party (Brazil)
PROFAVELA	*Programma Municipal de Regularização de Favelas* – Municipal Programme for the Regularisation of Favelas (Brazil)
PT	*Partido dos Trabalhadores* – Workers' Party (Brazil)
RDP	Reconstruction and Development Programme (South Africa)
SANCO	South African National Civic Organisation (South Africa)
SPARC	Society for the Promotion of Area Resource Centres (India)
UDF	United Democratic Front (South Africa)
UN	United Nations
UNCHS	United Nations Centre for Human Settlements
UNDP	United Nations Development Programme
UN-Habitat	United Nations Human Settlements Programme
URBEL	*Companhia Urbanizadora de Belo Horizonte* – Upgrading Company of Belo Horizonte (Brazil)
USAID	United States Agency for International Development (USA)
WSSD	World Summit on Sustainable Development

Chapter 1

Introduction

1.1 Stagnation in the development of South African informal settlement intervention?

The officially unplanned, illegal occupation of urban and peri-urban land for residential purposes is an ongoing phenomenon of South African towns and cities. Has government intervention with regards to this phenomenon changed significantly since the closing period of National Party rule in South Africa? The position in this book is that, while significant change towards more equitable access to housing has been achieved through the restructuring and budgetary allocations in the first decade of democracy, a departure did not occur from the particular informal settlement intervention approach introduced through the policy of 'orderly urbanisation', which, after the mid-1980s, replaced the 'influx control' policy that had restricted African (black) access to urban areas in South Africa.[1] The informal settlement intervention approach developed in the late apartheid years, and its continuity into the current National Housing Policy is briefly spelt out in order to introduce the concern this book sets out to address.

While ending the threat of repeated repatriation of unwanted urbanites (particularly women and children), '*orderly urbanisation*' embodied more subtle forms of restriction and control to the urban and urbanising poor (Budlender, 1990:74; Lemon and Cook, 1994:333). Its approach was to allow for 'controlled squatting' on designated land, through the 'upgrading' of invaded land or the 'orderly development' of uninhabited land (Cooper *et al.*, 1987:342). 'Home-ownership' and 'realistic standards' were to apply to these developments (*ibid.*:333), while implementation was to occur through the private sector (*ibid.*: 333, 334). In practice, this allowed for considerable ambiguity with regard to informal settlement. Thus, intervention in the late 1980s ranged from repression/demolition to attempts at upgrading (Harrison, 1992:18). However, the mainstream intervention practice was to afford selected informal settlements transit camp status until such time as a site and service project was elaborated for relocation. Only where relocation was heavily contested, were localised solutions eventually sought.[2] The primary focus was on quantifying demand and developing market-driven mechanisms for the delivery of serviced sites at scale on peripheral land.

A proposal for streamlining funding for the delivery of serviced sites within the policy framework of 'orderly urbanisation' was put forward in the late 1980s by an influential private sector initiative, the Urban Foundation. This proposal was accepted by government in 1990 through its funding commitment to the Independent Development Trust (IDT), which was set up to implement the approach developed by the Urban Foundation (Adler and Oelofse, 1996). The IDT's funding mechanism for low income development, which was intended to replace the inequitable, complex and duplicating subsidy mechanisms developed through apartheid policies, took the form of a uniform 'capital subsidy'.[3] It was allocated to a developer on behalf of the individual household, and covered the cost of a peripherally located serviced site with freehold tenure. The residents, on whose courage (and of course desperation) informal settlements had come into being, were thus reduced to subsidy beneficiaries in the externally and technically defined delivery projects.[4] Though including 'community participation' (*ibid.*:118), the predetermined project cycle and delivery product left no space for the definition of development objectives by informal settlement communities, which were relatively well organised mainly through the civic movement within the United Democratic Front's collective struggle against the oppressive apartheid state.[5] Likewise, the technocracy of the intervention approach left no trace of collective popular initiative and innovation, whether it had been in the informal layout or in land-use arrangements.

After the 1994 elections, the content of the orderly urbanisation policy,[6] with regards to urban informal settlements, was consolidated through the national housing policy into a centralised system which dispensed capital subsidies, primarily to developers, through Provincial Housing Boards. The individual once-off capital subsidy amount was increased to include the provision of a basic 'top structure' or house, usually one-roomed, though in 1998 a minimum requirement of $30m^2$ floor space was introduced. Legitimising the inadequacy of the delivered housing unit, the policy was termed 'incremental housing'. With the launch of this policy, the Housing Minister indicated the intention of government to ensure conditions that would support the improvement of such starter houses by the residents (Buchanan, 1994). Government pledged to deliver one million such incremental housing units in its first five-year term (Department of Housing, 1994:22). This target was met two years late, and by 2002, 1.4 million subsidised houses had been built. While professing a commitment to 'a development process driven from within communities' (*ibid.*:23), the policy in 1994 went no further than stating that 'Government is considering the establishment ... of [a] housing support mechanism' (*ibid.*:53).

The mainstream intervention, then, has been the relocation of residents from informal settlements and other inadequate housing conditions to large-scale private sector-driven 'greenfield'[7] development projects primarily through the project-linked subsidy, the only subsidy mechanism operational at the launch of the new housing policy in late 1994, and to date comprising 82 per cent of all subsidies released. Subsidy mechanisms that were subsequently introduced are the individual subsidy in 1995 (a demand-side subsidy for the purchase of completed houses in the market), the institutional subsidy in 1995 (for the construction of rental or cooperative housing by social housing institutions), the subsidy for the upgrading of migrant labour hostels in 1995, and the People's Housing Process in 1998 (enabling the top-structure[8] component of the project-linked subsidy to be released separately for self-construction of the house) (Huchzermeyer, 2001:312). The Implementation Manual of the Housing Subsidy Scheme, setting out the rules for intervention through the capital subsidy mechanism, acknowledges '*in situ* upgrade of existing unserviced or minimally serviced settlements' as one of the forms of residential property to which the housing subsidy facilitates access (Department of Housing, 1995:9). However, it does not elaborate any specific procedure for such *in situ* intervention, other than suggesting it be undertaken through 'project-linked subsidy applications (home ownership)' or through 'institutional subsidies'. Notably, the manual does include a separate procedure for 'hostel re-development' (*ibid.*). By late 2003, no subsidy mechanism or framework had been developed for *in situ* upgrading or regularisation of informal settlements (also see Royston, 2002).

In South Africa, then, informal settlement intervention – which in this book means intervention in officially unplanned urban or peri-urban settlements that have resulted from land invasions – has been determined by mechanisms that were designed for the market-driven (though government-subsidised) delivery of new housing units. In practice, therefore, the standardised and product-oriented nature of the housing policy has required that informal settlement residents be relocated, if not to newly developed greenfield sites, then through the orderly re-planning of the informal settlement. Realities such as existing community organisation, collective and individual ideas for improvement, and fragile livelihoods depending on the informally established land-use pattern and inter-household ties, though pointed to by responsive academics, have largely been overridden by the mandate to deliver standardised units. Subsidy-funded intervention that would sensitively respond to the informal settlement reality, and build on and strengthen, existing community organisation and localised ideas, has been difficult to implement.

The starting point of this book is a recognition that the intervention paradigm of the first decade of democracy reduced the informal settlement question to that of delivering sufficient standardised housing units, thereby obscuring important socio-economic, socio-political and socio-spatial dimensions of informal settlement, and likewise of the intervention. It must be noted that aspects of this approach were successfully challenged by a 'landmark' ruling in the Constitutional

Court in 2000. The 'Grootboom' ruling stated that the government's housing programme was not meeting the immediate needs of people such as Mrs. Grootboom and some 900 other people who had been evicted from land they had invaded and who were subsequently camping in desperate conditions on a sports field in Wallacedene, Cape Town. The ruling took issue with the government's stance that meeting the immediate needs for shelter and basic services of such people would compromise the medium- to long-term objectives of the housing programme in terms of resource allocation (*Financial Mail*, 13 October 2000). On this basis, and in response to the Constitutional right to adequate shelter, which is to be provided progressively according to the resources of the state (Republic of South Africa, 1996, see especially Section 26), the ruling prescribes that the housing programme must plan not only for the medium- to long-term delivery of housing, but also for 'the fulfilment of the immediate needs and the management of crises', ensuring that 'a significant number of desperate people in need are afforded relief, though not all of them need receive it immediately' (quoted in the *Financial Mail*, 13 October 2000). However, in the judgement, the Court does not prescribe what measures the government should take in extending the housing programme to the most needy.[9]

The Grootboom judgement is liberal, rather than radical, in its request for crisis or disaster management, i.e. temporary relief for those living in desperate or life-threatening conditions. It does not call for reform of the system of access to urban land, or intervention in the urban land market. Notably, this latter position would be an appropriate response to Sections 9 and 25 of the 1996 Constitution (Republic of South Africa, 1996), which commit the government to enable equitable access to land, and to promote equality ('the full and equal enjoyment of all rights and freedoms'). These sections give the Constitution a 'transformative' nature by rejecting 'the social and economic status quo' (de Vos, 2001:260).

The new policy mechanism that was developed in response to the Grootboom judgement is primarily a mechanism for disaster mitigation. Only after the third democratic election in April 2004 did the national Department of Housing officially begin to develop a policy mechanism for *in situ* intervention in informal settlements that will provide people with a permanent solution to their housing problem, or give people long term rights to invaded land. Thus, the Grootboom judgement, though referred to as 'the most important judgement to date in South Africa's post-apartheid legal history' (Legal Resources Centre, 2002:4), has taken four years to impact on housing policy and informal settlements in particular.[10]

Part 1 of this book examines how an understanding of the socio-economic, socio-political and socio-spatial dimensions of informal settlement has, to a varying extent, shaped international thinking on informal settlement intervention. Part 3, reviewing South African literature and practice, in turn finds that recent scholarly insights in South Africa did not impact significantly on South African informal settlement intervention, confirming instead my concern that the South African intervention paradigm trapped administrators, policy makers, community-based organisations, and to a large extent academic researchers (who failed to articulate alternatives) in a vision of a standardised housing product. A further concern of this book is the evidence it finds, in the intervention experience, of an added distortion in informal settlement intervention resulting from the increased emphasis, since the 1994 elections, on 'provision' or 'building' of 'houses' – a key element in the 'Meeting Basic Needs' component of the ANC's Reconstruction and Development Programme (RDP) (African National Congress, 1994:7). Thus the universal fixation with the dwelling, or 'top-structure', has become the main determinant of the intervention. The individualised product-oriented confines of the intervention paradigm, and its emphasis on the dwelling, have been reflected in ambiguous official terminology, which draws no clear line between informal housing (i.e. shacks or shanties) on serviced sites, in the back yards of formal housing or in settlements resulting from the invasion of land. Inevitably, this has led to confusion, particularly in the scale of the informal settlement phenomenon in South Africa, and has obscured the need for intervention specifically tailored to this phenomenon.

The limitations of the terminology used in South Africa, and the implications for the informal settlement discourse, are expanded on in Chapter 6. However, as the problem of terminology cuts to the heart of my argument throughout this book, I will briefly spell out my concern and describe the terminology I have chosen to use in this book. As mentioned above, the term 'informal settlement' is confusingly applied in official language to shack housing, be it in backyards, on serviced sites or on invaded land. Though the term 'squatting' (synonymous to my use of the term 'informal settlement') has acquired strongly negative connotations in South Africa and is generally avoided, it does remain one of the few terms unambiguously referring to the unauthorised and officially unplanned occupation of land, and is thus still applied officially in South Africa to avoid confusion. In post-1994 legislation, the term 'squatting' has been replaced with the term 'unlawful occupation'. In this book, I use the term 'informal settlement' synonymously with 'squatting', and 'unlawful occupation' to refer to this form of unplanned settlement in South Africa. However, I use the term 'squatting' only when and where it captures the official attitudes that earned it a negative connotation. When referring to unauthorised and officially unplanned settlement in Brazil, I use the term 'favela' (without italics), a popularly derived Brazilian term that has no equivalent in the technically-inspired term 'informal settlement'.

Beyond the problem of terminology, the lack of urgency officially afforded to the informal settlement question in South Africa in the first decade of democracy is further reflected in the absence of policy debates directly addressing the phenomenon. Various recent policy debates and enquiries skirted the informal settlement intervention question, an example being enquiries into urban land tenure, countering the hitherto rural bias of land reform (see Development Works, 1998). Similarly, there have been policy enquiries into options for house construction, including the involvement of residents through a 'People's Housing

Process' (see National Ministry of Housing, 1998). While furthering important aspects of informal settlement intervention, the housing enquiries did not have, as their primary objective, a paradigm shift. Instead, they sought to work within the current intervention framework of the once-off capital subsidy system, therefore remaining confined to the paradigm of individualised, standardised and product-oriented intervention.

An important moment was reached with the closure of the first decade of ANC rule in South Africa. Ten-year policy reviews were being undertaken in all sectors. In the housing arena, they pointed to a level of dissatisfaction with the quality of housing that has been delivered since 1994. The national Department of Housing announced a delivery shift from quantity to quality, which would mark the next decade. However, it was only after the national election in April 2004, that the Department announced a major shift in its treatment of informal settlements. While much of the existing framework will be taken into the next decade, officials and practitioners are now challenged to move beyond this framework in dealing with informal settlements.

1.2 Confronting the South African intervention paradigm

This book explores new ways of approaching the informal settlement intervention question in South Africa, drawing on international debates and practice and on the particular informal settlement scenario in Brazil, where a responsive informal settlement intervention approach has been developed and practised, particularly in municipalities with strong Workers' Party (*Partido dos Trabalhadores* – PT) mandates. This provides a valuable contrast to the South African informal settlement intervention paradigm. Both the progressive Brazilian approach and the broader international approaches to informal settlement intervention[11] have evolved from a technocratic, externally defined and market-driven paradigm towards positions that, to a varying extent, acknowledge informal settlement as a social process. However, it must be noted that the technocratic approach continues to be practised by conservative elements, both in Brazil and internationally, through bilateral and multi-lateral agencies. With regards to the international positions, liberal academic enquiries since the 1960s, and in particular the urban poverty debate of the 1990s, have contributed to this partial shift. The development of the progressive[12] approach in Brazil in turn is largely attributed to a struggle of the organised working class civil society (including the informal settlement or favela movement), which has shaped the particular mandate of the PT and its associated scholars and practitioners. The decentralisation of administrative and policy-making powers of government in Brazil with the 1988 Constitution has allowed for the development of institutional arrangements for the implementation of responsive informal settlement intervention approaches in the small number of municipalities that the PT controls.

Recognising, on the one hand, the validity of treating informal settlement as a people-managed social process, and on the other hand, the important political dimension to informal settlement intervention, this book draws attention to the mind shift needed to develop space for more responsive and progressive intervention in South Africa. In order to do this, the book penetrates the intervention coalface in South Africa through a number of case studies that examine the interface between initiatives of organised informal settlement communities and the rigid intervention framework, thereby revealing the absurdities of the intervention practice of the first decade. Through its various components, this book exposes a strong neo-liberal agenda that was driving informal settlement intervention in South Africa, and related to this, shallow and largely unsubstantiated market-driven arguments in support of the intervention paradigm, obscured by people-centred rhetoric. An examination of the evolution of intervention paradigms, both internationally and in Brazil (contrasted with the evolution of the neo-liberal paradigm in South Africa), enables this study to realistically engage with the development of an intervention paradigm in South Africa that builds on informal settlement as a social and political process.

1.3 Some theoretical considerations on the question of informal settlement intervention

Enquiries into the question of informal settlement intervention have traditionally fallen into either the Marxist or the liberal framework, although common uncertainties associated with a rapidly changing globalising future appear to have more recently reduced the paradigmatic divides between scholars.[13] The question here, is how these paradigms relate to the topic of this book. Both the liberal and Marxist frameworks have contributed to an understanding of the informal settlement question. Concerned primarily with the contradictions in the capitalist mode of production, the Marxist framework has enabled an understanding of informal settlements as a manifestation of social exploitation by the dominant capitalist class. Marxist studies have focused on the socio-political rather than physical dimension of informal settlement, emphasising the role of informal settlement mobilisation as a means to incite fundamental societal change that would bring an end to capitalist exploitation. From the perspective of this framework, the alleviation of physical conditions within informal settlements (through measures such as infrastructural upgrading) is critiqued in its perpetuation of the status quo, and more strategically in its potential for quietening protest.[14] The liberal framework, in turn, implicitly accepts the capitalist continuum and its inherent exploitation, which leads to the ongoing formation of new informal settlements. Its studies on informal settlement intervention have sought not to fundamentally challenge the structure of society, but to reduce the consequences of exploitation in the reproductive sphere. Scholars working within this framework have enabled a better understanding of the coping mechanisms through which informal settlement residents survive on their minimal share in the economy. In the 1960s, such enquiries led social researchers to conclude that conventional 'squatter removal' and re-housing were doing more damage than good in the absence of meaningful economic upliftment of the beneficiaries. They suggested, instead, approaches that would build on processes already existing within informal settlements. This included dwellers' involvement in an approach broadly termed 'self-help'.[15]

Neither of these frameworks, however, informed the informal settlement paradigm in South Africa. Indeed, internationally, mainstream informal settlement intervention since the 1970s has been driven not by Marxist or liberal insights, but by a separate framework that is 'market-driven', or 'neo-liberal'. It discards the relevance of the Marxist perspective, but has adopted liberal ideas, though submitting them to overriding economic policies of structural adjustment, privatisation and the reduction of the role of the state.[16] The responsive 'self-help' approach developed by scholars such as Turner in the 1960s and early 1970s was thus reduced into technocratically defined 'sites-and-services' and 'upgrading' approaches, leaving little space for social processes. Largely associated with the World Bank, this neo-liberal framework, then, was the reference point in the development of the intervention paradigm in the first decade of democracy in South Africa.[17] Chapter 2 of this book examines the World Bank paradigm in greater detail, tracing its shifts in relation to critiques from the liberal and Marxist frameworks, and more recent critiques from cross-paradigmatic debates such as that on urban poverty in the early 1990s. The absence, largely, of such critiques in South Africa, and therefore of any significant scholarly pressure for shifts in informal settlement intervention in this country, gives some explanation of the current distorted intervention paradigm in South Africa that persisted up to 2004.

Further explanation of the distortion in the South African intervention paradigm is derived from a comparison of the evolution of the South African paradigm with that of a particular informal settlement intervention paradigm in Brazil, which, as mentioned earlier, is associated with the Workers' Party (PT). This diverges significantly from the neo-liberal paradigm in South Africa, drawing instead on the Marxist paradigm by emphasising the importance of social movements in achieving societal change. However, it does not discard the relevance of physical intervention in informal settlements. Its informal settlement intervention approach, and the institutional framework within which it is based, was developed, not from the ideas of liberal scholars such as Turner, but from the demands of the organised favela communities, whose autonomy is supported within the PT framework (see Abers, 1996). The position in this book is that the PT framework is of relevance to the South African informal settlement situation. However, its tenets are incompatible with the broader neo-liberal policy and associated regulatory framework in South Africa, which, with regards to the practical aspects of informal settlement intervention, has largely remained unreformed since the closing period of National Party rule. The finding of progressive Brazilian scholars that even within Brazil, the PT approaches cannot be implemented without 'a degree of critical consciousness on the part of both the local state and of the civil society' (Souza, personal communication, 1999),[18] then also applies to South Africa. By exposing the intervention paradigm in South Africa, in contrast to paradigms that more consciously engage with the question of informal settlement, this book seeks to arouse a critical awareness in South Africa of the need to support a paradigm shift.

1.4 On comparing informal settlement intervention in South Africa and Brazil

The cross-national comparison in this book, between the development of divergent informal settlement intervention paradigms in South Africa and Brazil (Part 2), is embedded in an understanding of the development of influential international positions on informal settlement intervention (Part 1). This in turn informs a closer examination of the micro-level informal settlement intervention situation in South Africa through literature and case studies (Part 3). The central question in the comparative section of this book, then, is why a restrictive informal settlement intervention approach is maintained, relatively unquestioned, in a democratised South Africa. Such an understanding is necessary in order to define what chances there are, realistically, of departing from the dominant framework. The comparative perspective of the contrasting situation in Brazil provides a useful tool to further this question. As Ribeiro (1994:65) argues, comparing Brazil and South Africa 'within an approach that is sensitive to both similarities and differences, may cast new and interesting light on internal processes of both societies, making their special traits stand out'. He adds that by looking at the other, 'we may be better able to look at ourselves and discover what we are all about' (*ibid.*). The purpose of the comparison in this book is to cast light on the 'special traits' of the South African informal settlement intervention situation, at the same time opening for consideration innovative alternatives from Brazil, though not separating these from the political context and consciousness that enabled them to be developed and consolidated. For one 'special trait' of the current South African situation, which is evident from the outset, is that while a policy shift is occurring in 2004, there may not be mainstream political interest in, nor bureaucratic support for, such progressive innovation. The conclusion, therefore, may not simply be that innovation be transferred from Brazil to South Africa. More importantly it needs to raise key questions which have to be seriously confronted by those hoping to further more democratic informal settlement intervention in South Africa. Such questioning might not necessarily come from within government. As Sitas (1998:49) has argued in conclusion to a discussion of the political transition in South Africa: 'Without a constant challenge from below, poverty, inequality and powerlessness will continue into the 21st century'.

The comparative approach in this book is tailored to the country of comparison, Brazil, and the parallels and contrasts it offers in relation to South Africa for furthering of the South African informal settlement intervention question. The broad parallels in socio-political process (nationally, throughout the 20th century), despite fundamental differences, justify pursual of the comparison. However, it is the contrasts in recent informal settlement intervention in the two countries that triggers interest in a comparison. An exploration of these contrasts through the broad parallels then exposes those 'special traits' in the South African and Brazilian societies that have conditioned the diverging informal settlement intervention.

A primary contrast between South Africa and Brazil is the diversity in informal settlement intervention in the latter, compared to the uniform intervention across South Africa. The range of informal settlement intervention across Brazilian cities from the capital-intensive demolition and replacement by high rise low-income housing blocks (Cingapura Programme of the centre-right administration of São Paulo – see Figure 1), to community managed improvement programmes (e.g., upgrading in the PT municipality of Diadema), is indicative of decentralised policy-making in Brazil. In addition, capital intensive comprehensive upgrading of selected settlements is guided and co-funded (through loans or grants) by bilateral or multilateral agencies (Guarapiranga Programme in São Paulo (see Figure 2), Alvorada Programme in Belo Horizonte, Novos Alagados programme in Salvador Bahia, Favela-Bairro Programme in Rio de Janeiro) adding a further level to the intervention debate and practice. With the exception of the Cingapura Programme of São Paulo (introduced in 1993), the tendency has been towards the recognition of informal settlements, and their improvement through a technical, social and legal intervention termed '*urbanização de favela*'.[19] This term should not be confused with the English term 'urbanisation', which refers to the difference in population growth in the city as opposed to the rural hinterland (see Hardoy and Satterthwaite, 1989). '*Urbanização de favelas*', instead, would translate into South African English as '*in situ* upgrading of informal settlements'. However, in Brazil, *urbanização de favelas* encompasses more than the often narrowly technical and standardised interpretation of '*in situ* upgrading' in South Africa. In Brazil it entails land regularisation, the extension of infrastructure (both with minimal disruption to the existing urban fabric), and social integration through the provision of educational and health facilities and social programmes – intervention of such multi-sectoral nature will only now begin to be piloted in South Africa. While many challenges, particularly legal, are yet to be resolved in relation to *urbanização de favelas* in Brazil (Fernandes, 1998), the intervention question there has progressed towards tailoring cross-sectoral interventions to the informal settlement reality.

It is, however, not only the intervention debates and practices in Brazil that differ from those in South Africa. The informal settlement process, from shack settlement (or shantytown) to the building of permanent structures, from borrowing or pirating of services to the formal reticulation of infrastructure networks, from illegal occupation to individual rights to irregularly laid out plots,

Figure 1: Cingapura Programme: the favela on the left side of the street has been replaced by low cost apartment blocks (Bairro São Luis, São Paulo).

Figure 2: Guarapiranga Programme: upgrading of Favela Dionísio (São Paulo).

Figure 3: Informal housing consolidation on steep slopes (Favela Fim de Semana, São Paulo).

Figure 4: Informal housing consolidation (Favela Monte Azul, São Paulo).

presents a further contrast to that in South Africa. In Brazilian cities this process has taken its course in a considerable number of informal settlements, even in São Paulo. In most instances, permanent dwelling construction does not await the formal extension of the service and infrastructure networks and the property cadaster. Thus the Brazilian term 'favela', first coined, popularly, in Rio de Janeiro around the turn of the last century[20] and since adopted into official language, has

Figure 5: Shack settlement under temporary legal status since 1985 (Bloekombos, Cape Town).

Figure 6: Shack numbering indicating temporary right to occupation (Bloekombos, Cape Town).

come to represent a brick and concrete jungle on steep slopes in the cities (see Figures 3 and 4),[21] although the term is also applied to recent, more peripherally located and less consolidated informal settlements.[22] When services and property cadasters are extended into favelas, such intervention takes consideration of the intricate pattern of land-use, circulation and permanent building that is informally established.

In South Africa, in contrast, informal settlements have remained as unserviced shantytowns or shack settlements (see Figures 5 and 6), often under the ambiguous status of 'transit camps' until replaced by (or removed to) formally laid out and standardised townships (see Figures 7 and 8).

Figure 7: Standardised housing delivery: capital subsidy housing (Delft South, Cape Town)

Figure 8: Housing options: capital subsidy units (Delft South, Cape Town).

The inflexibility of the South African intervention framework, as becomes evident in the discussion of the case studies in Chapter 7, has prohibited and effectively discouraged the construction of formal dwellings prior to the standardisation of the layout. This process neither took account, nor left any trace, of popular initiative.

I now turn to the broad societal parallels that enable a socio-political comparison around the contrasts spelt out above – they span historic, political and economic dimensions. Such parallels have been pointed out, for instance, by Lawrence (1994), who seeks 'contours' relevant to a comparison between the ANC in South Africa and the PT in Brazil. Many of these apply equally to a comparison of informal settlement intervention in the two countries. In broad terms, then, there are parallels in the succession of dominant politics and associated economies in the two countries. Colonial structures and values endured well into the 20th century, supporting the interests of key exports (coffee in Brazil, as opposed to gold and diamonds in South Africa) through which the economies 'experienced massive growth' (Lawrence, 1994:92). Coffee dominated Brazil's exports from 1901, reaching 53 per cent of the world's coffee (Burns, 1970:216). In South Africa, the discovery of diamonds had 'revolutionary' economic implications (Webb, 1983:171), with a 'shift in economic geography' in the second half of the 19th century from the coast to the interior (Lester *et al.*, 2000:97). However, it was the production of gold 'that was to prove far more significant than diamonds in transforming the economy' (Omer-Cooper, 1994:126). From 1917 to 1938, gold dominated South Africa's exports with an average of 60 per cent of total exports, peaking at 72 per cent by 1939 (Lumby, 1983:217). Diamond exports had peaked in 1925 with 13.2 per cent of total exports (1983:219).

In both Brazil and South Africa, these economies generated regional disparities and social inequalities. Enclaves of privilege, forming part of the global market, developed in vast disparity to the 'impoverished rural or semi-rural peripheries' (Lawrence, 1994:92). In Brazil, economic power was concentrated in the 'coffee triangle': São Paulo, Minas Gerais and Rio de Janeiro (Burns, 1970:220). The South African economy is dominated by the Gauteng Province, in which Johannesburg is located (Lester *et al.*, 2000:237). 'Gauteng' refers to the word 'gold' in the Nothern Sotho and Tswana languages (Reader's Digest, 1991).

In both Brazil and South Africa, industrialisation took place relatively late. Requiring adjustment in government priorities, it challenged some of the conservative structures. However, in both countries, attempts at liberalisation (in Brazil this included early upgrading of urban informal settlements) triggered an authoritarian period of extreme repression, replicating and sharpening social inequalities. Lawrence (1994) identifies, on the one hand, parallels in the politics and tactics of the National Party government in South Africa and the military dictatorship in Brazil, particularly in the central role of the military in government and, linked to this, the repression of political opposition. On the other hand, he parallels the partial democratisation of South Africa in the 1940s up to the switch to National Party rule and apartheid policies, and of Brazil's populist period from 1946 up to the take-over by the repressive military in 1964. In both countries this early democratisation was limited by restrictions on the political franchise. Literacy, as a voters' qualification criteria, was maintained in Brazil up to the late 1970s, achieving (as argued by Lawrence, 1994:93) a similar exclusion of the rural and urban working class population as did the withholding of the vote from the African (black) population, maintained until the early 1990s in South Africa (*ibid.*).

Importantly, the mid-1970s signalled change in both countries,[23] setting in motion a protracted process of democratisation, drawn out by periods of state ambiguity with particular implications for the informal settlement situation. In both countries popular resistance broke out in the mid 1970s, 'leading to the rise of radical mass-based movements from the eighties to the present' (Lawrence, 1994:93). Of particular relevance to the question of informal settlement intervention was community mobilisation around self-determined development objectives. In Brazil this included the organised demand for legalisation and upgrading of informal settlements. Parallels also lie in the responses to the popular development objectives, from repression to patronage and clientelism. In both Brazil and South Africa, the mass-based movements of the 1980s have become players in the democratisation, or 'redemocratisation' as it is termed for Brazil (for instance by Souza, 1997:181). However, in both countries the privileged elite has maintained considerable power – in Brazil through a gradual process of democratisation (Diniz, 1988:9; Sader and Silverstein, 1991:20), in South Africa through a negotiated process (see Bond, 2000; Marais, 1998). More recently in Brazil, the victory of Luís Inácio Lula da Silva's (popularly referred to as 'Lula', the presidential candidate of the PT) in the October 2002 federal election is seen as a further step in the consolidation of democracy in the country. In comparing this to the ANC victory of 1994, it must be noted that the accumulation of administrative and policy-making experience by the PT in various municipalities and states (or provinces) over more than a decade gives the party a more experienced and therefore matured entry into national government than the ANC in South Africa in 1994 (Rolnik, personal communication).[24]

Bond (2000), in the title of his book, refers to the change into post-apartheid South Africa as an 'elite transition', in which the neo-liberal policy GEAR (Growth, Employment and Redistribution) was able to replace the ANC's progressive RDP (Reconstruction and Development Programme) only two years after the ANC was elected into power. Bond (*ibid.*) dedicates a chapter to the process through which neo-liberal thinking on housing managed to displace the progressive concepts and approaches that had emerged during the socio-political struggle for shelter during apartheid. It is hoped that the PT in Brazil is better prepared to effectively reduce the power of elites (including their technocratic allies), who are interested in maintaining the status quo.

The research for this book preceded Lula's victory in the national elections. While I may make reference to policy developments in the newly created Ministry of Cities in Brazilia, the book cannot claim to fully acknowledge current efforts by the federal government at tackling the informal settlement intervention process to scale. However, the new developments at the level of federal government are an extension of the paradigm that was developed and tested by the PT at municipal and state level, and which I discuss in this book. It is the current engagement of the national Ministry of Cities with social movements in the policy-making process that requires a substantial study in itself.

It is interesting to note that as the first decade of post-apartheid democracy closed, South Africa and Brazil were seeking bilateral agreements on trade as well as social development. The South African Department of Housing, beginning to recognise the need for a more differentiated policy response to informal settlements, visited the Brazilian Ministry of Cities in October 2003. Bilateral discussions on informal settlement policy come at a time when the Brazilian Ministry is starting to develop a housing subsidy system, and is concerned not to incorporate the weaknesses of the South African scheme. This book may contribute to a clearer understanding on both sides.

Returning to the comparison, according to per capita gross national products[25] both Brazil and South Africa are ranked as middle-income countries, comparable with Chile, Venezuela, Poland, Thailand and Malaysia (Ministry of the Office of the President: RDP, 1995). Because of the vast economic disparities that developed and were maintained through uneven development throughout the 20th century, reference to average per capita income is of course meaningless without reference to the actual distribution of wealth. According to the Gini coefficient,[26] Brazil and South Africa display the highest degrees of inequality among middle-income countries. The top 10 per cent of the population receive almost half of the national income, leaving a large proportion of the population with little or no wealth (UNCHS (Habitat), 1996). While illiteracy rates for the two countries are similar (14.7 per cent for Brazil and 14.9 per cent for South Africa, projected for the year 2000 in the *United Nations Statistical Yearbook*), life expectancy in Brazil is one decade higher than in South Africa (on average 55 for South Africa and 67 for Brazil (United Nations, 1999)).

Given high levels of urbanisation in Brazil (the United Nations Statistical Yearbook projects that 81 per cent of the Brazilian population will be living in urban areas in the year 2000) and a high rate of urbanisation in South Africa (from 48.8 per cent in 1990 to 50.4 per cent in 2000 (UNCHS (Habitat), 1996), with an expected increase to 68.6 per cent in 2025 (UNCHS (Habitat), 1996)), the population living in poverty is increasingly concentrated in cities.[27] With an income distribution policy[28] that excludes increasing numbers from legal access to formal housing, the urban housing stock has come to reflect severe income disparity. In Brazilian cities the poor have found residence in slums or dilapidated inner-city tenements, in illegal subdivisions on the urban periphery, and in favelas. In South African cities, the equivalent accommodation has been in overcrowded migrant workers' hostels, in overcrowded and dilapidated township housing, and in squatter/informal settlements. Among these forms of illegal and semi-legal residence, informal settlements or favelas most visibly draw attention to poverty. In Brazilian cities such as São Paulo and Belo Horizonte, approximately 20 per cent of the population are housed in favelas (Taschner, 1997), with higher figures for the poorer cities in the north (Maricato, 2000). For South African cities such as Cape Town, the figure for squatter/informal settlements is estimated at around 10 per cent, though growing steadily (Abbott and Douglas, 1999).

The broad parallels then allow for a thematic and periodised exploration of the processes that have resulted in such a divergence in current informal settlement intervention across the two countries. It is by examining what appears similar, through the literature in and on each country, that the subtle or more blatant differences emerge, which enable the comparison to raise questions that may otherwise have remained absent from a debate on appropriate informal settlement intervention in South Africa.

How, then, does the comparison in this book relate to other Brazil-South Africa comparisons on topics associated with the informal settlements? Broadly, three comparative approaches can be identified in the relevant Brazil-South Africa literature, each with separate objectives. Firstly, the practical question of informal settlement intervention, and closely related urban issues, have been addressed by South African scholars through comparisons with Brazil (for instance Abbott *et al.*, 1997;[29] Arrigone, 1987,1996; Lubisch *et al.*, 1996; Mabin, 1991, 1992). Though presenting interesting alternatives and scenarios, and engaging at varying depth in a comparison between the urban contexts, these studies have not significantly challenged the current mindset on the urban informal settlement question in South Africa. In part, this may be due to the fact that they have neither sought to gain a deep understanding of the societies from and to which lessons were to be transferred, nor have they been situated within a broader socio-political debate. A separate set of comparative studies has indeed engaged deeply with aspects of the Brazilian and South African society (for instance, Marx, 1998; Seidman, 1990a, 1990b and 1994). Though contributing to a better understanding of the two societies, they have primarily sought to further understanding on universal questions rather than to confront particular concerns about South Africa.[30] The third comparative approach is at a political level, with interest in the Brazilian PT, both in a popular form within the trade union movement in South Africa (as described by Mayekiso, 1996) and in scholarly debates (Desai and Habib, 1994; Lawrence, 1994;[31] Mayekiso, 1996). It is this popular and scholarly debate, which has engaged realistically with the divergence in socio-political context between Brazil and South Africa, that is of direct relevance to the question of my study. My position with regards to this debate, however, is that it would be enriched by engaging with the concern of informal settlement intervention, a question that has remained largely untouched by progressive debates in South Africa.

1.5 From the international to the local: some remarks on the South African case studies

The case studies of current intervention practice in South Africa, discussed in Chapter 7, are preceded by a critical examination of the framework of recent scholarly thinking on the informal settlement question in South Africa (Chapter 6). What, then, should the case studies add to our understanding of the informal settlement question in South Africa? I do not claim that the case studies rectify the omissions and biases that I identify in the South African literature on informal settlements. However, there is one very powerful bias, which I argue needs to be confronted, in order to promote a real paradigm shift in South African informal settlement intervention. It is the degree to which informal settlement organisation and leadership has been either ignored or portrayed as a problem. In Chapter 6, I ask and to some extent answer why this is so, finding that it appears to have been convenient to the intervention paradigm. My case studies in Chapter 7 then are selected specifically from settlements where organised communities have, with some success, taken the initiative of driving their development, though inevitably coming up against the inflexible product-oriented intervention framework. In tracing the development process in four such settlements, the dictates of formal development, and the degree to which these override many of the people-driven initiatives, are brought to the fore. Inevitably, the case studies also expose conflicts and contradictions related to the people-driven initiatives and their strategies. However, my finding is that in many instances such contradictions are a result of the intervention framework. The experience in the four settlements then highlights the need for the paradigm shift that finally began to occur in 2004.

Which settlements did I choose to examine? With respect to settlement development, two broad types of initiatives exist in informal settlements in South Africa. Firstly, there are those linked to the 'people-driven' development thinking of the civic movement, and secondly, those associated with the Homeless People's Federation movement (which is supported by the NGO People's Dialogue), with a somewhat different interpretation of 'people-driven' development. Two significantly different settlements were chosen from each of these categories: the case studies of Weiler's Farm[32] in Southern Johannesburg and Gunguluza in Uitenhage are related to the civic movement, while those of Piesang River in Durban and Kanana south of Johannesburg are related to the Homeless People's Federation. In each of these cases I examined, through an account of the settlement history,[33] what obstacles these settlement/community-based initiatives experienced when trying to carry through their development objectives within the development framework through which government funding is accessed and development implemented. When seen from this perspective, the intervention framework appears grossly unresponsive to the informal settlement reality, making evident the need for a search for more appropriate informal settlement intervention in South Africa. It is at this point, that the progressive innovations from Brazil, in offering an alternative that gives space to organised informal settlement communities (though not directly transferable to South Africa), make a contribution to the informal settlement intervention question in South Africa.

1.6 Exploring appropriate informal settlement intervention: a map

Broadly, this study explores the question of appropriate informal settlement intervention in South Africa from the wider international debates, to a Brazil-South Africa comparison, and then to the local level of informal settlement intervention in South Africa. In Part 1 (Chapters 2 and 3), I ask how the question of appropriate informal settlement intervention has been developed in international debates, what influential positions and approaches have emerged and how these are critiqued. My reason for examining these debates and positions is that it is then possible to measure the South African intervention paradigm against the international shifts, this bringing to the fore the stagnation in the progression of the informal settlement intervention question in South Africa since the late 1980s up to the end of the first decade of democracy. Chapter 2 examines how the international positions and debates have shifted, asking too, to what extent South Africa and Brazil contributed to, and responded to, these debates. The urban poverty debates of the early 1990s are significant in challenging the paradigm of conventional project-oriented informal settlement intervention, and in promoting alternative approaches. These alternative approaches, as well as the conventional project-oriented approach, are the subject of Chapter 3, which identifies three broad categories of informal settlement intervention that have been internationally acclaimed, and hence evaluated and debated in the literature. Core aspects of each of these categories have in some form come to be practised in South Africa and in Brazil. An initial look at how these approaches are practised in these two countries introduces particular traits associated with informal settlement intervention in the two countries. In Brazil these approaches, and in particular the alternative approaches, are embedded in local government. This has not been the case in South Africa. Instead, the centralised intervention framework until recently left little space for any departure from the standardised product it sought to deliver. It therefore required a distortion of these 'acclaimed' approaches. This distortion, I argue, has affected even the alternative approach that has been developed independently of government (through the Homeless People's Federation/People's Dialogue alliance) and in opposition to its framework.

Part 2 (Chapters 4 and 5) explores the roots of the divergence in informal settlement intervention in Brazil and South Africa. To understand this divergence, it is necessary to trace the position that informal settlements have had in both the Brazilian and the South African society, since the beginning of the 20th century. My argument is that it is the long history of control in South Africa and, almost at the opposite extreme, the largely unchecked property speculation in Brazil, that have shaped similar levels of inequality, yet diverging informal settlement processes in the two countries. Chapter 4 compares the production of informal settlements in Brazil and South Africa, through themes of division and exclusion. This exposes the extent of government control in South Africa as opposed to government negligence in Brazil, each shaping, in a particular way, the informal settlement situation. Chapter 5 in turn examines the diverging societal responses to informal settlement, discussing to what extent organised informal settlement residents themselves took part in the definition of intervention approaches. My argument is that in this process of democratisation and supposed inclusion lie the roots to the contrasting informal settlement intervention repertoires (and the underlying paradigms) of the two countries.

Part 3 (Chapters 6, 7 and 8) turns to the current situation in South Africa, asking to what extent the informal settlement intervention question was being furthered in the first ten years after 1994. Chapter 6 examines the scholarly responses to the Urban Foundation-inspired paradigm of standardised informal settlement intervention (as currently practised). It identifies, on the one hand, flaws in the arguments that support the Urban Foundation paradigm for informal settlement intervention and, on the other hand, evidence of the inappropriateness of this paradigm for informal settlement intervention. It further identifies biases in the body of literature that prevent the furtherance of alternative intervention approaches. A different, though also limited, challenge to the current informal settlement intervention framework is found in the settlement-based initiatives that are attempting to define and control their own development. These are the subject of Chapter 7, which examines the interface between organised informal settlement communities and the intervention framework. There, my finding is that an important obstacle to the self-determination of development objectives by such organised communities has been the government's once-off capital subsidy funding structure, and the regulatory and institutional arrangements that have been designed for its implementation. The final chapter then draws together the discussion across this study, consolidating the argument for a paradigm shift in informal settlement intervention in South Africa.

Notes

1 See 1986 *White Paper on Urbanisation* and the 1986 *Abolition of Influx Control Act* with its amendments to the *Prevention of Illegal Squatting Act* in Cooper *et al.* (1987).

2 For instance in the Weiler's Farm settlement in southern Johannesburg, one of the case study settlements in Chapter 7 of this book, where only a portion of the residents could be coerced into relocating to the Orange Farm sites and services project.

3 Meaning a once-off grant to an individual household.

4 Though supporters of this policy might argue the status of residents was elevated.

5 See Adler and Oelofse (1996:118) for the arguments in support of the 'well-defined product'.

6 With the exception of its original maintenance of racial segregation of residential areas (Department of Constitutional Development and Planning, 1986).

7 'Greenfield' in South Africa refers to hitherto vacant land, as opposed to land already occupied by informal settlement.

8 In the South African intervention terminology 'top-structure' refers to all above-ground elements of a building.

9 The Grootboom case and other recent judicial responses to invasions and evictions are discussed in Huchzermeyer, 2003).

10 It is interesting to note that in contrast most municipal housing programmes in Brazil include sub-programmes for 'new housing delivery', 'intervention in areas of risk' and 'regularisation and upgrading of informal settlements'.

11 Here international positions refer to those represented, for instance, in the Habitat Agenda leading from the 1996 UNCHS (Habitat) conference in Istanbul, other UN declarations, World Bank policy papers, and scholarly debates in international journals.

12 Here referring to the political and not procedural meaning of the word 'progressive'.

13 See Burgess *et al.*, (1997), bringing together various angles of 'critical analysis of contemporary neo-liberal approaches' (*ibid.*:11) including those of liberal scholars such as Turner. Oestereich (1996:61), in relation to constructive preparations to the Habitat 2 conference, welcomes that scholars have become less distracted by ideological battles.

14 See Burgess (1982a and 1985) for a review of Marxist thinking on the subject of informal settlement intervention.

15 See for instance Abrams (1966) and Turner (1968, 1976).

16 See Petras and Leiva, with Veltemeyer (1994:65), for a summary of the neo-liberal framework.

17 From the late 1970s, the Urban Foundation, funded by the South African business Sector and hence supporting primarily market interests, promoted the liberal notion of orderly urbanisation with reference to international trends, which were being promoted largely by the World Bank. Though the Urban Foundation stated that it did not accept World Bank views 'in full' (Urban Foundation, 1991:53), it is generally perceived that the Urban Foundation operated within the World Bank paradigm (see Bond, 1995:158). The continuity from the early Urban Foundation thinking on informal settlement intervention, through the policy shifts of the final years of National Party rule, to the current National Housing Policy, is traced in Chapter 5 in comparison to the evolution of a contrasting paradigm in Brazil.

18 Professor Marcelo Lopes de Souza, geographer and urban planner in the Department of Geography, Federal University of Rio de Janeiro, was commenting

(by e-mail) on the prospects of having the Brazilian concepts and innovations of urban reform applied elsewhere.

19 It should be noted, however, that even in the case of the relatively conservative Cingapura Programme, the relocation of informal settlement residents to a separate location in the city was not considered acceptable.

20 The first land invasion to be named *'favela'* was that of penniless soldiers returning to Rio de Janeiro after crushing the sectarian uprising at Canudos in the North East of Brazil. The hill above Canudos, on which the soldiers had camped, was named 'Favela', after a shrub in which it was covered. As the returning soldiers were nick-named *'favelados'*, their informal residential settlement in Rio de Janeiro was then referred to as 'favela' (Mangurian, 1997). For an account of the battle at Canudos from the *Morro de Favela* (Favela Hill), historically faithful, though presented in the form of a novel, see Uys (1986).

21 This inspired books such as Drummond's (1981) *Architectes des Favelas* (Architects of the Favelas), analysing the physical consolidation process in Rio de Janeiro's well-known *favela Rocinha.*

22 It should be noted, however, that informal settlement processes vary considerably across Brazil. Thus the invasion of swamps and shallow bays (termed *'mocambos'* in Recife) remain as *'palafitas'* or timber structures on stilts. In Salvador-Bahia a slow process of land filling occurs under each *palafita*, with masonry structures built only after the invaded plot has been 'dried' or land-filled (Machado and Cardoso, 1995). In the case of Brasilia, informal settlements are not termed 'favelas' but *'invasões'* or 'invasions' (see Aubertin, 1992:463). A more recent Brazilian term for informal settlement is *'occupação'* or 'occupation' (see Souza, 1991:66).

23 Some analysts compare a drawn out political transition in Brazil from 1974 to 1988 with a brief five year transition in South Africa from 1990 to 1994 (see, for instance, Schmitter, 1996). However, for the purpose of comparing policies on informal settlement, a political transition in South Africa, though ambiguous, clearly began in the mid-1970s. This also is the position of Seidman (1990b) in her comparison of political unionism in South Africa and Brazil. She notes that in both Brazil and South Africa 'divisions between the state and dominant classes' in the 1970s 'created an opening for labour mobilisation' (*ibid.*:3). In both countries there is a relationship between unionism and community mobilisation in that period (*ibid.*:13), which is of relevance to a comparison of the informal settlement situation.

24 Since January 2003, Dr Raquel Rolnik is the Urban Secretary of the newly created national Ministry of Cities in Brazilia. In June 2003 she contributed to a workshop in Johannesburg on Urban Fragmentation.

25 Gross national product per capita in 1995 was 2.77 for Brazil and 2.67 for South Africa (Ministry in the Office of the President: RDP, 1995).

26 The Gini coefficient measures the inequality in a country's economy, taking into account income distribution and disparities. It is based on what percentage of

national income each subdivision in society earns; 0 represents 'perfect income equality', whereas 1 represents complete inequality (Lester *et al.*, 2000:232). According to the World Bank's 1997 World Development Report, South Africa was rated at 0.58 and Brazil at 0.63, compared with an average of 0.34 for countries of the Northern Hemisphere (2000:323). In the Southern Hemisphere, South Africa and Brazil may be contrasted with Zambia and Venezuela, both rated at 0.44 (Ministry in the Office of the President: RDP, 1995, with reference to World Bank, 1994).

27 The harshest living conditions, however, will still be found in rural areas.

28 With reference to the Brazilian government's agreement to structural adjustment policies, Chossudovsky (1997:177) points out that 'poverty was not only "the result" of the reforms, it was also "an explicit condition" of the agreement with the IMF'. The same may be said of the self-imposed neo-liberal policies adopted by South African government through the GEAR (Growth Employment and Redistribution) programme in 1996. Bond (2000:51) noted that in the year of its adoption the new policy already accounted for the loss of 71,000 jobs, with worse to follow.

29 Professor John Abbot of the Department of Civil Engineering at the University of Cape Town set up an action-oriented research programme in 1996 to analyse and draw upon the experience of the GIS-supported comprehensive upgrading approach of the Alvorada Programme in Belo Horizonte, Brazil (see Abbott *et al.* 2001). Local interest exists in the approach, particularly in one informal settlement in Cape Town with which the research programme created links, and a broad agreement for *in situ* intervention has been gained from the local authority. However, various factors, including the inflexibility of the official intervention framework, have been delaying the practical piloting of the approach. The questions raised in my study were inspired, in part, by involvement in this programme in 1996 and 1997, which included a visit to a range of informal settlement intervention programmes in São Paulo, Salvador Bahia and Belo Horizonte.

30 Seidman (1990a, 1990b and 1994) uses the Brazil-South Africa comparison to address the question of labour movements in newly industrialised countries. Marx (1998), comparing Brazil, South Africa and the United States, addresses the question of mobilisation from the perspective of racial identities and its relationship to enforced segregation and, implicitly, white supremacy.

31 Desai and Habib's (1994) suggestion of such a party for South Africa triggered Lawrence's (1994) comparison of the ANC with the Brazilian PT, in turn triggering Ribeiro's (1994) useful discussion on comparative approaches.

32 Also spelt 'Weilers Farm'.

33 Loosely structured interviews were conducted with key residents in the settlement initiatives, with Ward Councillors, officials of local and/or provincial government, development consultants and other relevant informers. Interviewing took place in November and December of 1998.

Part One

Debates and Practice: An International Perspective on South African and Brazilian Informal Settlement Intervention

Chapter 2

International Thinking: From the (Neo-)Liberal-Marxist Divide to Socio-Political Pragmatism

2.1 Introduction

For the purposes of this study, international thinking on informal settlement intervention is represented by the positions and debates of influential bilateral and multi-lateral lenders and donors, and by the discourse and polemics in international journals. This chapter examines the shifts in such international thinking. The question throughout this chapter is: Where is the South African informal settlement intervention paradigm of the past decade situated in relation to the international thinking? In other words: How does international thinking help us make sense of the informal settlement intervention situation in South Africa? The chapter introduces Brazil as a useful contrast to the South African situation, touching on how the two countries have differently responded and contributed to international thinking on informal settlement intervention.

The twin approach of sites-and-services and slum upgrading[1] has come to represent mainstream informal settlement intervention, promoted internationally and practised since the early 1970s. On the one hand, this approach may be considered an important benchmark in the development of informal settlement intervention, on the other hand, its mainstreaming into technocratic project-oriented delivery has, in many countries including South Africa, been accompanied by a stagnation in the development of intervention practice. Its shortcomings have long been the subject of much international debate leading influential agencies such as the World Bank to depart, in their policy papers, from its initial project-oriented tenets. This chapter starts by tracing the shift from public housing to the twin approach of sites-and-services and informal settlement intervention, and subsequently the adjustments and shifts beyond this mainstream approach. This is paralleled by the response, since the 1970s, of Marxist scholars. Importantly, an alternative category of approaches to informal settlement intervention, which is support-based rather than project-oriented, has come to the fore in various countries and is gaining increasing recognition. While the evaluation of these support-based approaches, in comparison to the project-oriented upgrading approach, is subject of the next chapter, this chapter examines the thinking that has promoted these alternative approaches internationally. Here, an understanding of informal settlement as a social process, rather than a physical condition, presents a challenge to externally defined project-oriented physical intervention. A further translation of this understanding into concepts of urban poverty, has assisted in promoting a recognition of alternative support-based approaches. To some extent this is reflected in the initiatives surrounding the Habitat 2 Conference in 1996. The divergence in the extent to which South Africa and Brazil participated in, and responded to, such initiatives gives more perspective to the extent of stagnation in the development of informal settlement intervention in South Africa.

2.2 Western solutions: from public housing to sites-and-services and slum upgrading

Shifts in informal settlement intervention have not been unrelated to shifts in perceptions of (and attitudes to) the phenomenon of informal settlement. In this sense, the inductive research of Western scholars in the 1960s, particularly on informal settlements in Latin America, had a significant impact on international thinking on how to deal with the phenomenon of unauthorised housing on illegally occupied land. For the first time, social insight into the functioning of informal settlements was being introduced into the international development literature and into international consultancy and advisory work, influencing the positions of the World Bank, the United Nations and other international agencies (see Ward, 1982).

Unplanned or informal settlement was a phenomenon uncommon to Western cities, thus unknown to its town planners whose urban wisdom was being transferred to the developing world. In the 1950s and 1960s the Western approach of quantifying deficit and mass producing public housing, closely associated with a faith in modernisation, was being promoted internationally (Pugh, 1995; Ward, 1982). This required demolition of substandard 'informal' housing and relocation of the population to designated development sites. However, these low cost public housing projects largely failed to meet the target population's need in scale, cost and location, thus never effectively replacing informal settlements. Instead, informal settlements grew and co-existed with the failed attempts at their replacement. Little understood, and to Western town planners largely unknown, the phenomenon of informal settlement was seen as a rural intrusion into the planned city (Ward, 1982). Socially it was associated with pathologies,[2] marginalisation, and receptivity to political radicalism (*ibid.*). Throughout the 1960s and 70s, the analysis or understanding of poverty was limited largely to economic rather than social indicators, the West promoting the misconception that poverty in the developing world would be eliminated through economic growth and modernisation, of which the benefits would trickle down to the poor. Further, poverty was not associated with cities, but was understood as a characteristic of rural areas, where indeed, the majority of the developing world population was concentrated, and where the productivity level of subsistence agriculture was low (Wratten, 1995). Urbanisation, implying the transfer of labour to 'high-productivity modern industry', was seen as the solution (*ibid.*).

This, then, was the context within which Western scholars in the 1960s sought to expose the misinterpretations of urban informal settlements by closely examining their functioning. From their insights they developed ideas of housing intervention that would build on existing processes underway within the settlement.[3] The central recommendations, mainly ascribed to John Turner (see Nientied and van der Linden, 1988), were that housing should be understood not merely as a product, but as a process, therefore acknowledging human, rather than merely material values of housing. Further, it was argued that individual human needs are diverse and changing, and therefore cannot be met by standardised procedures and products – instead, choice should be enabled. This was to occur through decentralised institutions, while the role of government should be in: a) the planning and delivery of bulk infrastructure; b) the formulation of proscriptive (as opposed to prescriptive) laws, defining boundaries between actions of people and of local institutions; and c) providing access, for the users, to 'the elements of the housing process' (Nientied and van der Linden, 1988:139, 140). In summary, the argument of the school of thought associated with John Turner was for greater autonomy or dweller control in housing intervention, be it in informal settlements, or on new development sites.

Various factors led to the adoption, but also distortion, of these ideas into mainstream international thinking. The failure of economic growth to redress poverty had become evident. Thus attention was drawn, in the 1970s, to the need for poverty alleviation policies to be explicitly targeted to the poor and to directly address 'basic needs' (food, water, shelter) (Wegelin and Borgman, 1995). This replaced the former exclusive reliance on the trickle-down of economic benefits and associated economic indicators of poverty. However, new poverty alleviation strategies were focused on rural areas, where the majority of the population still lived (Wratten, 1995:19). In the urban areas, in turn, the failure of the imported public housing approach in addressing the growing problem of urban informal settlement was becoming evident to governments and to international agencies such as the United Nations and the World Bank. The liberal scholars,[4] operating in advisory capacity to these agencies, were promoting the concept of greater dweller involvement in, and control over, the development process.

Van der Linden (1986:28) acknowledges that the 'Turner-school' no doubt had a strong influence on World Bank policy. However, the ideas of the 'Turner-school' were distorted. Firstly, they were conveniently collapsed with already existing 'self-help' housing concepts used in the West, which transferred responsibilities for housing that had traditionally rested with the state, onto the poor themselves (see Harms, 1982). Secondly, the World Bank moulded the self-help approach to its own neo-liberal framework, which relied on free markets, individualism, and payment by users (rather than state subsidies). World Bank lending required cost recovery. Therefore, if housing products were to be constructed through World Bank loans, they needed to be affordable to the poor (see Pugh, 1995). Important aspects of the Turner concept, such as sophisticated roles for government, and decentralised institutions enabling choice as well as dwellers' control over the housing process (and providing access to its various components), were thus discarded. Governments of developing countries were, at the time, pressing the World Bank to extend its development loans into the housing and infrastructure sector (*ibid.*). This gave the Bank, with its entry into the housing sector in 1972, considerable leverage to enforce, at least on a project basis, a departure from public housing and an introduction of the twin approach of sites-and-services and slum upgrading.[5] Upgrading was to deal with the existing inadequate and illegal housing, infrastructure and tenure conditions, while the delivery of sites-and-services at scale was to forestall the development of new informal settlements (Nientied and van der Linden, 1988).

The influence of the World Bank over international development thinking has been substantial. Baken and van der Linden (1993:1) refer to the Bank as 'a trendsetter for development thinking,' arguing that it has been giving direction to the consultant community, which is largely dependent on funding from the World Bank, as well as the United Nations family and European Economic Community and United States governments, which all 'largely follow the example of the Bank' (*ibid.*). The World Bank's influence over developing country policies, however, has been varied. While by 1990 it had directly participated in the finance of 'some 116 sites-and-services projects and complementary slum upgrading schemes ... in some 55 countries' (Pugh, 1995:36), this has not meant that governments and bureaucracies in these countries necessarily reformed their development approaches. Menezes (1995) mentions, with particular reference to sites-and-services, that such projects were often treated as exceptions to the regulatory framework. This realisation led to later shifts in World Bank urban policy, which placed the twin approaches of sites-and-services and slum upgrading within a wider policy framework (Pugh, 1995:67).

It is therefore curious that South Africa, which was denied World Bank loans until the mid-1990s, should, in the 1980s, reform its regulatory framework to adopt some central tenets of World Bank thinking with regards to sites-and-services. Indeed, the voluntary conformity by South African policy makers to

World Bank thinking has allowed its policy advisors to pick and choose. They largely ignored the one side of the twin approach, namely 'slum upgrading'. Instead, 'in-situ upgrading' in South Africa until recently was interpreted as the replacement of informal settlements by standardised serviced sites (currently amplified by minimal housing units through a capital subsidy). As I turn to the later adjustments to World Bank policy on informal settlement intervention, it is again evident that South Africa only selectively adopted World Bank policy regarding informal settlements, shying away from many of the policy adjustments that were introduced to the Bank as a result of hindsight and critique. South African policy makers therefore also ignored the various advancements in international thinking on informal settlement intervention, beyond the bifurcated project-oriented sites-and-services and slum upgrading approach. It is to these that this chapter now turns.

2.3 Beyond sites-and-services and slum upgrading: productivity and enablement or alternative approaches?

The twin approach of sites-and-services and slum upgrading, and the project-by-project manner in which it was first promoted by the World Bank in the 1970s, came under varied criticism in the international literature. One strand of criticism identified reasons for limited effectiveness of the approach, in the hope that the World Bank and other agencies that were promoting it would take heed and make adjustments. Such concerns first found space within various initiatives of the United Nations, and the platforms they created for international discussion. Thus the 1976 Vancouver conference (Habitat 1) organised by the UNCHS (Habitat),[6] where the World Bank presented 'some preliminary results' of its informal settlement upgrading projects as a 'revolutionary turn in the handling of the squatter problem' (Oestereich, 1996:57), also allowed discussion on many aspects of self-help that were not incorporated in the World Bank's pilot projects. I will first discuss the subsequent adjustments in World Bank policies, in light of their relevance to informal settlement intervention. Then I turn to the other strand of criticism, which came from Marxist scholars, before examining how these positions bear on an understanding of post-1994 South African informal settlement intervention.

Adjustments to World Bank policies

World Bank policy shifted in the early 1980s in two broad areas. While initially the sites-and-services and slum upgrading projects were carried out as pilot projects to demonstrate the approach, it was recognised that their adoption by governments required adjustments to housing policy frameworks (Pugh, 1995). At the macro-economic level, the World Bank was following the economic policy shifts of Western countries from welfare states to more market-oriented economies (Baken and van der Linden, 1993), thus imposing 'tighter fiscal and monetary policies, deregulation in financial markets, and anti-inflationary policies' on developing countries (Pugh, 1995:66). Structural adjustment (market efficiency and a reduction in the role of government) was therefore to replace the former 'basic needs' approach. A further shift occurred in 1986 with a focus on the development and growth of the housing sector and the urban economy as 'vehicles for promoting general economic growth and productivity' (*ibid.*:67). Central to this new focus was the concept of 'enablement', meaning the provision of a financial, institutional and legislative framework, 'whereby entrepreneurship in the private sector, communities and among individuals can effectively develop the urban sector' (*ibid.*:67, 68). This new approach of the World Bank saw the need to constrain the power of politicians, bureaucrats and governments, due to their perceived narrow interests (*ibid.*) The World Bank's shifting of housing responsibilities to the private sector represented a further departure from John Turner's proposals, which saw a clear role for the public, private and community sectors, with control resting with the latter (van der Linden, 1986:29, 30).

Although this further shift in World Bank policy (1986) coincided with the formation of the Urban Management Programme (UMP), a technical support collaboration between the World Bank, the UNCHS (Habitat) and the UNDP,[7] with the aim of developing 'a common approach to urban problems' (World Bank, 1991:83), the World Bank and UN organisations to a large extent continued to develop their policies independently.[8] Thus the concept of enablement was refined and elaborated by the UNCHS (Habitat), giving governments a new role as enablers or facilitators (Vaa, 1995:192).[9] Taking heed, the World Bank accepted in the 1990s that liberalism and enablement require 'good governance, institutional reform and sophisticated roles in government' (Pugh, 1995:68).

The experience of structural adjustment of the 1980s resulted in a growing recognition of its social costs by the end of the decade. This was accompanied by a growing awareness that the spatial concentration of poverty had shifted from rural areas to towns and cities (Drakakis-Smith, 1996:692). The attention of poverty alleviation was therefore turned onto urban areas. Moser (1995a:225) refers to this new focus in poverty agenda development as 'responses to cities in crisis'. Tools of poverty analysis and intervention, which had been developed through the previous focus on rural poverty, started to be applied to urban conditions (see Mitlin and Thompson, 1995), initiating a new discourse on 'urban poverty', prominent in the international literature, and in UNCHS (Habitat) initiatives in the late 1980s and early 1990s. This new concern too was incorporated into World Bank policy in 1991.

A brief review of the 1991 policy publication of the World Bank gives context to informal settlement intervention in the 1990s.[10] Four key areas structure this policy document. Firstly, *urban productivity* is to be increased by lifting the constraints to the urban economy. These constraints are understood as minimising the urban economy's contributions to the macro-economy. Lifting the constraints includes improvements to the regulatory framework to increase market efficiency. Secondly, ***urban poverty*** is understood as being manifested in the vast informal settlements 'outside the legal framework of the city' (World Bank, 1991:9), associated with the impact of structural adjustment. Separate policy areas are assigned for economic aspects of poverty, social aspects of poverty and safety net assistance. Thirdly, ***urban environment*** as a policy area implies recognition of the link between poverty and environmental degradation. Fourthly, ***urban research*** includes research on the urban poor and the informal sector, and the government role in processes of urban development and the urban environment (*ibid.*).

A careful reading of this policy suggests that the World Bank would see informal settlements treated as manifestations of urban poverty, and not as opportunities for urban productivity, i.e. for macro-economic growth. This requires that intervention be directed at the economic and social aspects of poverty, and would include some form of safety net. Informal settlement intervention is thus taken outside of the realm of private sector delivery of sites-and-services. I will return to this position in comparison to South African informal settlement intervention of the past decade, after having discussed a second strand of criticism levelled against the influential 'self-help' approach, namely that of the Western Marxist scholars.

The Marxist position

The 1970s Marxist position on informal settlement intervention presented (though only indirectly) a separate criticism of the World Bank approach. This strand of criticism identified root causes of poverty within the structure of capitalist society. In the 1970s Marxist urban analyses by French scholars, for instance Castells (1972), were placing the informal settlement phenomenon within the conflict between dominant and subordinate classes in capitalist society. Particular interest was in the social movements that emerged out of the struggles of the exploited, under-housed populace. The eradication of exploitation required a fundamental restructuring of society, and the social movements were seen to contribute to this.[11] Burgess (1977, 1978) applied the Marxist critique more directly to the intervention concepts being promoted internationally, engaging in an academic debate with Turner, not suggesting adjustments to Turner's intervention proposals, but attacking the framework within which they are based.[12] Marxist scholars did not see it as their role to develop alternatives to the self-help approach[13] – indeed, they rejected the depoliticisation of urban demand-making, inherent in the imposition of development approaches by the West. With regards to Turner's self-help approach, Burgess (1982b:467) traces this depoliticisation back to the 'vast body of bourgeois empirical literature in Latin American urban studies'. This, he argues, has failed 'to unite in one theoretical structure, an account of the low-income settlement process for the Latin American city with the political activities of the state and the various classes centred on their provision', thus artificially separating the settlement process from its political dimensions (Burgess 1982b:466, 467). Indeed, the contradiction in Turner's thinking lies in the fact that its radical aspects, namely autonomy or dweller control, together with the necessary release of resources, require radical political support. While Turner acknowledges the need for grassroots action and radical change in power structures, he assumes there would be sufficient space for incremental changes within the plurality of government (Grose, 1979:45).

It is then precisely the radical aspects of the self-help approach, whereby the grassroots would be truly empowered, that have not been incorporated into mainstream sites-and-services and slum upgrading as promoted by the World Bank. Instead, the twin approach promoted by the Bank has remained primarily concerned with economic efficiency and cost recovery.[14] However, even *in situ* upgrading of informal settlements, as promoted by the Bank, has required some acknowledgement of *de facto* rights of land invaders, and an engagement with the complexity of unplanned environments. It is the less complex sites-and-services component of the Bank's twin approach that has found support with conservative sectors of society, particularly the construction industry, which recognises major profit-making opportunities in its mass delivery. Indeed, as will be evident in Chapter 5 (tracing policy evolution in South Africa in comparison to Brazil), the stakes of the construction industry[15]are considered a major interest behind the current informal settlement intervention approach in South Africa, which is distorted into the delivery of sites-and-services with a minimal housing structure.

While it was not the prerogative of the Western Marxists scholars to put forward alternative informal settlement intervention that would be internationally promoted, alternative approaches (though also along the lines of 'self-help') that may be broadly associated with the political left were developed in various countries, often in close collaboration with grassroots organisations and their demands.[16] More explicitly, they emerged in opposition to the conservative interests of private sector or government bureaucracies that support conventional technocratic top-down approaches. To some extent these alternative approaches have been embraced by the international literature (see for instance Denaldi, 1997; Hasan and Vaidya, 1986; Pathirana and Sheng, 1992).[17] They have been evaluated against the conventional or mainstream approach, and suggested as alternatives. Chapter 3 of this book thus examines two broad categories of informal settlement intervention, one the conventional externally defined and project-based upgrading, the other being support-based (either government-initiated or CBO/NGO-initiated). It may be observed that the political dimensions of these alternative approaches, i.e. the political space within which they were developed and implemented, and the political strategies on which they depend, are still not adequately addressed in the literature. Instead, these approaches are promoted largely through the international discourse of the 1990s on urban poverty.

The contribution of this new discourse on human vulnerability and resilience associated with the many-dimensional processes of informal settlement (to which I turn in more detail below), is that it presents a powerful argument for alternative approaches, therefore for releasing informal settlement intervention from the dictates of broader macro-economic agendas. It is of particular relevance to South Africa, where not even 'upgrading' (as the more responsive aspect of the World Bank-promoted twin approach), which might be less driven by macro-economic concerns than the mass delivery of sites-and-services, is practised. As argued before, slum upgrading has to engage to a far greater extent with the realities of informal settlement and the many associated dimensions of poverty, since it cannot easily impose ready-made solutions, as does the sites-and-services approach. Upgrading, too, due to the complexity of the environment in which it intervenes, is less easily quantifiable, therefore less attractive to the profit-driven interests of the private sector. Nevertheless, upgrading at scale may indeed provide opportunities for profit-making by the construction industry. This will be evident in the discussion of the Brazilian informal settlement intervention in contrast to that in South Africa, to which I now turn.

Situating South Africa and Brazil

Where is the South African informal settlement intervention of the past decade situated in relation to current positions? With regards to earlier World Bank policy, an obvious conformity lies in the neo-liberal framework, with housing delivery through the national housing budget intended to contribute to the macro-economy.[18] Within this framework, significant roles and opportunities have been afforded the private/profit-making sector, with mainstream intervention having been developer-driven. Thus the individualised capital subsidy, through which housing delivery (and informal settlement intervention) has been financed, may be considered not so much a safety net than a government commitment to boost the macro-economy, through the construction industry which contributes to urban productivity. Understandably, the construction industry has not been interested in implementing complex, socially responsive *in-situ* upgrading that would minimise social disruption and build on existing processes in informal settlements. Instead, the state of the art remained unchallenged for the first decade after 1994. Informal settlements continued to be replaced by standardised sites-and-services, albeit with a minimal housing structure.

This was a far cry from current World Bank policy which, as mentioned earlier, would have informal settlements treated as manifestations of urban poverty, intervention therefore being released from the broader agendas of macro-economic growth. As will be evident in Chapter 3 of this study, the project-based and externally-defined comprehensive *in situ* upgrading of informal settlements, as promoted by the World Bank within the twin approach mentioned earlier, remains product-driven, the intervention process (including community participation) being tailored to project efficiency rather than to poverty alleviation. The alternative approaches, also examined in Chapter 3, are then more in line with the current policy that the World Bank professes to have adopted for informal settlement intervention.

Brazil provides an interesting case, first as a contrast to the dominant South African informal settlement intervention, and second as an indication of the distance between current World Bank policy and the intervention for which it provides finance. As is discussed more explicitly in Chapter 5, a left-oriented sector in Brazil, in close collaboration with the organised informal settlement population, has developed an alternative approach to informal settlement intervention, in which poverty alleviation is a central concern. The few municipalities with a strong PT mandate have consolidated experience in this form of intervention. However, conservatively run municipalities, particularly the wealthy municipality of São Paulo 1993 to 2000, have made use of selective informal settlement intervention as a tool for increasing urban productivity, thus for boosting the urban economy through the construction industry. The 'Cingapura' Programme which, since its inception in 1993, demolished highly consolidated favelas and replaced them with standardised high-rise low-income blocks of flats, with a considerable boost to the construction industry, was in part financed through the World Bank/Interamerican Development Bank (José, personal communication, 1997).[19] The programme was the principal flagship in the election of the two successive mayors Maluf and Pitta (Corsalette and Lopes, 2001). A subsequent evaluation by the Interamerican Development Bank identified serious contracting problems with the Cingapura projects, and with cost recovery, as beneficiaries were expected to pay for the units over several years (*ibid.*). Non-compliance with planning regulations, particularly regarding open space requirements (Leon, 2000) and an emerging illegal market for the Cingapura flats (Jornal da Tarde, 2000) are some of the post-Cingapura challenges faced by the current administration, which has instead focused its attention on regularisation and upgrading of favelas (Corsalette and Lopes, 2001).

Another World Bank-financed programme during the Maluf and Pitta administrations of São Paulo was the Gurarapiranga Programme. This conventional project-based and product-oriented upgrading targeted 180 favelas (548,000 people) within a water catchment basin in the South of São Paulo (França, 2000; Yamazaki *et al.*, 1996). In 1997, it was already evident that resident participation had been sidelined due to the rigid time constraints associated with the civil works contracts through which the programme was being implemented (Araújo, personal communication, 1997).[20] After their completion, no funding remained for the important socio-environmental education, which had been designed to accompany the programme. Clearly, this had been less of a political priority than the awarding of lucrative construction contracts. Currently, it is feared that the omission of the socio-environmental aspects will affect the sustainability of the Guarapiranga intervention (Abiko, personal communication, 2002).[21]

The civil works-oriented approach to informal settlements, be it the replacement of informal settlement by serviced sites or by high-rise flats, or through externally defined and tertiarised upgrading projects, has clearly survived the recent shift in World Bank policy, and continues to be supported through international finance. The conservative interests it serves makes externally driven intervention a powerful approach, that would obscure rather than expose the realities of informal settlement. It is around such powerful interests that the development of informal settlement intervention has stagnated in South Africa. This leads me to ask in which way the urban poverty debate may contribute to challenging such stagnation.

2.4 Contributions of the urban poverty debate: recognising alternative intervention approaches?

While in the late 1960s and early 1970s John Turner directly inferred an intervention approach from his investigations into the housing processes in informal settlements, the informal settlement enquiries of the 1980s and 1990s have been more cautious. Primarily, they have exposed many dimensions of complexity and change, though identifying processes that appear to apply universally to informal settlements. Concepts have been developed for an understanding of the strategies by which poverty is handled in informal settlements, also enabling a conceptualisation of the social impact of intervention programmes, or other processes of change. No clear answers are provided for appropriate intervention. Indeed, the intervention principles that logically lead from urban poverty enquiry raise many unresolved questions about roles and procedures. These are diametrically opposed to the conventional intervention apparatus, including funding structures, regulatory frameworks, the decision-making structure, and roles and functions of professionals. I argue that the main contribution of the urban poverty discourse is not that of generating alternatives, but of supporting diverse initiatives that have developed in informal settlements in various countries, in opposition to conventional externally defined and product-oriented intervention. However, the political dimension, i.e. the political support and strategies on which these approaches depend, remains largely absent from the urban poverty discourse.[22] I first discuss the various dimensions of vulnerability that urban poverty enquiries have associated with informal settlement, before turning to the concepts that have crystallised, and the implications for intervention. Finally, I examine the international platforms on which the poverty discourse has found space, and to what extent South Africa and Brazil have participated and contributed.

Understanding informal settlement as a social process (vulnerability)

A first set of processes may be identified around the formation and growth of informal settlements. This phenomenon can be explained as resulting from an imbalance between the rate of urbanisation and the nature of urban development.[23] Two characteristics apply for most cities in the developing world. Firstly, formal land release and infrastructure provision are not in balance with rates of urbanisation. Secondly, the cost of authorised housing is excessive in relation to the wage structure (Amis, 1989:17). An aspect that is intrinsically tied to informal settlement formation, therefore, is a population increase in the poorest sector of the population, which is not matched by the supply of affordable housing delivery. Increase in demand in the 'poverty' sector of housing can be related, on the one hand, to economic recession, which decreases the level at which housing is affordable, thus pushing the lower middle-class into the housing sector previously occupied by the poor, and in turn displacing these into more marginal housing conditions such as sublet rooms or new peripheral informal settlements (Volbeda, 1989:158). On the other hand, economic changes trigger the migration of the poor into the city – severe rural poverty will cause movement to the cities, irrespective of the economic development in the cities themselves (Drakakis-Smith, 1996:676). The dynamics around urbanisation then comprise one set of long-term processes or changes that bear on the formation of informal settlements, and are beyond the control of the poor, therefore placing them in a position of vulnerability.

While there is a body of literature examining the social processes surrounding migration, also indirectly related to informal settlement (see for instance Amis, 1989; Beall, 1993; Gilbert, 1994; Gilbert and Gugler, 1992; Hardoy and Satterthwaite, 1989), I now turn more specifically to processes around the actual formation of informal settlement. Alsayyad (1993) identifies four processes of informal settlement formation: a) gradual, whereby individuals spontaneously seek shelter by gradually invading land, avoiding confrontation (for examples of this he draws mainly from the Middle East, but also from Latin America); b) communal, whereby the act of invasion is coordinated and collective (here he draws on examples from Venezuela; c) mobilised, whereby political parties or other agents initiate the invasion as a means of social mobilisation (examples being taken from Colombia); and d) generated, whereby invasions are endorsed officially or unofficially by the government (Alsayyad, 1993:35). However, a more important differentiation in the settlement formation process, with regards to vulnerability, may be whether or not it is linked to financial transactions.[24] Amis (1984) argues that where subsistence shelter (or access to shelter without a financial transaction) does occur, this is likely to be a transitional phenomenon, as commercialisation and political integration seem inevitable. This leads Amis to a main concern in his work on informal settlements in Kenya, namely the mechanisms of commercialisation and their implications for the poor. Amis finds a gradual change from communal to private rights to land in informal settlements in Nairobi, albeit in the absence of legal title to land – residual subsistence housing is replaced *in-situ* by rental units, the profitability of such activities lying in the high demand for accommodation (*ibid.*:89). Amis thus summarises: 'yesterday's squatter is today's tenant' (*ibid.*:90). Indeed, while very few data are available on rental markets in Africa, it is believed to be the most common form of tenure in many African countries (Tipple and Willis, 1991:128). Returning to the concept of vulnerability in the housing market, it appears common across the developing world, that sublet rooms in informal settlements rank lowest in the housing hierarchy, and are most often occupied by female-headed households, which are generally amongst the weakest competitors (Volbeda, 1989:162; Yapi-Diahou, 1995).

Insights into the functioning of housing markets in informal settlements, and the processes that surround movement in these markets, are crucial, if we are to gauge the impact or appropriateness of intervention. Vulnerability within these markets is important evidence against the often-held neo-liberal assumption that the principles of middle-income property markets apply to, or can be imposed on, informal settlements. Chapter 6, examining South African literature on informal settlements, discusses the extent to which such assumptions have driven and supported the dominant South African informal settlement intervention. Such intervention ties beneficiaries not only into fully registered freehold title, which is costly to transfer, but also into a system of rates and service charge billing.[25] Amis (1984) raises concern about the compromises households have to make when under pressure to pay high rentals. The same concern would apply to any new expenses imposed through an intervention. Amis (*ibid.*) also finds a nutritional compromise evident in child malnutrition. Thus he warns of 'a relatively well housed but malnourished population' (*ibid.*:95). Further, when the nutritional compromise does not free sufficient money to cover the cost of housing, the poorest are pushed out of the market and in turn seek subsistence shelter on the city's periphery (*ibid.*:94). A more complex interpretation of the consequences of financial pressures is through the gender-division of labour within the household. Reichenheim and Harpham (1991) find that mothers, forced to seek work outside of the home while still responsible for their own domestic work and child rearing, may be strained to the extent that their mental health is impaired. Such insights address the common assumption that 'women have plenty of time to spare for community participation' (Volbeda, 1989:160), particularly in 'participatory' intervention. The insecurities associated with financial pressures and associated threats of displacement (i.e. insecurity of tenure), are a further component that may cause mental health problems (mainly depression) among women in informal settlements (Reichenheim and Harpham, 1991).

Risk and insecurities (meaning the exposure to changes that are beyond the individual or household's control) are an important aspect of vulnerability related to informal settlement. Beyond the psychological risks already mentioned, the health and survival risks associated with inadequacies in the physical environment in informal settlements have been relatively well documented (Diaz, 1992; Fadare and Mills-Tettey, 1992; Hardoy *et al.*, 1990). They are, for instance, inadequate sanitation, contaminated standing water, poor ventilation, inadequate insulation of shelter, inflammable building material and geological instability or flooding. These obvious inadequacies indicate further dimensions of health compromises taken by those joining a land invasion or gradual expansion of an existing informal settlement.

Further dimensions of risk and insecurity play themselves out in the settlement cycle,[26] which Volbeda (1989) finds paralleled in the family cycle, seeing as it is often newly formed, young households that will compete for land in an invasion (see also Hardoy and Hardoy with Schusterman, 1991; Shakur and Madden, 1991). Important here, is the shifting between different forms of compromise, as the dimensions of vulnerability change. That intervention itself may introduce new dimensions of vulnerability is a reality which, in the standardised intervention framework of South Africa, has not been considered, nor been taken into account in project evaluations (see Chapter 6). Volbeda's (1989) observations, then, are that during the expansion stage of the family, when household demands on the women are strongest, women are most likely to stand together in a struggle for living space. Thus women's survival networks often go back to the invasion period of their life, which is followed by a stage of consolidation of family size, housing and networks. Economic recession will impact on the form and speed of physical consolidation, and will cause those unable to consolidate to be squeezed out of the owner-occupying sector in the settlement. The stage of settlement legalisation often coincides with the stage in the family cycle when financial burdens are greatest, as children require education, and are not contributing substantially to the household income. During such pressures, it is common for male heads to leave the household.[27] Female household heads, firstly, seek new economic opportunities, often at the expense of living space (rooms are sublet or home enterprises initiated), and secondly, turn to neighbourhood networks for support. New pressure arises as benefits from these networks in turn require contributions. Competition continues as adult children seek their own accommodation and the fragile elderly finally rejoin the weakest sector, requiring support from other household members (Volbeda, 1989).

A further important factor of change (and therefore vulnerability) in informal settlement, and again of particular relevance for the question of intervention, is the relationship between settlement community and the state. The degree of community organisation, on which the relationship with the state depends, is subject to various conditions. Firstly, there may be government strategies to dampen such organisation. One common strategy is 'clientelism', which Alsayyad (1993:36) defines as politicians taking 'advantage of the urgency of the needs of the urban poor to advance their own needs'. Another is the co-optation of settlement leadership through promises of personal favours or political gain, while a further strategy is repression (Gilbert, 1994:134, 135). Secondly, the informal settlement cycle bears on the level of organisation – in the initial stages of the settlement formation, and at times of threat to its continued existence, popular participation in community politics is usually high (*ibid.*). Levels of mobilisation are reduced with: a) the domestic responsibilities of daily life; b) with social stratification as temporary households (tenants) with short-term interests infiltrate the settlement; and c) with party political competition (*ibid.*). Thirdly, outside intervention in the form of paternalist charity may dampen participation by fostering mistrust (Hardoy and Hardoy, 1991). The vulnerability of the poor in relation to the state then is increased as accountable and cohesive community organisation is eroded. That such cohesion can be eroded by insensitive state intervention is clear. In South Africa, state orchestrated erosion of community cohesion (the tactic being referred to as 'divide and rule') through to the closing years of National Party government is well documented in the local literature (see Chapters 5 and 6). In Chapter 6, I argue that ongoing erosion of community cohesion through the dominant post-1994 South African intervention framework, which has still required considerable social disruption through settlement replanning, partial relocation and individualisation, has been left largely unchallenged in the South African literature. This gives particular relevance, in South Africa, to the concepts of urban poverty to which I now turn.

Urban poverty concepts and their implications for intervention

How, then, have insights of complex social processes in informal settlements been conceptualised in the urban poverty discourse so as to challenge the entrenched and persistent bias to economic rather than social analysis of poverty? One set of concepts is directed at clarifying the condition of vulnerability or insecurity. Another set is directed at resilience, or the ability of the poor to act against insecurity, rather than become its victim. Intervention, based on these concepts, would be cautious not to create new dimensions of vulnerability, instead acting to strengthen resilience. Interest in strengthening resilience, of course, implies that such intervention, though multi-dimensional, will not remove all aspects of insecurity, therefore not challenging fundamentals of the exploitative framework as such. Nevertheless, Drakakis-Smith (1996:686) argues that, for the urban poverty concerns to be taken seriously, 'fundamental questions of human rights and democracy' will have to be addressed.

Vulnerability, or the 'condition of insecurity' (World Bank, in Moser, 1997:60), is conceptualised through short-term shocks and long-term trends, both acting to increase exposure and defencelessness. Those at the receiving end of shocks and trends adjust by entering into compromises and dependencies. Amis (1995:149) defines shocks as 'short term incidents that push a previously self-sufficient household over the edge'. He finds that shock or stress events that have the greatest impact on households are illness and the loss of an income earner. Compromising responses to such events are the increase of female employment and indebtedness. He emphasises that 'shocks are the most important element of urban poverty and protecting the urban poor from such shocks is a critical policy area' (*ibid.*:156). Trends, in turn, may be long-term changes caused by policies such as structural adjustment, which affect the labour market. Other trends are related to the increasing commercialisation of urban assets, with the result that the urban poor have to purchase services and basic needs that they previously accessed free of charge (Amis, 1995:149).

Resilience, in turn, is defined as the means of 'exploiting opportunities and resisting or recovering from the negative effects of the environment' (Moser, 1995b:2). Here the concept of asset ownership at the level of individuals, households and communities represents resistance to insecurity (ibid.). Moser (1995b and 1997) lists the following assets which partly define vulnerability and partly explain responses to vulnerability: firstly, ***labour***, meaning the poor's ability to mobilise additional workforce, mainly that of women, and in severe cases that of children; secondly, ***human capital***, meaning the income earning capacity related to levels of social infrastructure, services, health, skills and education; thirdly, ***productive assets***, primarily housing, but also land, which have direct implications for a households' ability to earn an income; fourthly, ***household relations***, meaning household composition and structure, which can be changed or adjusted to reduce vulnerability; and lastly, ***social capital***, being the relationship between people in the community, through social networks, reciprocal arrangements and trust. Moser (1995b) emphasises that these assets should be analysed at the level of the individual, the household and the community.

Chambers (1995) and Amis (1995) interpret the concept of assets differently to Moser (1995b and 1997). They differentiate between tangible assets, namely stores and resources, and intangible assets, namely claims and access. These can be seen to supplement Moser's assets in determining livelihood capabilities or the ability to cope with shock. Amis notes that assets of the urban poor are more monetised than those of the rural poor, a factor that is reflected in the widespread commodification of urban housing,[28] which is referred to above as one of the long-term trends that can push households into dependency. Amis further concludes that the urban poor are less likely than the rural poor to have communal assets to fall back upon. Therefore, debt (or credit) can be a critical survival strategy of the urban poor, in coping with shocks and trends (Amis, 1995:154).

Resilience, as well as vulnerability, are further linked to the concept of entitlement, which captures the degree to which households, or individuals within households, have command over resources (Wratten, 1995:18). A difference in entitlement among individual members of a household, which may be linked to household survival strategies, means that poverty may be experienced with different intensity within the same household (Wratten, 1995).

What, then, are the implications of these social concepts of urban poverty for the intervention debate? Poverty alleviation, guided by an understanding of these concepts, will seek to understand vulnerability in relation to the local dimensions of shock and broader dimensions of trends, and the resilience inherent in the ownership of, and entitlement over, various forms of assets. It will intervene to reduce vulnerability and strengthen resilience. The danger of poverty alleviation intervention impacting negatively on multi-dimensional asset ownership applies particularly where economic indicators of poverty dominate. Housing intervention in particular has a tendency to be designed around economic factors, such as the household's assumed ability to repay. In addition, technical assessments concerning the required improvement of housing and infrastructure often justify the destruction of existing environments and with it a complexity of fragile social assets, in favour of standardised developments.

Literature of the past decade suggests a new agenda for poverty alleviation, which challenges professionals and politicians alike. Chambers (1995), a main proponent of this new agenda, identifies four broad aspects. Firstly, he argues that intervention based on the social concepts of urban poverty must be people-centred, participatory, empowering and sustainable (Chambers, 1995:200). He draws attention to measures that have low financial costs, yet 'make a big difference to the poor' (*ibid.*:201). He lists: 'Rights, security, the rule of law, information, access, changes in procedures, removals of restrictions, polite behaviour by officials, timing actions for the right season, timely delivery, providing diverse "baskets of choices"' (*ibid.*). Secondly, Chambers argues for analysis by the people themselves, and refers to the techniques of participatory rural appraisal (PRA), which are increasingly applied in an urban context (*ibid.*). Thirdly, he argues that 'every activity should be carried out as low down as feasible', this requiring 'decentralisation, democracy and diversity' (*ibid.*:202). This corresponds with Douglas's (1992:25) call for 'a mode of planning which moves away from the paternalism of societal guidance designed and carried out by the state and corporate economy toward one which emanates from processes of social mobilisation'. He adds that this requires hierarchical and non-democratic structures of government to be opened up (*ibid.*). The fourth aspect of the 'new' poverty alleviation agenda is directed at the role of professionals. Here Chambers (1995:203, 204) calls for a self-examination by professionals, for a greater awareness of their deceptions and the limitations attached to their terminology and use of concepts, as well as their relative positions of power over the destinies of the poor in the development process. He calls for greater levels of 'participatory management' in the entire range of development institutions (*ibid.*:204). This would require a move away from top-down approaches to 'interactive learning' not only at universities and colleges, but also between professionals and the poor (*ibid.*).

While Moser (1995c) emphasises the need for cross-sectoral approaches to poverty alleviation, Wegelin and Borgman (1995) extend this to local government, for which they perceive a central role in cross-sectoral coordination of poverty alleviation. Thus a further aspect of this new agenda may be associated with the functioning of local government, and its interface with poverty.

It may be noted that these concerns are neither new, nor restricted to the international development community, on whose publications I have been drawing in this section. Particularly questions around the role of professionals or 'intellectuals' in relation to the poor or 'popular class' were furthered by the progressive arm of the Catholic Church in Brazil since the late 1960s, when the appropriate relationship between pastoral agents and ecclesiastic base communities in poor urban neighbourhoods was being sought (see Mainwaring, 1984). Remaining, however, with the recent international debate on urban poverty, I now turn to the international platforms through which urban poverty concerns have been promoted, examining the different extent to which South Africa and Brazil participated and contributed.

International forums for urban poverty debates: involvement by South Africa and Brazil

The most visible international forum promoting urban poverty concerns since the late 1980s has been the UNCHS (Habitat), with numerous international declarations committing developing world governments as well as multi- and bilateral agencies to urban poverty alleviation. In 1988, the *Global Strategy for Shelter for the Year 2000* (UNCHS (Habitat), 1991) was endorsed, drawing urgent attention to the shelter needs of the urban poor. In 1992 the United Nations Conference on Environment and Urban Development (UNCED),[29] hosted in Rio de Janeiro, resulted in the *Agenda 21*, which gives support to the tenets of the Global Shelter Strategy (among other international declarations) (UNCED, 1992). Further declarations resulted from preparatory events leading to the 1996 Habitat 2 conference of UNCHS (Habitat), such as the Recife Meeting on Urban Poverty held in March 1996, attended by 35 countries. The resulting *Recife Declaration* (UNCHS (Habitat), 1996b), titled 'Urban Poverty: A World Challenge' includes, among its focus areas, the need to understand the unity and diversity of poverty, the need for new relationships with the poor in order to transform public and private action, and a central role for local government (UNCHS (Habitat), 1996b).

A more complex agenda resulted out of the Habitat II conference itself. The *Habitat Agenda* (UNCHS (Habitat), 1996c) only indirectly refers to informal settlements, focusing instead on enabling aspects such as building of local government capacity for governance and management, the reform of cadastral systems, streamlining of land registration procedures, the revision of by-laws and building and planning standards. Once addressed, these would ease informal settlement intervention as well as the release of new serviceable land and provision of affordable shelter. The twin approach of sites-and-services and slum upgrading is no longer promoted as the solution to informal settlement or urban poverty. Instead, the Habitat Agenda states 'there are no universal solutions that can be fairly applied' (UNCHS (Habitat), 1996b:7). This lines up with the Best Practice initiative (or competition) of Habitat 2, which invited developing country governments to document innovative and successful practices in areas such as poverty alleviation and shelter provision and submit these for scrutiny by a panel of experts, which would select a list qualifying for Best Practice awards to be presented at the conference. With the focus on sharing experiences, knowledge and skills, new initiatives were born out of the Habitat 2 conference, one being the International Forum on Urban Poverty (UNCHS (Habitat), 1996d). The theme of urban poverty thus remains a driving concern.

Another initiative born out of Habitat 2 is 'Cities Alliance/Cities Without Slums', launched in 1999 to support the implementation of the Habitat Agenda. Cities Alliance receives support from the World Bank and UN-Habitat, as well as grants from a number of northern hemisphere governments. As a global alliance of cities, this initiative aims to improve conditions for the urban poor by promoting: a) city development strategies; and b) city-wide and nation-wide slum upgrading (Cities Alliance, 2002). This gives support to the fulfilment of the 'Cities Without Slums Action Plan', which was endorsed by 150 heads of state at the UN Millenium in September 2000. The millennium goal of achieving by 2020 'a significant improvement in the lives of at least 100 million slum dwellers' (United Nations, 2000) was reaffirmed by the commitment of the World Summit on Sustainable Development (WSSD) in Johannesburg in September 2002, with reference to the Cities without Slums initiative (United Nations, 2002).

The divergence between participation of South Africa and Brazil in the preparations for the Habitat 2 conference and subsequent initiatives gives a useful indication of the different extent to which debates on urban concerns had matured in the two countries. This also places into context informal settlement intervention practice in each of the two countries. In South Africa, the Minister of Housing, on request by the UNCHS (Habitat), took the lead in the South African preparations for the Habitat 2 conference (von Broembsen, 1999). Meetings were convened in the various provinces and a country Action Plan submitted, as requested. No South African publication was made available on this plan[30] or the initiative as a whole. Nor did it spark much debate in civil society.

Subsequently, however, the Urban Development Framework (Department of Housing, 1997) was launched as the South African government's response to Habitat 2 (though based on the draft Urban Development Strategy that preceded Habitat 2),[31] with no reference to urban poverty concepts and poverty alleviation approaches promoted at Habitat 2. In line with conventional thinking of the

1970s, the Urban Development Framework makes reference to the pathologies of shack dwellers, stating that in informal settlements 'social disintegration, high levels of unemployment and crime are rife' (Department of Housing, 1997:5). Although the framework notes that upgrading of informal settlements is an important aspect of 'undoing the Apartheid City', there is no framework or guideline as to how this is to occur (*ibid.*:13). Surprisingly, however, in the continued absence of any programme for the improvement of living conditions in informal settlements, a study in 1999 commissioned by the Directorate of Human Settlement Policy and Integration of the Department of Housing made the finding that South African housing policy was in line with the Habitat Agenda (CSIR, 1999).[32]

Brazil, on the other hand, generated several publications, primarily leading from active responses to Habitat 2 from civil society. The documentation of 'best practices' across Brazil, irrespective of their acceptance by the Habitat 2 selection committee, was compiled into a valuable resource on Brazilian urban practice, including the wide range of Brazilian informal settlement intervention (see Bonduki, 1996). The context of the intense Brazilian response to Habitat II was the Urban Reform Movement,[33] which disagreed with the government's Action Plan (in preparation for the Habitat 2 conference). This it saw as 'a sum of sectoral policies', not reflecting the richness of the country's debate (Federação Nacional dos Arquitetos e Urbanistas, 1996:22). It therefore turned the Habitat 2 conference into 'an unique opportunity for uniting sectors of the Brazilian society around the urban and housing issues' (Maricato, 1996:10). As it had been sidelined in government's official elaboration of an Action Plan, the urban reform movement developed its own proposals, negotiating these with the government. For the purpose of developing such proposals, it united religious, popular, class and non-governmental organisations in preparation for the Brazilian Conference on Habitat, with mobilisation through the four largest urban movements (Federação Nacional dos Arquitetos e Urbanistas, 1996). The conference, focusing on the democratic management of cities, was the largest Brazilian meeting thus far regarding urban reform. Internal disputes within the urban movement were overcome by a common understanding of the political importance of the event (*ibid.*). The conference became the main topic of the local press, while international meetings brought the Brazilian discussion closer to the international debate and 'reaffirmed the maturity of the Brazilian position' (*ibid.*:22).

A further initiative (and resulting comprehensive publication – see UNCHS (Habitat), 1995), reflecting the richness in urban informal settlement intervention experience and debate in Brazil, was a preparatory seminar titled *Challenge of the Informal Town: Routes Towards the Integration of Peri-urban Settlements*, organised jointly by organisations involved in favela upgrading in Belo Horizonte, including the Italian NGO AVSI, and supported by the

UNCHS (Habitat) and the Italian government (UNCHS (Habitat), 1995). It reflects the debates on the social, legal, technological and managerial techniques that have been developed for the purposes of informal settlement intervention in Brazil. Unquestionably, then, debate on the informal settlement question in South Africa, when compared to Brazil, has indeed stagnated. Urban poverty, as a cross-sectoral concern, has yet to capture the attention of the South African government and civil society alike, and be applied to the question of informal settlement intervention. Parts 2 and 3 of this book give some explanation as to why this is the case.

More recently, the Cities Alliance has offered both countries the opportunity to engage in the promotion of slum upgrading. Cities Alliance acknowledges the innovative slum upgrading experiences that have been developed in Brazil (Cities Alliance, 2002). The Alliance is also supporting the process of developing a national slum upgrading strategy for Brazil. In cities such as Salvador Bahia, where upgrading was hitherto practised on a pilot project basis in selected settlements, Cities Alliance is supporting a city-wide approach to slum upgrading (*ibid.*). In São Paulo, Cities Alliance is supporting the new *Bairro Legal* (Legal Neighbourhood) programme, which replaces the Cingapura Programme of the previous administration. In June 2004 the Cities Alliance website (www.citiesalliance.org) lists four programmes that it funds in South Africa, none of which are slum upgrading programmes. However, one of the programmes is the preparation of a Southern African Cities Alliance, to be based in Pretoria. At the time of going to press in June 2004, a technical advisor from the new Southern African Cities Alliance was assisting the Department of Housing in developing a policy for informal settlement upgrading. While this is an important step, Brazil remains far in advance of South Africa in responding and contributing to this global programme.

2.5 Conclusion

Informal settlements may be viewed either as physical environments, deficient of basic infrastructure and services, or as complex and changing social processes that play themselves out in intricate spatial arrangements. The former view would have external agents intervene through provision of the lacking infrastructure and services, treating residents as passive recipients in technologically designed interventions. Primary concerns of intervention would be around technological efficiency. The latter view would have agencies in close alliance with the residents, intervene by communicating with and encouraging organised residents' initiatives, recognising their endeavours for improvement, acting on their demands, while also responsive to their vulnerabilities. Its central concern would be to build long-term capacity among the residents for ongoing survival and upliftment.

This chapter has examined how these opposing views and the associated approaches have been promoted internationally, discussing the role of: a) Western academics in challenging the public housing approach in the late 1960s and early 1970s by presenting alternative intervention ideas, though with little reference to the political implications (as pointed out by Marxist critiques); and b) the World Bank in distorting these ideas into externally designed and technologically driven interventions in the form of the twin approach of sites-and-services and slum upgrading. Concerns for poverty alleviation at the time focused on rural areas, leaving urban informal settlement intervention in the realm of housing and infrastructure development. Subsequent shifts in World Bank policy incorporated growing concern in the international development community over the ineffectiveness of isolated sites-and-services and slum upgrading projects, thus incorporating them into a wider review for more supportive urban policy frameworks. A further shift came with the emergence, in the late 1980s, of urban poverty concerns, with a particular emphasis on understanding (and acting upon) poverty as a process rather than a physical condition. This led to the incorporation of urban poverty concerns into World Bank policy, which now no longer views informal settlements within the technocratic framework merely as technically deficient environments, but instead within the framework of urban poverty, thus recognising the complexity of social processes and the need to intervene responsively.

While the World Bank does not discard its previous technocratic framework, still emphasising the importance of infrastructure delivery, it no longer promotes this as the solution to existing informal settlement. The Bank acknowledges that informal settlements are a manifestation of poverty, poverty in turn being associated with the adverse effects of structural adjustment. By ascribing to the concerns of the urban poverty debate in relation to informal settlements, the Bank implicitly separates informal settlement intervention from its policy component of boosting urban productivity (and thereby the macro-economy) with which it associates infrastructure delivery. Implicitly, it supports alternative intervention for informal settlements that seeks to reduce vulnerability and increase resilience. Such approaches have been developed in various countries, in alignment with the poor, and in opposition to conventionally promoted technocratic intervention, which serves the profit-making development sector. Being based on the concepts of urban poverty (though not necessarily consciously so), such intervention is diametrically opposed to the externally designed and technologically driven sites-and-services and slum upgrading projects. Thus responsive, urban poverty-oriented World Bank policy in the area of informal settlement may be regarded as mere rhetoric, responding to the intense concern over urban poverty in international platforms created by the UNCHS (Habitat). Indeed, the Bank continued to finance project-oriented and technologically- and profit-driven informal settlement intervention, for instance in São Paulo, Brazil. Nevertheless, the Bank, through the Urban Management Programme collaboration, and through the support of initiatives such as the Cities Alliance, is committed to bringing its policies closer to the thinking in the UNCHS (Habitat) and UNDP.

While such contradictions cause relatively slow change within structures such as the World Bank, the progressive sector of Brazilian society appears to be quite far ahead. Having developed an alternative approach to urban governance, and having conquered the political space (in a handful of municipalities),[34] for the institutional framework to support this approach (which includes a particular form of informal settlement intervention) it has been able to consolidate and document a poverty-oriented and democratic experience which is gaining international recognition (see, for instance, and Douglass and Friedmann, 1998; Sandercock, 1998). Informal settlement intervention in South Africa in turn stagnated around the paradigm of sites-and-services, which was imposed on informal settlements. For the first decade after 1994, there continued to be little will to depart from this simplistic framework (creating many opportunities for the profit-making development sector, which in its own interest is opposed to change) to, instead, implement the more responsive, and indeed more complex, twin approach that includes upgrading (as promoted by the World Bank since the 1970s).[35] Even less has there been awareness of the poverty concepts associated with vulnerability and resilience, and the support-based intervention approaches that would be built around these concepts. Thus, in South Africa, informal settlements continue to be conveniently perceived as technically deficient environments. While Part 2 of this study (Chapters 4 and 5) examines the development of such divergence in informal settlement intervention thinking (and experience) between South Africa and Brazil, bringing this in relation to the socio-political process in the two countries throughout the 20th century, the following chapter picks up on the conventional World Bank-promoted informal settlement upgrading approach, contrasting this with the alternative support-based approaches (from various countries) that have been acclaimed in the international literature. It refers to similar approaches in Brazil and attempts to implement such approaches in South Africa, noting however, that the latter have been distorted by the universal fixation on the housing product (a minimal house on an individual serviced plot), associated with the individual entitlement to a once-off capital subsidy and the powerful technocratic framework to which this is linked.

Notes

1 In the current UN definition, a 'slum' is a residential area that meets all of the following criteria: poor quality of built environment, inadequate access to water and sanitation, overcrowding, and insecure tenure (Badiane, 2003). This definition differs from the traditional definition of a 'slum', namely a formerly adequate residential building or neighbourhood that has deteriorated to the extent that improvement is not possible. By declaring an area a 'slum', the logical intervention

that followed was slum clearance. 'Slum upgrading' would be a contradiction in terms if this definition were to apply. Informal settlements in South Africa largely fall within the current UN definition of slums. The term 'slum upgrading' can therefore be taken to mean informal settlement upgrading.

2 Such as alcohol and drug abuse, crime and violence.

3 See Abrams (1966), Mangin (1967), Turner (1968), Turner and Fichter (1972).

4 Though the school of thought associated with scholars such as Turner and Mangin is referred to as 'the liberal approach' (Nientied and van der Linden, 1988:139), it may be noted that John Turner's ideology is that of 'limited anarchy' (Grose, 1979:64). Burgess (1982b:468), from the Marxist perspective, refers to it as 'bourgeois empirical theory'.

5 The term 'twin approach' is used, for instance, by van der Linden (1986:29). The approach of 'sites-and-services' is defined by the World Bank as: 'Government assembles the land and provides the basic infrastructure but relies on self-help for superstructure [or dwelling] construction ... [C]osts are minimised by self-help construction, and also by reducing standards (both in layouts and buildings)' (Menezes, 1995:1 – the author is an official of the World Bank). The term 'slum' usually refers to a built environment in its final decaying stage, whereas an 'informal settlement' would be an initial stage (Turan, 1987:77). However, the term 'slum upgrading' in the international intervention discourse has included intervention in what is commonly (and in this study) referred to as 'informal settlement'.

6 United Nations Centre for Human Settlements (Habitat), which in January 2002 was transformed into the United Nations Human Settlement Programme, UN-Habitat. Oestereich (1996:56) notes that around 1970 the term 'human settlements' as 'embracing urban and rural settlements' had become fashionable, while the added term 'Habitat' is believed to acknowledge awareness of the dependence of humans on the environment.

7 United Nations Development Programme.

8 UMP publications have sparked some confusion between the policies of these organisations and the UMP – see Cohen and Leitman (1994); Jones and Ward (1994); Lee (1994).

9 This was included in the Global Shelter Strategy for the Year 2000, endorsed in 1988 (UNCHS (Habitat), 1991).

10 Titled *Urban Policy and Economic Development: an Agenda for the 1990s* (World Bank, 1991).

11 See for instance Zukin (1980), reviewing 1970s writings of Marxist scholars such as Castells.

12 This debate is reviewed by Grose (1979) and Nientied and van der Linden (1988), both articles concluding that it was not a constructive debate, as each tended 'to avoid the other's central issue' (Grose, 1979:66).

13 Burgess (reviewed in Grose, 1979:55) does, however, imply that he measures Turner's approach (including security of tenure, which Burgess argues fosters indi-

vidualism), against the improvements that may be achieved through 'co-operative community organisations' and the associated collective consciousness.

14 See van der Linden (1986:30).

15 Represented, with other business sectors, by the Urban Foundation.

16 Harms (1982:20) acknowledges that self-help, when initiated by people themselves as collective self-help, can be 'a tool in the class struggle from below', potentially increasing self-determination, whereas if individualised self-help is initiated by the state, it can be 'a tool in the class struggle from above that attempts to increase integration into the existing social order and to perpetuate capitalist accumulation and domination'.

17 Note that in many cases it is non-Western researchers that submit such experience for international attention.

18 See Department of Housing (1994:26) where commitments are made for the South African housing policy to contribute to the programmes of the RDP, one being 'building the economy'. See also Jones and Datta (2000) for a comparision between the World Bank policy and the South African housing programme.

19 Maria José was working at a consultancy contracted to give social work assistance to the Cingapura Programme beneficiaries in their relocation from temporary housing (after the demolition of the favela) to the high-rise flats.

20 Ricardo Araújo was working in a consultancy firm, which had been contracted by the Municipality of São Paulo for the approval of plans of the Guarapiranga Programme. Most administrative aspects of the programme had been tertiarised.

21 Professor Alex Abiko is Head of Civil Engineering, Escola Politécnica, University of São Paulo. He has been involved in evaluating the Guarapiranga Upgrading Programme.

22 Indeed, a recent meeting of the Network-Association of European Researchers on Urbanisation in the South (N-AERUS) identified (among other concerns) the need for an increase in 'the amount of research on political issues, particularly on the relationship between urban strategies and the interests of important political actors' (N-AERUS, 1999:2).

23 'Urbanisation' meaning the difference in growth of urban population, as opposed to rural population. Such difference arises out of number of births as well as migration (Hardoy and Satterthwaite, 1989).

24 Yapi-Diahou (1995:25) refers to the commonly held 'myth of free land'.

25 Although indigent policies are realistically applied in some municipalities. One example is the Municipality of Uitenhage, where needy individuals from settlements such as Gunguluza (one of the case studies discussed in Chapter 7) may apply for temporary exemption from rates and service charge payments.

26 Alsayyad (1993) describes the settlement cycle as follows: a) land invasion; b) social formation; c) physical consolidation; and d) urban maturity.

27 Amis (1996:280) notes the same tendency in informal settlements in Kenya.

28 This finding is supported by Drakakis-Smith (1996:693) and Wratten (1995:25).

29 Though itself not an initiative of UNCHS (Habitat).

30 In a telephone enquiry with the Ministry of Housing in November 1998, no information could be obtained regarding the South African preparations for Habitat 2, nor of initiatives leading from it.

31 At a March 1999 conference van Broembsen (Director of Human Settlement Policy, National Department of Housing, Pretoria) presented the national Urban Development Framework as 'South Africa's response to the Habitat Agenda', yet made no reference to the contents of the Habitat Agenda (van Broembsen, 1999). The Urban Development Framework itself (Department of Housing, 1997), makes scant reference to the Habitat Agenda. The executive summary is introduced with a quote from Paragraph 5 of the Habitat Agenda promoting cities as 'engines of growth', and its main text includes three Habitat Agenda slogans ('adequate shelter for all', 'the development of sustainable human settlements' and 'people build cities' (*ibid.*:1)).

32 For a discussion, see Huchzermeyer (2001).

33 Souza (1999:1) explains that Brazilian Marxist intellectuals had shifted from denouncing urban planning as an instrument of capitalist interests at the expense of the poor, to accepting 'in principle the representative democratic regime', though not necessarily giving up 'their commitment to a radical transformation of society'. Thus progressive academics and town planners developed instruments of 'urban reform', as part of a national movement with the purpose of influencing the content of the 1988 constitution. While the 'front' of the Urban Reform Movement has since been transferred to municipal level, where, in accordance with the new constitution the challenges of poverty reduction have to be faced, nation-wide debates continue to take place (*ibid.*:2).

34 And in late 2002 at federal level.

35 Early in 2004, the national Department of Housing, in collaboration with the South African Cities Network (co-funded by Cities Alliance), issued a call for tenders for the development of a policy proposal for informal settlement support. In May 2004, this was paralleled by a process within the same government department to develop a policy that would enable *in situ* upgrading in informal settlements.

Chapter 3

International Practice: Imposed Comprehensive Upgrading versus Support-Based Approaches

3.1 Introduction

Leading from the debates in the previous chapter, the point of departure in this chapter is that externally imposed replacement of informal settlements by standardised sites-and-services (with or without formal house structures) in the same or another location, is not a solution to existing informal settlements. Such intervention, though heavily subsidised, is generally not conceived of in the interest of the occupants, particularly where relocation involves freeing illegally occupied land for profitable development (see Durand-Lasserve and Pajoni, 1995:25). It takes account neither of intricate spatial and social arrangements and their relationship to the livelihoods of residents, nor of the ideas of the residents, their initiatives and capacities for improvement. This chapter, then, examines those intervention approaches, acclaimed and evaluated in the international literature, that engage with the existing situation in informal settlements. As concluded in the previous chapter, two broad categories have emerged for such intervention. One is concerned primarily with technological deficiencies, thus packaging a once-off physical intervention. For the purposes of this study it is referred to as comprehensive externally designed upgrading. The other is socially or radically inspired, concerning itself primarily with the people that experience the many and changing dimensions of poverty. This I refer to as support-based intervention.[1] Extending the enquiry of the previous chapter, the question here is: What is known about these approaches, that helps us think differently about the South African informal settlement intervention situation?

In the previous chapter, I introduced the support-based category as an 'alternative' to the World Bank-promoted twin approach of sites-and-services and slum upgrading. I pointed out that these alternative support-based approaches emerged in various developing countries with socially or radically oriented practitioners seeking solutions in close alliance with the poor, and since the late 1980s have been increasingly recognised and promoted internationally through the discourse on urban poverty. It is through this focus on the complexities of urban poverty, that the comprehensive externally designed and the support-based approaches have been subjected to evaluations in the international literature, questioning not only the effectiveness of cost and technologies, but also the social processes through which the intervention occurs, and which the intervention sets into motion, these being of direct relevance to the reduction of poverty. Other concerns in the evaluations have been the impediments to mainstreaming the various approaches, in relation to the alarming scale of settlement outside of the official/legal framework. Inevitably, such evaluations examine the structure of government, its bureaucracies and frameworks.

Among these alternative support-based approaches, I differentiate between those initiated by government and those initiated by non-governmental organisations.[2] The distinction is particularly relevant to questions regarding the appropriate institutional framework. While government-initiated support-based approaches are accommodated within some form of institutional framework (that may be evaluated), the NGO-initiated support programmes often operate outside of, and in opposition to, unresponsive institutional frameworks. Both government and NGO-initiated support-based approaches respond to and encourage collective initiatives of organised communities. The government-initiated support programmes have developed bureaucratic mechanisms to channel government resources into the support of such collective initiatives, whereas the NGO-initiated approaches depend on: a) the resources of the poor; and b) external, mainly international donor funding. However, the NGO-initiated approaches mostly do work towards being appropriately institutionalised and thus towards securing government resources for community-based initiatives. The obstacle in this regard is that the particular nature of their funding requirements is largely at odds with conventional bureaucratic procedures (see Anzorena *et al.*, 1998).

This chapter examines evaluations and discussions of approaches in the three categories I have mentioned (comprehensive externally designed upgrading, and government-initiated support-based approaches and NGO-initiated support-based intervention). I present the main characteristics of each intervention category through a typical example from each. The Madras Slum Improvement Programme serves to illustrate externally designed comprehensive upgrading as promoted by the World Bank in the 1970s. Components of the Sri Lankan Million Houses Programme serve to illustrate government-initiated support-based intervention. And the Orangi Pilot Project of Pakistan in turn serves to illustrate the characteristics of NGO-initiated support-based intervention. Other cases documented in the international literature are drawn into my discussion to illustrate within each category the diversity and in part the limitations. I further make a connection, within each category, to intervention experience in South Africa and Brazil. I argue that in South Africa, all three approaches have been attempted or introduced, but have been distorted or restricted through the rigid framework of the once-off capital subsidy system. The support-based approaches in South Africa (both government- and NGO-initiated), though modelled on the international experience, have been unable to effectively address aspects of informal settlement improvement other than house construction once the settlement layout has been standardised. I substantiate this argument through the discussion of South African case studies in Chapter 7. In Brazil, in turn, experiences with informal settlement intervention in all three categories have been developed. I make reference particularly to the case of Belo Horizonte, where limitations associated with the ambitious Alvorada Programme, an externally designed comprehensive upgrading programme, have led the municipality to develop institutional mechanisms for support-based alternatives.

3.2 Externally designed comprehensive upgrading

Externally designed comprehensive upgrading seeks, within a relatively short period, to transform an illegal and substandard environment to acceptable standards through a capital-intensive intervention. As mentioned in the previous chapter, the relevance of this approach has been questioned by academics and practitioners. On the one hand, problems inherent in the approach have prevented externally designed comprehensive upgrading from achieving its own objectives. Usually introduced through pilot projects to test or demonstrate technologies and approaches, it has seldom been replicable at the broader scale (Durand-Lasserve, 1998:238). On the other hand, it does not acknowledge the social reality in informal settlements. Sirivardana and Lankatilleke (1988:7) thus state that the approach is based on an 'implicit ideology of paternalism, social control and non-reciprocity between professionals and "helpees"'.

Although the approach, as promoted by the World Bank in the 1970s in parallel to sites-and-services, has been replaced within World Bank policy by less project-oriented urban reforms, comprehensive upgrading continues to be practised in many countries and financed by international agencies such as the World Bank. Much favela upgrading in Brazil has displayed the very characteristics of the 1970s projects that piloted comprehensive upgrading, whereas in South Africa many of the deterministic elements of this approach, which to a large extent are associated with the prescribed planning and implementation procedure, have been encompassed in the post 1994 South African housing policy, although this has not promoted *in situ* upgrading as such. In this section I present the Madras Slum Improvement programme in India as a typical model of comprehensive upgrading as promoted by the World Bank, while exploring adjustments that have been made to the approach through the cases of the George upgrade in Lusaka (Zambia), and in the Alvorada Programme in Belo Horizonte (Brazil).

The comprehensive upgrading model: slum improvement, Madras India

The Madras Slum Improvement Programme initiated in 1977 illustrates the classic components and sequence of comprehensive upgrading. The aim of the World Bank in funding the programme was, firstly, to demonstrate feasibility and replicability of non-subsidised low-cost technology, and secondly, to reorient government policy in the housing sector. The programme relied on cost recovery (this comprising material, labour, contractor's profit and government overheads) from the resident households via a deposit, monthly instalments and maintenance charges (Hasan and Vaidya, 1986).

The methodology applied by the metropolitan authority responsible for the Slum Improvement Programme was as follows: Settlements were selected externally according to criteria such as location and physical condition. A cut-off date was set for household eligibility, barring newcomers from project benefits. Once identified for upgrading, the local leaders were given the task of promoting the programme, while the programme officials played the role of providers and the residents that of beneficiaries. A conventional planning and implementation approach was applied, commencing with the surveying of existing services and plots, and the enumeration of households. This formed the basis for an externally designed layout proposal presented to the residents for approval, followed by the estimation of the construction cost, official approval and formal tendering by contractors. The construction by contractors and service providers, and the signing of a lease agreement and associated payment of a deposit by the beneficiaries, preceded the formal hand-over of the project to the municipal corporation for maintenance. Accompanying the infrastructure upgrading were social programmes directed at small business development and maternal and child health care. Ongoing monitoring and evaluation remained the responsibility of the metropolitan authority (Hasan and Vaidya, 1986).

The critical evaluation of the Madras slum improvement experience by Hasan and Vaidya (1986) identifies the lack of involvement by the local community as the main factor responsible for limited success. Coupled with lack of capacity and coordination in the government departments, this has led to the deterioration of the programme's infrastructural benefits. Thus, as local level organisation was not developed, and residents were excluded from any responsibility in the upgrading process, the 'beneficiaries' expected the authorities to take full responsibility for the maintenance. As a result, then, the residents' commitment to regular payments was low. Hasan and Vaidya (1986) emphasise that, prior to the intervention, local community structures had indeed taken responsibility for a degree of maintenance and construction within the settlement, also collectively lobbying for land rights. The costs of these collective activities had been shared among the residents. Such initiative, however, had been thwarted by the Slum Improvement Programme.

The characteristics of the Slum Improvement Programme, which to date comprises the mainstream approach to *in situ* upgrading of informal settlements in many countries, are: a) external project identification; b) a project sequence starting with social and physical surveying, followed by design and cost estimation with some form of community consultation, and then conventional tendering and contractor delivery of civil works;[3] and c) delivery of formal tenure as a means to tie residents into regular payments. Variations in other examples of comprehensive upgrading, to which I now turn, have been either in the degree of involvement of the community after external project identification or in the institutional arrangements through which informal settlements are incorporated into the legal framework.

Degree of resident involvement

As the comprehensive upgrading methodology is essentially based on that of conventional infrastructure delivery[4] with the main difference being the presence of a resident population, the scope of resident involvement does not go beyond the promotion of the programme objectives.[5] Resident participation serves two purposes, the first being to narrow the gap between those responsible for the planning decisions (planning and engineering professionals) and those living in the settlement. Rakodi (1981:61, 62) thus refers to the 'flow of information' from the residents to the planners to improve the planners' technical decisions, and from the planners to the residents to convince residents of the 'rationality' and 'public interest' of the decision-making. In the Alvorada Programme (Belo Horizonte, Brazil, initiated in 1994) two innovations are applied to this end. On the one hand, detailed information gathering (requiring contact with each beneficiary household) and computerised data management have enabled design decisions to be more sensitive to the local social and physical conditions. On the other hand, the interdisciplinary professional team includes social workers as intermediaries between the programme and the residents. The social work component combines the development of community organisation (for collective resident participation), with individual beneficiary access to the project staff via a resident social worker, also providing access to socio-economic upliftment programmes (Novara, personal communication, 1997).[6]

The second purpose of resident involvement is to ease project implementation. Beneficiary involvement in construction works is mainly practised not out of the principle of resident empowerment, but where it is considered as contributing to the product-oriented project objectives.[7] This is illustrated by the partly World Bank-funded Guarapiranga upgrade programme in São Paulo, where the contractor draws a quota of labour from the resident population because this eases entry for the construction works into less accessible sections of the settlement (Araújo, personal communication, 1997).[8] In the case of the Alvorada Programme in Belo Horizonte it was said that while the employment of the local population in the construction activities is not enforced, contractors do give preference to local residents when recruiting labour. The labour recruitment agency run by the programme's social workers for the purposes of socio-economic upliftment, however, did not link up with the temporary employment opportunities generated through the upgrading works (Pinheiro and Andrade, personal communication, 1997).[9]

Clearly, there are benefits to resident participation within the continuum of comprehensive upgrading. These have been recognised and discussed in the literature. In the interesting, and much evaluated comprehensive upgrading of George settlement in Lusaka (Zambia),[10] infrastructure construction took place partly through mutual self-help. Specially trained community development workers had the role of stimulating 'a process of self-determination and self-help within the projects' through activities such as 'mutual self-help trench digging projects' (Jere, 1984:59, 61). This, coupled with a strong tradition of mutual help in the settlement, was found to have encouraged the residents to take some responsibility for ongoing maintenance of the works when it became evident that the local authority did not have the capacity to fulfil its mandate (Rakodi, 1981). Similarly, in the case of the Kampung Improvement Programme in Surabaya, Indonesia, where construction was by outside contractors, some responsibilities, such as the planting of trees, were placed with the residents. Maintenance of the trees, communal baths and toilets and the collection of garbage were later handled by the residents on an ongoing basis (Silas, 1992).

While the extent to which public participation is incorporated into development programmes depends partly on the degree to which the dominant political orientation supports participatory democracy, the structuring of external funding may be the decisive limitation to resident involvement. Both Rakodi (1981) and Jere (1984), in their evaluations of the upgrading of the George settlement in Lusaka, emphasise the need for greater flexibility in funding from organisations such as the World Bank, in order to allow for meaningful local participation. On the one hand, time schedules need to be flexible, as 'participation by residents *can* be time-consuming' (Jere, 1984:67, emphasis in the original). On the other hand, 'less detailed project planning and estimates' should be required before the signing of loan agreements (Rakodi, 1981:77). While these recommendations were made in the early 1980s and official World Bank policy has been amended since (see Chapter 2), World Bank as well as government funding in many countries in the 1990s continued to be made available under tight time schedules and with prescribed planning and implementation procedures. In South Africa, the rigidity of the IDT (Independent Development Trust) capital subsidy scheme in the early 1990s (see Chapter 5) and currently the capital subsidy system of the 'incremental' housing policy have frustrated locally defined objectives and approaches for *in situ* upgrading (see discussion on the attempted Besters Camp *in situ* upgrade, in Chapter 6). Similarly, the World Bank-funded comprehensive upgrading of numerous favelas in the Guarapiranga basin (the Guarapiranga Programme), as mentioned in the previous chapter, side-lined resident participation due to rigid time constraints imposed through the civil works programmes (Araújo, personal communication, 1997).[11]

A further limitation associated with the conventional finance mechanisms of comprehensive externally designed intervention is related to the need for a comprehensive cost estimation before finance is approved. This, with the external selection of settlements for upgrading, leads to the denial to the resident population of information on official intentions to upgrade. Thus, in the case of the state (or provincially) funded upgrading of the favela *Fim de Semana* in São Paulo,[12] residents in the densest section of the settlement were busy investing in concrete and brick improvements to their homes, while planning consultants (on their drawing boards) were identifying the very same area as particularly insalubrious, therefore proposing its removal and the relocation of the affected residents within the project area. The planning and social work consultants, wary of raising expectations, were unable to inform the residents of the planned intervention until such time as the construction costs were estimated (on the basis of their proposal) and the funding approved.[13] Rakodi mentions a similar dilemma with the George upgrade in Lusaka, where 'it was considered desirable not to raise the expectations of squatters, who had been promised upgrading on previous occasions, before the loan funds were guaranteed to be available, and so decisions on project components and mode of implementation were taken by the project planners' (Rakodi, 1981:70). Rakodi questions the value of the information on resident priorities which the planners of the George upgrade derived from secondary sources such as documented political activity by the residents, media campaigns, self-help projects and an earlier sample survey. She argues that this could not successfully replace direct consultation with the residents (*ibid.*).

It thus appears that there are significant obstacles to meaningful resident involvement within the framework of comprehensive externally designed upgrading. From the following section, it becomes evident that even where innovations have been applied to institutional arrangements for such upgrading, key aspects of the approach remain unsuccessful, this supporting the need to explore alternatives.

Institutional arrangements

In the evaluation of the Madras Slum Improvement Programme discussed earlier, the problem of lack of capacity and coordination within government was raised. I now examine two institutional responses to this and other bureaucratic demands of comprehensive upgrading, one from the George upgrade in Lusaka and one related to the Alvorada Programme in Belo Horizonte, before turning to the demands of comprehensive upgrading on regulatory and tenure frameworks.

The challenge of coordinating between the different sectors involved in the comprehensive upgrading intervention was addressed in the case of the George upgrade in Lusaka in the 1970s by creating a separate Housing Project Unit within the City Council. The purpose of this unit was to avoid 'the usual local government bureaucracy', and to enable resident participation (Jere, 1984:59). However, the hand-over of the completed projects from the Housing Project Unit to the City Council was not successful, one reason being the lack of funds for ongoing maintenance (Jere, 1984:64). As participation through the unit had not gone beyond the agendas of the project management (though I made mention above of some mutual self-help implementation), the residents had not acquired the necessary skills to take full responsibility for the maintenance of the infrastructure themselves. Both Jere (1984) and Schlyter (1981) identify this problem in their evaluations of the George upgrade, relating it, on the one hand, to the lack of resident involvement (which I referred to above) and, on the other hand, to the lack of appropriate institutional reform.

The institutional context of the Alvorada Programme in Belo Horizonte, Brazil, then, is an example of relatively far reaching institutional reform to accommodate comprehensive informal settlement upgrading. I will briefly review the steps in this reform, before turning to those institutional aspects of comprehensive upgrading in Belo Horizonte that have remained unresolved. In 1983 pressure from civil society, in association with unique political circumstances, had led to the passing of a municipal law in Belo Horizonte for the regularisation of favelas (Lei PROFAVELA – *Programa Municipal de Regularização de Favelas*), introducing a land use zoning category[14] that recognised favela residents' rights to the land they occupied (see Afonso and Azevedo, 1987; Fernandes, 1993). While the favela movement (which included the influential *Pastoral de Favelas*, an initiative of the progressive arm of the Catholic Church) set a 10 year target for the regularisation of the city's 120 favelas (Bernareggi, personal communication, 1997),[15] lack of political will, coupled with complicated bureaucratic procedures, was delaying implementation (Afonso and Azevedo, 1987). Problems experienced with the *ad hoc* titling of land had led to the adoption of integrated intervention in the form of comprehensive upgrading. This in turn required intersectoral coordination, which under the existing bureaucratic system further slowed down implementation. The favela movement responded, on the one hand, by requesting technical support from a Catholic NGO AVSI from Italy (Bernareggi, personal communication, 1997). On the other hand, it proposed the creation of a separate public body charged with the implementation of the PROFAVELA Law (Afonso and Azevedo, 1987:134). This resulted in the creation, in 1985, of URBEL (*Companhia Urbanizadora de Belo Horizonte* – Upgrading Company of Belo Horizonte).

Various circumstances then led to the elaboration of a comprehensive upgrading approach within the municipal upgrading company URBEL. While the Italian NGO was initially working in alliance with the *Pastoral de Favela* movement, the disbanding of the same in 1986[16] led to an alliance, instead, between AVSI and URBEL. Thus favela intervention was no longer controlled by organised public demand. Instead, URBEL and AVSI worked towards improving the upgrading approach, recognising major advancement in data capturing and management through the introduction of GIS (geographic information systems) technology. The victory of the PT (Workers' Party) in the 1993 municipal elections in Belo Horizonte in turn led to a political commitment to the implementation of the PROFAVELA Law. In this context, the Brazil-Italy cooperation was seen as an opportunity for piloting, in three favelas within the municipality, the GIS-supported comprehensive upgrading methodology. This took form in the Alvorada Programme (Novara, personal communication, 1997). The programme was in part funded by the Italian government (URBEL, 1996).

Based on the tenets of the PROFAVELA Law, the Alvorada Programme intervention recognises the rights of favela occupants to legalisation of their residence in the favela. Where geo-technical risks (primarily due to occupation on steep slopes) or the introduction of access routes (which double up for service reticulation) required the removal of some of the existing houses, their relocation was guided by the principles of: a) minimising social disruption by relocating affected residents within the settlement or as nearby as possible; b) involving affected residents in the decisions over the place and form of relocation; c) basing the size of the reconstructed dwelling on the size of the original dwelling (subject to minimum standards); and d) providing temporary housing in the interim (Capitanio, personal communication, 1997).[17] While sound in principle, such housing tenets comprise an ambiguous cost factor in a project-based intervention, as their expense is quantifiable only once geo-technical tests are undertaken, infrastructural designs elaborated, and decisions made over the partial relocation. A further cost ambiguity is caused by unforeseen delays in project implementation, requiring extension to the time span for which temporary housing is provided and managed (*ibid.*).

Delays in the implementation of the Alvorada programme in Belo Horizonte were a cause for concern to URBEL and to the Italian NGO. The pilot projects were intended to be completed in the three-year period from 1994 to 1997. However, in 1997 physical implementation was underway only in one of the three settlements. Several factors were associated with the delay in implementation, these leading to rethinking on the question of appropriate intervention. Besides political interference in the transfer of national funding via the State of Minas Gerais to the Municipality of Belo Horizonte (Valdares and Alvarenga, personal communication, 1997),[18] funding shortages were ascribed to unanticipated costs in the intervention. The required relocation of 10 to 15 per cent of households in order to carry through infrastructure upgrading was established only after initial budgeting (Jacinto, personal communication, 1997).[19] The latter experience again places in question the appropriateness of applying a conventional infrastructure delivery procedure or project cycle (preliminary planning and cost estimation followed by funding approval and then implementation) to informal settlement intervention that aims to be socially responsive. The cost ambiguity was then amplified by the ambitious scale of the pilot project, which sought to benefit 4,400 households (Valdares and Alvarenga, personal communication, 1997). Further, it was recognised that, in the quest for broad-based political support, there is a tendency within administrations to spread resources thinly over a large number of favelas, rather than concentrating resource allocation in a few individual settlements (Novara, personal communication, 1997). While other concerns, such as the lack of professional capacity and procedural norms, were being creatively addressed by URBEL and AVSI, who were arranging training and research through a partnership with the Pontifical (Catholic) University of Minas Gerais (Novara, personal communication, 1997), the unresolved concerns over resources had led both URBEL and AVSI to explore alternatives to comprehensive upgrading. I return to this thinking below, under government-initiated support-based approaches.

In the case of Belo Horizonte, I mentioned regulatory reform through the adoption of the PROFAVELA Law. This law, when applied to favela areas, recognises permanent but officially substandard houses and layouts, exempting them from the general planning standards and norms that regulate urban development, and replacing these with special norms issued by decree, together with the approved spatial plan (which is based, as far as is practical, on the existing land-use in the settlement) (Prefeitura Municipal de Belo Horizonte, 1985). Similarly, in the case of the George upgrade in Lusaka, Zambia, popular building standards were accommodated 'by declaring the settlements "improvement areas", in which the official Zambian building regulations do not apply' (Schlyter, 1981:51). The flexibility in land use in these areas was further maintained by issuing residents with 'a licence giving them the right to occupy the land on which their houses were standing for a period of thirty years' (*ibid.*:50). The 'absence of defined plot boundaries' enabled the continuity of the particular use of domestic space that had developed in the informal settlements of Lusaka (*ibid.*:51).

The innovative tenure arrangement in the Lusaka upgrade stands in contrast to the cumbersome conventional approach of issuing individual freehold titles to informal settlement households. Durand-Lasserve (1998:244) points out that security of tenure, from a 'conventional legal perspective' is 'achieved by the use of slow, costly and complex procedures'. It is widely held that full individual title is required, even though 'the residents of illegal settlements would prefer a simpler solution meeting their basic requirement of freedom of the fear of eviction' (Durand-Lasserve, 1998:244). Thus the decision to deliver individual freehold title in favela regularisation in Belo Horizonte in response to pressure from the favela movement, probably occurred in the absence of any viable official alternative. Fernandes (1998:5) criticises the 'lack of creativity' in formulating legalisation policies in Brazil, where 'most proposed legal solutions are still deeply conditioned by traditional ideas of individual property ownership, when the collective dynamics of life in favelas suggests different, still largely unexplored possibilities'.

The expense of formalising tenure (be it through a leasehold or freehold title) has generally been justified through the need to tie households into the system, which allows the collection of regular service payments. However, as in the case of the Madras Slum Improvement Programme mentioned above, such cost recovery has generally been low. In the case of the George upgrade in Lusaka, low payment rates are ascribed to various factors. Jere (1984:67) lists 'inadequate debt collection machinery; the inability of some residents to pay even if they wanted to; poor maintenance of services by authorities; non-delivery of certain services which had been promised; lack of continued community education and ineffective sanctions against defaulters'. Rakodi (1981:75, 76) adds further reasons for low payment, namely 'the perceived unfairness' of the payment system, the 'lack of a tradition of payment', and the contradictions between the multiple roles of politicians who were needing to secure votes, advocate 'for more efficient service provision' and collect debt. Bringing the non-payment in relation to the social concerns associated with urban poverty that I discussed in the previous chapter, Rakodi (*ibid.*:75) notes that a high proportion of the residents would have to compromise on other essential expenditure in order to make regular payments. Schlyter (1981:51) emphasises the detrimental nutritional compromises this may lead to, while Asthana (1994:69), reviewing integrated slum improvement in Visakhapatnam, India, raises concern over indebtedness of the poorest households and associated displacement and gentrification. In the case of Belo Horizonte, a different dynamic impacts on the recovery of costs from beneficiaries. Politicians, wary of losing support from the favela constituency, were resisting the enforcement of property tax payments after the expiry of the five year exemption after upgrading (as stipulated in the PROFAVELA Law, see Prefeitura Municipal de Belo Horizonte, 1985). The same non-enforcement applied to the payment of the small symbolic sum that beneficiary households were to make at hand-over of the property title. Government subsidisation in this case was not planned. Instead, it was the outcome of the political reality of clientelism (Bede, personal communication, 1997, 1999).[20]

With growing evidence of the serious shortcomings of comprehensive upgrading as practised in the cases referred to above, there is a need to consider alternatives. I have mentioned that such a reconsideration was taking place in the municipality of Belo Horizonte. I return to its contents in more detail below. At a more general level, there has been a call for the current debate to 'break with traditional urban and land upgrading which has dominated this century'.

Instead, it is suggested that the city be viewed differently, 'considering it essentially as the product of the urban society which inhabits it' (Durand-Lasserve and Tribillon, 1995:35). This challenges externally defined upgrading procedures, and the conventional institutional frameworks to which they are tied. While not condoning the urban society that produces informal settlements, the position in this study is that the alternative support-based approaches to informal settlement intervention, both government and NGO-initiated, must be considered, as they constitute a fundamental break with conventional thinking and practice. Realistically acknowledging informal settlements as products of the urban society, these approaches intervene to strengthen the societal position of their inhabitants on an ongoing basis, rather than submitting them to once-off physical upgrading through externally defined procedures.

3.3 Government-initiated support-based intervention

It is partly the direct experience of shortcomings with conventional comprehensive upgrading that has led administrations to explore alternative informal settlement intervention approaches. This has meant a departure from the conventional project cycle or procedure for a once-off physical intervention designed externally and delivered by commercial contractors. Instead, the intervention is broken into individual components that may be managed from within organised settlement communities. In this section I discuss the support-based experience of the National Housing Development Authority of Sri Lanka[21] as a model of government-initiated support-based intervention. Its particular relevance to the current intervention situation in South Africa is related to an initiative within the South African national Ministry of Housing, that has developed, and since April 2001 has tried to mainstream, a support-based housing approach as an alternative to housing delivery by commercial contractors. This initiative was advised by Lalith Lankatilleke (seconded to the South African Ministry of Housing by the UNCHS (Habitat), to set up and head the People's Housing Partnership Trust in South Africa), who had direct experience as Deputy General Manager of Urban Housing Development in the National Housing Development Authority in Sri Lanka.

The divergence between the Sri Lankan approach and that implemented to date in South Africa (the latter focusing on house construction through the capital subsidy) gives some indication of the constraints of the policy framework in South Africa. The development of Brazilian support-based approaches, and its association with left/progressive opposition politics, in turn gives insight into the political challenges related to the institutionalising of support-based intervention approaches (here I discuss innovations of the PT local administrations in São Paulo and Belo Horizonte). I pursue this theme in greater detail in Part 2 of this study, where I compare the socio-political evolution in Brazil and South Africa in relation to informal settlement intervention throughout the 20th century. My argument in doing so is that for support-based intervention to be seriously considered, the debate must be lifted above the mere merits of techniques (which is the focus of this chapter) to take into account the socio-political dimensions around which the official adoption of alternative intervention approaches hinge.

Support-based intervention through the Million Houses Programme in Sri Lanka

Within the Million Houses Programme of the Sri Lankan National Housing Development Authority, support-based intervention is divided into separate processes. The three sub-components discussed here are Community Action Planning (land regularisation and 'blocking out' or layout planning), Community Contracts (the construction of collective infrastructure) and the People's Housing Process (house construction). By separating these activities, and submitting each to a people-driven process, a break is made with the characteristics of once-off comprehensive upgrading, namely external project identification, the conventional project cycle, and the rigid procedures and time frames related to comprehensive cost estimation.

The concept of 'support' in this intervention approach is described by Sirivardana and Lankatilleke (1988:15) as covering 'a wide-ranging variety of non-dominating but facilitating processes, which assist the local bodies, communities and families in playing the deciding and doing roles'. This requires a 'non-dominating and sensitive professionalism of supporting individuals and groups ... the opposite of the traditional, packaged, all-knowing professionalism, where the bureaucrat and technocrat have all the answers' (*ibid.*:19). It also requires community development, which spans across the different components of the programme, with the formalisation of existing leadership into Community Development Councils (CDCs) that are formally recognised in the policy of the Urban Housing Sub-programme. CDCs are given general roles of organising community matters, primary health care, savings and other economic issues (*ibid.*:6), as well as specific roles in relation to the three support-based components covering layout planning, the construction of communal infrastructure and the building of houses. Institutional restructuring for this support-based or participatory approach entailed the formation of Housing and Community Development Committees at municipal level, charged with programming and monitoring. At the national level, it entailed the development of small housing loan packages, as well as guidelines and procedures for local authorities charged with implementation (Sirivardana and Lankatilleke, 1988). I now turn to the concept of support in relation to each of the three support-based components of the Sri Lankan Million Houses Programme.

Land regularisation through 'community action planning'

The support-based approach to the legal definition of land rights within the Million Houses Programme is through community action planning. This commences with the definition of planning principles and technical guidelines with the community via workshop interaction. Once it is ensured that all residents understand the agreed principles, layout planning is undertaken on the ground. This entails decision-making between neighbours over the exact positioning of boundaries, with officials giving technical assistance during this process. The physical dimensions are subsequently verified by the officials against the collectively agreed-upon layout principles, before land surveyors record measurements, place permanent boundary markers, number the plots and prepare cadastral plans for the registration of title deeds. The community-based layout planning also entails the alignment of roads, the placement of toilets and wells, the placement of refuse bins (determined by women as the direct users), the reticulation of electricity (guided by an engineer), and the placement of public buildings and open space (National Housing Development Authority, 1988).

Clearly this approach is time consuming for both residents and those officials that are directly involved. The National Housing Development Authority (1988), however, found this justified for two reasons. One, the process as a whole was found to be faster than the conventional external planning procedures. Two, residents were found to be satisfied with their direct involvement in detailed layout decision-making, an aspect that beneficiaries of comprehensive externally designed upgrading are largely denied.

Construction of collective infrastructure through 'community contracts'

The support-based approach to the construction of collective infrastructure is through the direct awarding of construction contracts to organised community groups (Community Development Councils – CDCs), thus heavily relying on trust in the ability of residents to effectively take on responsibilities that, with conventional comprehensive upgrading, are placed in the hands of commercial contractors. Indeed, it was lack of trust in commercial contractors, with a record of high profit margins and low quality of work, that led the National Housing Development Authority to opt for the awarding of construction contracts to community groups (Pathirana and Sheng, 1992).

The community contract procedure allows CDCs, jointly with the National Housing Development Authority, to identify construction projects, these being individual civil works, for instance a community facility, drain or footpath, with a limit on the maximum cost. A bill of quantities and cost estimate are drawn up for individual construction projects by the authority, who then invites the CDCs into a contract. Once this is signed, a community fund is established. After introductory training workshops the CDC is given the freedom to recruit and pay skilled labour at its own discretion. The CDC may draw labour from local residents, from outside, or may sub-contract the entire work to others. Payments are made by the National Housing Development Authority to the CDC in accordance with the phases of work, and subject to the authority's satisfaction with and approval of the work (Pathirana and Sheng, 1992).

As with the support-based approach to land regularisation or layout planning, this approach to basic infrastructure delivery was found to be faster than delivery by commercial contractors, as it excludes tender procedures. Likewise, resident satisfaction was found to be high. Indeed, the National Housing Development Authority found the majority of the work to be of good quality. Beyond time and quality, other direct benefits to residents and the authority could be identified. Residents were afforded the opportunity for temporary labour, for the development of skills and, if the contract work was profitable, for reinvestment in further collective improvements. To the authorities, in turn, it was beneficial that ongoing responsibility for the constructed facilities remained successfully with the CDC. Such responsibilities comprise the collection of money from the users, organisation of cleaning and repairs and notification of the municipality when necessary, for instance for the collection of sewerage (by truck). An important contrast then to conventional once-off upgrading intervention is that investment in community development and training through the community contracting system sets in motion a long-term process of settlement improvement (Pathirana and Sheng, 1992).

House construction through the 'People's Housing Process'

The support-based house construction approach of the National Housing Development Authority is based on the recognition that the production of the majority of housing is in the absence of government intervention, thus through a 'people's housing process' (Sirivardana and Lankatilleke, 1988). Rather than to parallel this with a government process of housing production, the decision was taken to give government support to the existing process, primarily through information and training. In contrast to the conventional top-down dissemination of educational material such as posters and pamphlets, the Housing Information Service developed practical tools to assist families with budgeting, construction and small loan repayment (*ibid.*). Self-construction to lower-than-conventional standards was legalised through a provision in the building regulations. Where settlements have been regularised through community action planning, specific building codes, and the means through which they are to be enforced, are formulated with the community representatives (Mitlin and Thompson, 1995:244).

Of the three support-based components of the Sri Lankan Million Houses Programme, the People's Housing Process has been incorporated into the South African national Housing Ministry, and developed into a workable alternative to housing delivery by commercial contractors. It appears that in South Africa, as in the documented case of Sri Lanka, unsatisfactory delivery by commercial contractors led the national housing authority to increasingly rely on community-based construction (through the People's Housing Process) as a means to reaching its housing target (see Pathirana and Sheng, 1992:4). A significant distinction between the official people's housing processes in the two countries, however, lies in the system of financial support. The South African People's Housing Process is moulded to the dictates of the once-off capital subsidy, while in the Sri Lankan case, longer-term support is provided through credit. It is therefore also the dictates of the capital subsidy system and the associated regulatory framework that have prevented the government-initiated support approach to function as a form of informal settlement intervention in South Africa. Instead, as will be evident in the case study discussion in Chapter 7,[22] informal settlements have been replaced by an externally planned standardised layout, and infrastructure has been delivered though the commercial contract procedure, before housing support was permitted to take place. Thus the conventional project cycle or procedure in South Africa has not been successfully challenged.[23] Understandably, then, community action planning and community contracting, as in the Sri Lankan support-based intervention, have as yet not found space in the South African informal settlement intervention framework. It is thus relevant to turn to the very different framework, both from South Africa and from Sri Lanka, within which government-initiated support-based approaches to informal settlement intervention have found space in Brazil.

Government-initiated support-based intervention in Brazil

As with the Sri Lankan experience, the benefits of a support-based approach in Brazil have been found to lie in rapid production, quality of workmanship and level of organisational capacity obtained within the community associations (Bonduki, 1993:57). However, the institutionalisation of support-based development approaches in Brazil did not emerge merely out of pragmatism on the side of central government, as appears to be the case in South Africa (with the People's Housing Process), and as the documentation on the Sri Lankan Million Houses Programme suggests. Instead, in Brazil a support-based, community-controlled approach was developed out of a strong demand by housing movements (Bonduki, 1993). Thus the concept of *'auto-gestão'* (self-management), giving organised communities control over all aspects of their development, was first developed in the early 1980s within the housing movements of São Paulo, out of an awareness of the exploitative aspects of self-construction (i.e. use of future occupants' labour) in externally designed and managed development projects (*ibid.*). This then led to 'a collective process of production of an entire residential area, managed by a co-operative or community organisation charged with all aspects of the productive process' (*ibid.*:57 – my translation from Portuguese).

Politically, the self-management concept was coupled with an awareness of the housing crisis, and of the need to create autonomous space for community organisation (Bonduki, 1993), these being concerns of the left-oriented PT, which had been formed in 1980 (see Abers, 1996). The self-management concept was therefore first institutionalised at local government level in those municipalities over which the PT gained control through municipal elections. In São Paulo this occurred with the Erundina administration (PT) from 1989 to 1992, and was subsequently discontinued with a swing back to more conservative municipal policy (see Bonduki, 1993; Denaldi, 1997). In the case of Diadema,[24] the PT won control of the municipality as early as 1983, with several consecutive PT administrations allowing for relative continuity of the self-management approach (Denaldi, 1995). While self-management was originally piloted for new housing areas (Bonduki, 1993), it was applied to favela intervention with the first PT administration in Diadema (1983 to 1988) (Denaldi, 1995). As the approach relies on high levels of community mobilisation, self-managed intervention is not viable in all favelas. Therefore, it is offered as an option to externally managed construction, be it through external labour or through the involvement of local residents in the construction (Denaldi *et al.*, 1997).

The overall approach, then, to informal settlement intervention in Diadema was not that of comprehensive upgrading in a small number of pilot projects, but instead gradual intervention through community managed processes in a large number of settlements (Denaldi *et al.*, 1997:46). For this purpose, the first PT administration of Diadema introduced a law to allow for land use concessions to favela residents, while its successor introduced Special Zones of Social Interest exempting favela intervention from conventional development standards (Denaldi, 1995), as pioneered in the Municipality of Belo Horizonte in the form of the PROFAVELA Law.[25] Through such institutional means, the 1989 to 1992 administration of Diadema supported (with municipal resources and not external or foreign finance) intervention in 80 different favelas (Denaldi, 1995).

In 1997, the PT-aligned administration in Belo Horizonte was reflecting on its experience with comprehensive externally designed (and internationally subsidised) intervention through the Alvorada Programme (which at the time and as mentioned above, had led to physical intervention in only one of three settlements). Within the municipality, self-management for the development of new housing areas had already been institutionalised and implemented in association with the annual participatory budget allocation process (*Orçamento Participativo*), whereby housing demand is channelled into a decision-making process involving organised civil society and local government. This budget allocation process occurs through a series of well-publicised public meetings in which development projects are proposed and elected by organisations of civil society, thus contributing to transparent administration and dialogue between civil society and local government (Bretas, 1996; Souza, 1999, 2003). However, in 1997 self-managed projects (with resources procured through the participatory budget process) had as yet not been applied as a form of informal settlement intervention in Belo Horizonte (Magalhaes and Puertas, personal communication, 1997).[26] To enable this shift, the municipality, in collaboration with the Italian NGO AVSI and its CAD and GIS computer technology, was developing a broad brush holistic plan (*'plano global'*) for each favela,[27] based on a preliminary survey, and identifying the broad technical constraints and opportunities around which community-based organisations can then articulate individual development projects, for example, drainage works, water reticulation roads, steps, pavements, etc. (Bede, personal communication, 1997).

In South Africa, it was the absence of any such government-initiated support-based housing intervention in the early 1990s that led to the formation of an NGO-initiated support-based approach through the People's Dialogue/ Homeless People's Federation alliance, modelled largely on Asian experience. As evident from South African case studies discussed in Chapter 7, this approach in South Africa has been largely restricted by the capital subsidy framework from achieving support-based informal settlement intervention other than house construction once the settlement has been formally replanned and infrastructure delivered through an externally managed process. It is relevant, then, to contrast the South African NGO-initiated support-based experience with that developed in other contexts. It is to this that I now turn.

3.4 NGO-initiated support-based intervention

Governments commonly cause two key problems for informal settlement residents and their community organisations. One is the vacuum created by non-intervention, with residents facing either ignorance or hard-handed repression. Even in cities where governments have articulated comprehensive upgrading programmes, these seldom reach more than a small percentage of informal settlements, leaving many to their own devices or struggling against eviction. The other is the social damage caused by inconsistent intervention. Due to the heavy reliance on external finance, be it national or international, comprehensive upgrading may be discontinued when such funding is delayed or cut as a result of political changes. A documented example of such damage is from the Barrio San Jorge in Buenos Aires, Argentina, where constant political change has resulted in little continuity in social policies and intervention. This has caused discouragement and resignation among low-income groups (Hardoy and Hardoy with Schusterman, 1991).

In this context of non-intervention by government and discouragement of the informal settlement residents, non-governmental support programmes have emerged with two objectives. Firstly, they attempt to challenge the poor to explore what they are capable of achieving without the assistance of government, and to empower them to successfully engage with government to win support for their self-defined local objectives. With the growing awareness in the international development community of urban poverty processes, success with the various approaches that have been developed to this end has been documented in the international literature (Bolnick, 1996; Cabannes, 1997; Environment and Urbanisation, 1995; Schusterman and Hardoy, 1997). Secondly, they attempt to challenge funders to reform the regulations to which their finance is tied, that is to break with the product-oriented funding mechanisms designed for the conventional contractual procedures of comprehensive upgrading (see Anzorena *et al.*, 1998).

The Orangi Pilot Project

Possibly the best known non-governmental support programme is the Orangi Pilot Project (OPP), initiated in 1980 in an informal settlement of 800,000 people in Karachi, Pakistan. Its central thrust is 'the creation of effective local organisation and dissemination of technical skills among local people' (Hasan and Vaidya, 1986:226). The project was initiated around the need for appropriate, affordable sanitation solutions in a context where foreign-funded intervention was offering conventional sanitation which the residents would not be able to maintain, and at a cost they could not afford to repay (Environment and Urbanisation, 1995:228). The OPP set out to break technical, economic, psychological and sociological barriers in order to enable residents to take control of their sanitation problem. This involved research into a simpler and more affordable sanitation system, convincing the residents of the benefits of taking control of their sanitation problem, and creating levels of organisational structures to take collective responsibility for the various levels of the sanitation system, this also requiring technical and managerial training (*ibid.*). Thus, the main inputs were in research, 'extension' (organisational development) and support or guidance (Hasan and Vaidya, 1986:226).

The sanitation planning and installation is managed at the organised street level, similar to the community contracts of the government-initiated Sri Lankan approach, with technical support from the OPP staff. However, two distinctions must be made between the OPP and the Sri Lankan government-initiated support approach. Firstly, while the Sri Lankan programme channels government funding into basic infrastructure construction, such funding in the case of the OPP is generated by the residents, with only the OPP support operations being externally funded. Hasan and Vaidya (1986:227) point out that 'through proper research, extension and support, OPP has managed to make a break-through in a self-managed people's programme without subsidising actual work. OPP subsidy has been only in research and extension; construction has been carried out entirely through local resources'. Secondly, while infrastructure developed through community contracts is officially recognised in Sri Lanka, the sanitation installations through the OPP, while functioning well, remained unofficial, though disposing waste water into the existing waste water drainage systems which lead to waste water treatment plants. The newsletter of the Asian Coalition for Housing Rights (Housing by People in Asia, 1998) has highlighted the determinism of conventional infrastructure programmes in Karachi in the face of existing people-managed systems of the OPP. An externally planned sewerage upgrading programme funded by the Asian Development Bank had taken no account of the well functioning sewer lines laid by the residents, and instead set out to duplicate these with a capital intensive sewerage approach. In 1998, opposition to the capital intensive project by the Orangi Pilot Project and other organisations had led to an official commitment to integrate the existing sewerage system (*ibid.*:15).[28]

While official acceptance of the OPP approach has been reluctant, demonstration of the successful sanitation solution has led to widespread demand from informal settlement communities for support from the Orangi Pilot Project (Hasan and Vaidya, 1986:227). The project has expanded to develop further programmes for low-cost house building, health and family planning, women's work centres, family enterprises and social forestry (food gardening and tree planting), while also introducing a rural pilot project (Environment and Urbanisation, 1995).

Common principles of NGO-initiated support-based approaches

Various non-governmental support programmes have developed in Asia, Latin America and Africa. They appear to have in common not a unitary methodology, but universally applicable principles through which a variety of approaches have been developed, depending on the localised deprivations as well as localised innovations of the poor themselves. The central principle is that of trust in the abilities of the poor, with the aim, therefore, not to provide for them, but instead to increase the options open to them. To this end, initiatives of the poor are encouraged and improved through appropriate organisational development, financial, technical and managerial training, and by increasing their ability to effectively interact with authorities.

One approach that has been developed to encourage the poor in their abilities has been that of exchange at the grassroots level, initiated in Asia by Father Jorge Anzorena (Bolnick, personal communication, 1998[29]). This has led to the formation of the National Slum Dwellers Federation in India, linking increasing numbers of informal settlement communities within India. Activities of the Federation are supported by the NGO SPARC (Society for the Promotion of Area Resource Centres), which seeks to empower women by linking isolated communities, and to support the existing efforts of communities by setting up resource centres (Environment and Urbanisation, 1990:91). The development of savings schemes as a means of mobilisation are central to the approach (Bolnick, personal communication, 1998).

International networking of this Indian NGO/Federation alliance led to the development of a similar approach in Southern Africa in the early 1990s, with a network comprising people in South Africa, Namibia and Zimbabwe (see Bolnick, 1993). The circumstances that led to the emergence of the Homeless People's Federation/People's Dialogue alliance in South Africa are discussed in Chapter 5, in comparison to the emergence of government-initiated support-based favela intervention through the PT in Brazil. In Chapter 7, the interface between the Homeless People's Federation/People's Dialogue initiative and the rigid government capital subsidy framework is examined through case studies, my finding being that the Federation activities appear to be distorted into primarily house construction due to the entitlement of low income households to the once-off capital subsidy (the Federation/NGO alliance has creatively negotiated access to the capital subsidy for its members). It is important to note, however, that due to the principle of networking and exchange at grassroots level through the Homeless People's Federation, the concept of non-governmental support is gaining increasing recognition among the poor. While still largely misunderstood by officials and planning professionals in South Africa (Bolnick, personal communication, 1998), this presents a growing challenge to the conventional project cycle that relies on external project identification and design, and implementation by commercial contractors.

A further common thrust of NGO-initiated support-based intervention is that of credit and savings mechanisms. International exchange and debate around the question of appropriate finance has sparked the development of new initiatives. Thus, a 1993 workshop on alternative housing finance funded by the International Habitat Coalition and attended by representatives from South Africa, Namibia, Mexico, India, Thailand, Colombia, England, Brazil and the Philippines, 'resulted in the idea of creating an alternative housing finance strategy in Fortaleza [Brazil] based partially around credit' (Cabannes, 1997:45). The *Casa Melhor* ('Better House') programme, supported by the French NGO 'Group for Research in Technological Exchange' (GRET) and the Brazilian NGO 'Cearah Periferia' (Centre for Study, Coordination and Reference concerning Human Settlements) in Fortaleza, enables low-income earners particularly in favelas in Fortaleza to access a combination of savings, subsidy and credit to improve their houses (Cabannes, 1995a, 1995b, 1997). Due to the government subsidy component in the funding scheme, a partnership with the local authority was required for the programme. Cabannes (1997:52) highlights the breakthrough of the programme as representing 'the first time in Brazil that a municipality has been willing to offer loans to those living in informal squatter areas who are without land titles. And despite a deep-rooted distrust among low-income households for government savings schemes, people are now encouraged to save – and in so doing to obtain public finance for housing' (*ibid.*). This poses a challenge to South African local government, which has yet to set a precedent of tolerating permanent house construction before township establishment and standardisation of settlement layout, and then of accommodating such permanent structures in the regularisation process (as will be evident in the case study discussion in Chapter 7). Another innovation of the GRET-Cearah Periferia support to the popular movement in Fortaleza is that of offering training for community leaders. The Urban Planning and Popular Research Course is designed to improve active community leaders' abilities to propose development ideas, to negotiate with public authorities, and to manage development projects. This is coupled with popular study centres and a fund for popular publications (Cearah Periferia, 1995).

Clearly, the diverse activities within the category of NGO-initiated support-based informal settlement intervention require very different funding arrangements from the conventional project-based and product-oriented funding requirements of externally defined comprehensive infrastructure upgrading to which national and international funding organisations have become accustomed. Despite the diversity among the NGO-initiated support activities, common funding principles may be identified. As inflexible funding mechanisms remain a significant obstacle to the expansion of NGO-initiated support-based intervention in informal settlements, and likewise to the adoption of support-based approaches by governments, I will briefly examine the debate on such funding requirements.

Common call to funders by the supporting NGOs

While much of the literature on NGO-initiated support programmes focuses on successful intervention as a means to promote relevant alternative approaches, not all support-based intervention can display tangible results. The ten year experience of support to the Barrio San Jorge informal settlement in Buenos Aires, Argentina (Hardoy and Hardoy with Schusterman, 1991; Schusterman and Hardoy, 1997), exposes the challenges to support-based intervention in the face of extreme poverty, low levels of organisation and ambivalent government interventions. The finding is that over the ten years the NGO IIED-America Latina (International Institute for Environment and Development – Latin America) was giving support to the settlement residents, no ways were found for accelerating the process of improvement in the settlement (Schusterman and Hardoy, 1997:119). While some progress has been made over the 10 years, the NGO staff warn that 'the reconstruction of social capital could take very long, even longer than NGO support staff will stay in communities, than aid agency officers will remain in office, or than development banks and governments will sustain their own policies' (Schusterman and Hardoy, 1997:119). Based on their experience, Schusterman and Hardoy (*ibid.*) make a call for external funding to be long term and flexible, not bound to individual projects and not requiring visible results. They argue that unless such change in external funding takes place, the temptation will always be, even for supporting NGOs, to seek communities that display conditions that will make such results likely. From their experience in Barrio San Jorge, they admit that:

> Many a time we have been tempted to give up and move to work in a community with a high level of organization, located in a municipality where local government is more responsive. Only our commitment to working with people who not only live in absolute poverty but also are least likely to receive support from government agencies and international donors prevented us from doing so (Schusterman and Hardoy, 1997:119).

The common call to funders in Anzorena *et al.* (1998) (representing various NGOs supporting development processes in informal settlements across the developing world, including those I have referred to in this chapter) is for new channels of finance. They highlight the constraints that funding organisations face, on the one hand, having 'to show demonstrable results quickly', and on the other hand, needing to reduce staff expenditure, i.e. increase the amount of funding managed by each of their staff members. 'Within such constraints it is easier for them to fund a few large, standard, capital projects' (Anzorena *et al.*, 1998:177). The authors contrast such projects with the achievements of community-based support initiatives in reducing poverty, these typically having begun 'with a relatively small amount of funding from some international agency' for an activity 'for which there was no support from local government. But once the initiative was established and had demonstrable achievements, there were increased possibilities for negotiating support from national or local sources' (*ibid.*:179).

Anzorena *et al.* (1998) summarise the main challenges to those funders that seek seriously to tackle urban poverty reduction: a) the individuality of the funding requirements of each initiative; b) the tendency for these initiatives to require funding for long term social processes rather than short-term projects; and c) the unpredictability and often immediacy of the funding requirements. The authors challenge donors to 'recognise the importance of channelling resources direct to low-income groups and their organizations' (*ibid.*, 1998:184) (rather than channelling resources to external consultants and commercial contractors). At a city level they suggest the setting up of local funding sources, which would be informed as to what is locally required to 'promote effective and inclusive urban development', and would then 'support initiatives that address such needs' (*ibid.*:184, 185). They further suggest 'intermediary institutions through which all official donors could channel funds to reduce urban poverty in any particular city' (*ibid.*:185). This discussion of alternative funding mechanisms is of particular relevance to the question of appropriate informal settlement intervention in South Africa, where the rigidity and product-orientation of the once-off capital subsidy, as the national funding mechanism for informal settlement intervention, has resulted in standardised intervention products. As will be evident from the case study discussion in Chapter 7, this has applied even in settlements where the Homeless People's Federation (supported by the NGO People's Dialogue) has been seeking alternative poverty-oriented means of settlement improvement. There I argue that the Federation members' entitlement to the capital subsidy appears to have channelled Federation activity into a very restricted focus on achieving the largest possible house product within the subsidy amount. In drawing attention to this distortion, my intention is not to discredit the substantial contribution of the Federation in South Africa, but rather to highlight the far-reaching impact of the once-off capital subsidy system as the only mechanism for government funding to be channelled into informal settlement intervention in South Africa.

3.5 Conclusion

The discussion of informal settlement intervention experience in this chapter suggests that in order for such intervention to impact positively on the processes of poverty, there has to be a shift away from comprehensive externally designed and managed intervention in selected settlements through once-off capital intensive projects. Such intervention fails to meaningfully take into account residents' needs, realities, ideas and capacities. Nor does it realistically consider institutional limitations in two important areas: a) that of ongoing maintenance of the investment in physical infrastructure; and b) that of replicating the externally imposed procedure in proportion to the scale and rate of growth of the informal settlement phenomenon.

Alternative approaches have been developed and institutionalised in various countries, each arising out of particular socio-political circumstances. These approaches have in common that they provide a longer-term support to informal settlement residents (and their organisations) for the gradual transformation of their social and physical environments. In Brazil, such alternative approaches have found political support from within the PT, and have therefore been institutionalised and practised in municipalities with mandates of the PT. In 2001 they were included in the new federal law, the 'Statue of the City' (Instituto Pólis, 2002). In Sri Lanka, in turn, support-based informal settlement intervention (in the form of community action planning, community contracts and a People's Housing Process) is incorporated into the policy of the National Housing Development Authority. South Africa, which likewise has a centralised housing policy, has drawn on the Sri Lankan experience, however, to date adopting only the house construction component (the People's Housing Process) from the Sri Lankan model. I argue that the South African housing finance framework, the once-off capital subsidy system, is at odds with some of the key support-based tenets of the Sri Lankan model. The South African framework, therefore, has only allowed for a people-centred house construction process (in South Africa likewise termed the 'People's Housing Process') once an informal settlement has been externally redesigned to a standardised layout, and conventional infrastructure has been delivered by external and usually commercial civil contractors. Community decision-making over layout dimensions around the existing pattern of land occupation, as in the case of the Sri Lankan Community Action Planning, has had no space in the South African framework. Nor has the identification and management of infrastructural projects by organised communities been possible in South Africa.

In contexts where governments have not shown willingness to support people-managed processes for the improvement of informal settlements, NGO-initiated support approaches have emerged, fulfilling the important function of assisting informal settlement residents in strengthening their position in society and in relation to the state. In the case of the Orangi Pilot Project in Pakistan, in the context of deterministic state intervention that takes little account of the needs and capacities of the poor, such an initiative supports the development of collective sanitation systems. In Fortaleza, Brazil, it trains community leaders in urban planning, thus strengthening their ability to develop ideas for improvement, to propose projects, to negotiate with government and to manage project implementation. In South Africa, in the context of a centralised and deterministic framework for intervention, an alternative support-based non-governmental initiative has likewise emerged (prior to the incorporation of the People's Housing Process into the national housing policy). However, as is evident from the case study discussion in Chapter 7, its activities are largely dictated to by the official framework. The entitlement to the once-off capital subsidy system has channelled much of the activities of this non-governmental initiative into house construction, in competition with both the mainstream housing delivery by commercial contractors and the government's People's Housing Process (all competing for capital subsidy allocations). The many important aspects of support-based informal settlement intervention that would take into consideration the collective needs that may be expressed, for instance, in the informal pattern of land use, have been overridden by an individual entitlement (through the product-linked capital subsidy) to a standardised plot with individualised access to conventional services, and to a house. Thus informal settlements have been remodelled into highly individualised and standardised settlements in which the support-based house construction may then take place. A stark contrast is presented by the Brazilian experience, which allows for house construction (in Fortaleza even with government assistance) prior to government intervention in the form of settlement formalisation. Early permanent house construction in Brazil thus forecloses subsequent standardisation of layouts.

The right to housing, then, in the favela context in Brazil, is interpreted not as the right to a standardised housing unit replacing the informally developed environment, as through the implementation process in South Africa. Instead, it is interpreted in Brazil as the right to have the permanent house legalised, or as the 'right to occupation' (see Aubertin, 1992:475). In Belo Horizonte this right was recognised in the PROFAVELA Law. Comprehensive intervention in the case of the Alvorada Programme (in Belo Horizonte) further responded to this right by compensating those households whose houses were demolished in the interest of collective infrastructure and access. Their original living space was rebuilt (at project cost) within the same settlement or as nearby as possible, thus minimising social disruption – a stark contrast to the standardised and uncompromising government intervention framework that I examine through the South African case studies in Chapter 7.

It is the wide disparity between South Africa and Brazil displayed in the current informal settlement intervention situation, which I have introduced through an international discussion in this chapter, that the following two chapters of this book seek to address. By examining the emergence of informal settlements in the two countries, and the similarities and contrasts in societal responses to this phenomenon, Chapters 4 and 5 give insight into the particularity of the contrast between Brazil and South Africa with regard to informal settlement intervention. This then enables a deeper and more critical examination of current debate and practice in relation to informal settlement in South Africa, in Part 3 of the study.

Notes

1 The term 'support paradigm' is used by those aiming to promote the merits of such alternative intervention as opposed to 'conventional thinking and planning approaches' – see Lankatilleke (1990:24). From the perspective of resident involvement, the support-based approaches have also been referred to as 'participatory', in contrast to the less participatory comprehensive upgrading – see Mitlin and Thompson (1995).

2 In developing a method-based planning framework for informal settlement upgrading, Abbott (2002a:320) warns of a paradigm that defines the government-community relationship only as a duality. Instead, he argues that it should be acknowledging that there are a range of government-community partnerships that lie 'between the extremes of government/agency controlled, and NGO-driven community-based' approaches. The government-initiated support-based intervention experiences that I refer to fall within this range of partnerships.

3 Sirivardana and Lankatilleke (1988:7) refer to this as a 'centralised project cycle'.

4 Survey, planning/design, cost estimation, detailing, tendering, construction and hand-over.

5 At a broad level such 'participation' has been severely critiqued, for instance by Azevedo (1998:264), in contrast to frameworks that afford civil society a role in the definition of policies and priorities.

6 In 1997, Enrico Novara of the Italian NGO AVSI (Voluntary Association for International Service) was Coordinator of the Alvorada Programme which was

being undertaken in partnership between the NGO, the Municipality of Belo Horizonte and other organisations.

7 An exception being South African policy, which explicitly prescribes local employment by contractors (Department of Housing, 1994:24). However, the meaningfulness of such a policy within a framework that denies residents' any definition of intervention objectives (see case study discussion in Chapter 7) must be questioned.

8 See endnote 20 of Chapter 2.

9 Flávia Lúcia Coelho Mota Pinheiro (Social Assistant) and Izabel de Andrade (Civil Engineer) were officials of the Belo Horizonte Municipality's housing and upgrading company URBEL (Companhia Urbanizadora de Belo Horizonte), and in 1997 were working in the site office at favela Senhor dos Passos, the first settlement to benefit from the physical improvements of the Alvorada Programme.

10 See for instance Jere (1984), Martin (1987), Martin and Ledogar (1977), Pasteur (1979), Rakodi and Schlyter (1981) and Schlyter (1987).

11 It should be noted that liberal arguments continue to be put forward in support of extending conventional methods of project elaboration and execution into informal settlements. See, for instance, Pamuk and Cavallieri's (1998:459) evaluation of the Favela-Bairro Programme in Rio de Janeiro.

12 This settlement was to be upgraded as a pilot project of the programme '*Sanear São Paulo*' of SABESP (*Saneamento Básico do Estado de São Paulo* – Basic Sanitation of the State of São Paulo) (Scazufka, personal communication, 1997 – Mauro Scazufka was an architect with the consultancy Diagonal, tasked in 1997 with the planning and cost estimation for the physical upgrading of favela *Fim de Semana*).

13 This contradiction was pointed out on a site visit to favela *Fim de Semana*, São Paulo, 11 July 1997, with the project staff of the consultancy Diagonal.

14 Originally this zoning was termed Special Sector 4, (Prefeitura Municipal de Belo Horizonte, 1985), but is now referred to as *Zonas Especiais de Interesse Social* – ZEIS (Special Zones of Social Interest) (Bede, personal communication, 1997, see endnote 20). The original cut-off date for favelas included in this zoning was in 1981. In 1986 it was extended to include more recent land invasions (*ibid.*).

15 Father Bernareggi was Coordinator of the *Pastoral de Favelas* in Belo Horizonte until its crumbling in 1986. He has remained strongly committed to its revival.

16 This is associated with the order by a newly elected conservative Bishop (believed to be acting in the interest of the land speculating class which was increasingly threatened by the consequences of the PROFAVELA Law), that the city-wide network of ecclesiastic base communities in favelas (the *Pastoral de Favelas*) be dismantled and recreated according to new district boundaries of the Church – none of the districts had the capacity to maintain the ecclesiastical base community (CEB) structures in favelas, once the city-wide structure was dismantled (Bernareggi, personal communication, 1997).

17 Giorgio Capitanio, an architect with the NGO AVSI in 1997, was involved in the planning and implementation of the Alvorada Programme.

18 Pio XI Procopio de Alvarenga, was Director of URBEL in 1997. Jessica Valdares was Coordinator of the Planning Section.

19 Claudinea Ferreira Jacinto was Coordinator of the Alvorada Programme at URBEL in 1997.

20 In 1997, Monica Cadaval Bede was Technical Director at URBEL. In 1999, she was Secretary of the Municipal Council for Urban Policy in Belo Horizonte.

21 Mitlin and Thompson (1995:243) refer to this as 'one of the most comprehensively documented examples of participatory methods in urban development'.

22 Particularly in the case of the Gunguluza settlement in Uitenhage.

23 In the policy process on informal settlement upgrading that was being developed in mid 2004, this aspect was also not being challenged.

24 Diadema is one of the important cities in the industrialised region of São Paulo referred to as ABCD ('D' standing for 'Diadema'). It was out of the metal worker's union militancy in this region that the PT was born, thus Diadema became one of the strongholds of the Workers' Party throughout the 1980s and up to 1996, when the Brazilian Socialist Party (PSB – *Partido Socialista Brasileiro*) won the municipal elections (see Kowarick and Singer, 1994; Sader and Silverstein, 1991; Saule Jr., 1998). In Chapter 5, I discuss the particular local government context which allowed the PT to take control over Diadema in 1983. It may be noted that in 1996, 30 per cent of Diadema's population was living in favelas (Saule Jr., 1998:13).

25 As mentioned above, also see Fernandes (1993).

26 Maria Cristina Fonseca Magalhaes was Coordinator of the Section for Enterprises in 1997, and Antonia Puertas was Coordinator of Self-management, both at the Upgrading Company of Belo Horizonte, URBEL.

27 In 1995 there were 139 favelas in Belo Horizonte, accommodating a total of 337,000 people (17 per cent of the city's population) (Prefeitura Municipal de Belo Horizonte, 1995).

28 Also see Abbas (1998).

29 In 1998 Joel Bolnick was Executive Director of the South African NGO People's Dialogue which supports the Homeless People's Federation – these two initiatives emerged together, drawing on the Asian NGO-initiated support-based experience, particularly that of grassroots exchange.

Part Two

Brazil and South Africa: A Comparative Socio-Political Perspective on the Evolution of Informal Settlement Intervention

Chapter 4

Division and Exclusion: The Production of Informal Settlements in South Africa and Brazil

4.1 Introduction

Informal settlements by definition result from the exclusion of a section of society from the formal processes of settlement formation. This chapter examines how this process of exclusion has differently shaped the informal settlement situation in Brazil and in South Africa. The exclusionary socio-political processes discussed in this chapter form the basis for an understanding of the more compromising societal responses to informal settlement in the two countries. These are subject of Chapter 5. The aim across these two chapters is to grasp the roots of the significant divergence of current informal settlement intervention in Brazil and South Africa so as to thereby develop a critical position regarding the South African situation.

In Part 1 of this book I examined intervention debates and experiences by those directly concerned with the question of informal settlement intervention, identifying shifts, themes and tendencies in interpretations of the informal settlement phenomenon, intervention thinking and practice. At that level I have introduced differences between South Africa and Brazil in relation to international debates and practice. In Part 2, I step back and examine the position of informal settlements within broader society in South Africa and Brazil. The questions here are: How was the informal settlement situation shaped in these two countries? Why have particular informal settlement interpretations dominated? And why have particular intervention approaches developed and been afforded political space? In this chapter, I examine societal themes associated with exclusion that have played themselves out relatively unchallenged from the beginning of the 20th century up to the mid-1970s, when signals of democratisation and 'inclusion' emerged both in Brazil and in South Africa. Chapter 5 then examines the different societal responses to informal settlement within the processes of democratisation or 'inclusion' in the two countries, and the informal settlement intervention approaches that have thus been developed and afforded political space. My position is that the difference in processes of 'inclusion' in Brazil and South Africa is partly rooted in the divergence in the processes of exclusion, which I contrast in this chapter.

First, I examine, for South Africa and Brazil, broad contrasts in the processes of exclusion (social, economic and political), which are inextricably tied to the production and perpetuation of informal settlements. In South Africa, these processes have been marked by legislated racial control deliberately creating racial divisions. In Brazil, unchecked market forces or speculation resulted primarily in class-based divisions. A degree of controlled and racially based exclusion in Brazil's history, and increasing class-based exclusion in South Africa, however, add societal complexity to the informal settlement question. This leads to varying interpretations and consciousness of these processes, in challenging the societal conditions that produce and maintain informal settlement. While a comparative discussion of societal responses to the processes of exclusion follows in Chapter 5, this chapter is a periodised comparative examination of the largely uncompromising forces that have both produced and reproduced informal settlement. Contrasting exclusionary measures in the pattern of land regulation in the two countries set the basis for diverging informal settlement processes. Commonplace, however, are the unrelenting removals and displacement, which recur in this comparative discussion. Here I trace the sharpening of oppressive intervention through a political swing to the far-right (in both countries), preceded, and followed, by state ambiguity with respect to informal settlements, giving limited space to a more compromising treatment. It is such gradual compromises from the mid-1970s onward that leads into Chapter 5, which (as mentioned above) more explicitly examines the emergence of the current informal settlement intervention repertoires in South Africa and Brazil in relation to interpretations and consciousness of the processes of exclusion discussed in this chapter.

4.2 Societal themes surrounding informal settlement in South Africa and Brazil

Social divisions creating and maintaining exclusion

For the largest part of the 20th century, political regimes in Brazil and South Africa have not only caused the production of informal settlements, but have also intervened to exacerbate rather than alleviate informal settlement conditions. This practice of socio-political exclusion, which is directly tied to the exclusive maintenance of privilege for a portion of society, has taken a different form in South Africa than in Brazil. In South Africa, exclusion has been distinguished by:

a) its racial nature; and b) the rigorous means by which it was legislated and thus controlled by the state. In Brazil, exclusion has been characterised primarily by unchecked exploitative market forces or speculation. It is relevant to unpack these opposing processes, as they have shaped contrasting consciousness of exclusion, and therefore of the phenomenon of informal settlement. This in turn has produced divergent intervention thinking, thus giving background to an understanding of the contrast in current intervention in South Africa and Brazil.

In South Africa, racial exclusion was regulated through the legal framework. This encompassed restrictions on political activity, on employment, commercial and investment opportunities, on social relations and spatially on access to accommodation in the city. Such state intervention interfered with the processes by which market (or capitalist) forces shape class divisions in society. By rigidly discriminating against blacks, the state induced a white race unified across different classes and cultural identities. Racial exclusion thus served to avoid class consciousness and inter- and intra-class conflict in South Africa (Marx, 1998:14, 15). Marx notes that while racial segregation served the economy in that it supplied cheap black labour, there were economic costs associated with the maintenance of the racial order. To some extent, then, the South African state subordinated economic interests to its racially-based social plan, part of which was to create unity within the white 'race' (*ibid.*). This in turn led to unforeseen social complexities. By the late 1940s, the modern economy had engendered 'new class forces' which were flourishing within the racial framework, posing a new threat to white domination (Mamdani, 1996:95). The National Party in the early 1950s responded to this threat by submitting these class-based forces (that had emerged among the African (black) population) to tribal confines, there 'contained by traditional authorities' that themselves depended on the South African state (*ibid.*). A white race, unified across class differences, could thereby dominate over a tribally divided black race.[1]

Divisions among Africans (blacks) were further fostered by the South African state through selective rights to the city. Linking such urban rights to employment situation, place of birth and past duration of the urban sojourn, a division was fostered between a (relative) elite of permanent African (black) urbanites, and temporary and illegal African (black) urbanites, whose tribal identities were maintained (see Lemon and Cook, 1994; Posel, 1991). Differential rights to the city were further polarised into separate forms of urban accommodation: a) those with formal leases to public housing; b) those residing legally in single-sex hostels; and c) those residing illegally, either in back yard shacks of formal housing areas, in overcrowded hostels (later spilling into shacks surrounding hostel buildings), or in shacks on invaded land. In the 1980s, such divisions were furthered deliberately as a means of gaining control over the growing African (black) anti-apartheid protest which had emerged in the UDF (United Democratic Front). In the reproductive sphere this took the form of the civic movement. Measures applied to win selective support for the apartheid government were, for instance, the upgrading of townships (see Boraine, 1988), the affording of restricted political expression to Africans (blacks) with permanent urban rights through the creation of 'black local authorities' (Omer-Cooper, 1994:229; Shubane, 1991:67), and the introduction of market delivery of African (black) housing, by definition exclusive to the relatively well employed (Crankshaw, 1993). At the same time, the patterns of African (black) employment were changing. A fall in the demand for unskilled jobs, and therefore lower wages, was contrasted by an upward mobility into semi-skilled and skilled jobs (Crankshaw, 1997). This led to a rise in class differentiation among Africans (blacks), with the result that class has increasingly become a barrier among those more broadly discriminated against by race (*ibid.*).

In Brazil, in turn, exclusion was primarily a matter of class. Similar to the ruling white South African minority of the mid-20th century, the Brazilian elite of the late 19th century, having experienced slave uprisings, was fearful of a unified black consciousness (Marx, 1998:15). Its response, however, was not to divide the African (black) population, but instead to incorporate racial difference into a national identity. In effect, the Brazilian state denied the existence of racial inequality, and promoted miscegenation as a means of 'whitening' and unifying the population (*ibid.*). Economic interests were allowed to play themselves out through a largely unrestricted class-based exclusion.[2] Nevertheless, there is evidence of racially discriminatory state practice, legislated political exclusion and state control over the reproductive sphere in Brazil. However, these measures in Brazil primarily served capitalist interests, and did not systematically dictate to the market, as they did in South Africa. Since they add complexity to the question of exclusion and its relationship to the production of informal settlement in Brazil, it is important to discuss them briefly.

The European racial doctrines of the 19th century, which legitimised South African racial practice, had likewise been imported to Brazil in the 19th century (Burns, 1970:264) and determined, for instance, the exclusive immigration of European workers to Brazil after the abolition of slavery. It is interesting to note that with the estimated 3.6 million Africans (black) imported as slaves to Brazil, whites constituted a minority until the early 20th century, after which almost 4 million Europeans were encouraged to immigrate to Brazil.[3] This resulted in the current ratio whereby whites barely constitute a majority (Oliveira, 1996:73, 74). As in South Africa, a coding of racial categories was developed in Brazil. However, this was not applied 'as a basis for domination' (Marx, 1998:15). Instead, the racial doctrine began to be rejected by the beginning of the 20th century, in favour of a national identity that acknowledged the contribution of Africans (former slaves) to Brazilian society. Referring to Brazilian publications of the beginning of the 20th century, Burns (1970:268) writes that 'racist doctrines seemed to 20th century Brazilian intellectuals as one more European effort to subjugate their country'.[4] The dominant view is that racial inequality, though present in Brazil, is produced by poverty, and perceived inferiority is associated with class rather than with race (Burns, 1970:268). However, this has been challenged as the 'myth' of 'racial democracy', with evidence of subtle but persistent policies aimed at 'whitening' the Brazilian population and reducing black collective consciousness (Carneiro, 1996:179; Marx, 1998:15). A combination of class- and race-based exclusion therefore exists in both South Africa and Brazil, though with different emphases.

Turning to legislated exclusion, labour laws regulating 'the exploitation of labour' were introduced by Vargas' *Estado Novo*[5] (Kowarick and Bonduki, 1994:128). Further, a limitation on the political franchise, in the form of a literacy criteria, was applied in Brazil until 1979. The limitation on the franchise largely denied the rural peasant population and the urban and urbanising poor a voice through the vote, thus reinforcing class-based domination. Lawrence (1994) compares this form of discrimination to the racial limitations on democracy in South Africa – in both cases mostly the non-white and largely illiterate sector of the population was excluded. Burns (1970:271) notes that in 1920 more than 64 per cent of the Brazilian population above 15 years of age was illiterate, while by 1970 this still applied to half of the Brazilian population (*ibid.*:5). As the first Brazilian ruler to capitalise on working class or popular support, rather than exclusively that of the elite, Getúlio Vargas, in his 15 year rule from 1930 to 1945[6] introduced the franchise for working women (*ibid.*:300), and through his education programmes[7] achieved an increase in the electorate. However, legislated political exclusion in Brazil returned in an almost absolutist form during the military dictatorship, with a complete ban on political activity applying from 1968 to 1974. This was also a period of extreme repression exercised towards favela residents, with large numbers of forced removals. Valladares and Figueiredo (1983:74) draw attention to 'the political/electoral significance of favela constituencies', with the result that 'extensive removal policies can only occur when favela populations lose their bargaining power represented by the vote'.

The denial of such political bargaining power has allowed for repressive informal settlement intervention in South Africa for the greater part of the 20th century. However, it is less through political exclusion than through political patronage, that uncompromising aspects of informal settlement intervention have endured beyond National Party rule in South Africa. In this regard, parallels may be suggested between current South Africa and the pre-1964 populist period in Brazil, which is described by practices of 'clientelism', 'patronage' and 'systematic co-optation of the working class' (Souza, 1993a:195 – my translation from German). It is in the ambivalence of the populist period that relocations from selected centrally located favelas to segregated 'proletarian parks' were enforced in Rio de Janeiro,[8] not unlike the continuing current mainstream practice in South Africa of relocating informal settlement residents to peripherally located housing developments through the housing subsidy framework. In their management, the Brazilian 'proletarian parks', however, have parallels with earlier South African practice, with control and discipline having been exercised over residents' lives. Even access to these segregated settlements was regulated by identity documents (Leeds and Leeds in Souza, 1993a). Though in vastly different dimensions, the Brazilian and South African histories therefore do share themes of social control around the question of informal settlement.

Returning to the current situation, socio-economic exclusion remains evident in both South Africa and Brazil in the high degree of inequality, although both countries have undergone democratisation and have abandoned legislated political exclusion. Among middle-income countries, South Africa and Brazil display the highest levels of inequality according to the Gini-coefficient (Ministry in the Office of the President, RDP, 1995). In both countries 10 per cent of the population control approximately half of the country's wealth (UNCHS (Habitat), 1996a). Physically, such exclusion is manifested in informal settlements and other deprived forms of urban residence. As discussed in Chapter 2, international debates around the politically neutral term *'urban poverty'* have drawn much attention to this condition in recent years, in the hope of channelling much-needed intervention or 'alleviation' in this direction. However, as will be evident in this and the following chapter, the question of informal settlement intervention in South Africa, as in Brazil, has been inextricably linked, not primarily to international debates and declarations, but to national, regional and localised socio-political dynamics, where the struggle for inclusion takes place. Inevitably, in the context of maintained socio-economic exclusion, the attainment of living space and improvements thereof depends, to a large degree, on forms of patronage by politically influential figures. Intervention is arranged with the purpose of securing political loyalty, and to counter class-based challenges to the socio-economic order. This leaves little space for organised informal settlement communities to articulate their own development objectives (invariably based on their own experiences) and to have these translated into responsive intervention approaches. In this context, then, the political space won by the PT (Workers' Party) in Brazil in the 1980s and 1990s and translated into non-patronising democratic urban practices grounded in an awareness of class-based exclusion are of significance. While the emergence of the PT and its approach to informal settlement in Brazil is discussed in Chapter 5, my discussion now leads to questions around the awareness of exclusion by class and race, and its relationship to the challenging or perpetuation of the informal settlement situation.

Interpretations and consciousness – implications for redressing exclusion

While for Brazil a 'more formidable barrier than race may well be class' (Burns, 1970:269), the relationship between class and race in the analysis and redressing of exclusion in the country remains unresolved. The PT leadership has been criticised for 'a consciousness of class' at the expense of 'a consciousness of race' (Marx, 1998:259). The question here remains: Which consciousness is more relevant in challenging the exclusion that is manifested in the informal settlement phenomenon? Certainly the deracialisation of the South African state has not led to the elimination of the phenomenon of informal settlement, with poverty (and in effect class) remaining the primary barrier to adequate residential conditions. With reference to the class-based struggle from within racially mixed favelas in Brazil as opposed to the race-based struggle from within the racially uniform ghettos of the United States, Oliveira (1996:72) suggests that 'political engagement around class issues' may impact more effectively on policy-making than that centred around race. This is the position of the PT in Brazil, and that of the Brazilian left more generally (Marx, 1998:259, 260). Souza (1999:4) makes direct reference to the engagement of 'alternative planners' of the Brazilian left with the concept of class and the 'conflicts and tensions that are inherent features of class societies'. He argues that as practitioners they 'do not aim at the building of harmony through instrumental rationality; instead, they contribute to a process of negotiation and regulation during which the contradictions become explicit and the options can be freely debated on the basis of political transparency and participation of the ordinary citizens' (*ibid.*:4, 5).

Indeed, the Brazilian intellectual left has politically engaged with and furthered (among other things) the demands of those housed in informal settlements. Critical analysis in South Africa in turn is particularly sensitive to the complex questions of race, ethnicity and identity that the South African situation raises.[9] As is evident in the discussion of South African literature on informal settlement in Chapter 6, the South African intellectual left has not significantly furthered the informal settlement intervention question. Instead, this literature is dominated by neo-liberal or market-oriented arguments that are not based on a consciousness of class. In Brazil, there is an intellectual awareness that the main cause of deprivation and impoverishment is the result of various forms of tolerated exploitation of the working class, through low wages, lack of efficient and affordable transportation, and negligence in the provision of housing, thus reliance on people's own resources in acquiring land and constructing houses (see Kowarick, 1985). There is an awareness that workers and the urban unemployed were left to their own devices, and were progressively displaced to the expanding urban peripheries through unchecked property speculation of the land-owning class. This process of exploitation in the reproductive sphere or 'in the community' (as opposed to the workplace) has been conceptualised by Brazilian urban sociologist Lúcio Kowarick as 'urban spoliation' (see Kowarick, 1979, 1985, 1997, 2000), a concept that has focused the analysis of informal settlements and other forms of residential deprivations in relation to class conflict and notions of citizenship.[10]

Political programmes addressed at the informal settlement situation have been driven by two opposing interpretations. One sees the harsh experience of a low quality of life for a large proportion of the urban population as a consequence of class-based exploitation, the other (dominant among the formally housed) sees the informal settlement phenomenon as a threat to the security, health and well-being of formal, mainly middle-class society. Sachs (1981:24), for instance, identifies two tendencies in the Brazilian debate on informal settlement, one seeking to humanise favelas, the other unrealistically wishing to eliminate the phenomenon. These opposed views may be compared to two separate discourses which Kowarick and Ant (1994) identify around the phenomenon of overcrowded inner-city tenements or '*cortiços*' of São Paulo in the 1930s. One associated *cortiços* with exploitation, and at the time was also calling for their eradication (i.e. replacement with adequate living conditions), the other associated *cortiços* with epidemics and disorder, and, driven by the fear of contamination, was calling for the segregation of workers' residential quarters from those of the middle-class (Kowarick and Ant, 1994:65–67). The representations of informal settlement as class-based exclusion on the one hand, and of threats to the middle-class, on the other, may each create political pressure for government intervention. The intervention ideas they produce are opposed – one seeks improvement and integration, and the other wishes to remove the phenomenon of informal settlement from the middle class existence. Complexity is added, however, as the state may also view informal settlements as a cheap labour pool, as is illustrated in the case of Rio de Janeiro in the 1940s: Souza (1993a:198) highlights the paradoxical situation whereby the well located favelas were, on the one hand, unpleasant to the middle-class and obstacles to the real estate, yet on the other hand, a cost-free solution to the problem of workers' housing; this resulted in variations in state intervention, depending on subtleties of political conjuncture and location of the favela (Souza, 1993a:198).

Thus, for reasons of discriminatory political representation or exclusion, government intervention has mostly been driven by the perception of informal settlement as either a threat or a convenient labour pool, and not by the experience of poor living conditions or a conviction of class-based exploitation. The inclusion of the informal settlement reality into government priorities, therefore, requires an intense struggle against the practices of socio-political exclusion. In South Africa, a largely unchallenged neo-liberal intervention programme imposes middle-class assumptions on the informal settlement reality (as will be evident in the discussion of South African intellectual debates in Chapter 6). In Brazil, the PT, backed by a cohesive body of intellectuals that are aware of the functioning of class division within capitalist society, has developed and implemented, at municipal level, urban practices grounded in an awareness of the reality of class-based exclusion and of practices of patronage and clientelism that largely maintain such exclusion. In order to understand the different histories from which the neo-liberal approach developed in South Africa, as opposed to the PT's awareness in Brazil, this chapter turns to a periodised discussion of the opposing processes of explicit exclusion from the beginning of the 20th century to the mid-1970s when signals of a gradual shift towards political inclusion started to emerge in the two countries. This is followed in Chapter 5 by an examination of the subsequent processes of 'political opening',[11] within which the mainstream neo-liberal approach to informal settlement in South Africa and the PT's approach in Brazil developed.

Before turning to the periodised discussion of the socio-political processes, it is relevant to emphasise two further distinctions between South Africa and Brazil. They are the military and the Catholic Church, which have acted as significant socio-political forces in Brazil, and as such have no direct equivalent in South Africa. Both have, in specific periods, impacted on the informal settlement situation in Brazil, the military furthering conservative middle-class interests, the Catholic Church in turn furthering the demands of the favela residents.

The military in Brazil has functioned as an independent political force, with interests vested in the status associated with its ranks, as well as in the progress of the middle groups (neither the extremely wealthy former coffee plantation owners nor the impoverished former slaves), and later the urban middle-class, from which they were mainly drawn (Burns, 1970:202). As its loyalties thus shifted, the military repeatedly supported undemocratic change of government. This occurred first with the overthrow of the monarchy in 1889 when the military sided with the Republicans, in 1930 with the overthrow of the republic, in 1945 to end the 15 year rule of Vargas, in 1954 to end the subsequent populist presidency of Vargas, and in 1964 overthrowing a radicalising government and establishing dictatorial powers in 1968 (Burns, 1970).

The Catholic Church, in turn, was independent of the Brazilian state since 1889, and despite attempts by the state to maintain power over it, was able to support societal causes in opposition to the state (Burns, 1970:206; Vink, 1985:97). In 1922, the Catholic Church turned its attention to the plight of the poor. This coincided with the formation of the Communist Party, which likewise addressed itself to social inequalities. Both were situated in a larger movement that was protesting against the increasingly inefficient republic, leading to its overthrow in 1930 (Burns, 1970:281). The Catholic Church and the Communist Party have been instrumental in organising communities in the unserviced subdivisions and favelas on the urban peripheries – in the 1920s, the Catholic Church started by organising 'Workers' Circles' running cooperatives and social services (*ibid.*:281). While the Communist Party was repeatedly banned (until legalisation in 1985), the Catholic Church maintained legitimacy and was therefore able to ensure continuity of progressive community organisation, even during the most repressive years of the military dictatorship in the late 1960s and early 1970s (Banck and Doimo, 1988:75; Mainwaring, 1984). By the late 1970s, progressive political movements took over the function of organising and defending the socially excluded. The Church, however, retained an influential role, particularly within the PT, in which many Catholic activists, pastoral workers, nuns and priests found a political home. Through their involvement in the ecclesiastic base communities (*Comunidade Eclesial de Base* – CEB) they 'tried to counterbalance, so to speak, the negative influence of party bureaucracy', promoting instead 'the principles of base democracy' (Banck and Doimo, 1988:75). The signifcant role of the Catholic Church in relation to favelas, in comparison to a more fragmented role of diverse denominations in South Africa, will be particularly evident in the discussion of societal responses to informal settlement in Chapter 5, whereas that of the military forms part of the discussion of the production of informal settlements in the following section of this chapter.

4.3 The production of informal settlements in South Africa and Brazil

Setting the pattern of ownership, distribution and regulation of land

Since the 19th century, informal settlements have been an element of the Brazilian and South African urban landscape. In the colonial centre of Rio de Janeiro, as in Cape Town, informal settlements are first associated with the abolition of slavery (Harrison, 1992:15; Oliveira, 1996:74) and the subsequent lack of official urban socio-economic integration, including legal access to land. From this common starting point, different processes in the pattern of land distribution, ownership and regulation in the two countries have caused the informal settlement situation to diverge significantly. We must bear in mind, however, that the contrasting processes (legislated racial segregation and control as a means to protecting white privilege in South Africa, and the process of uncontrolled land speculation by the land-owning class in Brazil), though each shaping the phenomenon of informal settlement in a particular way, have compelling similarities in outcome at the end of the 20th century, with respect to poverty, inequality and urban socio-economic segregation (as partly noted in the previous section). Land-related legislation of the early 20th century forms the basis of these opposing, yet similar, trends.

In South Africa, the expansion of the white domain to its current boundaries occurred through a land distribution pattern that formed the basis of white privilege throughout the 20th century. Africans (blacks) were restricted to 'native reserves' while the system of migrant labour ensured non-permanence of their much needed presence in urban areas, where they served the interests of mining and industry, and were to be housed in segregated areas. The 1913 Land Act entrenched permanent racial separation and prohibited blacks from purchasing or leasing land outside of the designated reserves. This Act, and the 1923 Natives (Urban Areas) Act, are referred to as the 'key pillars of segregation' in South Africa

(Omer-Cooper, 1994:169). The equivalent legislation regulating land in Brazil, and ensuring privilege of the land-owning class, was the civil code of 1916, legislating that 'the economic uses to which a given property can be put are determined by the individual interests of its owner' (Fernandes and Rolnik, 1998:143), thus attaching absolute rights to private property. This allowed for an unchecked land speculation process, continually displacing informal settlements from profitable land. In South Africa and in Brazil this early legislation later became the basis of land regulation during both countries' far-right authoritarian regimes (of the 1948 to 1994 National Party rule in South Africa[12] and of the 1964 to 1984 military dictatorship in Brazil).

Thus, while in the early 1900s planned, racially segregated city structures were established throughout South Africa, Brazilian cities remained largely unplanned into the 1960s, although inner cities were subjected to avenue/transport planning (see Taschner, 1995:187, 188). The practice of letting inner city tenements (*cortiços*) to a maximum number of low-income tenants meant that, in the early years of industrialisation, São Paulo was 'not a highly segregated city' (Kowarick and Ant, 1994:62). In the city of São Paulo, the overcrowded tenement was the main form of low-income housing up to the 1950s (*ibid.*), and the first informal settlements were noted only in the 1940s (Taschner, 1995:189). In cities such as Rio de Janeiro and Belo Horizonte, where informal settlements were common since the late 19th century, these had to give way repeatedly to administrative buildings, or speculative development as the occupied land became profitable for formal up-market development (Taschner, 1995). In South Africa, illegal 'squatting' and racially mixed sub-letting in slums in turn fell victim to deterministic intervention aiming to racially segregate the urban sphere. Such action was justified by concerns for public health, with the outbreak of plague in 1904 (Parnell and Pirie, 1991:130), and until the promulgation of the 1923 Natives (Urban Areas) Act it was supported by legislation such as the Location Acts of 1902 and 1905 in Natal, modelled on the example set by the Cape Colony (Davies, 1991:76).

Evictions were common in both countries. However, South African urban control was more severe than the displacement caused by the Brazilian urban land speculation, as it legislated exclusion from the economic benefits of the city. The Natives (Urban Areas) Act not only legislated for segregated urban environments, but also restricted African (blacks) access to cities through municipal employment registers, whereby unregistered Africans (blacks) could be removed from urban areas (Davenport, 1991:8). The Act further enabled local authorities to control trade in African (black) 'locations', and municipal monopolies on the sale of traditional beer increasingly became a means of raising revenue for the administration of African (black) 'locations' (*ibid.*). The acquisition and accumulation of economic benefits with an African (black) urbanisation process, i.e. the integration of urbanising Africans (blacks) into the urban socio-economy, was therefore prevented. The implementation of this law across South Africa's cities led to the removal of cross-racial sub-letting in inner-city slums and the creation of peripherally located townships (Cook, 1991:29; Hattingh and Horn, 1991:147; Parnell and Pirie, 1991:131). Forced removals were increased with the Slums Act of 1934, based on the Cape Town City Council's recommendations to Parliament (Cook, 1991:29). At the same time, insufficient formal housing production and the harsh control exercised over African (black) townships led to the formation of new informal settlements.

While policies in South Africa did not change course in the first decades of the 20th century, in Brazil the military overthrow of 1930, with the installation of Getúlio Vargas, first as chief of a provisional government, later as dictator and thereafter as elected president, led to some change in policy. Vargas' balance of power depended on support from business, labour, the military and the nationalists (Burns, 1970:303). He therefore introduced 'contradicting and inconsistent' policies, his state never 'submitting itself exclusively to the immediate aim of any single class' (Bonduki, 1994:100). Thus the 1930s saw attempts at urban land-use planning, and in Rio de Janeiro the application of land-use zoning as a preventative measure against favelas (Oliveira, 1996:75). However, 'neither this legal instrument nor constant police intervention aimed at destroying the rudimentary houses built by the poor prevented the increase of favelas in the city' (*ibid.*). Other policies at the time were directed at the needs of the poorly housed population. These included a decree to regulate the land sales to low income people on the urban peripheries, a home loan system and subsidised housing programmes (Bonduki, 1994:100, 101). Significant, too, was an adjustment to the rights associated with property, with the introduction in the 1934 Constitution of the concept of a 'social function' of property, requiring private property to serve not exclusively the economic interest of the individual owner, but to submit to the social interests of the broader public (Fernandes and Rolnik, 1998:145).[13] As the legitimacy of his continued rule depended on a degree of support from labour, Vargas introduced 'a new form of clientelism' into Brazilian politics, with the 'distribution of houses' through government programmes proving 'highly useful for the creation of political support for the regime' (Bonduki, 1994:101). This dynamic entered South African politics in a significant way only with the adoption of universal adult franchise. Thus in the run-up to the first fully democratic national election in 1994, the National Party government made generous housing concessions to new coloured and African (black) constituencies in order to secure votes (Tomlinson, 1995:8). In Chapter 5, I return to the clientelist relationship between the Brazilian state and civil society in the period of rule by Vargas and subsequent governments up to the 1964 overthrow by the military, examining how they both encouraged the organisation of favela communities, and gave favela residents some say (though very limited) in the definition of state intervention.

Pressures of industrialisation

In South Africa, as in Brazil, informal settlements mushroomed in the 1940s. With the exception of Rio de Janeiro's large informal settlements spreading over inner city hillsides, informal settlements in Brazilian cities have tended to be relatively small and spread across the urban periphery. To date few favelas in São Paulo consist of more than 1,000 dwellings, the majority comprising less than 100 houses (Mautner and Bueno, 1994). In contrast, the nature of formal land development in South African cities meant that informal settlements tended to develop in large concentrations on segregated portions of peripheral land. In Durban, the 1940s squatting concentrated in Cato Manor, initially outside the municipal boundaries (Hindson *et al.*, 1994). In Cape Town, it extended along the railway line on the eastern edge of the city, from Retreat to Windemere, where alone 20,000 shacks were concentrated (Cook, 1991:29). In Johannesburg, it concentrated on the western edge of the city, where land had been purchased by the municipality for the establishment of townships (Parnell and Pirie, 1991), which later became known as greater Soweto.[14]

In Brazil, the mushrooming of informal settlements in the 1940s was only in part the result of massive migration to the cities. The shortage of formal housing has also been linked to the contradictions in populist policies during the Vargas rule. Bonduki (1994) argues that the tenancy law, passed in order to foster popular support, indirectly led to a shortage of housing and the formation of informal settlements. This law was intended to control rent in the tenements or '*cortiços*'. However, as the provision of tenancy to the low-income population thereby became unprofitable, the production of private tenements declined, and private urban investments instead were made in industry. A dramatic housing shortage ensued in the 1940s, intensified by the influx of rural people into the cities, and sparking unplanned development on the urban periphery (Bonduki, 1994). This took two forms. On the one hand, portions of land were invaded (forming favelas). On the other hand, small unserviced plots were sold unofficially through illegal subdivisions,[15] as a process of private speculation. Successive governments' seemingly laissez faire attitude to this uncontrolled, 'anarchic' production of the urban periphery is interpreted as a deliberate encouragement of 'this type of housing as the only way of maintaining in the cities the growing waves of new inhabitants at as low a cost as possible to the authorities' (Kowarick and Ant, 1994:68; also see Seidman, 1994:211). It may be noted that for São Paulo in the period from the 1950s to the early 1970s, unauthorised subdivisions were the most common form of low-income access to urban land (Imparato, 1998:2). In 1979, when a law was finally passed to criminalise the action of illegal land-subdividers, unauthorised subdivisions comprised 35 per cent of São Paulo's urban area (*ibid.*). While the 1979 legislation is said to have reduced the rate of unauthorised subdivision, the rate of land invasion in turn has increased (*ibid.*).

Turning to South Africa, industrialisation brought a trend towards economic realism in the 1940s and associated with this a pause in implementation of some of the harsh policies applying to the African (black) urban existence. The operation of pass laws was temporarily relaxed to facilitate the unprecedented urbanisation that was responding to the labour demand of the industrial boom of the war years (Omer-Cooper, 1994:183). This temporary relaxation was followed by recommendations to the ruling United Party in 1948 by the Fagan Commission that urbanisation 'should be facilitated to satisfy the labour needs of industry and that the urban black population should be recognised as a permanent part of the urban population' (*ibid.*:188). Though rejected by the white electorate in 1948, the contents of the Fagan Commission were essentially those introduced again through the policy of 'orderly urbanisation'[16] in the 1980s.

A swing to the far-right

Instead of liberalisation and orderly urbanisation, the franchised section of South African society in the late 1940s chose the policy of apartheid (separateness), put forward by right wing Afrikaner intellectuals of the National Party in opposition to the United Party government (Omer-Cooper, 1994:192). This racist policy was translated into a complex legislative system, which set aside and protected the most attractive portions of the urban areas as enclaves for the development of an exclusive white property market. While the thorough, racially discriminatory framework that was created in South Africa had no equivalent in Brazil, a compelling parallel with the conservative project of the military dictatorship in Brazil (as from 1964) may be seen in the degree to which the system supported the interests of real estate. Under the apartheid plan, South African cities were restructured along racial lines, through a determined project of state intervention removing racially mixed slums and informal settlements from desirable land to make way for white business and residential investment, while a comprehensive regulatory framework of racial exclusion was consolidated for the maintenance of segregation. In Brazil, urban spatial restructuring took the form of state intervention in the removal of slums and informal settlements. However, the state did not enforce an urban spatial framework to regulate subsequent development.[17] Instead, the military regime returned to the contents of the 1916 Civil Code, discarding the concept of social function of property and reinstating highly individualised rights to private property (Fernandes and Rolnik, 1998). This gave virtual autonomy to land speculators, and resulted in the displacement, peripheralisation and segregation of the working class. Under both regimes, any form of popular protest was repressed.

It is estimated that at the National Party's entry into the South African government in 1948, 58 per cent of the urban African (black) population was illegally occupying unserviced land (Posel, 1991:20). Particularly women and children in this squatter population were considered, by the new rulers, as unnecessary to the urban economy, and therefore programmes were directed at their removal and restriction to their rural areas of origin. New acts were introduced for population registration, the promulgation of racially exclusive 'Group Areas', and the control of influx to the cities (preference being given to already urbanised labour). Fully urbanised Africans (blacks) were afforded the right to live in the segregated cities irrespective of employment, whereas new arrivals were not permitted to settle permanently (*ibid.*:21). Thus permanent residential rights of Africans (blacks) who had lived and worked in an urban area for a number of years were extended, permitting them also to raise their children in the city (*ibid.*), while at the same time influx control was tightened through an amendment to the system of passes, placing severe restrictions on the urban sojourn of migrant labour (Omer-Cooper, 1994). I have already mentioned the divisions that such biased policies fostered within the urban African (black) population. It follows that any form of radical political opposition to these policies, including African (black) trade union activity, was outlawed (*ibid.*).

The first stage of apartheid, the height of legalised discrimination and segregation, lasted through the 1950s and was based on an ideology of white supremacy. In Brazil, the military government, though not considering itself racially supreme, viewed 'the bulk of the population as ignorant and backward', while politicians were regarded as 'inherently opportunistic and corrupt' – the only civilians trusted by the rulers were 'industrial entrepreneurs and foreign-trained intellectuals and high-skilled technicians' (Bolaffi, 1992:101). Thus the regime 'attempted to establish complete tutelage over the country and the whole civilian society' (*ibid.*). Control over political activity was progressively increased, first through the banishing of politicians that were seen as corrupt or subversive (*ibid.*), and by 1968 through the temporary shutting down of congress and suspension of the Brazilian Constitution, and with it most political and civil rights (Sader and Silverstein, 1991:20).

The scale of squatter removal during the first decade of military dictatorship in Brazil was similar to that in the first decade of National Party rule in South Africa. For Rio de Janeiro, removal figures from 1963 to 1972[18] are in the order of 23,000 units (Seidman, 1994:213), affecting over 120,000 people. In Cape Town, between 1957 and 1961, 100,000 coloured and Indian people were relocated to segregated residential areas, while on average 9,000 Africans (blacks) were repatriated yearly to the rural reserves Transkei and Ciskei for five years (Cook, 1991:32). In Durban, the entire informal settlement of Cato Manor, comprising a population of 120,000 was removed between 1958 and 1960 (Hindson *et al.*, 1994:325, 327).

In both Brazil and South Africa, the removals were accompanied by a massive low-income housing thrust. The state production of South African townships could thus be compared to the housing estates created by Brazil's National Housing Bank (*Banco Nacional da Habitação* – BNH).[19] However, in South Africa and in Brazil the removal of informal settlements outstripped the production of formal low-income housing[20] and led to renewed land invasions in less obtrusive locations. Thus while Rio de Janeiro's southern zone was 'temporarily effectively cleared of squatter settlements ... new favelas sprung up in less-coveted areas of the city' (Seidman, 1994:213). During the removal of Cato Manor in Durban to the township of KwaMashu in the nearby Mlazi reserve, some 30,000 people 'dispersed and relocated outside of the process of official removals' (Davies, 1991:327). However, the situation in Durban was atypical of South African cities. Most urban areas were not bordered by rural reserves, and urban removals often implied repatriation to distant reserves. If Durban, with its neighbouring rural reserves was at one extreme, then Cape Town was at the other, with a distance of 900km to the nearest rural reserve. For Pretoria these reserves were in commutable distance from the city, while for Johannesburg, they were at a distance of at least 100km. This spatial differentiation became more significant with policies of the later phases of apartheid, when these reserves were officially 'urbanised'.

In Brazil the mismatch between removal and production of houses was a result of the tolerated deviation from the intended low-income housing goal. The National Housing Bank (BNH), which operated on compulsory deductions from workers' salaries through the Housing Finance System (*Sistema Financeiro da Habitação* – SFH), financed instead the production of middle-income housing (Bolaffi, 1992:102). The unattended housing need in Brazil led to further unplanned, tolerated and officially ignored expansion of the urban periphery. Seidman (1990b:10) thus compares the apartheid state's role in the production of African (black) townships to 'the role of Brazil's military state in creating the urban "periphery" – the huge sprawl of working-class housing, tenements and informal *favelas*, denied adequate services or security of tenure'.

While aspects of the living conditions might be comparable to the Brazilian periphery, the South African (black) townships were characterised by vastness of scale, uniform and wasteful planning standards and full segregation from white residential areas. 'Buffer strips', several 100 metres wide, were established as 'ideological friction-prevention zones' (Krige, 1991:109), spatially separating different 'Group Areas'. In the 1980s, with the increasing population pressures in townships coupled with government ambiguity and growing ideological redundancy of the buffer zones, these offered space for extensive informal settlements. An urban characteristic of South Africa today, therefore, is the band of informal settlement surrounding formal townships. The wasteful spatial standards applying to undeveloped 'public open space' and road reserves too were subject to reinterpretation under the pressures of the 1980s, with 'interspersed squatting' on unused land within townships.

Urban distortions

The second phase of apartheid, the guise of continued white control through the concept of racial self-determination or separate development (1960 to the mid-

1970s), brought new and lasting effects on South African urbanisation patterns. In this period, the South African government deliberately displaced rural labour tenants and 'squatters' (so-called *'surplus people'*) from white-owned farms, and from other rural areas where Africans (blacks) had legal title (so-called *'black spots'*), to African (black) reserves (Lemon and Cook, 1994:323). Close on a million people were relocated in the 1960s (*ibid.*), thus being driven into poverty and dependence in the rural homelands, which were henceforth to be 'urbanised' under the policy of 'territorial separateness' (Hattingh and Horn, 1991:149), also justifying the freeze of African (black) housing production in 'white' cities. While the reserves had previously been under white trusteeship, the policy of Separate Development was to afford them independent status. This was ridiculed, however, by the imposition of prime-ministers and appointment, in the Assembly, of chiefs, who henceforth supported the concept of separate development (Omer-Cooper, 1994:213).

In Brazil, particularly during the military dictatorship as from 1964, rural displacement led to urban distortions of a different sort. While displaced urbanisation (through 'urbanisation' of the homelands) has since marked the South African urban structure, Brazilian cities were distorted in scale. Rural land ownership patterns, technological advances, economic policies and rural labour practices conditioned migration to the Brazilian cities (Chossudovsky, 1997:185; Sader and Silverstein, 1991:59; SELAVIP, 1981:6). Sader and Silverstein (1991:59) point out that 95 per cent of arable land was owned by five per cent of the Brazilian population, while only 'about one-fifth of the potentially productive land was regularly worked. The rest lay idle while Brazil spent billions of dollars importing foodstuffs'. Redundant rural populations were thus added to the industrial labour reserves on the urban peripheries, which for that purpose were the equivalent of the 'urbanised' homelands in South Africa.

The non-production of housing in South African urban areas increased the pressure on existing urban townships, particularly where 'bantustan' boundaries were not in commutable distance from the city. It appears that Cape Town displayed the harshest urban conditions for Africans (blacks) – for many households the investment or consolidation base (officially in the homelands) was to be at a distance of 900km from the household's economic base, which remained the city. Inevitably, these households sought an urban foothold. With the relatively small scale of the formal African (black) townships in Cape Town, African (black) 'squatting', alongside coloured informal settlement, remained a visible characteristic of the 'white' city of Cape Town throughout the 1960s and 1970s. The repressive state intervention applied to the Cape Town informal settlements, and the state's gradual response to the evidence that these people had nowhere else to go, is significant as it eventually led to the reluctant acceptance of the presence of Africans (blacks) in the city and province for which 'the gradual removal of all Africans' had once been envisioned (South African Institute of Race

Relations, 1956:2). This meant policy concessions, and the introduction of a combination of intervention approaches that to date form the essence of the informal settlement intervention repertoire. They are selective informal settlement freeze, tightened control and the ambiguous 'transit camp'. It may be noted that the concept of 'transit camp' had been previously applied in the late 1940s and early 1950s as a temporary measure in dealing with existing 'squatters'. In Cape Town, the Nyanga Transit Camp,[21] established in accordance with the 1951 Prevention of Illegal Squatting Act, was envisaged to accommodate 17,000 people, who from there were either allocated a formal house or were repatriated to the 'bantustans' (Awotona *et al.*, 1995:2-5; Fast, 1995:142). The equivalent or precedent in Johannesburg was the strictly controlled Moroka Emergency Camp, established to the southwest of the city as early as 1947 (Fast, 1995:142; Parnell and Hart, 1999:375).

Signs of 'political opening'

In both Brazil and South Africa, the mid-1970s signalled the beginning of a gradual process of 'political opening'. In South Africa, the shifts in government approach to informal settlement through the 1970s and into the 1980s were indicative of this ambivalent and protracted process. Coloured 'squatting', which in Cape Town took the scale of around 150,000 people as opposed to 30,000 African (black) 'squatters' in 1977 (Ellis *et al.*, 1977:2), had become a growing concern to the state. In 1974, the government decided to freeze the coloured 'squatter' population across the country, registering the shacks, and imposing an interim service charge, until formal housing allocation (*ibid.*). With the delivery of formal housing, the number of registered shacks in Cape Town was reduced from 27,000 in 1974 to 7,800 in 1981 (Howe, 1982:6). However, the official freeze bore no relation to the actual housing need hidden in overcrowded formal housing. As from the 1974 freeze, new coloured 'squatters' were treated under the same preventative legislation as African (black) 'squatters', and in the absence of any alternative, 'squatting' for African (black) and coloured people alike became a life of repeated harassment, demolition and reconstruction of shacks. In the face of this reality, though not in acknowledgement of its actual cause, influx control was extended to coloured people entering Cape Town – in an amendment to the Prevention of Illegal Squatting Act, the employment of coloured people from outside of Cape Town without certification of being 'properly' housed was criminalised (*ibid.*:39). At the same time, legislation over demolition of shacks was progressively tightened, and mass demolition or bulldozing of large 'squatter settlements' was accompanied with the arrest and repatriation of African (black) women and children. However, removal to the Transkei and Ciskei was vehemently resisted, as families refused to be torn apart (Howe, 1982).

What remained unresolved (as is common with 'squatter policies' involving an informal settlement freeze), was the waning legitimacy of the 1974 cut-off date, in relation to the continuing growth of coloured informal settlement. For Cape Town, an extension of the cut-off date could not be applied, as under existing policies Africans (blacks) could not be afforded the same urban rights as coloureds. Admitting to losing the battle against African (black) 'squatting' in Cape Town, the government set a new precedent by assigning Crossroads (a vacant area adjoining the existing African (black) township of Nyanga) for the temporary relocation of African (black) 'squatters' from the Brownsfarm informal settlement. In 1976, Crossroads was proclaimed a *'transit camp'*, accommodating over 3,000 shacks (Cole, 1986; Weichel *et al.*, 1978).

The Crossroads transit camp became the subject of ambiguous intervention as government was reviewing its position on African (black) housing, and in the 1980s bore the brunt of the government's new tactics of co-optation. The uncertainty of the status of 'transit camp', which was afforded many informal settlements in the 1980s, has required the ongoing struggle for the full recognition of rights to land, and for the individual household implies the postponement of any strategic longer term decision-making. Nevertheless, the 'transit camp' has endured in the informal settlement intervention repertoire to date, now officially termed 'reception area'.[22] This continuity of intervention is a result of the third phase of apartheid, that which introduced orderly urbanisation (which I alluded to in Chapter 1). However, in the mid-1970s, concessions such as the proclamation of the Crossroads transit camp were signs not only of transition towards a new phase of apartheid, but also of a gradual and inevitable crumbling of the power of the National Party.

In Brazil, the gradual process of political opening introduced in 1974 was out of 'the regime's own confidence that its opponents were thoroughly defeated and conditions for a long period of capitalist expansion established' (Sader and Silverstein, 1991:20). Subsequent economic and political pressures then forced the way to further reform in Brazil (*ibid.*). In South Africa, in turn, the state in the mid-1970s was more directly forced to react to a complex set of pressures, both from the African (black) opposition movement and from industry (Omer-Cooper, 1994:223–6). In effect, then, in both Brazil and South Africa, the state increasingly was adjusting to societal responses to the harsh conditions its policies had produced and reproduced. Increasingly, initiatives from outside of government influenced official informal settlement intervention policy. A contrast, however, exists between the resulting intervention approaches in South Africa and Brazil, this being the subject of Chapter 5.

4.4 Conclusion

In South Africa, the processes of exclusion, which have been manifested in informal settlement, have taken different forms to those in Brazil. I have discussed in this chapter how the South African situation was primarily marked by racially based exclusion, as opposed to the mechanisms of class-based exclusion that characterised Brazil. Thus, class barriers in Brazil are contrasted with racial barriers in South Africa. Class barriers in South Africa were, however, introduced, first deliberately by the apartheid state's tactics of divide-and-rule of the African (black) population, and subsequently sharpened by the market as it increasingly gained access to this divided sector of society. Barriers have further been created through the urban structures that have been shaped by social exclusion throughout the 20th century. In South Africa, the racially segregated spatial pattern to date is maintained through class-based segregation, affordability being a major barrier to residential mobility (Houssay-Holzschuch, 1999). In Brazil, the speculative process of urban spatial formation, which has likewise resulted in distinct class-based segregation (Souza, 1993a), also creating a degree of racial segregation (Telles, 1994:191), has remained largely unchallenged by state intervention. Both spatial processes were implemented through extensive relocations and displacements, never resolving the informal settlement situation, instead replicating it in increasingly distorted dimensions. Interests that were served by such distortions were never those of the broader public. In Brazil, the privilege of a class-based elite was upheld, and in South Africa, that of a white minority.

In both countries tendencies towards greater inclusion, driven by the interests of industry and stability, were overturned by a swing to the far-right, reinstating ultra-conservative policies of the early 20th century, for instance, around land-related legislation and political rights. Gradual 'political opening' after the mid-1970s in both countries then reintroduced policy directions of those earlier liberal tendencies. In Brazil, clientelism characterises particularly informal settlement intervention in that period, while in South Africa, the policy of 'orderly urbanisation' introduced new, more subtle forms of bureaucratic control, though increasingly deracialised. The following chapter examines the differences in societal responses to informal settlement that gained space through political opening as from the mid-1970s. The dominance of neo-liberal informal settlement intervention proposals in policy negotiations in South Africa contrasts with the clear articulation and promotion, through the PT, of progressive governance and intervention proposals, based on a consciousness of mechanisms of exclusion and of class barriers. The variation in awareness of the exclusionary processes discussed in this chapter then appears to have determined the shape of societal response to informal settlement, and therefore what is considered appropriate intervention in South Africa and Brazil.

Notes

1 Mamdani (1996:96) draws direct parallels between this practice and the concept of 'indirect rule' practised by the British in colonial Africa. He thus argues against the particularity of the South African experience, and instead equates it with colonial experience across the African continent.

2 With reference to the pre-1964 populist period in Brazil, Alves (1989:279) mentions the dependency of the process of capital accumulation on 'state structures capable of ensuring a high rate of exploitation'.

3 Immigration took place between 1880 and 1930 (Oliveira, 1996:74).

4 A separate interpretation is that of Marx (1998:15), who argues that 'Brazilian elites found that they could maintain their long-established social order of white privilege without enforcing racial domination'.

5 *'Estado Novo'* or 'New State' refers to the 1937 to 1945 dictatorship (see Bonduki, 1994).

6 Vargas ruled again from 1951 to 1954.

7 The centralised schooling system served primarily to foster nationalism (Burns, 1970:303).

8 This affected eight favelas in Brazil between 1941 and 1943, and is interpreted as a concession by Vargas to elite interests (Souza, 1993a:196).

9 Lawrence (1994:95) argues that in South Africa 'the discourse on class distinctions has been often blurred by – indeed, almost to the point of being indistinguishable from – that of "racial identity"'.

10 The concept of citizenship in Brazil refers 'both to the membership in the political community of all Brazilians that guarantees them the right to voice, and to residence in a locality' (Friedmann, 1998:25).

11 The term 'political opening' (*abertura*) was coined in Brazil in 1974 by General Ernesto Geisel, the then military head of state, in his announcement of a gradual process of reinstatement of political rights (Sader and Silverstein, 1991:20). In my interpretation it may also be applied to the protracted and ambiguous process of reform by the National Party in South Africa through the third and final phase of National Party policy initiated in 1973/74, which Omer-Cooper (1994:223) refers to as 'multi-racial co-optation'. This reform was driven by deep economic and political crisis. It led to the first temporary concessions to illegal squatters (Crossroads Emergency Camp in Cape Town) in 1976, a gradual reform of property rights and urbanisation policy with a milestone in 1986 (the White Paper on Urbanisation), and eventually the unbanning of African (black) political movements in 1990.

12 It may be noted that certain land-related reforms were introduced by the South African government as from the mid-1980s.

13 Though progressive in content, the practical meaning of a 'social function of property' was only clarified in the 1988 Constitution. Thus the relationship between the 1916 Civil Code, which attached highly individual rights to private property, and the definition of the social function of property in the Constitution from 1934 onwards remained largely unresolved until a new legal framework was drawn up in the Constitution of 1988 (Fernandes and Rolnik, 1998:145).

14 The name Soweto was derived from the first two letters of the words 'South Western Townships'.

15 Dishonest speculators, referred to as '*grileiros*' (meaning 'crickets', as they were believed to darken the false documents they used in the transactions by burning crickets) would acquire parcels of land on the urban periphery, illegally subdivide the land and trick individuals into believing in the legality of their purchase of the land (Imparato, personal communication, 1997 – in 1997 Ellade Imparato was giving legal support to residents of illegal subdivisions in São Paulo's Eastern Zone through the NGO CEPAR – the Center for Studies, Research, Assessment and Consulting on Urban Reform and Citizenship).

16 Meaning the controlled settling of new arrivals to urban areas, and not to be confused with the Brazilian term '*urbanização*' applied to the upgrading of informal settlements.

17 Although the urban planning discipline flourished during the repressive years of the dictatorship, urban masterplans that were elaborated were never implemented (see Bolaffi, 1992:103).

18 In Rio de Janeiro, favela removal programmes had intensified as from 1960 (Valladares and Figueiredo, 1983:73). The peak of state removal of favelas was between 1968 and 1973 (Souza, 1993a:204).

19 However, in concept the BNH housing delivery might have more in common with that of the current South African housing policy. The BNH promised home ownership to low-income households (though on a mortgage system and not through a once-off household subsidy as is currently the case in South Africa), at the same time 'channelling non-inflationary financial assets to the building industry and large contractor companies' (Bolaffi, 1992:100).

20 However, low income housing production in Brazil ebbed off faster than in South Africa, where planned townships were nevertheless produced at a vast scale.

21 Until 1973 the area was operated as a transit camp (Fast, 1995), and in later years a portion that remained undeveloped was named KTC (Kakaza Trading Company). This became the locale of 'uncontrolled squatting'. In 1986 the KTC squatter settlement was subject to the tragic state orchestrated Crossroads squatter conflict (Cole, 1989), and since the early 1990s it is being reshaped (and de-densified) into a formal standardised site and service area through the ambitious Serviced Land Project (Awotona *et al.*, 1995).

22 In the late 1990s, five 'reception areas' had been set aside in and around Johannesburg, for the temporary settlement of homeless people, who's names were then entered on the official housing waiting list (*Mail & Guardian*, 11 to 17 June 1999).

Chapter 5

Inclusion or Patronage? Emergence of the Current Informal Settlement Intervention Repertoire in South Africa and Brazil

5.1 Introduction

In South Africa, the centralised informal settlement intervention framework of the past ten years has been dominated by neo-liberal notions. In Brazil, a strongly decentralised framework allows space for socially oriented, progressive and democratic practice at municipal level. In the previous chapter I argued that this contrast may be partly rooted in the diverging processes of exclusion that have differently shaped both the informal settlement situation and the consciousness thereof within the various sectors of society. In Brazil, informal settlements are more consciously associated with an exploitation of the working or 'popular' class, whereas a consciousness of racial barriers in South Africa has resulted in a racial (and to a lesser extent a class-based) understanding of the informal settlement phenomenon. This chapter examines in more detail, how the Brazilian and South African societies have responded differently to the phenomenon of informal settlement, and how these responses have developed into the current intervention repertoires in the two countries. The aim thereby is to develop a critical position on current informal settlement intervention in South Africa, which is then deepened in the following chapters that turn more specifically to the South African thinking and practice. The leading question in this chapter therefore is: What critical aspects of the South African informal settlement intervention paradigm are exposed through a comparison between the emergence of South African and Brazilian intervention approaches?

This chapter is addressed through two broad enquiries. Sections 5.2 to 5.4 examine the range of responses within civil society to the phenomenon of informal settlement. There, returning first to the 1940s, I trace contrasts between societal responses during populism in Brazil and limited economic realism in

South Africa, through subsequent repression in both countries, to the responses that developed in the 1970s and 1980s with the (re-)emergence of unionism, community mobilisation, political activity, NGOs and private (business) sector initiative. Section 5.5 then examines the extent to which these responses from civil society were adopted into a process of government reform, and the extent to which they have thereby shaped the current informal settlement intervention repertoire. This outcome is largely defined by the process through which such reform look place. In the Brazilian case, re-democratisation, constitution-making and decentralisation, in which an organised progressive sector of civil society participated with well-articulated and consistent demands, were important processes where civil society exercised influence over the state. In South Africa, the process of change took place primarily through negotiations, largely dominated by the strong position of the private sector, which gave little space to the more fragile proposals put forward by the left-oriented civic movement (and later by the People's Dialogue/Homeless People's Federation). Through this comparison, I draw attention to the important influence of critical progressive urban thinking on informal settlement intervention in Brazil, and the absence of a strong articulation of equivalent thinking in South Africa. Chapter 6 takes this further, by examining the South African informal settlement literature of the 1990s, and Chapter 7, by examining current South African intervention practice.

5.2 The liberalising post-war years: different forms of patronage in Brazil and South Africa

As mentioned in the previous chapter, the 1940s in Brazil and in South Africa saw an unprecedented growth in informal settlements in the rapidly expanding cities. In both countries, the mobilisation of informal settlement communities was characterised by patronage, though of a different kind. In Brazil, patronage was exercised by the state which depended on support from labour (during the Vargas dictatorship, 1937 to 1945), and later depended more directly on electoral support from the literate sector of the informal settlement population (during the 1945 to 1964 populism). In South Africa in the 1940s, in the absence of African (black) political rights, patronage was exercised by individual 'squatter leaders'. I will briefly discuss, how each of these forms of mobilisation responded to the particular socio-political context.

While Vargas, during his 15 year rule of Brazil (1930 to 1945), had introduced clientelism to ensure political support of his regime, and created an 'official apparatus' for the organisation of labour (Kowarick and Bonduki, 1994:128), it was only in the populist period after his rule and up until the 1964 coup, that demands of organised communities were translated into government programmes. For the short period of its unbanning from 1945 to 1947, the Brazilian Communist Party (*Partido Comunista Brasileiro* – PCB) became 'the primary proponent of issue-oriented movements' (*ibid.*, 129), setting up 'Popular

Democratic Committees' (CDPs) within communities, coordinated by a centralised and disciplined structure at municipal level (*ibid.*). Unlike the anarchist movement earlier that century, the PCB was holding the state responsible for inadequate housing conditions. Its aim was 'to take over the state and strengthen it', and the activities of the CDPs had to submit to this overall strategy (*ibid.*:111). Souza (1993a:199) notes that in the 1947 elections it was particularly from the favela population that the PCB won votes in Rio de Janeiro. Although CDPs were repressively disbanded with the banning of the Communist Party later in 1947, the 'practice of addressing problems to the state left a very deep impression in local grassroots organisation' (Bonduki, 1994:111).

In the following period (1947 to 1964), neighbourhood associations were encouraged, and were used clientelistically by city governments (Kowarick and Bonduki, 1994:130). They 'tended to become vehicles of political support for populist governments, rather than institutional conduits for working-class pressure' (Alves, 1989:278), although their roles varied according to the orientation of individual governors or mayors. These tendencies are illustrated by the case of Belo Horizonte (as described by Afonso and Azevedo, 1987), where a strong favela movement resisted expulsions and organised overnight invasions, thus challenging the status quo. As from the mid-1950s, it received support from the progressive sector of the Catholic Church. While the official intervention approach remained that of relocation to new housing, the demand from within the favela movement was for legalisation and regularisation of land occupations. A mayor, elected with strong support from favela residents on promises of regularisation, once in office responded by clientelistically handing out plots and apartments to those favela residents to which he had links. Those less favoured invaded land in order to create pressure for action on the election promises. This in turn was tolerated by the state governor, who opposed the Belo Horizonte mayor (Afonso and Azevedo, 1987:116–8). In Rio de Janeiro, it was through an agreement between the Catholic Church and the municipality in 1955, forming the '*Cruzada São Sebastião*', that several favelas benefited from improved basic services without disruption of the spatial layout, i.e. *in situ* upgrading (Taschner, 1995:203). The municipal policy towards favelas in Rio de Janeiro, however, remained that of relocation (*ibid.*). Ambiguity thus characterised informal settlement intervention of that period.

Government concern with popular housing receded in the late 1950s and early 1960s, with government interest instead being diverted to modernisation and the automotive industry, and the construction of the new capital city of Brasilia (Taschner, 1995:204). However, the Cuban revolution in 1959, and the urban reform of Fidel Castro, inspired a progressive movement of urban professionals and 'fostered utopias about the future of Latin American countries' (Maricato, 1996:8). In 1963, progressive Brazilian architects convened a seminar on 'Housing and Urban Reform', based within a larger movement promoting

'Basic Reforms' (*ibid.*:7). The content of the urban reform proposals in the 1960s was that of centralised planning and strong intervention by government to ensure access to land and housing for the low income population (*ibid.*:9), notably very different from the thinking in the urban reform movement that re-emerged in the 1980s to which I return later in this chapter. Ironically, these early urban reform proposals were translated into the national housing policy of the subsequent military regime (Maricato, 1996:9; Souza, 1993b:213). Housing provision through this policy, however, exposed 'an extravagant distance between discourse and practice', which Maricato (1996:9) refers to as one of the 'hallmarks of Brazilian society'.

In South Africa in the 1940s, political exclusion[1] required informal settlement mobilisation of a different sort from that of Brazil. Stadler (1979:93), analysing the informal settlement dynamics in Johannesburg from 1944 to 1947, speaks of 'squatter movements' (note the plural), driven by individual leaders. These movements depended on the particular orientation and power of their leader, an example being the well known James Mpanza, who mobilised the frequently referred to 'Sofasonke Party' (Harrison, 1992:12; Mamdani, 1996:98; Stadler, 1979:94). Such mobilisation comprised the recruitment of a following by the leader, sometimes in authoritarian style, the collective invasion of land and the maintenance of autonomy from the municipality. Autonomy was enabled through the density of the occupation and the authority exercised by the leader (Stadler, 1979:94). While Bonner (1990:97) makes mention of individual squatter leaders at the time having set up food cooperatives, which might suggest socialist orientations, it appears that the squatter mobilisation did not entail political conscientisation of the followers. Instead, it created a dependency on the tactics and vision of the leader. With political disenfranchisement, the possibility of squatter demands being taken up as contending policy proposals, as was the case in Brazil, did not exist in South Africa. Indeed, squatters at the time were considered less than human – the official process undertaken to identify individual perpetrators of the pass laws was officially referred to as 'culling'[2] (Stadler, 1979:101).

Within this context, the particular form that squatter mobilisation took in Johannesburg was the only effective means of securing living space for the landless urban African (black) population. Patronage by the squatter leaders may have some parallels in Brazil with the middle-men or '*grileiros*'[3] that illegally sold land to the working-class on the urban periphery. However, this was an officially tolerated and even deliberately encouraged process that relieved the state of the acute housing shortage (Kowarick and Bonduki, 1994:125), whereas squatting in Johannesburg in the 1940s provoked confrontation with the state. Indeed, by 1948 the state had gained control over most of the Johannesburg squatter movements, their members being resettled in municipally controlled emergency camps. Mobilisation, then, took the form of rent strikes within these camps, and therefore renewed confrontation with the state (Stadler, 1979:103).

The relationship between the favela movement and a broader left-oriented movement in Brazil, with the progressive sector of the Catholic Church and political parties of the left, did not have an equivalent in South Africa. The South African squatter movements avoided compliance with the African National Congress (ANC) and the Communist Party, the two main African (black) political organisations at the time (Sapire, 1990a). The ANC had been founded in 1912 by an elite of Western-educated Africans (blacks), strongly supporting the civilised values on which 'white' society 'claimed to be based' (Omer-Cooper, 1994:162). Initially they sought the extension of equal rights to all in the civilised sector of society (*ibid.*), not dissimilar from the limited franchise applying to Brazilian society at the time. It was only with the harsh racial discrimination experienced across the black social spectrum, that the ANC identified with the 'wider African population' (*ibid.*). Thus, in 1943 the ANC drafted a Bill of Rights, which included universal political rights. The ANC continued to pursue moderate liberal principles, though with pressure from the more radically inclined Youth League it adopted tactics of mass passive resistance, and reluctantly participated in mass protest action initiated by the Communist Party (*ibid.*). However, Stadler (1979:108) notes that the ANC, though concerned with miners' strikes, 'does not seem to have taken up the issue of squatting'. The same appears to have applied to the Communist Party at the time (*ibid.*).

While political leaders of the ANC 'drew on Christian values for the building of a broader political community' (Walshe, 1997:384), the religious landscape in South Africa did not allow for the Catholic Church to play a role equivalent to that of its Brazilian counterpart. Across the denominational diversity of the Christian faith in South Africa (Calvinist, Catholic, Protestant, Pentecostal and independent African-initiated churches), political convictions and affiliations varied significantly. Bonner (1990:104) speculated on the intersection between the squatter movements of the post-war years and the African-initiated churches, which 'blossomed' simultaneously among the urban poor. He noted parallels between the squatter leaders and the 'charismatic prophet-type leaders' of these religious congregations (*ibid.*:192). Notably, most members of the African-initiated churches adopted an apolitical stance (Walshe, 1997). The significance of this becomes clear when one realises the scale of this religious movement. In the mid-1950s, membership of the African-initiated churches was estimated at two million (Bonner, 1990:104), with an increase to 10 million by the late 1990s (Anderson and Pillay, 1997:233).

5.3 The re-emergence of mobilisation from the 1970s: new responses to informal settlement?

In both Brazil and South Africa, the social mobilisation in the work place and the community, which had developed in the post-war years, was repressed with the political swing to the far-right (1964 in Brazil, 1948 in South Africa). Some of the earlier (post-war) political trends around informal settlement, however, endured or re-emerged with gradual political reform after the mid-1970s. In Brazil, clientelism and patronage again characterised the relationship between favela communities and the state. In South Africa, the informal settlement question remained largely ignored by African (black) oppositional politics, although increasingly informal settlements became the locale of politically motivated confrontation between community and state. In Brazil, progressive mobilisation confronted the dominant practice of clientelism, and aimed to replace the associated political patronage with political inclusion and self-determination through the concept of participatory democracy. In the 1980s, the newly formed PT (Workers' Party) became the political vehicle for the promotion of the autonomy of grassroots or 'base' organisations,[4] and their direct participation in the definition of intervention programmes. In South Africa, progressive thinking on alternative forms of local governance was developed within the civic movement. However, continued government repression in the 1980s, and professional patronage into the 1990s, left little space for the emergence of alternative practice. In Section 5.4, below, I turn more directly to the patronage entailed in the influential thinking on informal settlement intervention put forward by the Urban Foundation, a neo-liberal private sector initiative, which strongly promoted a technocratic solution to informal settlement, namely the delivery of sites-and-services through the individualised capital subsidy.

The Catholic Church and favela mobilisation in Brazil

The Catholic Church in Brazil played an important role in organising and conscientising at the grassroots level, and in building an understanding of the exploitative nature or injustices of capitalism as it was playing itself out in Brazil. Repression by the military, as well as the 1968 decision by the Latin American Bishops' conference in Medellín, Columbia, to serve the cause of the poor, led to an 'internal transformation' of the Catholic Church (Alves, 1989:286; Mainwaring, 1984:98; Sader and Silverstein, 1991:58; Vink, 1985:100). Throughout military repression, a degree of community mobilisation was kept alive through the ecclesiastic or Christian base communities (*Comunidades Eclesial de Base* – CEBs), which the emerging Catholic left had first set up in the early 1960s as a new means of working with the popular sectors, thus overcoming the previous paternalistic practices of the Church (Mainwaring, 1984:97, 98). As 'the only institution in civil society that had sufficient autonomy vis-à-vis the state to continue progressive pedagogic work with the popular classes', it had become by 1973 'the most significant institution defending human rights' (*ibid.*:98). The concept of Christian base communities or CEBs was extended into the informal settlements through the '*Pastoral de Favelas*',[5] which provided structured space for debate on the situation in informal settlements. The 'democratic participatory practices' developed by the CEBs in favelas and elsewhere had no precedent in the pre-1964 popular organisations (*ibid.*:100).

After the first relaxation of repression in 1974, the political role that the Church had fulfilled was taken over to some extent by unions, political parties, neighbourhood associations and progressive professional groups (Mainwaring, 1984:98). However, the Church continued to play an important role in 'strengthening the struggles of unions, peasant leagues, and neighbourhood associations' (*ibid.*). What, then, were the Church's responses to the favela question? Three examples illustrate that the Church confronted the question of social rights related to land and housing, thus the legal position of favelas, besides the continuing role of the *Pastoral de Favelas* in community organisation, formation of leadership and articulation of, and lobbying for, localised development objectives. In the case of Rio de Janeiro, the Archdiocese created a juridical service in 1978, with lawyers fostering 'a critical consciousness' among favela residents (SELAVIP, 1981:8). Together with the *Pastoral de Favelas*, the aim was to ensure that favelas were not removed, that paternalism (or the solving of problems from outside) be avoided and that existing socially responsive laws be implemented and new laws be enacted (*ibid.*). In the Diocese of Vitória, the Church undertook particular activities around the question of housing rights, promoting the concept that invasions by poor people are not a crime but an act of survival, and therefore a human right. It therefore challenged the government to become involved not through its police force, but through social welfare (*ibid.*:9). In Belo Horizonte, the *Pastoral de Favelas* was increasingly engaged with the question of rights to land, whereas a separate movement of favela residents, the Union of Workers of the Periphery (*União dos Trabalhadores da Periferia* – UTP) was concerned with the more immediate demands generated by evictions, for instance, the demand for better compensation (Afonso and Azevedo, 1987:122).

In terms of rights to occupied land, the long-standing popular demand was for individualised freehold title or home-ownership. Bolaffi (1992:100) notes that in 1961, a survey by the American Institute of International Relations had concluded that 'one of the most frequent aspirations ... of the Brazilian urban population was to own a house'. This it associated with 'conservative political attitudes', and indeed such correlation had inspired the home ownership thrust of the military dictatorship (*ibid.*). However, Kowarick and Ant (1994:71), acknowledging the widespread home ownership aspiration, place this trend in relation to exclusion and insecurity faced by the urban working-class. Thus they argue that 'it is surely not for ideological reasons alone that workers set their sights on freeing themselves from the obligation to pay rent' (*ibid.*). With this understanding, then, the progressive sector of the Catholic Church, and the left-oriented professionals supporting the favela movement and its demands, sought to promote instruments that would enable favela residents to gain individual freehold tenure. Some opposition was voiced from an ideologically focused left sector, wishing instead to promote forms of communal tenure in the expectation that individual home ownership would lead to a demobilisation of the working-class (Michelini, personal communication, 1997).[6] Its proposals, however, found no popularity among the favela population. More rigorous opposition was in turn voiced from the conservative land-owning class, which saw its real estate interests impeded by the proposed instruments for favela land regularisation (*ibid.*).

From the mid-1970s, there were endeavours to unify the various localised urban struggles, including those for rights to land. Through the land-related initiatives of the Catholic Church, and in particular a 'National Network for Urban Land' (*Articulação Nacional do Solo Urbano* – ANSUR),[7] which was created in the early 1980s, a national Urban Reform Movement was initiated, as a counterpart to the movement advocating agrarian reform (Maricato, 1994:310). In 1988 this movement, through the participation of various popular and professional national entities including the Movement for the Defence of Favela Residents (*Movimento de Defesa do Favelado*), submitted a constitutional amendment on urban reform, supported by 160,000 signatures (*ibid.*). Central aspects of this proposal were, on the one hand, the social function of property and of the city and, on the other hand, popular participation in the definition and management of urban policies (Lago, 1992:42), i.e. democratic urban management through structures such as democratic councils, public audiences and popular referendums (Maricato, 1994:311). With specific regards to the favela situation, the movement was promoting mechanisms for the regularisation of land (*ibid.*), thus reflecting the localised struggles I have referred to above. The overriding objective of the urban reform movement remains that of achieving a more just city, thus combating two processes that have shaped the Brazilian city: on the one hand, the excessive real estate speculation, which has resulted in both over-densification and the holding of vacant land; on the other hand, the inequitable spatial distribution of public investment in infrastructure (Souza, 1993b:208).

The contribution of legal and planning scholars of the left was in the articulation of urban reform instruments that would address popular concerns. Being oriented to the overriding concern of social justice, these alternative professionals, unlike their conventional rational counterparts in Brazil, emphasise the 'political-technical process' of planning rather than the 'technical product' (Souza, 1999:4). Concerning their relationship with the popular class, Souza (1999:4) argues that: 'Alternative planners are not afraid of conflicts; instead of conceiving disharmony as an undesirable and avoidable thing (as conventional planners do), they know that conflicts and tensions are inherent features of class societies'. The understanding, then, is that harmony cannot be built through 'instrumental rationality' (*ibid.*). Instead, these alternative planners 'intend to contribute to a process of negotiation and regulation of conflicts during which the contradictions become explicit and the options can be freely debated on the basis of political transparency and participation of ordinary citizens' (*ibid.*). The orientation of these alternative Brazilian professionals, in their consciousness of class and conflict, contrasts with the product-oriented professional input in South African urban reform with regards to informal settlements. I will emphasise this point below, particularly with regards to the 'professional' position developed by the influential Urban Foundation. In Chapter 6, I more specifically trace the scholarly thinking behind this approach, finding there the professional endeavour to stabilise mobility and inter-community conflict and violence through a technically defined intervention product: the serviced site with individual freehold title.

It should be noted that apart from the mobilising activities of the Catholic Church through CEBs, the late 1970s in Brazil saw a strong growth in resident associations, this being ascribed to both the worsening conditions in favelas as well as the 'political opening' which allowed the earlier populist relationship between state and citizens to re-emerge.[8] Support for community associations came both from politicians, for whom they represented a vehicle for making themselves known and to lobby for support, and from the state programmes that laid increasing emphasis on 'participatory' approaches (Afonso and Azevedo, 1987:124). A different political vision for community organisation and its relationship with the state then emerged with the formation of the PT in 1980. Though having its roots in the 'radical labour union movement that emerged in south-eastern Brazil's heavy industrial sector at the end of the 1970s', the PT had been formed in an alliance between the labour unions and other progressive and radical groups in Brazilian society, including the progressive arm of the Catholic Church (Abers, 1996:36).

Politicisation: the PT approach in Brazil

The PT is considered 'a novel development among Brazilian institutions' for three reasons (Keck, 1992:239): firstly, it set out to express at a political level 'the interests of workers and the poor'; secondly, it strove to be 'internally democratic'; and thirdly, it emphasised accountability to its members. These concerns have remained central to the party's identity (*ibid.*). The particular concept of the PT therefore lies in the role it foresees for grassroots organisations. Abers (1996:37) defines this concept as 'autonomous grassroots control and direct participation', noting, however, that the party's heterogeneity did not lend itself to an official ideology. Indeed, it shunned 'the elitism, dogmatism, and revolutionary vanguardism of earlier Brazilian socialist parties' (*ibid.*). Autonomy of the grassroots movements (as opposed to their integration into the ruling system) was then considered necessary for the active participation of the population in the implementation of democracy (Wolf, 1994:348). The party's decentralised and democratic internal structure (Abers, 1996:37) reflected its vision for governance: on the one hand, the party was to be carried by the base movement, on the other hand, it was to take the demands of the base movement into the political system (Wolf, 1994:350).

Mainwaring (1984:115) notes that in its early years, the PT was 'explicitly more concerned about conscientisation and supporting popular movements than about coming to power in the short run'. Popular awareness grew over the difference between the PT approach and the patronage and clientelism offered by other politicians (Seidman, 1994:209). Conscientisation also encompassed a broad anti-capitalist sentiment through an awareness of the exclusionary process of capital accumulation in Brazil (*ibid.*:225). The concepts of class and citizenship were popularised and 'increasingly appealed to a constituency that found itself excluded from the benefits of capitalist growth' (*ibid.*:227).

Although the PT had won control over the municipality of Diadema as early as 1982 (as noted in Chapter 3), and two further municipalities in 1985, it was only in preparation for the 1988 municipal elections that 'the PT began to define what a PT municipal administration should look like' (Abers, 1996:37). Abers lists the PT's key governance principles as 'decentralisation of power, government accountability to autonomous social movements, and a reversal of priorities away from elite groups toward the poor and disadvantaged' (*ibid.*:37, 38). Popular councils were to play an important role in controlling the decision-making of the municipal administrations (*ibid.*). In a practical sense, then, the PT hoped to challenge the widespread practices of clientelism, both in the deals between leaders of residents' associations and politicians (with electoral support being exchanged for promises of development) and in the deals between the business sector (particularly construction and real estate) and politicians, with business giving financial support to political campaigns in return for 'the right to reap super-profits in overcharged government contracts' (*ibid.*:42). Both these forms of clientelism were bearing on the informal settlement situation, and on the form that intervention was taking.

The civic movement response in South Africa

Before returning to the institutionalisation of the PT's alternative concepts in Brazil later in this chapter, I now contrast the Brazilian societal responses with those that emerged in South Africa as from the mid-1970s. As in Brazil, the societal responses to informal settlement in South Africa were embedded in oppositional politics. A clear distinction, however, emerged between the response of the white liberal opposition and the African (black) community-based opposition. In 1976, in reaction to the instability sparked by the brutal police massacre of protesting school children in Soweto, Johannesburg, the white business sector in South Africa created the Urban Foundation (Urban Foundation, 1994). This private sector initiative, which I discuss in more detail below, undertook policy-oriented research on questions of urbanisation (including informal settlements), and proposed and piloted a neo-liberal informal settlement intervention approach. The African (black) opposition responded to informal settlements through the civic movement, which had emerged in African (black) townships in the late 1970s (Shubane, 1991:64). From 1983, the civic movement was coordinated by the newly formed UDF (United Democratic Front),[9] which also spread the movement beyond formal townships into informal settlements. This included the new generation of informal settlements that emerged with the administrative ambiguities of the 1980s (see Crankshaw, 1993:49).

The civic movement received support, through a response from the sympathising professional sector, with the formation of development NGOs. However, as I argue below, development thinking within these NGOs appears to have been closer to that of the Urban Foundation than the civic movement in practice. A later societal response to the persistence of the informal settlement phenomenon was developed in the early 1990s in the form of an internationally inspired social movement, the Homeless People's Federation. The community-based responses of both the civic movement and the Homeless People's Federation have sat uncomfortably with the well financed and thus slickly articulated proposals of the Urban Foundation which were embraced by the dominant African (black) opposition movement, the ANC-SACP-COSATU[10] alliance. The Urban Foundation proposals thus informed current South African housing policy, and by implication, policy on informal settlement. This demonstrated that the informal settlement question remained on the fringe of dominant African (black) politics into the 1990s.

Turning to the activities of the civic movement in the 1980s, it must be noted that while developing its own longer term ideology and concepts on development, the movement was primarily required to respond to immediate circumstances created by ambivalent state reforms. A widespread cause of contention was the implementation of 'Black Local Authorities' (BLAs) in African (black) townships in 1983, which had previously been administered by officials of white City Councils, Administration Boards or Divisional Councils (McCarthy, 1992).[11] Elections of the new BLA councillors were severely boycotted by the contesting constituencies (Shubane, 1991:68). Notably, only 'Section 10' residents, meaning those with permanent urban status, were afforded political expression through these local elections (Omer-Cooper, 1994:229; Shubane, 1991:67). A related point of contention was the raise in rent and services charges. This increase was introduced by the new BLA councillors who were faced with virtually no revenue base, as their constituencies were separate from business and industrial areas (McCarthy, 1992).[12] Further contention among urban African (black) communities arose from the establishment of tricameral parliament in 1983, giving preferential treatment to coloureds (through the House of Representatives) and Indians (through the House of Delegates), by allowing these groups control over their budgets and priorities. While this bode well for the production of coloured and Indian housing, it had no impact on the inadequate African (black) housing stock (Parnell, 1992). Instead, the African (black) residential sphere was subjected to the privatisation of state assets in the area of housing and transport. African (black) housing stock was thus sold to legal occupants, and government expenditure on commuting was reduced through the privatisation of bus companies and the promotion of the informal combi-taxi industry (McCarthy, 1992).

The civic movements' response (and that of the UDF) was to orchestrate boycotts in order to cripple the BLA structures.[13] Rent boycotts had been organised since the early 1980s.[14] However, incidents such as brutal police intervention in rent marches in 1985 led to calls for more comprehensive challenges. Besides consumer boycotts of white outlets, this included the creation of alternative governance structures. The civic movement thus encouraged participation in its street and section committees, the boycotting of police stations by taking disputes to 'people's courts', and attempts at people's education associated with the boycotting of government schools (Boraine, 1988). These alternative structures or people's initiatives, however, were not given space to govern.[15] From June 1986 they became the target of a nation-wide state of emergency. Thirty-four townships across South Africa were designated 'strategic bases', from which the security forces believed they could 'regain control' over the African (black) population (*ibid.*:1). One so-called 'oil spot' was the Crossroads transit camp adjacent to the Cape Town township of Nyanga (Cole, 1989).

The state approach was that of creating division through repression and selective co-optation.[16] While the BLA structures in themselves were a means of dividing the urban African (black) society by privileging those with permanent status, from whom the state was hoping loyalty 'in defence of the system' (Omer-Cooper, 1994:227, 228), in 1986 the security forces intervened directly. Control by the civic movement was crushed through the isolation of townships (for example, disconnecting telephone lines), a ban on public gatherings, house-to-house searches and detention of civic and youth leadership, trade unionists and members of street committees (Boraine, 1988). Divisions were then fostered through selective improvement of infrastructure and facilities in townships (with central government funds) (*ibid.*). Tragically, groups of vigilantes emerged, many of which sided with the security forces and attacked ANC supporters (Omer-Cooper, 1994:239). The most publicised case possibly was that of the war in the Crossroads transit camp in Cape Town. In Durban, these dynamics, which 'assumed the character of a long running civil war' (*ibid.*) had a particular bearing on informal settlements. Seeing as this dynamic has led to a widespread assumption (particularly by the middle-class, including urban researchers, as will be evident in Chapter 6) that informal settlements *per se* are associated with violence, it is relevant to briefly review the shifts in such violence in the Durban situation.

As a result of the state's undertaking to incorporate Durban townships[17] into the Inkatha-run KwaZulu, conflict shifted from protest (boycotts) against the apartheid state to a struggle between the UDF and Inkatha[18] (Hindson *et al.*,

1994:338). This violence then shifted increasingly from Durban's core townships to the squatter settlements of KwaZulu, taking the form of mutually destructive clashes between communities of different squatter settlements, and squatter settlements and townships, though also including clashes between townships and hostel residents (*ibid.*:340). Harsh measures employed under the state of emergency led to the removal of virtually all UDF leadership from townships. This promoted the spread of lawlessness and brought the youth constituency to the fore. Thus UDF-supporting youth, 'joined at times by criminal elements' came 'to dominance in most of the formal townships', whereas Inkatha leaders re-emerged in the squatter settlements 'where they teamed up with local shack lords' (in control of single sites), and 'warlords' (in control of entire settlements) (*ibid.*). Within this conflict, Inkatha was given support first by the South African police and later by the KwaZulu Police (founded in 1987). However, by the late 1980s the had ANC won over large portions of the squatter periphery, whereas 'Inkatha retreated into fortress-like pockets of ground' (*ibid.*:41).[19]

The shift from Inkatha control over informal settlements to that by the UDF with its civic structures brought with it the particular ideology of the civic movement. Firstly, this meant democratic representation of communities. It should be noted, however, that this did not always materialise. Van Horen (1996:13), analysing the change from Inkatha to ANC control in the Besters Camp informal settlement in the early 1990s, points out the limitations of what was described as 'democratic' at the time: 'In the absence of adequate organisational structures, or reporting lines and lines of accountability, power cliques operating under the banner of the ANC or civics were in many instances no less guilty of violent intolerance of dissenting viewpoints, than their Inkatha predecessors had been'. Secondly, the UDF and civic structures introduced free access to land. In informal settlements, this meant a shift from rental tenure towards a system that may be associated with 'communal land holding in rural areas', with entry through sponsorship and screening (Cross, 1994:180). Again, clandestine selling of sites in ANC-aligned settlements was not entirely out-ruled (*ibid.*:34).

Turning, then, to the development thinking in the civic movement, ideas of grassroots democracy and the decommodification of land may be considered central concepts. Mayekiso (1996:21), writing about his first hand experience within the civic movement in the Alexandra township of Johannesburg, which is considered one of the most militant areas in South Africa (Mayekiso, personal communication, 1998),[20] mentions that as early as 1985 the Alexandra civic (then called the Alexandra Action Committee – ACC), was discussing its role in community development. Grocery cooperatives for the unemployed, centres providing after school care, and other communal self-help projects were considered. However, such early work on a popular development programme was thwarted by the state-orchestrated violence that diverted the attention of the civic movement (*ibid.*). Nevertheless, decommodification of basic needs commodities, including land and housing, remained central to the development ideology of the civic movement into the 1990s (Mayekiso, 1996:155, 165). This, then, is a remarkable contrast to the Brazilian popular movement that was demanding individual freehold tenure. As will be evident in the discussion of the Urban Foundation thinking, it was the private sector in South Africa that advocated the concept of individual freehold title and 'home ownership' for informal settlement residents. In my analysis of the South African research literature on informal settlement in South Africa in Chapter 6, I return to the simplistic thinking behind the home ownership concept.

Support to a people's movement or deradicalisation? The development NGOs

Early development endeavours of the civic movement, particularly from within informal settlements, found support from sympathetic development professionals in various cities. Thus, besides church organisations and humanitarian NGOs such as the Black Sash,[21] which were engaged in non-political relief work in assistance of informal settlement communities, a new form of 'development NGO' emerged in the 1980s. In 1982, the Built Environment Support Group (BESG) was created at the University of Natal (Durban). This was followed in 1985 by the founding of Planact in Johannesburg, and in 1986 the Development Action Group (DAG) in Cape Town.[22] Starting on a voluntary basis, these groups formalised with time into largely foreign aid-funded NGOs. The formation of DAG was directly linked to the 'squatter crisis' in Cape Town: during the Crossroads war, activists had directed a petition at development professionals to refuse participation in government plans to reorganise the Crossroads transit camp without involvement of the original squatter population. After consultation with the civic organisations and the UDF, DAG was formed to 'contribute to the growing resistance to undemocratic planning methods used by the State to achieve its own political objectives' (DAG, 1996:4). DAG's role is said to have varied according to the demands directed at it from the grassroots. Its activities thus ranged from the formulation of upgrading approaches in resistance to squatter removals, technical input in the drafting of legal documents in resistance to squatter demolitions, advice to civic organisations, drafting of fund raising proposals and, increasingly in the late 1980s, assistance to communities in development negotiations (*ibid.*).

Why did such NGO support not lead to an implementation of communal or decommodified development programmes as the civic movement envisioned? In part, this may be explained through the shifts in relationship between the development NGOs and the communities they were serving. In the early years of these NGOs, they operated in direct partnership with the civic movement. However, the state's endeavour to regain control over the townships, leading to the elimination of the civic leadership in the second half of the 1980s, left the development NGOs without a 'client base' (Abbott, 1996:200). Abbott notes that whereas those NGOs that directly promoted community organisation and media presentation were considered serious threats to the state, the development NGOs operated 'in a political space which allowed them a significant amount of freedom of action' (*ibid.*). They therefore found various ways 'to continue their operation and to grow over the period of oppression' (*ibid.*). The shift was one from a means towards an end (which was defined by the civic movement), to an end in itself. Towards this latter end, the Urban Sector Network was formed in 1988, enabling cooperation and coordination between the various localised development NGOs across South Africa (DAG, 1996:9), thus strengthening an independent nation-wide development NGO movement. In the late 1980s, when the civic leadership was released from detention and could rebuild the civic movement, civic organisations were increasingly in a position to focus on development rather than resistance. However, the development NGOs had by then developed a language and agenda of their own.

Development thinking in the Urban Sector Network NGOs towards the late 1980s and early 1990s was closer to that promoted by the Urban Foundation (which I discuss below), than that of the civic movement. Though respectful of the progressive contributions of development NGO staff, Mayekiso (1996:258), from his own experience as both a Planact employee and a civic leader, critically observed that the NGO professionals were 'usually oriented towards the deradicalisation of the grassroots'. Thus 'many disagreements about strategy between the NGOs and civics ... flowed from professional arrogance and community vulnerability' (*ibid.*). The NGO bias to conventional neo-liberal (or deradicalised) development approaches had a further reason for existence. In 1990, the Urban Foundation's thinking on informal settlement intervention had been semi-institutionalised through the Independent Development Trust (IDT, to which I return later in this chapter), thus increasingly dictating the shape of development. The Urban Sector Network NGOs found a niche in project managing such development (this being financed through the IDT projects), thus placing themselves in an uncomfortable position between civics and a rigid development framework from which they were no longer independent. Although the Urban Sector Network NGO approach to project management was more participatory than that of conventional development consultants, the NGOs had to abide by the dictates of the development framework, including its time constraints and individualised site-and-service product. This, then, was the context in which conflict arose around the involvement of the NGO BESG in the Piesang River informal settlement – one of the case studies discussed in Chapter 7 (although this development was not funded by the IDT, it was contemporary, and based on similar tenets).

The People's Dialogue/Homeless People's Federation alliance in South Africa

A further societal response to informal settlement is the People's Dialogue/ Homeless People's Federation alliance which, though only emerging in the

1990s, developed an intervention approach that contrasts with that of the civic movement that I have already discussed, and more so with that of the Urban Foundation to which I return below. The radical nature of this approach, and hence its conflict with the current Urban Foundation-inspired informal settlement intervention framework, are aspects that I examine in relation to two of the case studies in Chapter 7. Here I introduce the alliance, and then place it in relation to the other strains of informal settlement intervention thinking in South Africa, and to that in Brazil.

As I have already briefly mentioned in Chapter 3, the People's Dialogue/Homeless People's Federation alliance in South Africa was inspired through an international network promoting and linking NGO-initiated support-based intervention initiatives among the urban poor. In 1991, an international meeting of 'people's networks', to which community workers of the Cape Town-based NGO Catholic Welfare and Development (CWD) were invited, led to the formation of a new network, the Southern African People's Dialogue for Land and Shelter (Bolnick, 1993). Supported by the German Catholic aid agency MISEREOR, this autonomous sub-committee of the Southern African Catholic Development Agency was to link informal settlement residents (and other similarly housed people) across South Africa and beyond. The objective was to empower such residents through an exchange of experience (*ibid.*).

Initially, civic leaders from across the country were invited to participate in debate on 'land and shelter' (People's Dialogue, 1991). However, the experience was that homelessness was not a topic that civic leaders were prioritising (Hunsley, personal communication, 1998).[23] Therefore, only individual civic leaders committed themselves to the new initiative. One such leader is the current president of the Homeless People's Federation, whose civic organisation in the Piesang River settlement in Durban has since disbanded. The Federation developed with no direct link to the civic movement. One reason for this was that the Dialogue/Federation initiative took into account what it perceived from international experience to be an 'organic link between women and shelter', therefore addressing itself primarily, though not exclusively, to women (Bolnick, 1993:99). It found that civic organisations in South Africa were in turn 'invariably controlled by men' (*ibid.*). Indeed, Mayekiso admits that the civic movement has been 'notoriously patriarchal,' an issue that only started to be addressed in 1994 (Mayekiso, 1996:253).

A further reason for the non-involvement of civic leaders and their structures in the People's Dialogue initiative, appears to have been the degree to which the civic movement was politicising development. The People's Dialogue initiative instead, was promoting the message that democracy would not necessarily deliver houses to the poor. Here, particularly the experience of continuing homelessness in India despite 40 years of 'democracy', impacted on the new initiative's thinking (Hunsley, personal communication, 1998). Instead of promoting a political solution, the attempt was rather to empower people to take control of their own situation. The People's Dialogue initiative was finding success in breaking through the situation of disempowerment, particularly of poor South African women, by exposing them to the achievements of poverty stricken women in other contexts, for instance through a mutual exchange programme with the pavement dwellers of Bombay (Bolnick, 1993). This recognition of people's own strength was coupled with a realisation of disengagement by those who 'control and contest power' (the initiative had sought dialogue with both the then government, and the contesting ANC) (*ibid.*:104). The conclusion was the need for a 'bottom-up' housing approach based on savings and credit groups. In 1993, a revolving fund was initiated through a grant from MISEREOR, and shortly before the 1994 elections, an umbrella for the savings groups was formalised as the South African Homeless People's Federation. The supporting professionals constituted themselves into the NGO People's Dialogue, with the sole function of assisting with the Federation's activities (People's Dialogue, 1995). Notably, then, this new NGO, in its direct alliance with the Homeless People's Federation, stands in contrast to the service-oriented development NGOs of the Urban Sector Network, which I discussed above.

Diametrically opposed to the Urban Foundation thinking, the premise of the People's Dialogue/Homeless People's Federation alliance was that 'people's direct participation in all aspects of the development of their own settlements' needed to be supported and sustained (Bolnick, 1993:94). In discussing the attempts at institutionalising this approach below, it is interesting to see how the Federation embraced the Urban Foundation-inspired capital subsidy as an individual entitlement. The case studies in Chapter 7 suggest that this individual entitlement has distracted the Federation's collective and radical development activities into endeavours to achieve the largest possible individual housing product through the subsidy amount, in direct competition with profit-driven initiatives. While reluctant to open itself to having this pointed out at the time of the case study research (late 1998), People's Dialogue has since recognised this limitation (see Bauman and Bolnik, 2001:110).

5.4 New forms of patronage: the influential business response in South Africa

In the 1970s in South Africa, as in Brazil, industrialists had begun to distance themselves from the military and apartheid regimes which were no longer serving their interests. Thus in both countries there emerged two broad forms of opposition to the state, one from business, the other rooted in social movements (Seidman, 1990b:12, 1994:101). Seidman (1994:101) notes that in Brazil a 'largely middle class human rights movement strengthened the business opposition'. However, the Brazilian literature appears to make no reference to an independent position on informal settlement intervention developed and advocated by the Brazilian business sector. In South Africa, by contrast, the business sector created the Urban Foundation as a liberal think tank on urban policy. Its proposal for informal settlement intervention has been particularly influential. In order to understand the drive behind this influence, it is relevant to first examine where the Foundation was situated within South African society, before discussing the position it promoted.

In 1976, the instability associated with the Soweto conflict had sparked a business conference on 'the quality of life in our urban communities' (Urban Foundation, 1994:25), which in turn led to the creation of the Urban Foundation as a non-profit organisation funded by leading South African companies spanning mining, construction, banking and retail.[24] Underlying this seemingly humanitarian concern, however, was an economic downturn, which industrialists in part associated with the instability in the skilled workforce, and limited consumer markets (Seidman, 1990b:8). Thus Seidman (*ibid.*) argues that industrialists in South Africa (as in Brazil) in the 1970s 'were far more concerned with improving their own economic prospects and access to state policy-making bodies than with overall democratization'. Indeed, South African business invested in upliftment and social advance (through the Urban Foundation) out of 'enlightened self-interest' (Seidman, 1994:135).

In its initial years the Urban Foundation initiated change in the areas of: a) employment, promoting the removal of job reservation; b) education, by mobilising for non-racial national education; and c) African (black) housing, by encouraging banks to provide end-user finance to black home buyers (Urban Foundation, 1994). For the poorer sector of the urban African (black) population, it promoted the concept of reduced standards of housing, and an individualised form of 'self-help'.[25] It further 'spearheaded' the search for a solution to the urban housing situation by launching a research and policy initiative on influx control and the role of cities, which in 1985 was formalised into the Private Sector Council on Urbanisation (Seidman, 1994:25). Indeed, most of the research on informal settlements in the 1980s and into the 1990s was commissioned by the Urban Foundation.[26] I examine and critique the more recent of these studies in Chapter 6. While the earlier studies uncovered many important aspects of the phenomenon of informal settlement, the research findings as such appear not to have influenced the policy proposals put forward by the Foundation. Much rather, the research appears to have been commissioned to substantiate a proposal that developed primarily from concerns for the position of the profit-making development industry and the commodification of the low-income housing sphere, and not for the informal settlement reality or the popular development concepts that were being debated in the civic movement.

It was also through the Private Sector Council on Urbanisation, that the Urban Foundation promoted permanent housing rights for urban Africans (blacks). In the latter half of the 1980s, it more directly promoted housing delivery by creating utility companies 'to scale up housing delivery for medium and low-income households', while also building capacity for low cost housing in the contracting sector (Urban Foundation, 1994). Seidman (1994:243) interprets the Urban Foundation's prioritisation of housing for African (black) workers as the business sectors' 'explicit hope of integrating an urban industrial labour force into capitalist South Africa'.

Turning, then, to the Urban Foundation's central intervention concepts with regards to informal settlements, which today essentially make up the national housing policy, it is striking to what extent product is emphasised, rather than process. According to its influential 'Proposals for a National Housing Policy' (published in 1990), a national housing programme was to operate on 'quantitative objectives' (Urban Foundation, 1990:ix). The product was envisaged as a serviced site, for which the local authorities were to be encouraged to accept 'appropriate' (meaning lower) 'servicing standards', to be upgraded over time (*ibid.*:x). Government funding was to be restructured 'so as to provide assistance to the urban poor on a wide scale through the introduction of capital subsidies on serviced sites' (*ibid.*), this applying to 'site-and-service and informal settlement upgrading' (*ibid.*:vii). Indeed, the proposals included 'upgrading of existing informal settlements wherever feasible, through, in particular, the provision of infrastructure services, secure tenure and access to appropriate housing subsidies' (*ibid.*:x). However, through the standardised capital subsidy system, with an individualised product orientation, the policy proposal set itself an obstacle to the actual *in situ* upgrading of informal settlements, if this were to mean minimal disruption to informally established settlement patterns: inevitably, the capital subsidy required the replacement of informal settlements with standardised serviced sites, as indeed has been the practice, thanks to the Urban Foundation, since the early 1990s.

Not surprisingly, the only support programmes envisaged in the 1990 proposal of the Urban Foundation were to 'protect consumers from exploitation and malpractices in the low-income housing market' (Urban Foundation, 1990:x). The neo-liberal nature of the Urban Foundation proposal lies, then, on the one hand, in the individualisation and commodification it foresees for the low income residential sphere, therefore, the transformation of informal occupiers of land into individual consumers of a standardised, technically defined and private sector delivered product. Associated with this individualisation and commodification is the favouring of individual title over communal ownership (*ibid.*:vi). On the other hand, the neo-liberal nature of the proposal lies in the stakes it places for the profit-making development industry. Indeed, no role whatsoever is foreseen for the popular sector, which in complete patronage is reduced to a uniform body of consumers. The proposal further indicates a complete ignorance of the institutional requirements of organised community groups: it bundles together entities such as 'community organisations, community-based housing agencies, non-governmental agencies' and 'utility companies' with 'commercial developers' under the category 'private sector' (*ibid.*:ix). The Urban Foundation therefore assumes that non-profit organisations all operate on the exact same basis as those of the private sector. The Foundation goes as far as to suggest that 'informal housing agencies ... must ... operate under the same rules as private sector actors' (*ibid.*:iv, v). Clearly, it is staking claims for the profit-making development industry. This powerful neo-liberal bias has transcended scholarly debates, as is evident in my analysis of the South African informal settlement intervention literature of the 1990s in Chapter 6.

The Urban Foundation's professional wisdom must also be seen in the light of international thinking in the late 1980s and early 1990s, which I discussed in Chapter 2. There I noted that even the capitalist-driven World Bank (since 1972 promoter of the product-oriented twin approach of 'sites-and-services and slum upgrading') had, by the beginning of the 1990s, admitted in its policy papers to the limited success of its early approach, and was instead promoting social processes of poverty alleviation. Where, then, did the Urban Foundation advisers derive their folly or naiveté? Various factors come to mind. Firstly, they lacked engagement with the shifts in international debates and practices. Secondly, they lacked a consciousness of the functioning of class within an unequal society, thus unquestioningly accepting the practice of patronage by the business and professional sector over the working-class 'communities'. This was legitimised through their commitment to denounce racial discrimination. Indeed, they appear to have been unaware of the adversities of capitalist agendas for the working-class, i.e. the inherent exploitation. Thirdly, then, due to a lack of consciousness of class division, they saw little reason to engage with the development thinking of the civic movement. The deep resentment that the Urban Foundation professionals had for the civic movement, which becomes evident in the process of institutionalisation which I discuss below, further indicates how uncommitted these professional advisers were to a true process of democratisation.

Societal responses to informal settlement in South Africa, then, were diverse and opposing, indeed conflicting. While the civic movement was envisioning the decommodification of land and shelter, and development was to be undertaken and controlled by organised communities, the Urban Foundation envisioned individualised and commodified intervention through the 'private sector'. I turn next to the process through which the Urban Foundation proposal on informal settlement intervention was institutionalised into the current housing policy, and that of the civic movement marginalised. I contrast this with the process in Brazil, through which the progressive concepts of the PT were indeed institutionalised, with particular implications for local government.

5.5 Institutionalisation of societal responses

The processes of transition or democratisation in South Africa and Brazil took different forms. The most striking contrast is the trend towards decentralisation in Brazil, as opposed to a high degree of centralisation in South Africa. This contrast has important bearing on the processes through which the societal responses to informal settlement were institutionalised in the two countries, and explains many of the contrasts in current intervention practice. I will briefly discuss decentralisation and centralisation, before examining in more detail the process through which new policy on informal settlement intervention was institutionalised.

Diverging forms of democratisation and decentralisation in Brazil and South Africa

Both apartheid rule in South Africa and military rule in Brazil were highly centralised systems of government (Schmitter, 1996:10; Souza, 1997:32). In Brazil, the process of democratisation implied a process of decentralisation, restoring political powers to states and municipalities, whereas in South Africa, it was believed that an efficient centralised state would best address the racial and socio-economic imbalances brought about by apartheid. I will first examine the decentralisation process in Brazil, and then contrast this with government restructuring in South Africa, including recent neo-liberal tendencies which are invariably reducing the powers of all levels of the state.

In 1966, the Brazilian military rulers had abolished direct elections of mayors in those areas that were perceived as a threat to national security, this including most state capitals. Municipal executives were instead appointed by state governors,[27] who were likewise not directly elected. At the same time, the rights of the appointed executives or mayors in relation to the Municipal Council were increased, giving them power over the budget, and allowing them to 'submit legislative proposals and to veto laws approved by the Municipal Council' (Assies, 1993:42). In 1982, state governors were once again directly elected (Souza, 1997:101), and in turn nominated mayors for the state capitals and other municipalities falling under the security regulations (Assies, 1993:46). As mayors of other municipalities were directly elected, the PT was able to elect its first mayor in Diadema, as mentioned in Chapter 3. National security regulations were lifted only in 1985, allowing all municipalities to directly elect their mayor (*ibid.*:48). In this election, the PT won only two additional mayors, Fortaleza and Vila Velha (Abers, 1996:51). A popular struggle continued for further democratisation, with demands for political, fiscal, and administrative decentralisation. These demands, then, alongside the demands for urban reform mentioned above, were taken up in the 1988 Constitution (Souza, 1997:52), to which I return below.

Souza (1997) draws attention to the ambiguities surrounding decentralisation. The concept appeals to both the neo-liberal and left ideologies, in their concern over excessive power based with central governments. Analysing the effects of decentralisation in Brazil, she argues that it may not have been able to 'disintegrate old political coalitions or change the allocation of public resources' (*ibid.*:6). This leads her to associate decentralisation in Brazil with 'peripheralized federalism' and a 'paralyzed competitive arena' (*ibid.*). Indeed, many challenges remain. With regards to housing obligations, local governments are restricted by the absence of a decentralised, democratic national housing system (Saule Jr., 1998). In 1990 a petition with over one million signatures, calling for such a system to 'be integrated with the states and municipalities through housing councils and housing funds at state and municipal levels' was turned down (*ibid.*:3). Instead, a centralised bureaucratic system has impeded the utilisation of the national housing fund, which originates from a compulsory contribution from workers' salaries and from employees. Thus in 1995 and 1996, only one-fifth of the available national housing budget was spent (*ibid.*:2).

Souza (1997) argues that at a sub-national level, 'decentralisation and re-democratisation have caused diversity in the way the political system is operated' (*ibid.*:6, 7). Thus, with policy-making around the question of favelas taking place at the sub-national level, intervention may differ from one municipality to the next, and from one municipal term to the next. In the case of São Paulo, favela upgrading programmes including the concept of self-management were discontinued after one term of PT rule (1989 to 1993) and replaced by the Cingapura Programme of the conservative Maluf administration. As mentioned briefly in Chapters 1 and 2, this programme demolished visibly located favelas and constructed high-rise flats in their place. Delivery of this top-down intervention approach was through the construction industry, in total patronage over the favela population.[28] While continuity in local policy is not guaranteed through the decentralised system of government, political space may be contested at the municipal level for the implementation of progressive intervention proposals, such as those of the PT. Such contestation, however, requires a continuously high degree of conscientisation and politicisation of urban questions. This, then, is one important dynamic that is largely absent with the particular form of government in South Africa, to which I now turn.

In the South African transition, the particular distribution of power led to a very different debate around decentralisation to that in Brazil. In South Africa it was not progressive but rather conservative minority sectors of the society (primarily the National Party) that were calling for decentralisation and greater autonomy of local government, as a means to protect minority interests, and in effect minority privilege (Cameron, 1996:20). The ANC in turn traditionally had a centralised vision for the state, and while softening on this stance during the 1990 to 1994 negotiations, continued to perceive extensive devolution of powers as a mechanism 'to prevent the essential redistribution needed to ameliorate inequalities caused by apartheid' (*ibid.*:21). For the realisation of rights such as housing, a strong central government was considered necessary (*ibid.*). Indeed, the ANC continued to believe 'that central government should have the power to intervene directly in local authorities' affairs to ensure that such structures conformed to national development policy' (*ibid.*:35). In this sense, the Urban Foundation's national housing policy proposal of 1991, which I discussed above, was therefore compatible with the thinking of the ANC (I return to the negotiation process around housing policy below).

While constitutional negotiations were underway at national level, local or metropolitan level negotiations were likewise debating aspects of local government. The civic movement (since 1992 largely constituted into a unitary national body, the South African National Civic Organisation, SANCO – though individual civic organisations remained independent and others formed federated organisations),[29] disagreed with these local negotiations on two points. Firstly, as these negotiations preceded consensus at national level, SANCO regarded them as premature. Secondly, the township population was represented through the discredited BLA councillors, who were seen to favour the interests of the property-owning township dwellers over those living in back yard shacks, hostels and informal settlements (Mayekiso, 1996:218). Only with renewed rent boycotts in the townships in early 1992, in response to non-delivery by the BLA 'puppet councillors', did the message come across that 'progress toward democratic cities in the New South Africa' required the 'full and final resignation' of the BLA councillors (*ibid.*:225). This led to SANCO's initiation of national level negotiations on local democratisation through the Local Government Negotiation Forum. Reflecting a demand to overcome the racially defined infrastructure inequalities, which had been maintained through separate white and black local authorities, SANCO's primary demand was for 'single non-racial cities with single tax-bases' (*ibid.*:211). These principles were 'ratified in a deal by the multiparty constitutional negotiations, after some heated controversy toward the end of the process' in late 1993 (*ibid.*:225).

Cameron (1996:36) notes that the constitutional negotiations, primarily between the ANC and NP, led to a compromise and in many instances contradictory clauses with regards to the autonomy of local government. Further contradiction, particularly with regard to local autonomy and the role of civil society, has resulted from shifts in the ANC approach since it entered government in 1994. The RDP (Reconstruction and Development Programme), on the basis of which the ANC campaigned in the 1994 elections, ascribed an important delivery role to local government. However, this was primarily defined technocratically – urban policy in turn was to be determined at national level through an Urban Development Strategy (Chipkin, 1997:8). 'Autonomy' thus referred only to the 'operational independence' of local government. Within this context, 'community-driven development' came to mean the identification of needs and priorities for infrastructure through various forums (*ibid.*:9). Initially, these forums were envisaged as mechanisms for 'direct democracy', acting against the 'inherent class and race prejudice of representative democracy by monitoring and opposing such bias in the workings of local government' (*ibid.*:10). However, their function has increasingly been reduced to mere advisory bodies (*ibid.*).

Indeed, SANCO (the largest representative of the civic movement) experienced sidelining in the decision-making by the new government, this being justified through the provision that the government's RDP made for governance 'in consultation with organisations in civil society' (Seekings, 1997:12). A similar experience is that of the Homeless People's Federation, which likewise complains of being sidelined by the new government and its consultative bodies (People's Dialogue, 1995:9).

Chipkin (1997:10) highlights a key problem in the South African definition of local government, namely that it assumed 'that service delivery is in fact uncontroversial', or simply an administrative and managerial task. Inevitably, where local governments are not seen by individual organised communities to be performing their task, such communities have appealed to higher levels of government, which are considered 'more capable of addressing local needs' (*ibid.*:10). Indeed, this is the context of the case studies in Chapter 7, one of which examines an organised informal settlement community (Kanana, southern Johannesburg), which secured a development concession from national government; and another (Weiler's Farm, southern Johannesburg), which secured a commitment for development funding from the provincial tier. In both cases the relationships between the organised communities and local government have remained strained.

A further shift in South African policy towards decentralisation has been through the broad shift in macro-economic policy. While in 1994, the RDP (Reconstruction and Development Programme) was seen as the government programme required to drive a transformation to redress social inequalities and infrastructural backlogs in the South African society, the neo-liberal macro-economic strategy GEAR (Growth Employment and Redistribution), essentially promoting structural adjustment, was to take over this function in 1996. Thus economic growth is to drive transformation, with a more modest role ascribed to all tiers of government (Chipkin, 1997:7). The 1998 Local Government White Paper has translated this concept to the local level. Critiquing this policy paper, Bond and Mayekiso (1998:8) highlight its neo-liberal contents and warn of the problems around privatisation of municipal functions. They further warn of the demobilisation of labour and communities, which the policy implicitly requires in order for citizens to 'trust a largely technocratic process'.

This contrast in government transformation in South Africa and Brazil then helps explain the different processes of institutionalisation of non-governmental thinking on informal settlement intervention. Indeed, the liberal tendency of discouraging community mobilisation in South Africa is apparent in the patronage that the business sector exercised over the civic movement in housing policy negotiations. In Brazil, however, ongoing practices of patronage and clientelism (see Souza, 1997:3) reflect similar tendencies, discouraging conscientisation and politicisation of urban questions.

Institutionalising popular favela intervention demands in Brazil

In examining the Brazilian popular response to informal settlement above, I mentioned that decentralisation of power was one of the key concepts of the PT. Indeed, then, the constitution-making process, culminating in the 1988 Constitution, accommodated the concept of decentralisation. Souza (1997:73) notes that this was one area of general consensus in the constitution-making process, although ambiguities and contradictions around the concept prevailed. Of relevance to the governance concept of the PT was that local government was afforded 'the power to enact laws governing the use and development of urban space' towards guaranteeing the social functions of the city and its inhabitants' welfare (Fernandes and Rolnik, 1998:147). Towards this end, masterplans regulating urban expansion and development became obligatory for municipalities with a population above 20,000 (*ibid.*). The concept of 'social function' of private property, which had first appeared in the 1934 Constitution, was now given meaning through the masterplan, which was to stipulate such a function (*ibid.*). A further obligation attached to the concept of decentralisation, was that all three tiers of government were given responsibility in promoting the construction and improvement of housing and basic services, and in combating poverty and marginalisation (Fernandes, 1993:220). Concerning the Urban Reform Movement's demand for legal instruments to enable land regularisation of favelas, the 1988 Constitution includes 'the right to adverse possession' or '*usucapião*': after the uncontested occupation of up to 250m^2 of private property for a period of five years, the occupier has the right to ownership of that property (*ibid.*).

With the subsequent local government elections based on the Constitution of 1988, the PT presented 'the greatest electoral shock in the country's history' by wining mayoral office in 36 cities, including São Paulo, with over 15 million inhabitants, other state capitals Vitória and Porto Alegre, Brazil's largest port, Santos, the State of São Paulo's second largest city, Campinas, and various important industrial cities (Sader and Silverstein, 1991:98). With the challenge of translating democratic governance into practice, the Urban Reform Movement transferred its attention to the local level, where tasks such as democratic masterplanning and favela regularisation awaited (Souza, 1999:2). In the discussion of the PT's concepts for municipal governance earlier in this chapter, I mentioned the role the party envisaged for autonomous social movements and grassroots councils. The PT, then, promoted popular participation or public debate on the formulation of the annual municipal budget in São Paulo, Porto Alegre and Vitória (Assies, 1993:50). The PT's experience in such 'participatory budgeting' in Porto Alegre was of particular consistence and has drawn much attention (see Abers 1998; Souza, 1999; Zimmerman, 1998). More recently, the concept was introduced in Belo Horizonte, and has likewise been portrayed as a successful experience (see Bretas, 1996; Fernandes, 1996). Abers (1998:65) notes that the concept of participatory budgeting has recently been recognised as successful, even by parties in opposition to the PT. As an instrument of participatory governance it is therefore increasingly applied outside of PT municipalities. In Chapter 3, I discussed the endeavour of the Belo Horizonte municipality to specifically link the instrument of participatory budgeting to intervention in favelas, thus breaking with the practice of concentrating capital intensive comprehensive externally defined intervention in a small number of selected settlements.

With regards to land regularisation in favelas, the constitutional instrument of adverse possession (*usucapião*, through which favela households are to acquire freehold titles of privately owned land after an uncontested five-year period of occupation) requires the development of legal procedures before it may be implemented (see Imparato, 2002). Thus, adverse possession had as yet not been applied in Belo Horizonte in 1997, almost a decade after adoption of the constitutional amendment, as efforts were still underway to develop such procedures. Land regularisation was instead taking place in the legally less complicated situations, namely occupation of public land (Pinheiro and Andrade, personal communication, 1997).[30]

It is evident that the accomplishment of the Urban Reform Movement through the constitutional amendments of 1988 in itself remains meaningless unless these amendments are translated into legal instruments that enable implementation at the local level. Only in 2001, 11 years after promulgation of the Constitution, at the relentless demand of the National Forum for Urbãn Reform (*Fórum Nacional de Reforma Urbana* – FNRU) and against much opposition from the entities representing land owners, the construction industry and real estate agents, was the procedure completed for the approval of the City Statute (de Grazia, 2002). This national law 'aims to regulate the chapter on urban policy found in the 1988 Constitution' and 'provides consistent legal support to those municipalities committed to confronting the grave urban, social and environmental problems' (Fernandes, 2001). It was hoped that whereas political will for such socially-oriented legal endeavours had been largely restricted to the socially-oriented administrations, such as the PT municipalities, the City Statue would promote application of these instruments across Brazil. With the entry of the PT into federal government, new impetus was given through the creation of a federal Ministry of Cities in January 2003. The Ministry includes a Programme for the Support of Sustainable Land Regularisation. This has the role of enabling and promoting the implementation at scale of those aspects of City Statute designed for land regularisation. However, even under a PT-led government, any practical change to the status quo requires ongoing political consciousness within civil society of the urban challenge. In collaboration with NGOs and other institutions of the Urban Reform movement, the Ministry of Cities' current efforts at popularising the City Statue and involving organised citizens in the policy decisions of the Ministry are in response to this realisation. This contrasts to the very different route of institutionalising change in informal settlement intervention in South

Africa. Indeed, the dominant endeavour in South Africa has been to discourage politicisation in favour of a technocratic process driven by professionals, although throughout 2003 consultation and research on key areas of policy were gaining increasing recognition in the national Department of Housing.

Negotiation, patronage and transformation: institutionalising business demands in South Africa

In the discussion of the Urban Foundation above, I have already mentioned the particular housing policy proposal that the Foundation developed, and its provisions for informal settlement intervention. Here I will examine the undemocratic route through which this proposal was institutionalised in the first half of the 1990s, showing to which extent this sidelined existing proposals for alternatives. More detailed than my discussion of the Brazilian reform, this section in particular also forms the context for the critical discussions of South African informal settlement literature of the 1990s in Chapter 6 and of current South African practice through the four case studies in Chapter 7.

At a general level, the transition in South Africa from 1990 to 1994 is considered a 'process of pact-making', which 'not only paved the way to democracy but also limited it' (Friedman, 1996:45). I mentioned above that with regard to the constitution-making negotiations, the two main players were the National Party and the ANC,[31] their differences to some extent being accommodated in constitutional compromises. With regards to policy-making on urban informal settlement intervention, the divide in thinking however, appears not to have been between that of the ANC and the National Party. With the business sector as a major force in this policy arena, the thinking of these two political parties converged over the central ideas of the Urban Foundation. Vocal opponents instead appear to have been the civic movement and to a lesser extent the emerging People's Dialogue/Homeless People's Federation, both suspicious of the agendas of the profit-making sector, and calling instead for people-driven development.

The influence of the Urban Foundation over the National Party became evident in 1990 when, having gained confidence in the methodologies that the Foundation had piloted, the National Party government approached the Foundation's chairman, former judge Jan Steyn, for a proposal for a socio-economic upliftment programme. According to Nuttall's (1997) insider review of the programme, Steyn literally compiled the proposal over a weekend and within three days the draft was accepted by the National Party government and Steyn charged with its implementation. At Steyn's request, R2,000 million was committed by government to an independent development agency, the IDT (Independent Development Trust), which was to address poverty alleviation in the areas of housing, education, health/welfare and employment (Nuttall, 1997:10, 11).

The housing context at the time was complex and disjointed, housing being delivered by the separate houses of parliament, provincial administrations, homeland governments (through the Development Bank of South Africa – DBSA), and the South African Housing Trust (SAHT) (Nuttall, 1997:110). The IDT was seen as an instrument that could to some extent streamline delivery to the poorer section of society. Indeed, 100,000 households were to benefit. However, the development model did not reflect the experience of the target group, largely organised and represented by the civic movement. Instead, the IDT model reflected the values and thinking in the boardrooms of the establishment, as presented in Nuttall's book *The First Five Years: The Story of the Independent Development Trust* (1997), an unapologetic review of the apparently sincere, but naively misinformed (and therefore patronising) yet successful, attempts at influencing the post-apartheid poverty alleviation policies.

In line with the 1990 Urban Foundation proposal for a national housing policy which I reviewed above, the IDT delivery model was based on a 'capital subsidy scheme', delivering home-ownership of a serviced site. Qualifying criteria were first-time property ownership, monthly income under R1,000, age of household head above 21, and dependants forming part of the household. Such households were then subsidised to the value of R7,500 through a delivered serviced site. Applications were made on behalf of beneficiary groups by 'developers', these being either public authorities, private developers, utility companies or community trusts. A key criterion for the allocation of IDT funding for the implementation of a proposed project was evidence of the involvement of beneficiary communities. However, strict time constraints applied to the project formulation process (Nuttall, 1997:62). Such constraints in the blueprint then excluded the possibility of communities taking control of the housing process, thus reducing the people-centred ideals to mere rhetoric. Instead, project delivery was consultant-driven. A further criterion for funding allocation was the location of the project in relation to employment opportunities, social infrastructure and transport (*ibid.*). However, as land 'suitable' for less formal development was inevitably located on the urban periphery, or at best integrated with the existing poorly serviced townships, the IDT admitted to having 'a limited impact on urban integration' (*ibid.*:142). Indeed, despite legislative reform in 1991 (the White Paper on Land Reform, in conjunction with the Less Formal Township Establishment Act) for the accommodation of 'less formal' development, the same legislation protected existing land rights and interests of established communities (Harrison, 1992:19). In effect, then, a property market based on the spatial exclusivity of the 1950 Group Areas Act (though repealed in 1991 through the Abolition of Racially Based Land Measures Act) ensures that new low income development is separate from middle to high income housing and places of economic opportunities.[32]

The IDT capital subsidy scheme was targeted largely at informal settlements. The first of its initial 108 projects was the 'upgrade' of the Besters Camp informal settlement on the outskirts of Durban (Nuttall, 1997:28, 29). In Chapter 6, I discuss van Horen's (1996) evaluation of this project, particularly the implications of the IDT dictates on the intervention process. The largest IDT project was targeted at the Soweto-on-Sea informal settlement in Port Elizabeth, where 3,000 families were resettled from a flood plain and a further 7,000 received engineering services and freehold tenure through 'upgrading' (Nuttall, 1997:111). Less successful projects were located in what the IDT referred to as 'political hotspots' – Phola Park on the East Rand and Alexandra in Johannesburg (*ibid.*). Here the attempt was to implement capital subsidy projects via 'social compacts', agreements through which all stakeholders were to commit themselves to the development. Hindson *et al.* (1994:345) thus argue that it was 'from the experience of violence-torn communities' that an entire 'project cycle' was developed, 'beginning with mediation [and] the formation of social compacts'. In current policy, applications for development projects to be funded through individual households' capital subsidies must include a 'written social compact' committing all stakeholders to the proposed development. Of the 'community based partner' in the development, the application requires commitment 'to create a climate and environment that will be conducive to the efficient implementation of the project' (Department of Housing, 1995: VOL A-P2, page 11).

The IDT came under disrepute of the civic movement and of the Homeless People's Federation/People's Dialogue alliance, both rejecting the concept of providing high standards of toilets yet no houses. At a project level, civic structures clashed with the IDT on the consultant-driven nature of the development process. Various criticisms of the IDT policy (though presumably not those from grassroots) led the government to appoint the De Loor task team to investigate a National Housing Policy Strategy (Tomlinson, 1998a:138). Disagreeing with the resulting report,[33] the IDT with the DBSA decided in 1992 to initiate, with IDT funding, a National Housing Forum, in the hope of influencing the future South African housing policy (Nuttall, 1997:107).[34] Represented in this forum were the business community, building industry, financial institutions, development organisations and 'mass-based' political groupings (Lalloo, 1999:38; Tomlinson, 1998a:137).

Within these negotiations, then, the debate between SANCO and the IDT/Urban Foundation representatives polarised. SANCO criticised the market-oriented policies of the IDT and the fact that the capital subsidy scheme delivered 'toilet towns' rather than houses, which SANCO considered a human right (Nuttall, 1997:168). The IDT defended itself by listing its project outputs, which had benefited some '112,000 very poor families with the security of owning sites which had running water, proper sanitation and drainage, and road access in what were far more dynamic environments than the "toilet towns" which the Sanco president liked to portray' (*ibid.*). Clearly, the IDT was not prepared to reflect on questions of ideology and human rights, nor was it prepared to understand the actual grassroots experience from which SANCO was arguing. Mayekiso's (1996:271) perspective from within SANCO therefore was that 'the enemy now included a much more sophisticated crew of development technocrats even more intent on co-opting and forcing us to accept their capitalist agenda'. Indeed, Smith (1992:317) notes that negotiations were being disproportionately influenced by 'powerful vested interests,' through agencies such as the Urban Foundation, with the result that 'major challenges to existing property ownership' and to 'predominantly private sector solutions' were being precluded.

Perhaps most threatening to the IDT was not SANCO's request for people-driven development, which indeed was accommodated in the compromises and rhetoric of the NHF outcomes (see Tomlinson, 1998a:144), but SANCO's request for the democratisation of development financing, and therefore also of bodies such as the IDT and the DBSA (Mayekiso and Hanlon, 1994; Nuttall, 1997). For this purpose, SANCO was calling for a probe into their operations (Nuttall, 1997:170). Nuttall refers to this as 'continuing intrusions' into the IDT's 'affairs', and short of launching a counter-probe into SANCO's affairs (*ibid.*:177), publicly retaliated by emphasising 'the positive role played by the civic structures in assisting the IDT implement its site-and-service schemes across the country' (*ibid.*). This evident patronage that the IDT was exercising over grassroots communities and indeed their national representatives was sadly paralleled by internal inconsistencies and contradictions that emerged within SANCO, substantially weakening the organisation. The IDT in turn has survived, pledging its commitment to assisting the government in implementing the new Reconstruction and Development Programme (RDP) (Nuttall, 1997:191). Nuttall's book has the purpose of legitimising the organisation, and to this end is introduced as a contribution to a 'symbolic ritual cleansing process' of the IDT (Ramphele in Nuttall, 1997:3).

While explicit confrontation took place between the IDT and SANCO, there is evidence of more subtle manoeuvring of the negotiation process by the outgoing apartheid state and business interests, in order to ensure 'only nominal changes to the old apartheid order' (Lalloo, 1999:41). In what has been interpreted as an attempt by the National Party government to re-establish control over the policy-making process, the then Minister of Housing allocated funding to the National Housing Forum for a capital subsidy scheme (Adler and Oelofse, 1996:121). The Forum's longer-term policy negotiations were thereby distracted into practical decision-making on the immediate implementation of the funding (*ibid.*, also Lalloo, 1999:40). Lalloo (1999:42) also associates this manipulation with the Forum's failure to investigate means of spatially restructuring or integrating the segregated urban form, the over-emphasis on the individual capital subsidy having led to a perpetuation of spatial inequalities. Wilkinson

(1998:224) argues that the ANC's concern with redistribution, and therefore 'delivery' to the previously disadvantaged, further led to the sidelining of endeavours to redress the apartheid legacy of social and spatial division. Continuation of policy from the National Housing Forum with its particular dynamics, to the housing policy of the ANC-led government[35] was further guaranteed through the close working relationship between the new (post-election) Department of Housing and the National Housing Forum, the latter 'soon' being 'reconstituted as the National Housing Board' (*ibid.*:40).

The main difference between the earlier IDT approach and that of the new government's housing policy, then, was that the capital subsidy amount for the lowest income sector was increased to allow for a minimum top structure or 'incremental house'. As will be evident from the case study discussion in Chapter 7, much debate among housing role players and beneficiaries has been around the size of the top structure. Sensitive to the demand for bigger houses, the housing minister in the new cabinet, subsequent to the 1999 elections, has pledged to ensure that the building industry delivers a minimum of 30m^2 (see 'Towards Sankie's "Social Revolution"', *Mail & Guardian*, 25 June to 1 July 1999). Also associating community-based construction through the People's Housing Process with a larger top structure, therefore higher beneficiary satisfaction, the minister has pledged to particularly promote this housing approach (*ibid.*). I will briefly examine the emergence of government support to community-based housing, before closing with the growing inconsistencies in the civic movement and their implications for informal settlement intervention.

It is in the National Housing Board, constituted out of the National Housing Forum after the 1994 elections, that the emerging People's Dialogue/Homeless People's Federation alliance (with its alternative approach to housing) experienced being sidelined (People's Dialogue, 1995:9). Nevertheless, several years of consistently demonstrating people's ability to save and to construct houses, given the appropriate support, slowly led to recognition by government. At the 1994 Housing Summit, the new government had made a pledge to support a 'People's Housing Process' (Bolnick, 1996:155). Bolnick, from his position within People's Dialogue, however, found that 'this was little more than a poorly understood afterthought', indicating 'how weak the Federation's position was relative to the private sector, the public sector and others anxious to deliver housing "entitlements" to low income settlements rather than supporting them in defining their own solutions' (*ibid.*).

It was a gradual process that led to the accommodation of community-based housing within the new government's housing policy. This has taken two routes. One is direct support to the Homeless People's Federation. Initially, this was through a grant, augmenting the Foundation's 'uTshani Fund', the revolving loan fund into which daily savings of Federation members are deposited (see Phadu, 1997:78). Subsequently, direct government support has been secured through uTshani Fund agreements between the Federation and various (though not all) provincial housing boards, whereby the housing boards deposit individual members' capital subsidies into the uTshani fund, with house construction then administered through the Homeless People's Federation/People's Dialogue alliance. The other route has been the establishment of a People's Housing Process, with international support from the United Nations Development Programme (UNDP) and USAID for the formation of a 'People's Housing Partnership Trust', with the purpose of addressing 'institutional capacitation and empowerment at the provincial and local spheres of government and among NGOs to support the people's process' (Ministry of Housing, 1997:3). The People's Housing Partnership Trust operates in partnership with the Directorate of Housing Support, within the national Department of Housing. Staff secondment from the UNCHS (Habitat) to the trust (in the form of the Chief Executive Officer, Lalith Lankatilleke) ensured transfer of expertise from the government-initiated community-based intervention approaches of the Sri Lankan Million Houses Programme, which I discussed in Chapter 3. However, both the uTshani Loan agreements and the government's People's Housing Process then submitted to the overall framework of the capital subsidy system. In Chapter 7, I examine the restrictions this placed on the definition of local development by organised communities. Subsequent to my case study research, the alliance between Homeless People's Federation, People's Dialogue and the uTshani Fund was remodelled and clarified. The uTshani Fund now plays a stronger role in protecting and growing the Federation's assets, in supporting Federation projects and in acquiring land (Baumann, personal communication, 2003).[36]

Returning, then, to the inconsistencies within SANCO, these may well be associated with political co-optation and neo-liberal pressures. At its formation in 1992, SANCO had resolved to remain an autonomous civic movement. However, in the run-up to the 1994 elections, it decided to endorse both the ANC with its alliance partners and the RDP, seeing this 'in keeping with the civic movement's needs and aspirations' (Mayekiso, 1996:235). This was indeed a contradiction, given the degree to which the new ANC government subsequently embraced the IDT/Urban Foundation policy proposals for housing. Seekings (1997:12) argues that shifts in SANCO's position and problems in its organisational capacity have led to weak articulation in negotiations, particularly since 1994. In a bid to redress this situation in 1995, SANCO created a Development Research Institute (DRI) (paralleling a similar move in the labour movement), with the purpose of training and conscientising civic leadership on development questions (Mayekiso, personal communication, 1998; Seekings, 1997:14). However, the national office of SANCO, increasingly adopting a top-down approach for the organisation, while also implicitly endorsing neo-liberal tendencies within government, appeared to perceive the conscientisation of lower tiers of leadership within the organisation as a threat (Mayekiso, personal communication, 1998).[37]

The financial crisis that the national office was experiencing (partly due to an unsuccessful membership drive and a decline in foreign and local grants) then led to a controversy over a development research grant secured by the DRI. This caused increasing sidelining of Mzwanele Mayekiso within SANCO, and his eventual suspension in 1997 (Mayekiso, personal communication, 1998; also see Seekings, 1997:14). The suspension itself, however, being dictated by national office to the Alexandra branch of SANCO, violated SANCO protocol. In protest, this branch, followed by that of Soweto and Thembisa, withdrew from SANCO and reverted to its former local name (Alexandra Civic Organisation) (Mayekiso, personal communication, 1998).

Withdrawal of key civic structures from SANCO created space in early 1998 for the formation of a new non-unitary federation, the National Association of Residents and Civic Organisations (NARCO), with no political affiliation. Its aim is to promote the definition of localised development strategies, coordinating between civic organisations around common issues, and through the DRI (now run by a board of trustees of NARCO) to train local leaders (Mayekiso, personal communication, 1998; also see Bond and Mayekiso, 1998:8). During my 1998 case study research in the four informal settlements that I discuss in Chapter 7, I did not come across knowledge of NARCO, although the Uitenhage Branch of SANCO had heard of 'Mayekiso's new civic'.[38] The SANCO structure in Uitenhage, was neither aware of shifts in position at the national level of SANCO, nor did it appear to be affected by neoliberal tendencies itself. In the Weiler's Farm settlement in Southern Johannesburg, where the SANCO-affiliated civic organisation is independently acting as developer in a Provincial Housing Board subsidy allocation, community leaders likewise had no knowledge of inconsistencies at SANCO's national level. Thus the unitary and top-down nature of SANCO appears not to transcend or affect the entirety of the organisation. Notably, however, the organisers of the Kanana invasion (also a case study in Chapter 7), had been discouraged by SANCO from occupying the land they had identified, SANCO promising to negotiate for land on their behalf. As this did not materialise, the organisers eventually formed an independent organisation and went ahead with the invasion. The interface between organised informal settlement communities and the formal intervention framework is the topic of the discussion in Chapter 7. From that angle, I return to questions around the civic movement, as well as the Homeless People's Federation, both being represented in the case studies.

It remains to be mentioned that a new social movement was formed in South Africa in July 2001 around the question of access to land. The Landless People's Movement (LPM) is modelled on the Brazilian '*Movimento dos Sem Terra*' (MST – Movement of those without Land),[39] a rural movement that has an urban counterpart in the '*Movimento dos sem Teto*' (Movement of those without Roofs). Both Brazilian movements are closely connected with the PT. In South Africa, the

LPM is independent from political parties. It comprises primarily 'farm workers, labour tenants, restitution claimants, redistribution applicants [and] the rural poor living in former homelands', but also includes 'the urban poor living in informal settlements' (Mngxitama, 2002:10). Strategies of the movement to date have been largely around access to rural land. In the context of controversial rural invasions in neighbouring Zimbabwe, the movement occupies a difficult political space. Limited attention to questions of access to urban land by the LPM and by the less radical NLC (National Land Committee, a network of poor and landless people's organisations that has its origin in the 1980s in resistance to apartheid forced removals) were evident in their responses to the gradual invasion of rural-zoned land in Kempton Park on the outskirts of Johannesburg in July 2001. With the intense media coverage once the rate of occupation in Kempton Park escalated (then referred to as the 'Bredell' invasion), the newly formed LPM and the NLC voiced their concern over the slow pace of rural land reform (see 'Land Occupations are "Inevitable"', *Mail & Guardian*, 27 July to 2 August 2001). This did not acknowledge the reality that Bredell was an invasion by the poorly housed urban population, seeking an urban home to call their own. None of the civil society organisations alerted public attention to the unconstitutionality of the court ruling that led to the forceful eviction of all Bredell occupiers, even those that had rights due to having lived on the land for more than six months.[40]

5.6 Conclusion

In the introduction to this book, I mentioned that only in mid 2004 was a policy amendment for informal settlement intervention starting to be explored by the National Department of Housing. In this chapter, I have traced the process of continuity in informal settlement intervention from the late apartheid government into the democratic era in detail, contrasting it with the more profound process of reform in Brazil. I have, however, shown that due to the high degree of political decentralisation in Brazil, change towards a more progressive informal settlement intervention framework is politically vulnerable, thus requiring the ongoing politicisation of the urban question and conscientisation of citizens. Deeply critical urban socio-political analyses have thus appeared in the Brazilian literature, some of which I have drawn on in this and the previous chapter. Compared to the Brazilian situation, the urban questions predominantly posed in South Africa stand out as being technocratic and indeed depoliticised. I have thus examined the product-oriented, deterministic, neo-liberal nature of the dominant professional position on informal settlement in South Africa, placing it alongside fragile radical positions based in the grassroots organisations.

Early development thinking on grassroots autonomy and democracy within the civic movement in South Africa appears to have been largely overridden by the need for autonomy as a tool to protest against government control and repression, not dissimilar from the autonomy exercised by the squatter movements in the post-war years. With the lifting of racially based state control and repression, the demand then turned from that of grassroots autonomy and democracy to a focus on state delivery in order to redress the injustices caused by racial discrimination. The civic movements' alliance (through the dominant civic body SANCO) with the ANC and subsequently the new government was at the time not considered (even by progressive activists) as a form of co-optation. Instead, it was perceived as a means of ensuring delivery to the disadvantaged sector of South African society. Only subsequent to the 1994 elections have elements in civil society come to experience the dynamics of co-optation, clientelism and patronage. These in turn have formed a long tradition in Brazil, starting with the populist politics in the post-war years and re-emerging with political opening after the mid-1970s. Progressive thinking, demand-making and practice in Brazil has then embraced the concept that decentralisation of political and administrative powers, as an aspect of democratisation, may counteract the dynamics of clientelism and patronage. This position has as yet not entered the South African debate. Instead, the academic left, though sympathising with the slowly emerging NARCO initiative (the non-aligned federation of civic organisations) which supports grassroots autonomy, primarily argues for higher standards of delivery to disadvantaged communities. The People's Dialogue/ Homeless People's Federation in turn pursue their demands through apolitical lobbying, arguing that party politics is an inappropriate vehicle for the pursuit of poverty alleviation. The grassroots autonomy they seek is freedom from bureaucratic interference in their own development process, and not political autonomy. A more recent movement claiming to represent, among others, urban informal settlement residents, is focused mainly on the question of rural land reform.[41]

In the third part of this book, I turn to the South African scholarly debates that have emerged around the question of informal settlements in the 1990s, critiquing them in relation to the Brazilian positions and experiences that I have contrasted here, and the international positions I have discussed in Part 1. In Chapter 7, I discuss the post-1994 South African informal settlement intervention practice, with case studies of informal settlement intervention initiated by either the civic movement or the Homeless People's Federation. I thus examine the development process these community organisations are able to undertake, in relation to the dictates of the formal development framework and its particular structure of funding. This consolidates an argument for the need to release informal settlement intervention from the current housing subsidy framework in order to develop mechanisms more appropriate to the question of informal settlement in South Africa.

Notes

1 This refers to exclusion from national and municipal elections. A very limited degree of political expression was afforded the urban African (black) population

through the election of advisory boards. At the time, the ANC and the Communist Party were not outlawed (Stadler, 1979:109).

2 'Culling' is conventionally applied to the selection and killing of surplus animals from a herd.

3 See endnote 15 in Chapter 4.

4 The Brazilian term for grassroots, '*base*', is often adopted into English in texts on Brazil (see for instance Vink, 1985).

5 Through the *Pastoral de Favelas*, priests were given the responsibility for spiritual welfare of favela residents in their parishes, by setting up Ecclesiastic Base Communities (CEBs). Previously, the existence of favelas had not been officially acknowledged by the Church (Bernareggi, personal communication, 1997). Similarly, a 'Labour Pastoral' was later set up in the workplace, allowing unionists to 'reflect on their activities in the light of the Gospel' (Vink, 1985:107).

6 Dr Anna Conigliaro Michelini was speaking of her experience within the Italian NGO AVSI in supporting the struggle of the *Pastoral de Favelas* in Belo Horizonte in the early 1980s. In 1997 she was coordinator of the *Novos Alagados* project (favela intervention) for AVSI in Salvador-Bahia.

7 See Barbosa *et al.* (1997:30).

8 Assies (1993:40) refers to a 'neo-populism' that emerged with clientelism in the late 1970s, while Teixeira (1993:52) notes that in the 1990s the culture of clientelist politics is still dominant in various regions of Brazil.

9 McCarthy (1992:33) describes the UDF as a 'coalition of civic associations, smaller trade unions, and related groups,' noting that it was the first signal of 'an internal coalition of forces dedicated to the establishment of a strong unitary state pursuing non-racial and social-democratic policies'. Mayekiso (1996:67) notes that the UDF was in many ways the 'ANC's surrogate', coordinating 'the national protest campaigns against apartheid.' He too emphasises that it was 'a broad multi-class and non-racial coalition' (*ibid.*).

10 African National Congress – South African Communist Party – Congress of South African Trade Unions.

11 Divisional Councils were intended for the administration of non-urban areas, and were replaced by RSCs (Regional Services Councils) in the late 1980s.

12 The revenue dilemma was eased to some extent in 1984 by the state's decision to include BLAs into Regional Service Council (RSC) areas (Shubane, 1991:6).

13 In early 1985, the ANC had made a call for 'ungovernerability', thus spurring the boycotting that was already underway (Mayekiso, 1996:67).

14 Mayekiso (1996:98) notes that rent boycotts were supported by residents 'not only for political purposes', but also in response to declining income levels, therefore as 'a cry for economic justice'. Mayekiso thereby refutes the concept of a 'culture of non-payment' which is commonly associated with the continuing boycotting of rents.

15 Mayekiso (1996:67), referring to his involvement in the civic movement in the Alexandra township of Johannesburg notes that: 'Our most heady period of

township organizing was the few months in early 1986 when we could really claim that apartheid rule was being displaced, street by street, by our own form of self-government. It was a liberating experience, though it did not last for long'.

16 Interestingly, Mayekiso (1996:100) refers to the state's torturing and killing of leaders, and the selective distribution of handouts to its followers, as 'the "Brazilian Option"'.

17 This affected the townships of Lamontville, Chesterville and Clermont (Hindson *et al.*, 1994:338).

18 The Inkatha Freedom Party, 'representing black traditionalist interests' in KwaZulu and since 1994 in the new KwaZulu-Natal Province, is considered the 'third major political force' in South Africa's transition, alongside the National Party and the ANC (Friedman, 1996:49).

19 For instance 'Lindelani and Mshayazafa in Inanda, and also parts of Malukazi near Umlazi' (Hindson *et al.*, 1994:341).

20 Mzwanele Mayekiso, author, activist, urban planner and academic (and brother of the 1992/1993 president of SANCO Moses Mayekiso, who then headed SANCO Investment Holdings from 1995 to 2001), in 1998 was a leading activist in a new civic movement National Association of Residents and Civic Organisations (NARCO). Mzwanele Mayekiso then also headed the Development Research Institute, which gave professional support to the civic movement. The objectives of this institute have now been incorporated into the Centre for Urban and Built Environment Studies (CUBES) in the School of Architecture and Planning at Wits University, where Mayekiso teaches.

21 And in the Cape Town area the Catholic Welfare Bureau (later Catholic Welfare and Development) and the Surplus People's Project.

22 Other such development NGOs were Afesis-Corplan in East London and the Urban Services Group in Port Elizabeth. In Chapter 7, I make reference to the Urban Services Group's involvement with the Gunguluza settlement in Uitenhage, and BESG's involvement with the Piesang River settlement in Durban.

23 In 1998, Patrick Hunsley was president of the Homeless People's Federation, and resident of the Piesang River informal settlement. He was interviewed in connection with the Piesang River case study, which is discussed in Chapter 7.

24 Listed in Urban Foundation (1994:21).

25 As early as 1983, the Urban Foundation piloted self-help through the Khutsong project (Urban Foundation, 1994).

26 With democratic elections in 1994, the Urban Foundation was seen to have served its purpose and was subsequently disbanded. Continuity in policy related research has however been assured through other business-funded organisations such as the NBI (National Business Institute) and the CDE (Centre for Development and Enterprise).

27 Within the federal system in Brazil, 'state' refers to the tier of government that in South Africa is referred to as 'province'.

28 It may be noted that resistance to this approach from favela communities had led to the incorporation of partial favela upgrading alongside the construction of flats

within the Cingapura programme, one example being the intervention at Favela Piqueri (José, personal communication, 1997 – see endnote 19 in Chapter 2).

29 Seekings (1998) discusses the complexity of different civic bodies in Cape Town.

30 See endnote 9 of Chapter 3.

31 The third 'major political force', the traditionalist Inkatha Freedom Party, withdrew from the constitutional negotiations in 1993, only to recommit a week before the 1994 elections (Friedman, 1996:49).

32 Mabin (1993) illustrates retaliation of the property owning class in response to the official search for well located land for the orderly relocation of the 'Zevenfontein squatters' north of Johannesburg shortly after the abolition of Group Areas. See also Berrisford (1998:223).

33 The De Loor report did not foresee freehold tenure for the poorest sector of site-and-services beneficiaries (Adler and Oelofse, 1996:119; Nuttall, 1997:107).

34 Note that according to Lalloo (1999:38) the proposal for a National Housing Forum was made jointly by representatives of business as well as political and civic organisations, in a meeting in August 1991, set up by the DBSA and the IDT to discuss 'the problems of violence in migrant labour hostels'.

35 This policy was adopted through a national Accord between state, building industry, financial institutions and civic organisations (see Wilkinson, 1998:226), followed in late 1994 by a White Paper on Housing.

36 Ted Baumann, previously with People's Dialogue, continues to work closely with the Homeless People's Federation through Bay Research and Consultancy Services in Cape Town.

37 The neo-liberal tendency within the SANCO national office is also apparent in its decision in 1996 to launch a subsidiary company, SANCO Investment Holdings. Though portrayed as an empowerment tool towards a socialist ideal, the business arrangements include the harnessing of SANCO members' consumer power through membership deals imposing discounts on purchases and a compulsory funeral insurance (Seekings, 1997:18–22). These deals duplicate, and indeed compete with, the numerous funeral associations and other co-operatives existing at the grassroots levels (see, for instance White, 1998).

38 Indeed, NARCO has not expanded beyond Johannesburg and its leadership has been weak. However, there was a new attempt in 2002 to capacitate the leadership, and it is hoped that pressing issues around informal settlements may be promoted through this organisation (Mayekiso, personal communication, 2002).

39 Also translated as 'Rural Workers without Land' (Sader and Sliverstein, 1991:60).

40 The Bredell invasion and ruling, along with the Grootboom ruling and evictions from Alexandra, are discussed in more detail in Huchzermeyer (2003).

41 However, at the time of going to press, a new umbrella body was emerging, the Coalition of the Urban Poor, bringing together the Homeless People's Federation, the Landless People's Movement and others.

PART THREE

Towards Appropriate Intervention in South Africa

Chapter 6

South African Scholarly Thinking in the 1990s on the Question of Informal Settlement Intervention

6.1 Introduction

The 1990 proposal by the influential Urban Foundation for a national urban housing policy[1] may be seen as a benchmark in the South African informal settlement intervention debate and practice. On the one hand, it channelled government resources into the delivery of services and freehold title for those precariously housed in urban informal settlements. On the other hand, it entrenched a deterministic product-driven and individualised approach to informal settlement intervention. In Chapter 5, I reviewed the Urban Foundation's 1990 proposal and showed how it was translated into practice throughout the 1990s, first through the government-funded Independent Development Trust and, in the latter half of the decade, through its undemocratic institutionalisation into the national housing policy, sidelining fragile popular or mass-based alternative positions. I contrasted this with a very different intellectual engagement with the informal settlement intervention question in Brazil, and the democratic and decentralised institutionalisation of the resulting alternative approach into municipal governance programmes. In this third part of the book I depart from the comparison with Brazil in order to examine the current South African situation in more detail. The Brazilian scenario remains a point of reference, which supports the critical perspective I apply to the South African informal settlement literature in this chapter, and to the South African practice described in Chapter 7. Further critical perspective is gained from the international positions discussed in Chapters 2 and 3. The central question in this chapter is: How have scholarly debates in South Africa in the 1990s and beyond responded to the influential Urban Foundation promoted position and practice?

The bulk of the informal settlement research commissioned by the Urban Foundation was undertaken in the 1980s and cast light on diverse aspects of the unfolding informal settlement situation. From 1990, the Urban Foundation turned its attention to the formulation of a national policy, and being seen to have fulfilled its function, was disbanded after the 1994 elections. The main body of the Urban Foundation research on informal settlement itself is not the subject of this chapter. Here I examine a continuity of the Urban Foundation thinking throughout the 1990s through the work of liberal researchers. As academics, consultants or Urban Foundation staff, they had agreed with the liberal stance of the Urban Foundation, and through the Foundation, formed a unanimous position on low-income housing. They were then influential in developing this into the Urban Foundation model, which in the early 1990s was implemented through the IDT, and formed the basis of the Urban Foundation proposal for a national housing policy. Throughout the 1990s, their work has defended this position. I contrast this continuity in private sector orientation with research findings that have contradicted the positions that underpin the Urban Foundation model. While these findings expose serious flaws in the Urban Foundation position, it must be asked why such evidence did not impact on the informal settlement intervention paradigm in South Africa, which continued largely according to the rules set by the Urban Foundation in 1990.

This chapter starts by positioning the Urban Foundation paradigm, pulling together discussions from the previous chapters. I then review South African research literature that supports this position, critically examining the underlying arguments. Next, I turn to research that has contradicted the Urban Foundation position, and draw together evidence of the inappropriateness of the Urban Foundation-inspired intervention approach. Finally, I discuss why these critical research initiatives have had little impact on informal settlement practice in South Africa.

6.2 Positioning the Urban Foundation paradigm

In the previous chapter I presented the concepts of the Urban Foundation position, highlighting its neo-liberal or market-oriented nature. Central tenets were the emphasis on the private sector delivery of a standardised product, funded through a once-off household-based capital subsidy and, associated with this, the individualisation and commodification of access to land and basic services. In many respects, the Urban Foundation proposal of the early 1990s may be comparable to the benchmark in international practice, presented in the promotion of the twin approach of sites-and-services and slum upgrading by the World Bank in the early 1970s. Parallels lie particularly in the product-based and civil works oriented nature of the intervention. In relation to the discussion in Chapter 3, it falls into the category of externally designed comprehensive intervention, in contrast to the support-based intervention approaches. A difference between the

Urban Foundation model and that of the World Bank lies in the funding (see Jones and Datta, 2000). The World Bank envisaged this to be recovered from the beneficiaries, thereby burdening fragile household economies. The South African intervention through the Urban Foundation-inspired capital subsidy in turn is recovered from national coffers. Nevertheless, the delivery of individual freehold title through the capital subsidy in South Africa is intended to tie the beneficiary household into a system of payment of rates and service charges, likewise a form of cost recovery introducing a new financial burden to the beneficiary households.

In Chapter 2, I discussed the scholarly response to the World Bank-promoted position and practice. Important in confronting the product orientation of the World Bank's approach was the growing awareness in the 1980s that the spatial concentration of poverty was shifting from rural areas to the cities. With an increased emphasis on urban poverty, socially-oriented poverty analysis tools (first developed for the alleviation of rural poverty) were applied to urban areas. The subsequent urban poverty debate, partly coordinated or hosted by initiatives of the UNCHS (Habitat), including the articulation of urban poverty concepts for the various dimensions of vulnerability and resilience, then gave recognition to alternative support-based intervention approaches emerging in various developing countries. These alternative approaches, which I discussed in Chapter 3, focused on social processes rather than predetermined, standardised products. In Brazil, as discussed in Chapter 5, it was through the Urban Reform Movement that practitioners and researchers confronted the concerns of urban poverty articulated by numerous social movements. Through the political space contested by the PT, this movement then developed institutional responses to accommodate alternative forms of informal settlement intervention. In municipalities governed by the PT, this has led to responsive and less product-oriented informal settlement intervention that gives organised communities the opportunity to determine and manage the intervention process. In South Africa, in contrast, an externally defined, product-oriented informal settlement intervention approach, developed by the Urban Foundation, has been adopted into the national housing policy and has determined the nature of urban informal settlement intervention across all municipalities.

In Chapter 5, I discussed the route through which the Urban Foundation model was institutionalised into the national policy for housing delivery and informal settlement intervention. It is undeniable that the Urban Foundation position was extremely influential. However, various research initiatives in South Africa have exposed flaws in the Urban Foundation position. In the final section of this chapter I ask why such evidence has had little influence on the framework of informal settlement intervention in South Africa. At this point, it is relevant to illustrate the intellectual influence of the Urban Foundation position. My finding from examining the literature is that most South African research orients itself to the Urban Foundation, if not explicitly, then by using the ambiguous terminology that the Foundation coined in support of its paradigm. The result, on the one hand, is that by applying the Urban Foundation terminology, researchers submit (though not explicitly) to the intellectual approach that supports the content of the Foundation's proposal. On the other hand, research findings communicated through this terminology have been open to ambiguous interpretation, therefore resulting in a blurring of the real issues at hand.

A strong bias in the Urban Foundation's intellectual position was its view of the informal settlement phenomenon primarily from the perspective of the housing structures, thus perceiving a physical, rather than the socio-legal, socio-political and socio-environmental situation (the informal settlement problem, as understood by the Urban Foundation, was then to be solved by the construction industry). The Urban Foundation terminology, as set out in its 1991 report titled *Informal Housing Part 1: Current Situation*, therefore starts with the over-arching term 'informal housing', which it defines as 'shelter usually constructed with unconventional building materials acquired informally, that is, outside of the formal housing delivery mechanisms' (Urban Foundation, 1991:24). It then differentiates between various categories of 'informal housing'. One category is 'spontaneous' informal housing, this comprising both 'back yard shacks' (in the yards of formal township houses), and shacks in informal settlements (*ibid.*: 4, 6). The other category is informal housing on official serviced sites (*ibid.*:6). The Urban Foundation report then introduces confusion through the term 'free-standing informal settlements', which it first defines as 'clusters of informal structures located on tracts of land within formal townships, in buffer zones between townships, on undeveloped farm land, on tribal land close to urban centres, and on vacant land in formerly white, coloured and Asian areas' (*ibid.*:6).[2] In the same report, the glossary of terms then defines 'free-standing settlements' (note the confusing omission of the word 'informal'), as being either 'illegal settlements' or 'planned site-and-service schemes' (*ibid.*:24). In the same glossary, the definition of 'informal settlement' in turn is worded as 'settlements where communities are housed and located initially in informal housing' (*ibid.*).

From the perspective, then, of the Urban Foundation, the term 'informal', is equated with 'initial' or 'temporary', to be replaced by the 'formal'. Informal housing in the 1980s could be afforded temporary legal 'transit camp' status through the Prevention of Illegal Squatting Act and its amendments. Subsequent to 1991, 'less formal areas' could be afforded permanent status through the Less Formal Township Establishment Act (Republic of South Africa 1991).[3] The Urban Foundation term for 'informal settlement', based primarily on the temporary nature of the house, rather than legal status or other characteristics, then applied to the entire range, from illegal settlements and temporary transit camps, to permanent 'less formal' sites-and-services areas with informal housing.

The ambiguity between illegal settlement, transit camp, serviced sites, and also back yard shacks permeates informal settlement literature of the 1990s and to date.[4] This has led in particular to ambiguous statistics. One example that can be drawn from the introductory paragraphs of many informal settlement studies, is the unquestioned reference to a figure of seven million people. In some studies it is applied to the number of people living in informal (squatter) settlements, and in others to those living in informal housing structures including serviced sites and back yard shacks.[5] Not surprisingly, the source of the seven million figure is the same influential Urban Foundation (1991) report from which I have quoted the confusing definitions. It gives no evidence of seven million people living in unplanned or illegally formed informal settlements. Instead, it estimates that 'over seven million people live in urban informal housing', with reference to its 'informal housing' definition that includes shacks in back yards, in informal settlements and on serviced sites (Urban Foundation, 1991:4). In this estimation, the informal settlement population makes up an unqualified portion of the seven million people.

With the continued use of the confusing Urban Foundation terminology, there are to date no clear figures on the number of people living in unplanned, illegally formed urban informal settlements in South Africa. Subsequent to the 1991 Urban Foundation report, an influential reference on the 'current housing context' has been the White Paper on Housing (Department of Housing, 1994). It is clearly based on Urban Foundation terminology and concepts. Though attempting to up-date the statistics, it perpetuates the confusion by defining 'squatter housing' as shacks 'in free-standing squatter settlements ... and in the back yards of formal houses' (*ibid.*:9). For this category it provides an estimation of 1.06 million households, adding an estimated growth of 150,000 households per annum. Even the national population census of 1996 failed to give clarity on the national figure of people living in illegally formed informal ('squatter') settlements. The census collapses informal dwellings on serviced sites with those in 'squatter' settlements, though identifying a separate category for 'informal dwelling/shack in backyard' (Orkin, 1998). The figure for the former category is 1,049,686 households. Applying an average household size of 3.6 people for this category,[6] this results in a figure of approximately 3.8 million people. Of this, again, only an unqualified portion lived in unplanned informal settlements. Indeed then, even half a decade after the 1991 Urban Foundation report, there was no evidence of 7 million people living in informal settlements, as suggested by Gigaba and Maharaj (1996), Lohnert (1997), McCarthy *et al.* (1995) and Smith (1992).

While most informal settlement research in South Africa displays Urban Foundation influence by unquestioningly applying its ambiguous terminology, and therefore not contributing to the clarification of the informal settlement situation, it is possible to draw a distinction between research that explicitly supports the Urban Foundation paradigm and that which contradicts it. I examine these in turn, before discussing the limitations of the informal settlement literature in effectively challenging the entrenched framework of informal settlement intervention in South Africa.

6.3 Scholarly responses within the Urban Foundation paradigm

Most of the studies in support of the Urban Foundation paradigm are evaluations of the informal settlement intervention that took place either through the IDT capital subsidies or, after the 1994 elections, through the National Housing Policy's capital subsidy. These studies have examined the intervention experience primarily from the perspective of project managers and the private sector. A particularly influential[7] private-sector funded study by McCarthy *et al.* (1995) provides direct continuity with the Urban Foundation thinking. Bond (1997:93), critiquing this report from the perspective of the academic left, traces the association of the authors (as staff or consultants) with the Urban Foundation, the IDT and the National Housing Forum. Indeed, Bond labels them as 'some of the leading architects' of the post-apartheid housing policy, and in his review of the report points to 'the residue of UF [Urban Foundation] arguments and ideology' (*ibid.*). Bond critiques this report primarily on the deviation it promotes from the ANC's Reconstruction and Development Programme (RDP), which promised the mass delivery of housing to specified minimum standards. According to Bond's argument, McCarthy *et al.*'s (1995) presentation of informal settlement 'upgrading' and incremental housing delivery as having no alternative, has discouraged the exploration of mechanisms for the delivery of a higher standard of housing. The questions I ask of this and similar studies are not about the obstacles to adequate standards of mass housing. They are about the relevance of the Urban Foundation's approach as a universal model for informal settlement intervention in South Africa. I identify four areas of concern: first, the assumption that informal settlement intervention is simply another form of housing delivery; second, the dismissal of community-based organisation; third, the market assumptions that support the delivery of individual freehold titles; and fourth, the stakes placed for the profit-making sector.

Informal settlement intervention: simply a form of housing delivery?

A characteristic of the studies I review in this section is that they do not clearly differentiate between informal settlement intervention and the establishment of new development sites. This position agrees with the current standardised intervention through the capital subsidy, which indeed leads to the replacement of informal settlements with orderly township layouts. The only difference between this so-called '*in situ* upgrading' and greenfield development is that in the former case, the development site is already occupied. The social objective of minimal disruption to the informally established urban fabric (and to the intrinsic social ties), which defines upgrading or *'urbanização'* in Brazil, does not apply. Instead, a 'roll-over' procedure is common practice.[8] This means removal of all shacks from the land, their temporary reconstruction on nearby land, and the installation of layout and infrastructure according to conventional greenfield procedures. As the formal layout generally results in increased plot sizes[9] and wider access routes, dwelling densities are considerably reduced. Only a portion of the original population is then re-allocated sites within the 'upgraded' settlement. Others are assumed to be allocated sites elsewhere. Where original settlement densities correspond with those of planned settlements, shacks may be 'shifted' (and not entirely removed) in order to accommodate a standardised layout.[10]

In accordance with this practice, McCarthy *et al.* (1995:2, 3) state in their evaluation that 'once an informal settlement has been upgraded in-situ, it does not differ fundamentally from a settlement where housing has been delivered on an incremental basis'. The term 'incremental' refers to the current policy of delivering a serviced site with a starter house. McCarthy *et al.* (1995), in their lengthy study (for the National Business Initiative) which sets out to evaluate 'informal settlement upgrading and consolidation projects', include case studies of greenfield as well as so-called '*in situ* upgrading' projects. The 'Choice of Case Studies' (*ibid.*:9) gives no explanation of this, other than 'to provide a different perspective' and the conclusions of the study do not differentiate between what was found in the '*in situ* upgrades' as opposed to the greenfield situation.

The same limitation applies to the voluminous USAID-funded evaluation study by Mary Tomlinson, then of the Centre for Policy Studies (Tomlinson, 1995b, 1995c, 1996, 1997a, 1997b and 1998b). This study is not as biased in favour of the private sector perspective as that of McCarthy *et al.* (1995). It also examines the 'views' of government and 'beneficiaries' and is willing to point to contradictions in the policy. However, it too evaluates the national housing subsidy scheme without differentiating between so-called '*in situ* upgrading' and greenfield development. This delivery-oriented perspective on informal settlement intervention clearly does not seek to address the complex social, legal, political and economic realities of poverty, as manifested in informal settlements. It does not recognise the popular initiative that created the informal layout (the struggle of the Kanana settlement leadership in having their well planned informal layout recognised is discussed in Chapter 7). Nor does it accept popular ideas for settlement improvement. The obstacles identified through the delivery-oriented evaluations are those that impede formal delivery, rather than those experienced by the informal settlement households and their community representatives, in their endeavours to improve living conditions. The perception, then, of informal settlement as simply a form of housing delivery supports the private sector-oriented assumptions on community organisation, the land market and the role of the formal profit-making sector, which I discuss in the following paragraphs.

Dismissal of a role for community-based organisations

Studies in support of the Urban Foundation paradigm and the current informal settlement intervention approach argue for the relevance of an individualised intervention, therefore supporting the notion of a standardised, household-based once-off capital subsidy. Intervention structured in this manner makes the individual household a player in the development, alongside government and the delivering private sector. The role of community organisation and leadership is reduced to that of serving the project objectives. Thus McCarthy *et al.* (1995:69) recommend:

> Essentially civics need to withdraw from the managerial and financial aspects of the development process and focus essentially on ensuring full community participation in the development process while acting as monitor and watchdog over development and future local authority servicing and maintenance of upgraded areas.

This position does not allow for people's collective control over development, which, as Bond (1997:102) points out, is the objective of many civic organisations. The position of McCarthy *et al.* on the role of civics does not acknowledge the challenges that organised community groups in informal settlements present against the Urban Foundation paradigm (I examine such initiatives in Chapter 7). The Homeless People's Federation/People's Dialogue alliance, with its radical people-driven development approach and strong criticism of private sector interests in development (see People's Dialogue, 1994:14), are portrayed by McCarthy *et al.* (1995:39) as no more than 'an organisation mainly of women which seeks to promote housing through self-help saving and loans schemes coupled with collective construction'. The Tomlinson study likewise, though less explicitly, dismisses the relevance of community organisations in the housing subsidy interventions. Tomlinson's set of publications separately examine the views of implementers (1995b), developers (1995c), beneficiaries (1996), financial institutions (1997a), national and provincial legislators (1997b) and local governments (1998b), yet entirely omit the views of civic or other community-based organisations. Tomlinson does not explain this. However, she does state her view that alongside developers and 'others with an interest in particular forms of housing', civics pursue 'their interests in a way which disadvantages beneficiaries' unless sanctioned or given an incentive to act on the contrary (Tomlinson, 1996:51). Further, she suggests that government is 'perhaps the only institution capable of representing beneficiary interests' (*ibid.*:52). In a separate publication addressing questions of citizenship in a sites-and-services area, Tomlinson with Bam and Mathole (1995:57) state the same position in their conclusion, namely that 'communication between residents and the state is impeded by the existence of civic groups which seek to act as intermediaries between them and the state'.

The dismissal of civic and other community organisations as exploitative, corrupt and self-seeking obstacles to government delivery gives justification to an intervention approach that ensures that the government administration interacts (be it via a developer) directly with the individual beneficiary through a standardised capital subsidy (linked to freehold title), rather than with a collective community representation. This position has been justified particularly from studies that have examined the phenomenon of violence in the informal settlements in Durban in the early 1990s, concluding that informal settlements, due to the power of community representatives, are intrinsically associated with violence. Thus Morris (1992:97) states:

> As long as the inhabitants do not have an individual *de jure* right and *de facto* control over their own reproductive resources, shantytowns will always be intrinsically violent, since their reproduction is based on forcible control, patronage and arbitrary extraction of surplus in the form of cash, kind, labour or quasi-military service to those who control social resources.

Morris (1992:98) then recommends intervention that creates individualisation in informal settlements. Hindson and McCarthy (1994:28) argue along similar lines, concluding their synopsis of the informal settlement problem in Durban by stating:

> The challenge at present is to recast power relations within these communities, and more widely within urban areas, through the creation of rationalised, integrated and democratic local authorities which are accountable to residents. The reconstitution of local government in this way should entail a shift in power elites towards new governmental structures, and a shift from local political organisations towards individual residents who are the beneficiaries of development.

The recommendation, therefore, is to reduce the power and role of community-based organisations. This might be relevant in exploitative situations, assuming that local government councillors and officials are more committed to assisting individual informal settlement communities. However, as the case studies in Chapter 7 indicate, accountable civic and other community organisations do exist, as does local government incapacity and lack of will to act upon demands for informal settlement upgrading. In that context, a blanket reduction in the role of community organisations, as recommended by Hindson and McCarthy (1994), McCarthy *et al.* (1995) and Morris (1992), and implied by Tomlinson's various studies, clearly impacts negatively on the process of settlement improvement.

Market assumptions: support for individual freehold titles

Support for the individualised approach to informal settlement intervention through the capital subsidy then translates into support for the delivery of individual freehold titles. This is a theme in two evaluations of the Freedom Square informal settlement upgrading in Bloemfontein[11] (Botes *et al.*, 1996; Marais and Krige, 1997). Marais and Krige (*ibid.*) discuss the results of a post-upgrading opinion survey, on aspects most appreciated by the beneficiaries. An overwhelming majority is reported to appreciate land ownership above infrastructure and services. On this finding, the authors base their recommendation that 'ownership might be administratively advisable' (*ibid.*:186). However, the survey and the discussion in their paper fail to explore the concept of tenure security in the light of options to freehold title, be they leasehold, communal ownership or the formal recognition of the existing informal tenure system. Instead, they defend individual freehold tenure against their own evidence of its shortcomings. Acknowledging that 'a number of stands have been vacated since sites were registered in the names of the owners', they suggest that 'most residents do not have an understanding of the value of their sites' (*ibid.*:185).

This suggestion of ignorance on the part of the beneficiaries is based on questionable assumptions, which are invalidated through the evidence in the literature I review in the following section. The one assumption is that a property market, operating similarly to that in a middle-class suburb, is created by imposition of individual freehold titles on an informal settlement. Coupled with this are the assumptions, on the one hand, that the exchange value of an upgraded site is equivalent to the subsidy investment and, on the other hand, that the poor don't understand the market. Along these lines, McCarthy *et al.* (1995:22) then argue that 'people have an imprecise view of the market value of their properties (and this is especially true of the less educated)'. These authors ignore the basics of the functioning of property markets, namely that property value is related to the economic power of the demand. The researchers fail to acknowledge that in most instances there is no demand for buying into upgraded settlements at a price that would recover the subsidy amount. Indeed, it is not the residents, but the private sector-oriented researchers, who fail to understand the market. Moreover, the researchers show ignorance of the universally recognised problem of downward raiding, i.e. the selling of subsidised low-income units to middle income buyers who would be able to pay the subsidy amount or more.[12] McCarthy *et al.* (1995:57), by lamenting the lack of a 'viable market in housing within the informal settlements', are in fact promoting downward raiding and displacement.

Botes *et al.* (1996) present an even more questionable explanation of the vacating of sites by registered owners without selling. They argue that 'because delivery was free, some registered owners later simply abandoned their stands and vanished without trace ... If people had paid even a nominal amount for their stands, they would have made more of an effort to sell them when they moved away' (*ibid.*:463, 464). It is apparent that the evaluators have made no attempt to understand the reality of household mobility, a survival strategy that has been documented by socially-oriented researchers and to which I return in the following section. From the perspective of project management, Botes *et al.* (*ibid.*) portray this survival strategy as a ***problem***, not only after issuing of titles, but throughout the development process. Thus they state:

> Absentee shack-owners soon became a problem that the Problem Solving Committee had to deal with. A number of shacks, apparently deserted or at least temporarily abandoned, posed a financial threat to the development because the capital subsidy guaranteed by the Independent Development Trust would only be paid once ownership of the land had been transferred (Botes *et al.*, 1996:457).

From this perspective it is understandable that the authors do not articulate any need to revise the capital subsidy approach with its blanket imposition of individual freehold title. Instead they suggest that a 'monetary contribution may be required ... to entrench ownership of a stand' (Botes *et al.*, 1996:266).

Increased stakes for the private sector

The promotion of commodification and individualisation of land, and the flawed market assumptions supporting this, form part of a larger agenda of increasing the stakes of the profit-making sector through informal settlement intervention. Thus, with reference to McCarthy *et al.*'s (1995) report, Bond (1997:93) emphasises the powerful private sector interests that 'clouded the analytical judgement of the NBI researchers'. The private sector interests then are promoted at two levels. At one level are the direct stakes in the delivery process, which is funded through the individual household-based subsidies. Thus McCarthy *et al.* (1995:41) ensure that the 'private sector (business)' be included in the list of essential actors required to 'make upgrade a success'. They further argue that 'the role of the local authority itself has to change so that its role is very substantially modified ... [with] much stronger involvement of the private sector in development, servicing and maintenance' (*ibid.*:53, 54). At a separate level, McCarthy *et al.* (1995) promote individualisation and housing delivery on the grounds that it encourages consumerism among the beneficiaries. Thus they state that: 'Upgrading can unleash the huge consumer markets in informal settlements. The introduction of electricity, for example encourages the consumption of "white goods" [meaning refrigerators, stoves, washing machines and freezers], kitchen appliances, television sets, etc.' (*ibid.*:77).

In the following section I will discuss research evidence that confirms that the current intervention approach encourages individualism and consumerism (and debt). Indeed, we may assume that such intervention does contribute to the urban economy. However, in the absence of any direct economic upliftment accompanying the housing intervention, it must be asked how individualisation and commodification impact on people's ability to cope with ongoing poverty. Returning, then, to a question raised through my review of the current World Bank urban policy position in Chapter 2: should state-funded informal settlement intervention be designed primarily to respond to demands for growth in the urban economy (as implicit in the McCarthy *et al.* (1995) report, and indeed the current intervention approach in South Africa), or should it respond to the realities of poverty, as experienced by the inhabitants of informal settlements? This brings me to the research evidence in the South African literature that contradicts the market-oriented tenets of the current informal settlement intervention framework in South Africa from various perspectives.

6.4 Scholarly responses contradicting the Urban Foundation paradigm

While there are various studies and debates challenging the relevance of individual freehold tenure for informal settlement residents, no studies in South Africa have explicitly challenged the relevance of the Urban Foundation model as a whole for informal settlement intervention. I return to this point later in the chapter. In this section, I draw out from the literature empirical evidence that contradicts the various positions I have discussed above, which have been used to support the Urban Foundation model. A few studies have highlighted problems with the standardised product-driven funding mechanism for informal settlement intervention, some have cast light on the realities of civic or community organisation, various studies have pointed to the social impacts of the imposition of freehold titles and individualisation, and yet others have exposed the impacts of commodification and consumerism.

Questioning housing/service delivery as a means of informal settlement intervention

An important case for examining the relevance of the capital subsidy and associated delivery-oriented model of informal settlement intervention is that of Besters Camp in Inanda, Durban, documented by Merrifield *et al.* (1993) and van Horen (1996, 1999). The Besters Camp intervention was the first attempt at *in situ* upgrading in South Africa. Though initiated by the Urban Foundation in 1989, the initial stages of the intervention preceded the articulation of the capital subsidy approach by the Urban Foundation. The Informal Settlement Division of the Urban Foundation at the time was not dictated to by the model later promoted by the Urban Foundation, and could therefore explore an upgrading approach that was building on the '*de facto*' situation in Besters Camp. Indeed, 'the lack of local or national precedent provided Besters Camp with considerable room for manoeuvre in the formulation of the planning approach' (van Horen, 1996:22). Initially funded through a grant, the intervention allowed for the establishment of community facilities, including community halls, health and education facilities, and for the mobilisation of NGOs and government agencies' involvement in health and education programmes (*ibid.*:18). Planning principles that were adopted at this stage were grounded in an understanding of the constant social and physical change in the settlement. The 'ideal end state' was to be developed with the residents over a period of time, and was to be based on the existing layout (*ibid.*:20). External planning and imposition of a standardised layout was considered inappropriate. Planning itself was seen as 'only one element of what needs to be a multi-disciplinary approach to the upgrading process'. However, this responsive approach was stopped in its tracks in 1991 with a switch in the 'funding regime' from a relatively flexible grant to the IDT's capital subsidy scheme, requiring 'the delivery of serviced sites' and freehold tenure through a standardised household-linked budget (*ibid.*:18). As a result, the broader social and developmental aspects of the intervention were discontinued, and the intervention instead was limited to the delivery of services and freehold title (Merrifield *et al.*, 1993).

Merrifield *et al.*'s (1993) and van Horen's (1996) case studies of Besters Camp reflect doubt over the relevance of structuring informal settlement intervention as simply another form of housing or services delivery. This position is supplemented by positions in the recent urban tenure-related research and debate. Cross (2002), analysing the blockages in the delivery of secure tenure to informal settlement residents, suggests that access to secure tenure through the 'gold-plated vehicle' of the capital subsidy, which ties the delivery of freehold title to that of services and housing, neither meets the social reality in informal settlements, nor is it likely to reach the current and future scale of the informal settlement phenomenon. The reality of continuous social change, hence the limitations of a rigidly imposed inflexible intervention (as occurs through the capital subsidy), has led to proposals for an alternative approach to land management, based on the concept of 'social change' taking into account and giving support to existing community-based mechanisms of land control (Davies, 1998; Davies and Fourie, 1998, 2002). From the experience of the Durban-based NGO BESG (Built Environment Support Group), Marx (2003) calls for a support-based approach for informal settlements, arguing though that current policy in South Africa does make this possible. However, the relationship between the approaches advocated by Davies and Fourie and by Marx, and the national housing finance mechanism, the capital subsidy, is yet to be explored. I return to the tenure options, and in particular the evidence of continuous social change in informal settlements, later in this chapter when discussing research that has questioned the relevance of imposing freehold titles in an informal settlement intervention. Indeed, it is the attachment of freehold title to the capital subsidy, a central objective of the Urban Foundation,[13] that has been questioned most rigorously in the literature. It is through the case studies in Chapter 7, that I expose other obstacles that the capital subsidy approach places on meaningful informal settlement intervention.

Acknowledging the importance of community organisation

The Urban Foundation model associates violence and resulting mobility in informal settlements with the particular pattern of leadership and power that these settlements enable. The intervention then seeks to stabilise settlements by ensuring individual access to services and individual freehold titles. The assumption that imposed individualised development leads to settlement stability is contradicted by experience of the IDT-funded capital subsidy intervention in the Phola Park informal settlement on the East Rand near Johannesburg, documented by Royston (1993), Adler (1994) and Bremner (1994). In this settlement, the prospect of being tied to private plot ownership and payment for individual access to services (through the IDT-funded capital subsidy intervention) brought social division to the fore. While the majority of residents originated from back yard shacks in the neighbouring township and were willing to settle permanently, the same prospect deeply threatened the livelihood of a separate grouping, the migrants, who were planning instead to consolidate in the rural areas (Bremner, 1994). This was associated with the pressure of increasing dependency of a rural survival on wages from family members in the city (*ibid.*:37). A third grouping, illegal immigrants, were threatened by the enforcement of a registered title, as the survival of these immigrants depended on an unregistered existence. Thus Bremner (*ibid.*:40) argues that the very intention of creating 'stability, order and efficiency ... contradicted the function of the informal settlement in a sub-region where personal security was limited and economic opportunities scarce'.

The inflexible plans to impose freehold title and services on all households then undermined community cohesion at Phola Park. Royston (1993), in analysing the community organisation prior to the IDT intervention, notes that cohesion existed due to the unifying need for access to the city for survival. At the same time, the civic organisation had co-existed with a number of other organisational structures, including traditional as well as illegal groupings. It was the formal development process, requiring the civic organisation to represent all residents, that triggered conflict between the various groupings (*ibid.*). The finding that the Urban Foundation model is underpinned by a flawed assumption of community cohesion is supported by household level research in Cape Town (Spiegel *et al.*, 1994, 1996a). While not exploring the challenges of community organisation in the development process, the Cape Town study reveals a complexity of household ties among the African (black) urban population, often spanning the city and the region. This leads the authors likewise to warn policy makers of the assumption that people sharing one locality also share common interests and priorities regarding development.

The IDT intervention approach (the basis of the current intervention framework) was built on a flawed perception of community representation. Assuming community cohesion, it expected full community commitment to the development. The civic organisation was placed in a difficult position between a divided community it was to represent, on the one hand, and a disempowering project structure, on the other hand. With reference to the Phola Park case, Bremner (1994) mentions two aspects of the funding mechanism that undermined the civic organisation's role in the development. Firstly, rigid time limitations attached to the funding did not allow space for a community-driven process. Secondly, control over the capital subsidy funds was placed not with the community organisation but with developers and private consultants.[14] Bremner (1994:39) highlights the poor record of these private sector stakeholders: 'speculation, corruption, poor standards of work and unwillingness to facilitate community consultation'. Her conclusion then is that 'short term measures should have been adopted to address the immediate needs, while longer term solutions to political conflict, marginalisation, urban poverty and spatial segregation were worked out' (*ibid.*:41).

A similar recommendation results from a study examining the reasons for continuous on-migration by poor households in the Durban Functional Region (Cross *et al.*, 1994). Tying household mobility to the high incidence of violence in informal settlements (*ibid.*:95), the authors identify the need to stabilise the population. However, unlike the Hindson and McCarthy (1994) and Morris (1992) studies reviewed above, Cross *et al.* (1994) are cautious in recommending development as a means of stabilisation. As did Bremner (1994), they argue that development interventions are 'problematic since they may provoke violence and competition' (Cross *et al.*, 1994:95). Rather than promoting individualisation, they emphasise the importance of 'community capacity' in informal settlements 'to cope with service delivery and violence' (*ibid.*:96). Thus the core of their conclusion relates to the interface between development intervention and informal settlement leadership structures, whose credibility plays an important role in settlement stability. In a more recent study, Bénit (2002) examines how public intervention has led to increased community division in Diepsloot, Johannebsurg. Private property developers have exploited existing divisions within communities to influence local government decision-making, for example, regarding the relocation of squatters from land that can be profitably developed for others. The same settlement process is a case study in Beall *et al.* (2002), who examine the extent to which the Diepsloot Community Development Forum was able to engage in democratic decision-making.

The impact of formal development prospects on civic organisations is particularly evident in settlements that have been faced with official plans of relocation. Ardington's (1992) documentation of the Canaan settlement in

Durban discusses this point. A strong cohesion among the residents of Canaan had been fostered around the common threat of eviction. This was reflected in the formation of a settlement committee. However, as the invaded land was officially classified as not upgradable for low-income residential purposes, the official solution was to relocate the residents. Within this official process, the community organisation was expected to ensure that no further shacks were constructed in the settlement. However, neither the relocation site, nor the moratorium on formal construction (prohibiting even the construction of pit latrines), met the diverse realities of the residents. Community cohesion disintegrated once it became evident that the common resistance to eviction had failed – residents were once again needing to make individual decisions about their future. Thus Ardington (*ibid.*:33) concludes that 'Canaan, which appeared well on the way to developing a strong civic authority, is weak, divided and unable either to press its own demands or react to those of the authorities'.

In a study of the partial upgrading of the Greenpoint informal settlement in Khayelitsha, Cape Town, Oldfield (2002) traces the impact on the already fragile civic organisation, and residents' participation in the civic structures. A situation where only a portion of the informal settlement population benefits from the first phase of a capital subsidy housing programme is common. Oldfield (*ibid.*) shows how these partial benefits weakened the ability of the civic organisation to attract the remaining development that was required for all the families to be housed formally.

A further collective social relation that may be impacted upon by prospects of serviced site delivery in informal settlements is that between informal settlement residents and neighbouring communities. Crankshaw (1996) examines this through the case of the West Rand township of Bekkersdal, where social division and conflict exist between council tenants, home-owners, back yard shack tenants, 'squatters' and hostel residents. Crankshaw (*ibid.*) emphasises the threat that the population growth (through in-migration) in back yard shack accommodation and informal settlement poses to 'the ethnic and political dominance of established Bekkersdal residents' (*ibid.*:63). Crankshaw (*ibid.*) points to various reasons why the 'upgrading' of informal settlement in this context may polarise social divisions. On the one hand, such intervention 'could be interpreted by established residents as politically partisan' (*ibid.*:63). On the other hand, upgrading may be seen to encourage the formation of new informal settlements in anticipation of sites-and-services delivery. The resulting movement from backyard shack accommodation into new informal settlements may be perceived as undermining the private rental sector, in itself an important source of income. Crankshaw's (*ibid.*) recommendation, therefore, is that the benefits of upgrading should not be limited to the residents of one particular housing type.

Crankshaw's (1996) study gives some insight into the complex social relations surrounding informal settlements that are embedded in African (black) townships. More recently, Swart-Kruger (2002) examined social relations surrounding an inner-city 'squatter' community (in particular the implications for children) and later its peripheral relocation site Thula Mtwana near Weiler's Farm south of Johannesburg. However, most studies on the relationship between informal settlement and the neighbouring formal 'communities' have focused on invasions that challenged group areas (see Sapire, 1990b), and particularly the exclusivity of middle to high income areas (see Emmett, 1992; Gardener, 1992; Nathan and Spindler, 1993; National Housing Forum, undated; Oelofse and Dodsen, 1997; Saff, 2001). I return to the implications of this research bias below. A finding in economists Nathan and Spindler's (1993) study of the informal settlement intervention process in Hout Bay (a suburb of Cape Town) gives some explanation to this research bias, while also casting light on the nature of community organisation. Nathan and Spindler (*ibid.*) apply the theory of pressure group reaction, or pressure group competition, to the Hout Bay situation. In the context of waning repression of land invasions by government around 1989, they analyse how the threat that the land invasions posed to the property-owning class in Hout Bay induced mobilisation. A Property Rights Association was formed with the aim of asserting pressure on government to act against the invasion. 'In response to this induced rise in political pressure, squatters were induced to form a proactive lobby ... which would capture increased gains by increased cohesion' (*ibid.*:484). Government's response of reassigning public land for the permanent settlement of the squatters within Hout Bay in turn led to the formation of 'new counteractive and proactive lobbies' (*ibid.*:485). Nathan and Spindler (*ibid.*) therefore refer to a continuing process of adjustment, as 'new groups entered the political arena to protect self-interests or to gain new property rights'. This study then is a useful explanation for the attention informal settlements within formerly white Group Areas have received.

Questioning the relevance of freehold titles and individualisation

The aspect of the Urban Foundation model most challenged in the South African literature is that of imposing individual freehold titles on the informal settlement situation. This aspect has been questioned from various angles. Some studies have examined diversity at the household level, exposing a range in household types, changes in household composition, and mobility of households. These studies disagree with the notion of a stable nuclear household, to which the Urban Foundation model ties freehold tenure. While the Urban Foundation-oriented researchers portrayed social phenomena such as household mobility as a 'problem' in the development process (Botes *et al.*, 1996), these studies understand social change as a response to a complex condition shaped by various degrees of poverty and by regionally specific situations. It is the evidence of diversity, both locally and regionally, that renders questionable the blanket solution of delivering individual freehold titles to informal settlement residents. A separate set of studies has examined the informal system of tenure and land management promoted in informal settlements by the civic movement. These studies have highlighted the responsiveness of this system to the realities of urban poverty. Yet other studies have examined to what extent a legal 'property market' has materialised subsequent to the delivery of freehold titles. These studies expose in particular the misfit between the cost of legal transfer of property and the economic reality within which post-intervention mobility takes place.

In Cape Town, household change through the adjustment of household composition has been researched through the concept of 'domestic fluidity', as a coping strategy of the urban poor (Ross, 1993, 1996; Spiegel *et al.*, 1994, 1996a, 1996b, 1996c, 1999). Though not making explicit reference to the universal concepts of urban poverty that I discussed in Chapter 2, these studies give important insight into the mobilisation of the non-monetary assets of 'household relations' and 'social capital'.[15] The contribution that Ross and Spiegel, *et al.* make to the understanding of household relations as an asset of the urban poor, is in the finding that adjustments to household composition are made at an expense. The poorer households were found to remain unchanged for relatively long periods, as 'they could not afford to relocate members or to call on others who might have the resources to support them' (Spiegel *et al.*, 1994:14).[16] The Spiegel *et al.* (*ibid.*) study draws its conclusions from surveys across the range of African (black) low-income residential environments in Cape Town (family housing, back yard shacks, hostels and informal settlements). Their finding is that the poorest households, least likely to draw on adjustments in household composition, are most prevalent in urban informal settlements (*ibid.*:19).[17]

The impoverished context of a peri-urban informal settlement near Cape Town, with high tenure insecurity, is examined by Ross (1993).[18] This study found a more localised and thus affordable form of domestic fluidity, with considerable movement of individuals among homes within the settlements – so much so that Ross 'was led to argue that the very idea of household as a simultaneously co-residential, commensal and co-productive unit was wholly inappropriate' (Ross in Spiegel *et al.*, 1994). In relation to inter-household relationships, Ross found that 'the resources with which to sustain intense, long-term relationships of the type associated with kin networks were scarce. Consequently people often utilised other relationships of friendship and reciprocity' (Ross, 1996:60). It must be added, however, that the settlement Ross researched had a largely coloured population (Spiegel *et al.*, 1994:20), with the important distinction that origin and kinship ties are not comparable, culturally or in terms of distance, to those of the African (black) population researched by Spiegel *et al.*[19]

The importance of kinship ties to African (black) informal settlement households in Cape Town is evident from Lohnert's (1998) study in two informal settlements and one relocation scheme. Her finding was that both informal settlements contained concentrations of people originating from the same rural magisterial districts. Kinship relations had played an important role in people's residential decisions, and many households appeared to actively maintain such networks. Thus Lohnert (*ibid.*) highlights the importance of urbanised kinship networks within informal settlements. This leads her to question the practice of re-allocating sites,[20] as is commonly associated with the delivery of standardised plots with freehold tenure through the capital subsidy. She makes particular reference to the absurdity of the technocratic site allocation practice that applied to the sites-and-services scheme she surveyed, to which people from 14 different informal settlements within the Integrated Serviced Land Project (iSLP) area had been relocated (*ibid.*:388).[21]

A further condition, specific to the African (black) population, is the occurrence of households that are 'parts of spatially divided income-sharing units with bases in both urban and rural areas' (Spiegel *et al.*, 1996b:20).[22] The ongoing 'circulatory migration'[23] between the urban and rural base 'allows households to gain access to a wide variety of income-generating activities (and services such as schooling) and to "spread its risks" as far as exposure to the various sectors of the economy are concerned' (Spiegel *et al.*, 1994:9). The particular significance of informal settlements in the circulatory migration system is, firstly, that 'they make up much of the urban and peri-urban accommodation of the African population' and secondly, that they give 'access to a cheap place to live' (*ibid.*:10). However, Spiegel *et al.* argue that there is no clear evidence whether circulatory migration in South Africa is transitional and eventually leads to permanent migration (*ibid.*), as is assumed with the issuing of freehold tenure through the once-off capital subsidy. Again, it is the poorest households, that do not have the resources to travel, for whom the move to the urban area is permanent. Here Spiegel *et al.* (1999:153) refer to a 'fatalistic pragmatism rather than a belief that urban life is appropriate and right'. It is evident then that in Cape Town, where the rural base of migrants is likely to be at least 900km from the city, the cost of transport places a particular restriction on circulatory movement, thus giving urban poverty a dimension of deprivation that might not be as acute in other South African cities. The particular tenure needs of such households have not been explored in the literature. However, Ross's (1993, 1996) study (though examining a largely coloured and not African (black) community) made the finding, as mentioned above, that extremely poor households resort to more localised mobility and high degrees of household fluidity as a mechanism of survival. This does not suggest that tying such households to freehold tenure, in isolation of economic upliftment, is an appropriate intervention.

The regional diversity in poverty and coping strategies is a further challenge to the uniform delivery of individual freehold title. I have mentioned above that in the case of Durban, the particular phenomenon of 'on-migration' from one urban location to the next has caused concern among researchers. Cross *et al.* (1994) have explained the high occurrence of on-migration as a response to violence, and as a strategy to improve the residential situation. Again, the relevance of tying households to one locality through a once-off capital subsidy and freehold title is questioned (*ibid.*).

A further argument that has been made against the practice of tying households into freehold titles is based on the increasing evidence of household disintegration resulting from HIV/AIDS (Tomlinson, 2001). Not only does the economic disintegration of the household due to cost of medication and eventual loss of breadwinner lead to its displacement back into overcrowded rooms or informal settlements, but households themselves are transforming into new and transitional types of household. These households include people that are periodically ill or orphans from other households, or they may consist of infected and expelled individuals, or orphans fending for themselves, and households from which an entire generation is missing (Tomlinson, 2003a). Alarmingly, the prevalence of HIV infection in urban formal settlements in South Africa is currently estimated at 23 per cent (Thomas, 2003). Tomlinson (2003b) argues that government intervention should focus on the provision of water and sanitation, which is vital in the household-based caring for AIDS sufferers.

With the prevalence of household change in informal settlements, it has been asked how informal systems of tenure and land management have responded to this social reality. Cross (1995), examining informal urban tenure in the Durban Functional Region, illustrates how the informal tenure practices 'have adapted to mobility and to a considerable extent represent portable land rights' (Cross, 1994:187). They comprise 'systems of relative social rights, rather than systems of property rights' (*ibid.*). In Chapter 5 (and with reference to Cross, 1994), I have mentioned that the civic movement in the late 1980s came to control informal settlements on Durban's periphery, abolishing the practice that associated access to land with the payment of rent. Cross (1994) describes how the 'widespread urban system of rent tenancy' (*ibid.*:180) comprising the lodging of rooms, back yard structures, and site rental, with landlords making profits or securing business clientele, and shack lords securing political or personal support, gave way to a 'powerful social movement against the practice of paying rent for access to land' (Cross, 1995:31). The spread of the civic movement then comprised a shift 'away from the ethic of private tenure' (albeit rental and not freehold), towards a system that has similarities with communal land holding practices in African (black) rural areas (*ibid.*:34).

While appearing to draw on African (black) rural traditions, the urban informal tenure system promoted by the civic movement was not restricted to African (black) settlements. In Cape Town, a study by Dewar and Wolmarans (1994) documents four informal settlements in the Western Cape,[24] each with a mixed population of African (black) and coloured people, therefore no common reference to traditional rural practices. The tenure system described by Dewar and Wolmarans is that referred to by Cross (1994, 1995). Newcomers require introduction to the committee by a resident, are screened and then offered a 'choice of two or three sites', where possible in the vicinity of their sponsors, and in negotiation with the neighbouring residents (Dewar and Wolmarans, 1994:90). Precise boundaries are negotiated between neighbours, with the committee intervening in the case of a dispute (*ibid.*).

The informal tenure system as promoted by the civic movement provides free of charge access to land for the urban poor. However, it is not necessarily responsive to the most needy. Cross (1995) raises concern over the sidelining of single people in the entry process into informal tenure. Particularly single women, and women with young children, are not welcomed into established settlements, thus often having to resort to: a) 'clientship arrangements with established householders', frequently resulting in suspicion from established female residents; b) entry into new settlements that are still in the recruitment stage; or c) lodging and tenancy within an informal settlement, which then allows the collection of local information in the search for sites (*ibid.*:35). Thus, the finding from the international review of informal settlement research in Chapter 2 that lodging in informal settlements ranks lowest in the residential hierarchy and is largely occupied by women,[25] appears to apply to some extent to the South African situation.

While there are problems inherent in the informal tenure system, its responsiveness to those in greatest need is further impeded by official intervention that requires a moratorium on further construction. I have mentioned the practice of affording transit camp status to informal settlements. This is associated with the numbering of shacks and a freeze on shack construction, as a first step in a process of stabilisation that ultimately ties households to individual freehold tenure and regular service charges. The settlement committee (usually a civic organisation) is expected to enforce the building moratorium. Inevitably, this impacts on the ability of the informal tenure system to accommodate needy arrivals, while also changing the role of the committee from that of enablement to that of strict control. This role in turn is undermined by the pressing demands for living space. Dewar and Wolmarans (1994:81) describe the case where a settlement committee responded to the official imposition of a settlement freeze by prohibiting settlement growth. Ongoing densification then appeared to take place without consultation of the committee, as established households would cede portions of the land they were occupying 'to incoming friends or extended family who would construct their own shacks' (*ibid.*:92). In addition, lodging was being practised, with rent being paid 'in return for a bed or a room' (*ibid.*). Thus both the collective control over settlement expansion, and the concept of free access to living space, were undermined.

There is evidence, then, that the imposition of a settlement freeze may induce practices of subletting. Cross (1994:187) goes further to warn that the imposition of private title through the development process may 'contribute to a loss of equity and a re-emergence of rent tenancy'. This has parallels with

Mayekiso's (1996:163, 164) concern about new forms of exploitation induced through the privatisation of public housing in townships, and therefore the re-introduction of the exploitative landlord-tenant relationship in the back yard shack situation.

The impact of the commercialisation process induced through close on a decade of issuing of freehold title through the capital subsidy system in South Africa has not been adequately researched. Nonetheless, the misfit between individual freehold title and the reality on the ground has been pointed out, particularly with regards to the cumbersome system of title registration, thus refuting the property market assumptions made by the Urban Foundation-oriented researchers. In the case of Besters Camp, van Horen (1996:25) reports that subsequent to the expenditure of the R7,500 capital subsidy of the IDT on the delivery of services and individual freehold titles, beneficiaries were selling the serviced sites for R800 to R3,500. This, he argues, 'is marginally higher than average pre-upgrade house selling prices – hardly in keeping with inflation rates – and in any event considerably lower than the value suggested by the average [IDT] subsidy' (van Horen, 1996:25). Barry (1995), likewise questioning the relevance of the title registration system in the low-income context, mentions similar findings from Khayelitsha in Cape Town, where serviced sites were being exchanged informally for R600 to R1,000. Barry adds the useful detail that the legal transfer fee 'would probably be in excess of R400' (*ibid.*:154). Barry (1998:23) casts light on a further area of misfit. In a study of land occupation patterns in sites-and-services schemes, he found an alarming amount of dwellings (up to 28 per cent) encroaching over legal boundaries. While the causes of this phenomenon were still under investigation at the time of his writing, this finding clearly indicates that middle-class property-ownership behaviour does not necessarily apply to sites-and-services schemes in South Africa. It may be added that Davies and Fourie (1998:242; see also Davies and Fourie, 2002) acknowledge that formal tenure could 'revert to an informal form of tenure over time'. This is also a suggestion in recent tenure research on urbanised former homeland areas where freehold titles are being issued as part of a tenure upgrading process (Ambert, 2002).

What have been the recommendations by research that has questioned the imposition of freehold tenure through the Urban Foundation model of intervention? While Barry (1995) explores systems of communal land ownership, Cross (1994:188) recommends the formalisation of the informal tenure system, in other words 'a formal version of what impoverished shack communities produce for themselves'.[26] This, she argues, 'while disliked by planners, offers flexible site access to its users and can usually secure their rights in terms of accepted understandings against anything short of violence or government intervention' (*ibid.*:187). As mentioned earlier in this chapter, Davies (1998) (see also Davies and Fourie, 1998) developed a 'social change' approach to land management in informal settlements. This is tied back to a conscious redefinition of the term 'informal settlement'. Their use of the term is not based on the nature of the housing structure, but on the legality of the land occupation, and its relationship to the local authority. As opposed to the ambiguity of the Urban Foundation use of the term, their definition of 'informal settlement' consciously accommodates the concept of change by acknowledging a continuum of (il)legality and of development. Their approach to land management then allows for 'the transformation of indigenous land tenure over time' (Davies and Fourie, 1998:241). The approach seeks to draw together the 'extensive local knowledge' of community leaders, and official technical expertise (*ibid.*:242). The authors recommend that community-based land management systems are assisted 'even if they contravene existing legislation' (*ibid.*:243). In the South African literature reviewed, this then represents the only explicit proposal for a support-based alternative to the Urban Foundation approach to informal settlement intervention.

Exposing the impact of commodification on poverty

The relevance of individualisation and commodification of land has been questioned throughout the discussion above. Here I turn to recent studies that have critically examined the unleashing 'of huge consumer markets in informal settlements' through 'upgrading', as predicted by McCarthy *et al.*'s (1995:77) promotion of the Urban Foundation model. One anthropological study (Yose 1999 in Spiegel, 1999) examines the ways in which a relocation from an informal settlement[27] to a standardised 'incremental' housing scheme nearby impacts on lives and livelihoods. The study indeed confirms that consumer markets are unleashed. The orderliness and permanence of the new environment inspired modern aspirations. New furniture and appliances were being purchased on credit. The individualisation of access to services implied an individualisation of household chores such as laundry washing, which in the informal settlement had been conducted at public taps, with the sharing of bathtubs among women. Each household was now purchasing its own wash tub, this corresponding with 'a breakdown of the kinds of inter-household links that had previously prevailed' (*ibid.*:5). Households in the relocation scheme were clearly impacted upon by the individualisation, which directly undermined 'mutual assistance' or reciprocity. In addition, they were being burdened with down payments on their purchases. Some households incurred further expenses by transporting old furniture to distant rural homes (*ibid.*:6).

In discussing these findings, Spiegel explains that the perception of 'urban' among inhabitants of informal settlements and townships is associated with orderliness and individualisation, whereas informal settlements, though located in urban areas, are perceived as 'rural'. While not referring explicitly to the current model of informal settlement intervention which entrenches individualisation, Spiegel (1999:11), in his conclusion, refers to the 'confidence trick' of modernity. While promoters of the Urban Foundation model would argue that the modern lifestyle is what the poor aspire to and should not be denied, it is of course evident that in the absence of economic upliftment, individualisation is a burden to the urban poor. Spiegel notes that there is indeed evidence of 'popular suspicion of modernity' (*ibid.*). He implicitly supports community-based and communal alternatives by stating that: 'Once we can see people consciously recognising the cruel hoax that has been modernity's promise, we need also to take note that there is chance for them to begin to valorise other forms' (*ibid.*).

A related warning comes from Cross (2002:198), who presents evidence of beneficiaries of 'incremental' capital subsidy housing having 'moved out again after two months, reportedly due to cost factors that were unsustainable on the household's income.' Referring to Spiegel's (1999) paper on the implications of commodification, she adds the considerable drain that service charges place on household economies. This leads her to question official attempts at integrating the poor 'into the urban fabric by subsidizing the up front cost of their move from informal into formal accommodation' (*ibid.*:6). Those households that move out of the delivered housing due to economic problems 'will not be eligible for a housing subsidy again' (*ibid.*). Therefore, such a move 'may result in the permanent loss of tenure security' (*ibid.*).

I have noted in the discussion of tenure, above, that the impact of individualisation commences with the official numbering of shacks and imposition of a moratorium on building. With reference to this particular stage in the informal settlement process, Makhatini (1994) notes that the economic opportunities that are created by settlement growth, namely clandestine building activity and the growing demand for household commodities, are lost once the official numbering of shacks occurs and the settlement committee is given the official mandate to prevent further construction. While the individualisation process then removes economic stakes for the clandestine and informal sector, it promotes stakes for the formal private sector. That the private sector itself is not necessarily efficient and ethical in fulfilling its delivery role has been suggested by Bremner (1994), as mentioned earlier in this chapter. Cross (2002) gives evidence of how the cost of mismanagement by a private developer in Cape Town is borne by the beneficiaries. With the developer having 'folded his operation' due to overspending, and the municipality refusing to cover the 'cost overruns', the prospective home owners wait indefinitely for the completion of their capital subsidy units.[28] While warning also of illicit practices on the part of powerful community leaders, therefore sceptical of alternatives that place financial responsibilities with community representatives, Cross seriously questions the relevance of the 'route to tenure security' through the capital subsidy approach (*ibid.*).

6.5 Limitations in challenging the Urban Foundation paradigm

In the section above I have referred to a body of evidence indicating that the current model of informal settlement intervention in South Africa is based on flawed assumptions and is therefore not responding adequately to the realities of urban poverty as manifested in informal settlements. Why, then, has the Urban Foundation model for informal settlement intervention not been successfully challenged? In Chapter 5, I discussed the route through which the Urban Foundation proposal of the early 1990s was institutionalised into the current national housing policy, discarding alternative mass-based positions. I referred to the powerful interests that supported the Urban Foundation approach in the policy-making, and that sidelined alternative proposals. Critical academic positions in turn neither appear to have impacted independently on this process, nor were they explicitly supporting the popular position articulated by the South African National Civic Organisation (SANCO).

The comparison in Chapter 5 between the South African informal settlement policy formulation, and the process through which alternative governance approaches were institutionalised in Brazil, gives perspective to the South African scenario. In Brazil, progressive academics were able to exercise considerable influence on policy formulation by acting within a unified Urban Reform Movement which included popular movements. Although democratisation and the policy-making process in Brazil took a very different route from that in South Africa (as shown in Chapter 5), the comparison does raise the question: What is the role of critical academic research in informal settlement policy formulation? In Brazil, this role has been that of actively strengthening the collective endeavours of the working class and poor. In South Africa, while individual academic research initiatives have built relationships with informal settlement communities,[29] informal settlement research initiatives tend to be isolated from one another, and from the two main popular movements that apply to informal settlements, the Homeless People's Federation and the civic movement. This tendency to conduct *ad hoc* or isolated research[30] is perpetuated by overseas academic researchers, whose valid findings are lost to the South African readers, to the popular movements and indeed to the policy formulation process, as they are published mainly in learned overseas journals or presented at international conferences,[31] often not in a South African language. Where publications have been explicitly policy-directed,[32] the research initiatives have undertaken to represent the realities of the poor to the policy makers. However, the body of informal settlement research as a whole, does not adequately represent the informal settlement reality, as its coverage is incomplete and restricted by strong biases. I expand on these below.

As I have mentioned earlier in this chapter, it is the tenure aspect of the intervention question that has recently been debated, with some networking among researchers and discussions with policy makers.[33] It is also from the tenure perspective that alternatives to the Urban Foundation model for informal settlement intervention are being developed and promoted.[34] As yet, however, popular movements do not participate in this debate. Indeed, critical informal settlement research in South Africa has not strengthened popular movements in the policy-making process. It has also largely ignored pragmatic initiatives confronting the Urban Foundation intervention paradigm at a community-based level.[35] Instead, as argued by Adler (1994:110), research on the capacities of organised communities has tended to be based on research in particularly violent informal settlements.[36] This has skewed our understanding of community organisations, their vulnerabilities, and the role they are able to play in the improvement of living conditions in informal settlements.

A further bias in the informal settlement literature, mentioned earlier in this chapter, has been created by the tendency to research settlements that invaded formerly white 'group areas' or are located in formerly 'white' local administrations. This research bias applies to South African informal settlement data in general.[37] Everatt *et al.* (1996:8), comparing information on Ivory Park (a land invasion in a former white municipality) and Tladi-Moletsane (an invasion in the African (black) township area of Soweto), find that:

> The mere fact of being in a formerly white area means that although the residents were under-resourced, the local authorities had resources to survey the population within their areas. We know more about areas such as Ivory Park, only a few years old, than we do about our Soweto neighbours who have been living in suburbs such as Tladi-Moletsane since 1955.

The bias on the part of administrations is mirrored by the academic research community. This is illustrated in the Cape Town context, where much academic literature is available on the informal settlements in Hout Bay and their relocation site within that same suburb[38] (see Lohnert, 1998; Nathan and Spindler, 1993; Oelofse and Dodsen, 1997; Sowman and Gawith, 1994, among others),[39] and the Marconi Beam informal settlement in Milnerton[40] (see Lohnert, 1997, 1998; Saff, 1996, 1999; Yose, 1999). Little in turn has been asked about those settlements embedded in, or on the verges of, the African (black) townships of Nyanga, Guguletu, Langa and Khayelitsha.[41]

It appears that much of the research focusing on the interface between high income formal residential areas and neighbouring impoverished informal settlements in the early 1990s was conducted in the anticipation of future urban restructuring, with expectations that vacant land in proximity to high income areas would be developed for low-income groups. This vision of the future South African cities would have stemmed partly from an assumption in the early 1990s that the post-apartheid state would intervene in the urban land market, creating more equitable and efficient cities by removing many of the stakes that were upholding the privileged, exclusively white property markets. Partly, it would have stemmed from the precedent set by a small number of high profile land invasions within formerly white group areas, which induced municipalities to reassign land for low income residential purposes within the former exclusively middle- to high-income areas. It was perceived that these challenging land invasions and the subsequent allocation of land to low income groups represented the beginning of a new and growing trend. Sowman and Gawith (1994:561) thus argue that the relevance of their case study of the Hout Bay informal settlements and their relocation site lies in the fact that this is representative of 'a new pattern of urban growth'. However, such predictions have not materialised, nor has much research since the 1994 elections been conducted on how to deal with the 'interface' between high and low income settlements. Instead the reality of 'post-apartheid social polarisation' has drawn recent academic attention (see Lohnert *et al.*, 1998; Oelofse and Dodson, 1997; Singh, 1997). Nathan and Spindler (1993) correctly anticipated the actual post-apartheid property market mechanisms (explaining, in part, the continuing racial non-integration of the city). In 1993 they predicted 'new, countering, rent-seeking innovations and interest-group empowerment which may modify, stay, or even reverse the present course' (*ibid.*:490). The prediction was supported by evidence of 'changes in private behaviour and activity in Hout Bay', such as fencing and patrolling of privately owned vacant land, and pressure to develop vacant land 'in order to eliminate attractive squatting targets' (*ibid.*).

A further bias in the informal settlement research body then results from our lack of understanding of the dynamics of the post-1994 land invasions in relation both to the predicted 'counter-redistributive activities'[42] and to the deterministic intervention that sets out to stabilise and individualise settlement populations. Indeed, patterns of post-apartheid exclusion in relation to the informal settlement question have not been explored by critical scholars. Instead, unfounded statements, such as the following by Botes *et al.* (1996:456), in support of problematic official positions remain uncontested:

> Land invasions and illegal occupation of land, which started out as strategies to oppose apartheid structures, have since denigrated into a culture of entitlement and queue-jumping to gain access to development funding. This was acknowledged by late Joe Slovo, then minister of Housing.[43]

We therefore cannot presume that the needs of those participating in recent invasions are presented to policy makers through the research community.

Returning, finally, to the understanding we do have of the informal settlement reality, I have shown that the South African informal settlement literature gives important insights into the diversity of household situations, the variety of coping strategies, and their implications. This body of research, however, remains largely isolated from the international debate on urban poverty. It does not make use of the various concepts of vulnerability, resilience and social capital, which I discussed in Chapter 2. Only a very recent study by Thomas (2002) on social capital in the informal settlement of Siyanda, Durban, argues that an understanding of social capital in communities may lead to development initiatives that are based on realistic strategies. Abbott (2002a), drawing in part on discussions in Huchzermeyer (1999a), also makes reference to international debates on urban poverty in developing a methodology for informal settlement upgrading in South Africa. Internationally, debate around these concepts has assisted in drawing attention to the realities faced by the urban poor, has exposed the limitations of externally designed product-oriented intervention and has promoted alternative support-based approaches. While World Bank urban policy of the early 1990s responded by embracing the urban poverty concerns, South African policy, as I demonstrated in Chapter 2, primarily associates poverty in informal settlements with social pathologies. This indicates that the poverty insights represented in the informal settlement literature have had little impact on official positions in the 1990s.

6.6 Conclusion

In this chapter I have shown that the influential Urban Foundation position on informal settlement intervention is underpinned by unsubstantiated assumptions. Critical literature of the 1990s contradicts the Urban Foundation position, yet fails to impact substantially on the informal settlement policy-making, which, as I argued in Chapter 1, has remained on a continuum since the late 1980s. The need for a more flexible approach that is sensitive to the realities of poverty and to the particular collective social dynamics in and around individual informal settlements has been identified from various angles. However, the isolated way in which informal settlement research has been conducted in South Africa has meant that individual aspects of an alternative approach have been articulated in isolation of one another. It appears that successfully challenging the by now well entrenched Urban Foundation approach and mindset to informal settlement intervention, will require coordination among researchers in order to develop a cohesive and convincing position. Engagement with the international debates on urban poverty, and the concepts that have promoted an awareness of alternative intervention approaches internationally, would strengthen such a position. The development and promotion of an alternative then should not occur in isolation of existing popular initiatives struggling for the improvement of informal settlements.

In Chapter 7, I show how the household-based entitlement through the capital subsidy approach to informal settlements has shaped the strategies through which community-based initiatives currently seek improvement. There I argue that they are trapped into the framework of individualisation. A critical debate is therefore required in order to create a common academic, professional and popular awareness of the shallowness of the wisdom that underpins the

Urban Foundation approach. Indeed, of all role players, the academic discussion that I present in this chapter is of most direct relevance to organised informal settlement communities themselves. Firstly, they should not be required to accept the official position that informal settlement intervention is simply another form of housing delivery, therefore needing to replace all signs of popular initiative in settlement formation with a standardised environment consisting of freehold tenure, services and an incremental house. Secondly, they should not have to accept the dismissal of their ability to lead the process of improvement. Thirdly, the limitations of individual freehold titles should be fully understood before households are made to commit themselves to this form of tenure. Fourthly, there is no reason why the stakes of the private sector in the settlement improvement process should be increased if organised communities have the capacity to undertake their own settlement improvement. Likewise, the stakes of the formal retail sector (delivering, for instance, 'white goods') should not replace those of the informal sector, to which livelihoods in informal settlements are directly tied.

While this book does not seek to redress the research biases identified in this chapter, it does to some extent address the imbalance in understanding the capacities of community organisations, through four case studies in Chapter 7. These explore the experience of community-based organisations currently attempting to lead settlement improvement. While this chapter has dealt with the flaws in scholarly positions that underpin the Urban Foundation model, the case studies then bring to the fore the practical obstacles that have been created through the institutionalisation of the flawed Urban Foundation model into the national framework for informal settlement intervention. Of equal importance as the critical academic positions that I reviewed in this chapter, then, are the challenges represented by organised informal settlement communities intent on improving their living conditions.

Notes

1 See Urban Foundation (1990).

2 The Urban Foundation further differentiates between 'freestanding informal settlements' and 'scattered informal settlements', the latter being impermanent 'small clusters of informal structures often found in locales such as disused mines and on small-holdings' (Urban Foundation, 1991:6).

3 This act allows for the exemption of low income residential areas from formal township regulations, thus legally accommodating informal structures and low levels of infrastructure, though ensuring the possibility of 'subsequent upgrading of services' (Republic of South Africa, 1991:6).

4 For instance Tomlinson with Bam and Mathole (1995:8), in their report for the 'independent, autonomous research institution' the Centre for Policy Studies (CPS), confusingly speak of 'a serviced site in an informal settlement'. They refer to

sites-and-services areas as 'state-aided informal settlements' (*ibid.*:11). Beall *et al.* (2002:130) use the terms 'site-and-service settlement', 'informal settlement' and 'squatter area' interchangeably in their discussion of Diepsloot, Johannesburg.

5 Gigaba and Maharaj (1996:218) state in their introduction that 'about seven million people live in squatter settlements in South Africa'. The one source they cite makes no reference to this figure, the other (Hart 1992:23) speaks of 'over 7 million people ... in informal houses', using the Urban Foundation definition that includes legal and illegal forms of informal housing. Beavon (1992:232) states that '7 million urban people nation-wide live in shacks of one kind or another', whereas Smith (1992:2) mentions 'the spread of spontaneous "shack" settlements around the major metropolitan areas to the extent of accommodating an estimated 7 million or quarter of the African population today' (no source cited). McCarthy *et al.* (1995:1) state that 'during the 1980s ... more than seven million people were living in informal settlements in and around South Africa's urban areas' (likewise no source cited). Lohnert (1997:1) inflates the seven million figure without citing a source: 'The fact that about 19% of the country's population – these are approximately 8 million people – are living in informal or squatter settlements demonstrates the scale of the problem'.

6 As suggested in Mazur and Quangule's (1995) survey of Cape Town's low-income population.

7 Bond (1997) in his critique of this report, associates its influence with the high respect the authors enjoy as housing commentators in South Africa, and with the high profile launching of the publication.

8 For instance the Millers Camp, KTC, and other settlements within the Integrated Serviced Land Project (iSLP) in Cape Town (see Holistic Settlements, 1996). Note that Tomlinson (1996:59) refers to the iSLP as an 'upgrade'.

9 An exception being the Weiler's Farm case, discussed in Chapter 7, where remodelling of the entire settlement was justified due to the need to reduce the plot size to the maximum of $300m^2$ specified by the capital subsidy scheme.

10 An example is the upgrading of the Winnie Mandela Park informal settlement in the Khayalami metropolitan area near Johannesburg (Housing in Southern Africa, 1998). The project report explains that 'although the occupation was informal, there was quite a lot of order in the way the shacks have been laid out. This allowed a town plan to be designed which largely followed the existing layout. This presented problems to the project engineers ... as the long straight lines, which are usually built into town plan layouts, allowing economical servicing did not exist ... Inevitably there were shacks in the way of services ... To allow the installation of pipes, the concept of "shifting" was evolved after negotiations with the community. The object of shifting is to get the shack owner to move his shack to the nearest planned stand. The other option is 'moving' which means that the shack will have to be moved to another area altogether. Obviously the first option is used as much as possible' (*ibid.*:33).

11 Freedom Square is also one of the 'upgrading' projects in McCarthy *et al.*'s (1995) evaluation.

12 Bond (1997:96) raises this concern, with reference to the World Bank (1991), in his critique of McCarthy *et al.* (1995).

13 In 1994, the chairman of the Urban Foundation applauded that the 'acceptance of the capital subsidy approach also means acceptance of home-ownership for low-income households. This has been an UF [Urban Foundation] goal from the start and represents a key contribution by the UF to how South Africa will be structured in the future' (Urban Foundation, 1994). It is interesting to note that as early as 1977, the Urban Foundation chairman argued that 'the absence of meaningful provision for home ownership in our Black urban townships plays a significant part in the instability and insecurity so prevalent in these areas' (Ellis *et al.*, 1977:77).

14 These same mechanisms have been institutionalised into the current housing policy, and govern most informal settlement intervention projects.

15 With reference to Moser (1995b) I have discussed in Chapter 2 that, alongside infrastructure and services, housing and labour, the poor may capitalise on adjustments to household compositions and on inter-household reciprocity (the latter termed 'social capital').

16 In the context of violence and disruption of schooling in South African townships, the practice of relocating children to rural kin for schooling has been widespread. This practice was interwoven with the complex household relations that were necessitated by the migrant labour system, leading to what Spiegel *et al.* (1994:12) refer to as 'disrupted domesticity'.

17 It may be noted that a quantitative study of African household dynamics and mobility in Cape Town by Mazur and Qangule (1995:42) found that in terms of household income, informal settlement populations ranked higher than those of back yard shacks. However, the data analysis of this study is limited to the Urban Foundation terminology, thus failing to make a distinction between shacks in informal settlements and those on serviced sites. The study gives no distinguishable evidence of socio-economic conditions in informal settlements.

18 Also reviewed in Spiegel *et al.* (1994).

19 The rural areas of origin of the African population in Cape Town are at a distance of at least 900km.

20 Although Lohnert (1998) refers to relocation from informal settlements to greenfields sites, it may be noted that even in the case of 'upgrading', it is common practice to redesign settlements according to a standardised layout and then to re-allocate sites.

21 The iSLP is an ongoing project, initiated in the early 1990s to deliver serviced sites to all households living in shacks in the back yards and informal settlements of the townships of Langa, Nyanga and Guguletu. The iSLP operates its relocations from informal settlements to serviced sites/incremental housing units by assigning to the various informal settlements in the project area a 'fair' quota of sites in each of the big relocation schemes. Thus one informal settlement would be assigned 200 sites

in a relocation scheme 8km to the north, and a further 200 sites in a scheme 5km to the south (see Holistic Settlements, 1996).

22 With evidence from Mabin's 1990 migration study, Spiegel *et al.* (1994:9) state that households with multiple urban and rural bases are common not only to Cape Town.

23 In Durban this phenomenon is referred to as 'oscillatory migration' (see Cross, *et al.*, 1994).

24 The study is based on primary research in the settlements of Bloekombos (Kraaifontein), Sun City (near Somerset West) and Site 5 (Noordhoek) on the urban periphery of Cape Town, and Waterworks in the rural town of Grabouw. The study compares these settlements with historic data on the Crossroads transit camp.

25 See Volbeda (1989) and Yapi-Diahou (1995).

26 There is increasing interest in such a tenure system, even from within government (see Kuhn, 1999).

27 This research is conducted in the informal settlement Marconi Beam and its relocation site Joe Slovo Park in Cape Town.

28 Here Cross (2002) refers to a housing scheme in Macassar, in the south-eastern periphery of Cape Town.

29 Examples are firstly, the Urban GIS Research team in the Department of Civil Engineering at the University of Cape Town (under the leadership of Professor John Abbott from 1996 to 2002), which explored a GIS supported and community managed approach to informal settlement intervention with the residents of the Kanana informal settlement in Guguletu, Cape Town (see Abbott, 2002a, 2002b; Abbott *et al.*, 2001). Secondly, the Centre for Land Development, Housing and Construction at the University of Pretoria has been building a support-based relationship with informal settlement communities in the Eastern District Council, which functionally form part of the City of Tshwane (Pretoria) (see Waring and Allanic, 2001).

30 Thorold's (1997) very honest account of an anthropologist team's arbitrary attraction to an informal settlement that happened to be visible from their office windows, illustrates how informal settlement research comes to be conducted not with the aim of impacting on policy or supporting a popular struggle, but merely to satisfy academic curiosity.

31 I captured some of their findings (Bénit, 2002; Guillaume and Houssay-Holzschuch, 2002; Haferburg, 2002) in *Urban Forum*, 13(2), a special issue on 'Contemporary Processes in Informal Settlements in South Africa'.

32 As is the case with Spiegel *et al.* (1994, 1996a, 1996b, 1996c, 1999).

33 This debate has been sharpened through a workshop in 1999, 'Tenure Security Policies in South African, Brazilian, Indian and Sub-Saharan African Cities: A Comparative Analysis' (Johannesburg, 27 to 28 July, 1999, Institut Francais d'Afrique du Sud, Development Works, Johannesburg, Lincoln Institute of Land Policies, Cambridge MA, Department of Land Affairs, Pretoria, Centre National de

la Recherche Scientifique, CNRS, Paris), which is part of a larger study on 'Urban Tenure Research' (coordinated by Dr. Alain Durand-Lasserve of the Laboratoire Sociétés en Développement dans l'Espace et le Temps (SEDET) Centre National de la Recherche Scientifique (CNRS)-Université Paris VII, and Lauren Royston of Development Works, Johannesburg) aiming to redress the hitherto rural bias in land tenure reform in South Africa. Several of the papers have been recently published in Durand-Lasserve and Royston (2002).

34 See Barry (1995), Davies (1998) and Davies and Fourie (1998).

35 Literature on the Homeless People's Federation is mainly written by the staff of its supporting NGO People's Dialogue, while the civic movement's particular role in informal settlements as opposed to formal townships, has only been marginally researched.

36 Exceptions are Seethal's (1996) study of the collective achievement of the Otto's Bluff informal settlement and sympathetic civil society in Pietermaritzburg, in the context of political transition in the early to mid-1990s; and Pickholz's (1997) study of the role of politics and storytelling in the upgrading process of Oukasie near Brits.

37 It may be noted that urban administrations and other institutions have at various times commissioned comprehensive informal settlement inventories, see for instance Abbott and Douglas (1999), Gauteng Provincial Government (1997) and Henessy and Smit (1994). However, these are limited to descriptive background data derived mainly from aerial photography (thus rapidly outdating) and are generally not backed up with data from the field. Thus, while giving a quantitative overview, they do not redress the imbalance in understanding of social relations and community organisation.

38 Hout Bay is a formerly 'white' coastal suburb of Cape Town. Several small land invasions in picturesque settings emerged in the 1980s, resisting relocation to distant township schemes. Eventually a relocation site (Imizamu Yethu) was established within the formerly white group area of Hout Bay.

39 These studies listed above all (though not exclusively) examine the relationship between the 'invaders' and the established white community. It is not surprising that many of the researchers live in that particular suburb and have a direct (possibly humanitarian) interest in their own 'back yard'.

40 The Marconi Beam informal settlement located on privately owned industrial land in the formerly white suburb of Milnerton. A relocation was eventually arranged in a nearby residential and industrial development, although a portion of the original settlement remained.

41 One might note, however, that the ODA-funded study by Awotona *et al.* (1995, 1996, 1997) redresses this to some extent, by studying the range of low-income residential environments in Cape Town, and in more detail the complex mosaic of residential types in the Cape Town township of Nyanga East, including its informal settlements. However, this overseas initiated study too was *ad hoc* and poorly

disseminated, its working papers being obtainable only from the UK (at considerable cost). Studies focusing specifically on the current challenges faced by organised informal settlement communities within this fabric have only been undertaken recently (see Haferburg, 2002; Oldfield, 2002; Lohnert, 2003). A further research bias, identified by Simpson (1995), is that the informal settlement literature has tended to present 'squatting' as a black phenomenon, ignoring that it is common too among poor coloured people.

42 Nathan and Spindler (1993:490) argue that these 'counter-redistributive activities' might well collapse in the future, as has happened in other countries.

43 Botes *et al.* (1996) refer to the *Sunday Times* of 14 August 1994.

Chapter 7

Obstacles to Appropriate Intervention in South Africa: The Experience of Current People-Driven Initiatives

7.1 Introduction

The effect of the influential Urban Foundation proposal for informal settlement intervention has been experienced most strongly at the level of individual informal settlements. There, organised communities endeavouring to secure government commitments for the improvement of living conditions have inevitably interfaced with the Urban Foundation-inspired model of intervention. In this chapter, I examine the interface between the standardised intervention framework and four well organised informal settlement communities. In the previous chapter, I argued that the South African informal settlement literature has skewed our understanding of community organisations, either discarding their role in development or exposing their weakness through a bias on violent situations. My point of departure in this chapter is that informal settlement organisations are indeed key players, with relevant strategies for settlement improvement. Through the case studies, I expose, on the one hand, the distance between that which makes sense from the community organisation's perspective, and that which is imposed from the level of the national housing policy. Thus I examine challenges to the Urban Foundation inspired model of intervention from the level of organised communities directly experiencing its implications. These challenges supplement those in the South African informal settlement literature, presented in Chapter 6. On the other hand, I expose the impact that the national housing policy, with its household-based entitlement to the capital subsidy, has had on the thinking and strategising within these organisations. Due to the direct individual gain related to the household-based capital subsidy entitlement, community organisations tend eventually to work with, rather than to oppose, the restrictive framework. This, I argue, has limited the search for alternatives. As a result, the Urban Foundation-inspired framework for informal settlement intervention has been effectively challenged neither from the level of organised communities, nor through the South African literature which, as shown in Chapter 6, has remained fragmented and biased.

In South Africa, a number of informal settlements have been 'upgraded', meaning that a development solution is sought on the land that was invaded. In most cases, such settlement communities have resisted attempts at relocation, therefore having played an active role in determining the nature of the government intervention from which they are to benefit. This has entailed a range of challenges, firstly, to the *de jure* rights to the illegally occupied land; secondly, to the formal legal procedure that produces eviction orders; thirdly, to the formal delivery mechanisms that have favoured orderly relocations; and lastly, to the conventional mechanisms of resource or capital subsidy allocation.[1] However, the prescriptiveness of the intervention framework has required that the community-based organisations in such settlements be reduced to mere consultative bodies once a development commitment is secured through the Provincial Housing Boards which issue the capital subsidies. The settlement committees have then been expected to ensure the smooth implementation of an externally designed and standardised solution. The four settlements discussed in this chapter are of particular relevance, as their settlement organisations have managed to maintain an important role in the intervention, despite the restrictive development framework. It is therefore possible to examine their strategies in both challenging and cooperating with the formal model of intervention.

In some of the case study settlements, the earlier stages (particularly the resistance to removal) have been documented in academic literature or project reports. The recent and current development process in all four settlements, however, had to be accessed through in-depth interviewing with key players in the settlement organisations, supporting entities, the municipalities and other authorities involved.[2] Guided walks through the settlement allowed for more questions to be raised and issues to be pointed out. Case study drafts reflecting my understanding of the settlement process and the questions it raised were compiled for each of the settlements and circulated to the organisations in which I had interviewed.[3] Feedback has been incorporated into the discussion in this chapter. In many instances, the interviews covered conflictual situations. In order to protect the identities of interviewees in relation to such conflict, the approach in this chapter has been not to cite individuals, but merely to indicate the perspective from which particular views were expressed.

I introduce the case studies through the processes of settlement formation, turning then in more detail to the emergence of people-driven initiatives in the settlements, and the external support on which they have been able to draw. Next, I review the government intervention programmes to which these initiatives have secured access. This, then, forms the background for a discussion of the strategies through which the people-driven initiatives in the four case study settlements have sought to improve their settlements, and have engaged with the prescriptive formal development framework. I finally examine the impact that this framework, in particular the household-based entitlement to a capital subsidy, has had on the strategies of popular initiatives and of those entities which seek to support them. This leads me to identify limitations of these initiatives in fundamentally challenging the Urban Foundation-inspired approach to informal settlement intervention.

7.2 Emergence of the four case study settlements

Unique and diverse processes have led to the formation of each of the four case study settlements. However, two broad categories may be identified. The older settlements, Piesang River (Durban) and Weiler's Farm (southern Johannesburg), date back to the 1960s, and have their origin not in organised invasions, but in unofficial land agreements on farming land. Gradual growth led to subsequent increase in settlement size. In the case of Weiler's Farm, the availability of land allowed the settlement to expand at relatively low densities with dwellings being constructed on large, well-defined plots. In Piesang River in turn, sections of the settlement densified, despite relatively steep slopes. Wattle-and-daub dwellings are closely packed, with no private open space or yard surrounding individual homes. The more recent case study settlements, Gunguluza (Uitenhage) and Kanana (also southern Johannesburg), which formed in 1993/94, resulted from the organised invasion of unused land within established townships. In these two cases, the illegal land occupation was modelled on the formal layouts and densities of surrounding townships, thus creating suitable conditions for *in situ* upgrading. However (after resistance to eviction orders), the existence of 'invisible' cadastral boundaries and servitudes complicated the regularisation process in both cases. I will briefly sketch the emergence of each of the four case study settlements, before turning to the respective community initiatives that led to their current 'upgrading'.

The Piesang River settlement, near the township of Inanda (and the more recent township of KwaMashu) 25km to the north west of Durban City Centre (see Figure 9), derived its name from the river on the banks of which the settlement developed.[4] In the 1960s, an unofficial land sale took place between an Indian vegetable farmer and an African (black) individual who in turn subdivided and allocated land to other African (black) households, partly in return for payment. This was followed by the gradual uncontrolled settling on adjacent portions of land throughout the 1970s, seemingly tolerated by the state. In the early 1980s, as demand for housing increased, a new residential trend emerged with so-called 'train houses'. Outsiders would commission Piesang River residents to build rows of wattle-and-daub rooms, which these absentee owners would then rent out. Residential densities increased, with one-roomed units packed against one another. In the mid-1980s, an IFP[5] leader established control over Piesang River, and is said to have convened the first community meetings, arranged cleaning campaigns, and numbered the dwellings. He eradicated rent tenancy by forcing the owners of train houses to sell the rooms to their occupants. While such initiative was appreciated, the residents remember the IFP leader as a war fanatic. Eventually his house was burned and he was expelled from Piesang River. The settlement then reverted to its previous disorganised or anarchic state with rent tenancy re-emerging alongside intense informal business. The fast life, including 'gambling, drinking, stabbing and shooting', earned the settlement its alternative name 'Soweto'. The main street is remembered as a strip with various stalls, with people 'dancing, talking, just carrying on with life' – a 'continuous buzz' – attracting many people from outside the settlement. A new phase then began with the canvassing by the UDF and the formation of civic structures in the late 1980s, eventually leading to land regularisation and the extension of infrastructure into the settlement.

The Weiler's Farm settlement derives its name from the farm on which it located, 30km south of the Johannesburg city centre and 15km south of Soweto (see Figure 10).[6] In this case the farm owners (the Weiler brothers) had consented to 'illegal African tenants' living on their farm since the 1960s (Crankshaw, 1993:41). In 1985, the then landowner, an elderly Mr Weiler, abandoned the farm, permitting the 300 residents to remain living on the land (Black Sash, 1989:S4). With the subsequent lack of control, settlement on the land multiplied.[7] Weiler's Farm and similar uncontrolled settlements in the area grew in the second half of the 1980s, first attracting redundant farm workers from the area, and subsequently residents from troubled and overcrowded townships (Crankshaw, 1993:43). In the decision to move from townships to Weiler's Farm, the disadvantage of the remote location is said to have been outweighed by the prospect of a peaceful and free-of-charge family life.[8] By 1987, about 13,000 people had established themselves at Weiler's Farm (Budlender, 1990:67). A settlement leadership is said to have guided the settlement expansion. Its early responses to demands for social development are discussed below.

The more recent Gunguluza settlement derives its name from the highly respected Mrs Gunguluza,[9] one of three elderly people who in 1993 led the invasion and guided the expansion of the informal settlement. Gunguluza is located within a band of informal settlement that surrounds the township of KwaNobuhle,[10] 9km to the south of Uitenhage town centre (see Figure 11).[11] The land invaded by Mrs Gunguluza and others was earmarked for private sector delivery of higher income African (black) housing, in accordance with the official thinking of the late 1980s. This was to act as a buffer between the impoverished township and the nearby white farms.[12] Erven had been pegged in accordance with this plan. The up market development did not materialise, the unused land instead attracting criminal elements, as argued later by Mrs Gunguluza, who maintained that the invasion was motivated in part by the need to restore safety to the area. Unaware of the demarcated erven, Mrs Gunguluza with others invaded the section closest to the existing township, consciously mirroring the official township pattern, and thereby not deviating substantially from the officially planned and pegged layout.[13] The issuing of eviction notices, despite a policy 'not to evict as such', was threatening enough for Mrs Gunguluza to seek support from the Uitenhage branch of SANCO (South African National Civic Organisation), and for a joining of forces with other informal settlement

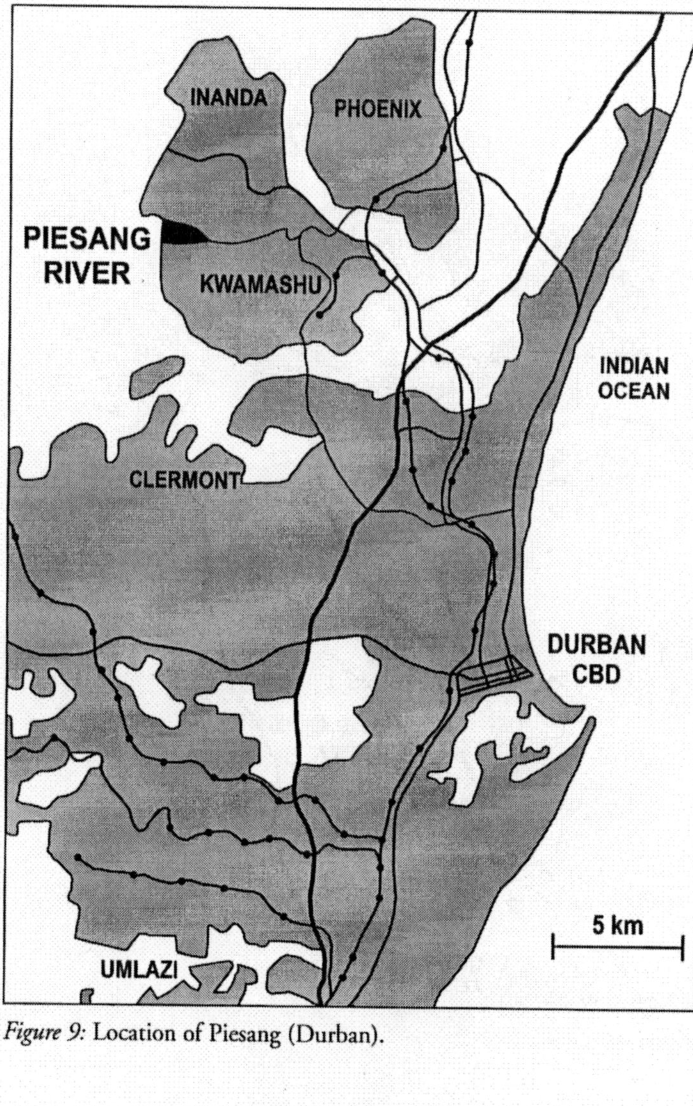

Figure 9: Location of Piesang (Durban).

communities through the formation of a 'Squatter Committee' (with representation from the SANCO branch). At that time, 50 shacks are said to have been constructed at Gunguluza, while several other settlements had emerged in KwaNobuhle.

The fourth case study settlement, Kanana,[14] was formed in 1994, although planning for the invasion had begun as early as 1991. The People's Dialogue (1997) documentation of the settlement process describes how dissatisfaction of the backyard shack residents[15] in the Sebokeng township (45km south of Johannesburg, 15km north of the industrial towns of Vereeniging and Vanderbijlpark – see Figure 12) in the early 1990s led to the formation of a committee, which planned the invasion of a vacant portion of land in the

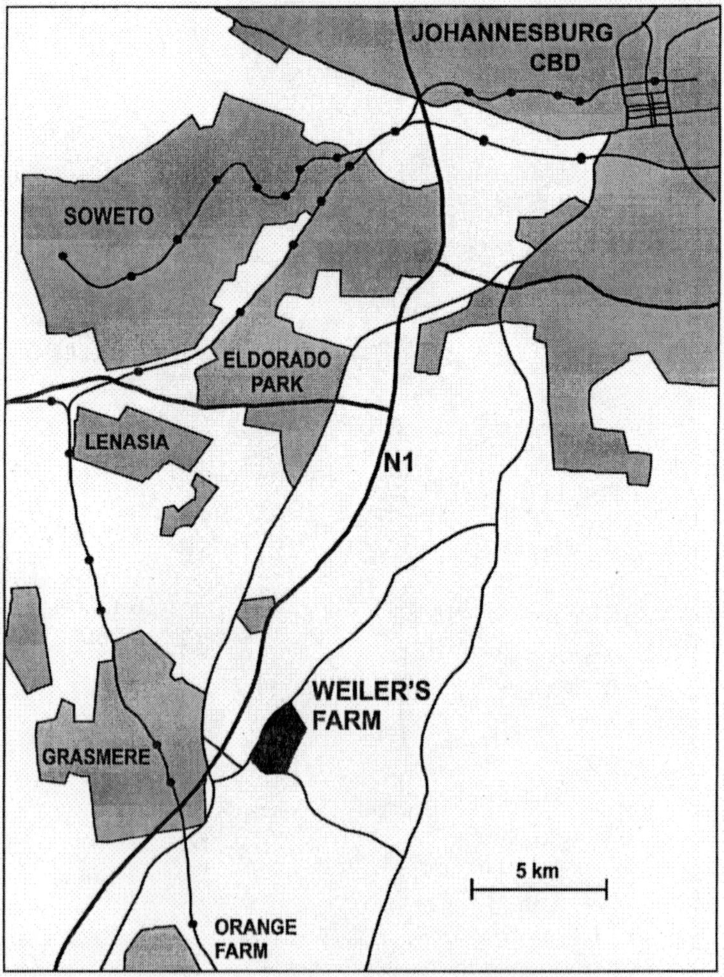

Figure 10: Location of Weiler's Farm (southern Johannesburg).

township. As in the case of Gunguluza, residents recall that the vacant land harboured criminals and was dangerous to cross. The civic leadership in Sebokeng, however, discouraged the invasion, suggesting instead that the committee join the civic structure, whose leadership would then negotiate for the land. By early 1994, the land was not secured. The committee then dissolved itself from the civic structure,[16] and proceeded to plan for the invasion to occur a few days prior to the first national democratic elections. As one interviewee stated, they were wanting 'to vote with something in our hand'.[17] The organisers of the Kanana invasion measured surrounding township layouts, and on this they based the informal demarcation and free-of-charge allocation of 1,500 sites to which backyard tenants relocated their shacks.

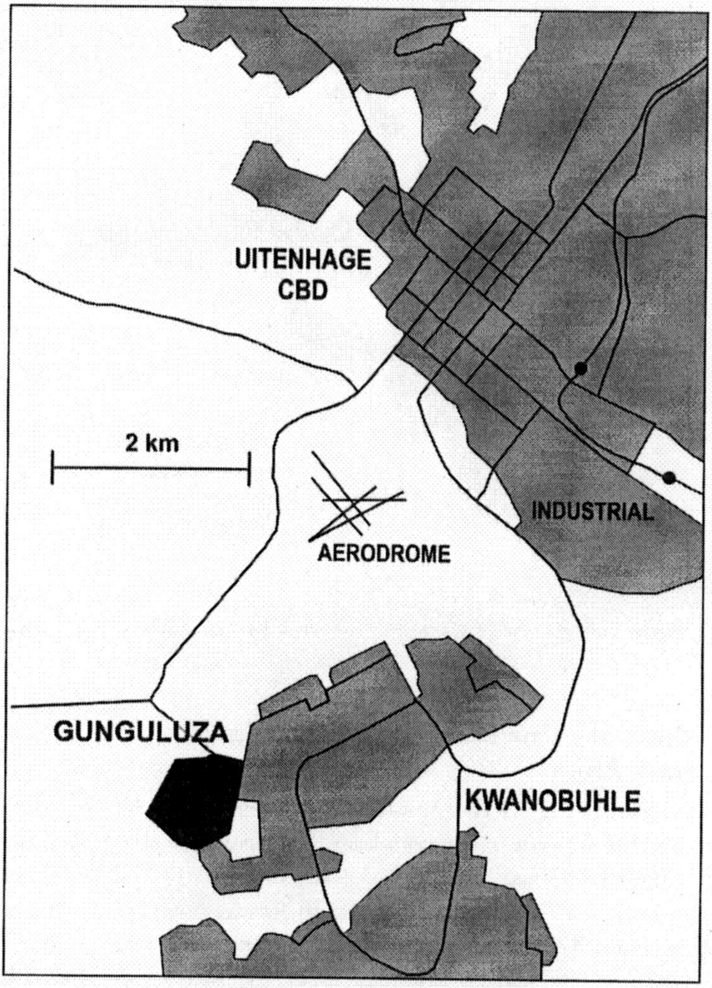

Figure 11: Location of Gunguluza (Uitenhage).

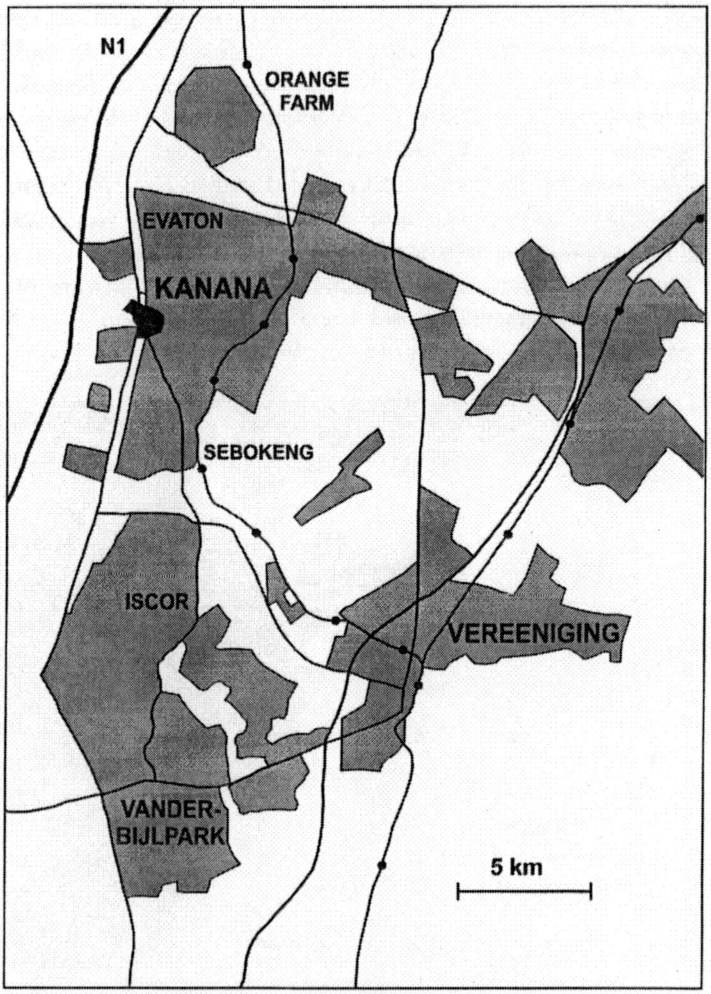

Figure 12: Location of Kanana (southern Johannesburg).

7.3 Forms of community organisation in informal settlements in South Africa

In order to introduce the community organisations in the four case study settlements, and the support initiatives which they have been able to tap, this section briefly contrasts the two broad types of community organisation committed to informal settlement improvement in South Africa. They are, on the one hand, the democratically elected representative committees, usually referred to as 'civic' organisations, and on the other hand, the membership-based Homeless People's Federation structures.[18] This section supplements the discussion, in

Chapter 5, of the emergence of these two forms of organisation in relation to the socio-political process in South Africa.

Representative structures: civic organisations or committees

By virtue of the representative approach, civic organisations or committees cover the entire settlement population, even where contesting organisations emerge, usually with opposing political affiliations. Through the civic structures, settlements are sub-divided into sections or blocks, each with an elected committee. Representatives of each of these committees make up the settlement committee or civic organisation. The committees at block or section level deal with day-to-day concerns within their area, while broader concerns are brought to the settlement committee, which in turn may tap into regional and national structures. As mentioned in Chapter 5, civic structures were set up in informal settlements through the UDF (United Democratic Front) in the 1980s, as it expanded from core townships into the more marginal urban areas. With the disbanding of the UDF (and the unbanning of the ANC and SACP) in the early 1990s, the civic movement created its own umbrella structure, SANCO. However, alternative umbrella bodies exist, as do independent civic organisations or committees. It may be noted here that although SANCO has aligned itself to the ANC since the run-up to the 1994 elections, SANCO-aligned civic organisations are not official party structures. While the four case study settlements do not all have a SANCO-aligned civic organisation, they all happen to be bases of strong ANC support. In each of the settlements, the development-oriented community organisations (be they representative committees or Homeless People's Federation structures) are supplemented by local ANC structures such as women's leagues, men's leagues and youth leagues.[19]

As discussed in Chapter 5, the civic movement, as from the mid-1980s, received support from the development NGOs that later constituted themselves into the Urban Sector Network. In the early 1990s, these NGOs were instrumental in assisting civic organisations secure government funding for development. I argued in Chapter 5 that the requirements attached to such development funding, and the niche that these NGOs found as project managers, led to externally designed, individualised development, as promoted through the Urban Foundation model. In the Piesang River case, as shown later in this chapter, tensions arose around this imposed development approach, particularly once the radical thinking of the People's Dialogue/Homeless People's Federation initiative encouraged the exploration of alternatives.

Membership-based structures: the Homeless People's Federation

In contrast to the representative structure of the civic organisations, the Homeless People's Federation operates on active membership based on daily saving.[20] Savings groups, consisting mainly of women, deposit their daily savings with

Federation bookkeepers on a weekly basis. The group structures have various functions. Similar to the section/block or street committees of the civic movement, though with a higher degree of active participation, weekly group meetings allow space for the discussion and resolution of day-to-day concerns, and the discussion of development issues. Beyond this, the daily door-to-door collection of savings by the group treasurer, always a woman, gives this person insight into the home circumstances of the group members. When individual households experience financial crises (reflected in their not being able to make daily contributions) solutions are sought in the weekly group meetings. Emergency credit for income generation is considered in these meetings, provided the member has actively participated in the group and has a sound understanding of the Federation philosophy.

Here it must be stressed that the activity of saving through the Federation is not one of accumulating individual capital, to be accessed at a later stage. Instead, the daily contributions go towards building an independent collective fund, which ensures Federation members continual access to low interest credit. Repayment of credit, together with daily saving, is supervised by the group bookkeeper. Separate credit mechanisms exist for emergency loans, small business loans (see Figure 13), and house-building loans. The savings activities are supported by the nation-wide Federation structures and the supporting NGO People's Dialogue. Learning between various Federation settlements is encouraged through exchanges. Where deemed particularly relevant, international exchanges with equivalent Federations (for instance in India) are funded through the internationally supported NGO People's Dialogue. It is through the

Figure 13: Local 'tuck shop' at Piesang River financed through a small business loan of the Homeless People's Federation.

networking and learning between settlements, therefore the breaking of isolation, that alternatives are promoted and a significant popular challenge may be posed to aspects of the Urban Foundation model.

The two case study settlements with Federation structures (Piesang River and Kanana) were recommended to me by the NGO People's Dialogue for the purposes of this research due to their high level of Federation membership. However, even in these settlements not all households decide to participate in daily saving. The Federation, though playing an important role in shaping development, can therefore not claim full representativeness of the informal settlement.[21] As will be evident in the case study discussion to which I now turn, this places Federation structures in a difficult relationship with government programmes that seek to interact with beneficiary communities via representative structures.

7.4 The case study settlements: people-driven initiatives and their external support

By tracing the emergence of the various forms of community organisation in the case study settlements, my intention is to illustrate that such organisation undergoes change. This bears on the effectiveness of the community organisation's development strategy, thus increasing or reducing its capacity to lead the development process. From the case study discussion that follows, it appears that such change is triggered in part by the development process, and in part by the form of organisation and the support it is able to secure. The discussion in this section then forms the background for the later enquiry into the strategies for settlement improvement, and the degree to which these have been shaped by knowledge of the formal development framework, and in particular the individual capital subsidy entitlement.

Piesang River: from civic organisation with NGO support, to Homeless People's Federation/People's Dialogue alliance

Of the four case studies, the most complex process of people-driven initiative and support has been that at Piesang River. Related to this has been a drawn-out process of formal development commencing in the early 1990s, and still incomplete at the time of interviewing late in 1998. In relation to the development process, change in the form of community organisation has strengthened the ability of many individual residents to acquire houses, while weakening their collective ability to resolve the infrastructure delivery and site allocation required by the official framework. The later discussion of popular strategies at Piesang River clarifies many of the seeming contradictions reflected in the changes in community organisation.

In the early 1990s, the civic organisation was supported by the NGO BESG (Built Environment Support Group) in its endeavour to secure government funding for development. Once this funding was obtained, the NGO was appointed as project manager, therefore changing its position in relation to the civic organisation.[22] A new entity was then introduced in the form of a development trust, intended as the vehicle through which the community was to drive the development process.[23] As the civic organisation at the time did not have the capacity to drive the development itself, the trust was created as a separate body, though placed under the civic's control alongside its various committees. The civic organisation then had the important role of linking the development project, through the area-based block structures, with the community. With the election of trustees, disunity within the community leadership came to the fore. From 1991, the People's Dialogue for Land and Shelter (later constituted into the Homeless People's Federation and its supporting NGO People's Dialogue) emerged in Piesang River, with a prominent civic leader becoming an important player in the Federation. BESG's perception then was that separate 'power bases' were constituted around the civic, the trust and the Homeless People's Federation.

While the approach to which BESG was contractually tied relied on a unified civic organisation that could pull through the agreements made at acceptance of the development funding, the reality in Piesang River was increasingly a divided one. Under such circumstances, BESG was indirectly required to drive the development. While the emerging Homeless People's Federation/People's Dialogue initiative had the intention of strengthening the existing development process, a radically opposed development thinking emerged, partly through exchange programmes with India. The new approach sought to build on residents' own abilities in planning, surveying and construction. With increasing contestation of the formal development project's approach in 1995, BESG found it appropriate to withdraw. While 80 per cent of the engineering works had by then been completed (thereby legally enabling the project managers to withdraw), official site allocation, 'de-densification', relocation and issuing of individual freehold titles were outstanding. The civic organisation and the trust subsequently collapsed, and the Homeless People's Federation emerged as the main organisation in Piesang River, its membership currently estimated between 75 and 90 per cent of the 1,600 households.

The Homeless People's Federation did not prioritise the completion of the original project, to which formal development funding had been allocated through the original project. Instead, it prioritised the construction of individual houses of its members. The former leadership divide re-constituted itself in the arena of house construction, as a separate NGO, Habitat for Humanity,[24] established itself in the settlement, offering loan funding for house construction.[25] In the denser sections of the settlement, formally pegged sites remained occupied by more than one household (see Figures 14 and 15). As a result, Federation and Habitat houses (see Figures 16 and 17) could only be constructed where respective member households occupied an entire site or could claim formal occupancy despite others sharing the site.

Figures 14 and 15: High residential densities at Piesang River, with multiple occupancy of the formally pegged sites.

Figure 16: Formal housing constructed through the Homeless People's Federation at Piesang River.

While the Federation was clearly more visible and influential in Piesang River than Habitat for Humanity, neither organisation could claim representativeness of the entire settlement population. It was the ward councillor, the official representative of Piesang River and surrounding township areas, who then endeavoured to arrange for the formal completion of infrastructure and site allocation, as foreseen by the original BESG project. In the continuing absence of any single structure able to represent the entire settlement in the completion of the abandoned project, the local authority (through a development consultant) eventually arranged the election of a representative development committee for the duration

Figure 17: Formal housing constructed through Habitat for Humanity at Piesang River.

of the project. At the time of interviewing, a site allocation committee had been elected to resolve the politically sensitive and socially disruptive question as to which households were to be affected by relocations to distant sites. No doubt this process will have further eroded social cohesion at Piesang River.

Weiler's Farm: civic organisation securing pragmatic support

The Weiler's Farm case contrasts in many respects with that of Piesang River. At Weiler's Farm, a representative community organisation had consistently improved its capacity to lead a formal development processes. When it finally secured a development commitment from the provincial authority, all aspects of the formal development process were placed in its hands. With consistent support, the civic organisation had then steered formal development within the confines of the capital subsidy development framework, while also considering the tasks that lie beyond.

Community representation at Weiler's Farm emerged in the mid-1980s when the farm had been abandoned by its owner. An 'informal committee' established itself (Budlender, 1990:77), and with the assistance of the Legal Resources Centre succeeded in confronting the eviction tactics of the Provincial Administration. The result was a sympathetic court ruling, the expropriation of the land from Mr Weiler and the affording of transit camp status to the settlement in 1987. Transit camp regulations required the constitution of a 'formal committee' with the purpose of representing 'the residents in dealings with the officials' (*ibid.*:77). The 'informal committee' then took over this function, therefore cooperating in the strict official control over the settlement, in the introduction of a monthly service charge, and in the planned relocation of households to Orange Farm 8km to the South (Mashabela, 1990). Resistance to the imposition of a service charge (in the absence of service delivery) led to the formation of a rival organisation, the 'Masakhane Association' (*ibid.*). In order to cover up its support for the then banned ANC, this organisation presented itself to officials as a funeral association. While various tactics (including beatings) coerced about 1,000 households to relocate to Orange Farm, new arrivals filled their space, the majority intent on remaining at Weiler's Farm. The original committee leadership appears to have relocated to Orange Farm, whereas the Masakhane Association leadership remained in Weiler's Farm, reconstituting into a civic structure (later affiliated to SANCO). Legal ANC structures were established with the unbanning of the party. Official plans for relocation remained beyond the 1994 elections.

Not supported by an Urban Sector NGO, the Weiler's Farm civic organisation independently created a Development Team, in order to seek ways of formalising the settlement. In the hope of support from influential ANC personalities in the wake of the 1994 elections, the civic leadership eventually made contact with a sympathetic businessman working at the ANC's headquarters in Johannesburg. Under his guidance, the civic organisation interfaced successfully with government structures, and in 1995 secured an approval, 'in principle', for 'upgrading' (Gauteng Provincial Government, 1998). While lack of will on the side of the local authority delayed further development decisions, the Weiler's Farm civic organisation improved its own capacity to lead the development. In 1996 the Development Team was re-established as the Weiler's Farm Planning Team, with a formal constitution (Rand Afrikaans University, 1997:3). Its structure of accountability is to the 'section committee' of the civic organisation, which consists of the elected heads of each of the ten settlement sections. Its objectives are the upliftment of the community through 'housing, development, job creation and training, education, health, sport and recreation, and safety and security' (*ibid.*). For the fulfilment of the housing and development objective it then registered a non-profit organisation, the Thuthuka Foundation.[26] Subscribers of the Foundation are the section heads of the civic organisation. Its two directors are a long standing community leader (and former voluntary teacher) and, by invitation from the community, the acquainted businessman. By this time, a trusting relationship had evolved between the civic organisation and the businessman, who had consistently committed time and resources to the support of the civic organisation and its structures. In contrast with the fragmented organisational situation at Piesang River, which required a development committee to be set up by the authorities, the Weiler's Farm civic organisation, through its Thuthuka Foundation, was in a position to drive infrastructure and housing development.

Gunguluza: representative committee supported by broader civic structures

Less complex, then, is the organisational context in the two more recent case study settlements. In the case of Gunguluza, I expand on the context of support, as this has enabled a relatively consistent involvement by the settlement organisation in the formal development process. The Gunguluza settlement is organised through a representative structure, with a committee consisting of elected heads of each of the five settlement sections. Essentially a civic organisation, the structure (calling itself simply a committee) has chosen to remain independent from the broader civic structures of SANCO in KwaNobuhle. Nevertheless, the SANCO local structure of Uitenhage has played an important role in supporting and guiding the Gunguluza committee in the development process. In the early to mid-1990s, this SANCO structure, with its various branches, was itself supported by the Urban Sector Network NGO, the Urban Services Group, based in Port Elizabeth. In the context of a non-functioning 'black local authority' for KwaNobuhle, the SANCO structure, with its NGO support, came to play a major role in the management of the township. The SANCO structure's position on informal settlement was to oppose relocation, advocating instead 'development where the people are'. This was coupled with a strong call for a 'people-driven' approach to development.

In accordance with this policy direction, SANCO then initiated the formalisation of the various land invasions in KwaNobuhle, including that of Gunguluza. In the surveying and record keeping of this process, Mrs. Gunguluza recalls having worked closely with the staff of the NGO Urban Services Group. However, once the formerly white and African (black) town councils were amalgamated into one Transitional Local Council, the involvement of the NGO in KwaNobuhle appears to have been at odds with newly elected councillors. For the NGO, its involvement came to a 'traumatic' end, whereas to the Gunguluza committee it seemed sensible that since local government elections, it has been working through the ward councillor and no longer through the NGO. In the local governance context of Uitenhage, the SANCO structure has maintained a uniquely strong position as representative of civil society and independent agent of development. It regularly interacts with the Uitenhage Town Council at ward level as well as at the level of full council. Uniquely, too, the official housing coordinator at the Town Council carries the housing-related portfolio at the Uitenhage local structure of SANCO. A strong support for people-driven development thinking is therefore reflected in the current policies of the municipality. It is the supportive approach of the local authority and the SANCO structures that has enabled the Gunguluza committee to work in close cooperation with the official structures.

Kanana: representative committee and Homeless People's Federation/People's Dialogue alliance

In the case of Kanana, the insensitive formal development procedure triggered a process of organisational change. As a result, a committed community organisation, which boldly planned and arranged the invasion and resolved eviction threats, has lost its capacity to drive the development which it had itself initiated. Of the four case study settlements, Kanana has posed the most comprehensive challenge to the formal development framework. While I return to the particular strategies of the Kanana leadership later in this chapter, it is important to note here that this challenge was not tenable. As a result of the individual capital subsidy entitlement and associated framework of development, support for the settlement leadership, its organisational structures and its challenging strategies were eroded.

From the outset, the Kanana settlement was organised through an Independent People's Committee, essentially an independent civic organisation. This representative structure has worked closely with the membership-based structures of the Homeless People's Federation. While the Federation, with support from the NGO People's Dialogue, was instrumental in securing a development commitment for the Kanana settlement, it was not able to drive the development process. A divide emerged in the settlement as newly elected ward councillors supported the conventional development approach, which was being challenged by the Federation. The Independent People's Committee split, and the membership of the Federation decreased, as the ward councillors were seen to be drawing supporters away (People's Dialogue, 1997). The Federation, challenging the official procedures for intervention, was in turn seen to be causing delays in the development. The settlement divide constituted itself geographically, the split occurring along a power line that happened to run through the invaded land. Separate 'Independent People's Committees' and ANC structures exist in the two areas, while Federation membership concentrates in the section referred to as 'Phase 2' of the development. It was in Phase 2, that I conducted interviews with the Federation and Independent People's Committee leadership.

7.5 Government intervention programmes in the case study settlements

Imposing individualisation: informal settlement intervention as a form of housing delivery

All four case study settlements (at the time of interviewing) were undergoing individualised development through the capital subsidies of the National Housing Ministry. The individual subsidies are released through the Provincial Housing Boards, which cross-check the eligibility of each individual household against a national database. It is thereby ensured that applicants have not previously benefited from housing subsidies. In most cases, local authorities have been expected to make a project-based application on behalf of informal settlement residents, who were then required to individually supply the household-based information on which the subsidy allocation is based. Excluded are those with household heads that are either not South African citizens, have no dependants, earn above a certain amount, or who themselves or their legal spouses have previously benefited from a government subsidy. Such households have been required to either buy into the project, or to move elsewhere. As it is impractical to base an intervention in an existing community on such grounds, officials in the case study projects had attempted to accommodate non-qualifying households. 'We arrange for them to adopt a child', was the response to situations where, for instance, elderly widows did not qualify as their children had formed their own households and might be applying themselves for housing subsidies.

In accordance with the Urban Foundation model, informal settlement intervention has been treated by the subsidy framework as a conventional housing project, as though development were to take place in a greenfield situation. Indeed, intervention in all four case studies, though officially referred to as 'upgrading', has resulted in the imposition of standardised conventional town planning layouts on the informal settlement pattern. In the case of Gunguluza and Kanana, the orderliness of the informal layout (consciously modelled on the surrounding townships) allowed for relatively little disruption (see Figures 18 and 19 for Gunguluza, and 20 and 22 for Kanana), although some households were required to 'shift' their shacks to ensure straight boundary lines. Project engineers explained the connection between the capital subsidy framework and their insistence on straight boundary lines. Due to the individual entitlement to a 'housing subsidy' of which a portion goes towards collective infrastructure, residents and politicians were requesting that the infrastructure expenditure from the subsidy be minimised, so as to maximise expenditure on the house or 'top structure'. Infrastructure costs could be saved by minimising curves in the underground reticulation of water mains and sewers. In this calculation, shack-shifting or relocation is not considered a cost factor.

In the case of Kanana, it was only through the insistence of the community leadership that the local authority eventually recognised the orderliness of the informal layout. In its application to the Provincial Housing Board, the municipality proposed a layout that takes no consideration whatsoever of the existing settlement structure (see Figure 21). Only after an aerial photograph proved to the engineers that the settlement was designed as if by an 'engineer's sketch' (see Figure 20), was the layout revised (see Figure 22). In the case of Piesang River, steep slopes and high residential densities (see Figure 23) required some deviation from conventional layouts, many of the pegged erven being accessible only by pedestrian walkways (see Figure 24). The densest section is handled through the conventional 'roll-over' procedure, whereby all dwellings are removed and a conventional layout is constructed. Despite significantly lower densities, this was the approach at Weiler's Farm where the informally established plot sizes are larger than the 300m^2 maximum stipulated in the capital subsidy regulations, requiring a complete remodelling of the settlement into a standardised plot layout (see Figures 25 and 26).

Within the Gauteng Provincial Government, an 'Informal Settlement Upgrading Programme' was articulated in 1996 (Gauteng Provincial Government, 1996), though since disbanded. This upgrading programme did not entail any deviation from the subsidy procedure. The programme merely redressed the

Figure 18: Gunguluza: orderliness of the original invasion (source: Russel Alison).

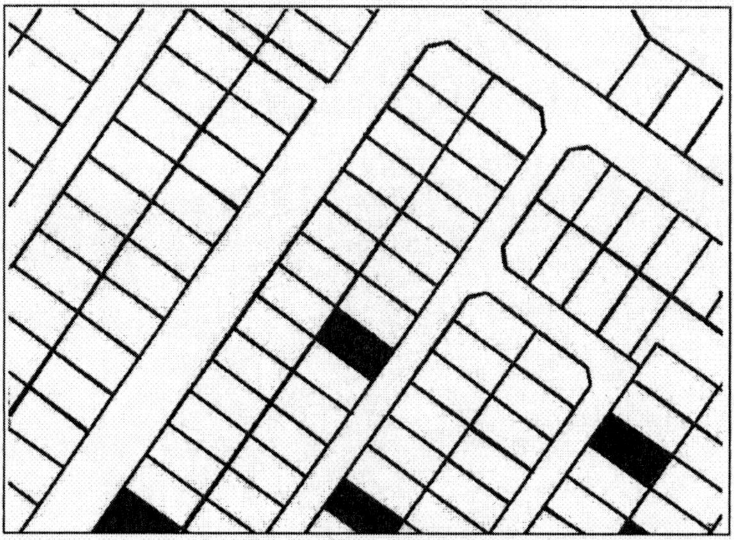

Figure 19: Gunguluza: the formal standardised layout (source: Uitenhage Municipality).

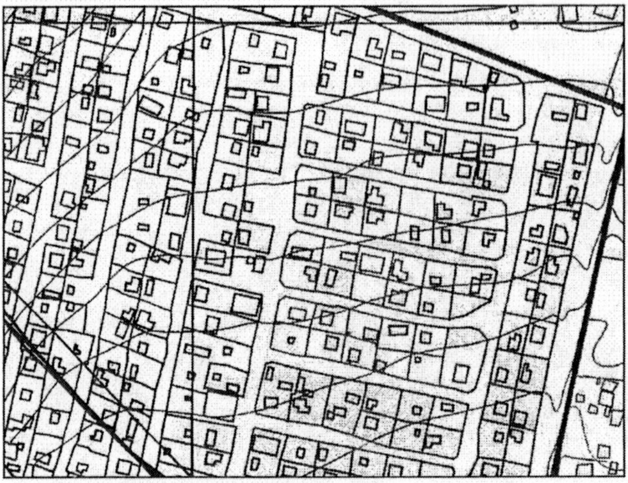

Figure 20: Kanana: layout of the original invasion resembling an 'engineer's sketch' (source: Urban Dynamics).

Figure 21: Kanana: formal layout design, as submitted to the Provincial Housing Board (source: Lekoa/Vaal Transitional Metropolitan Council/Urban Dynamics).

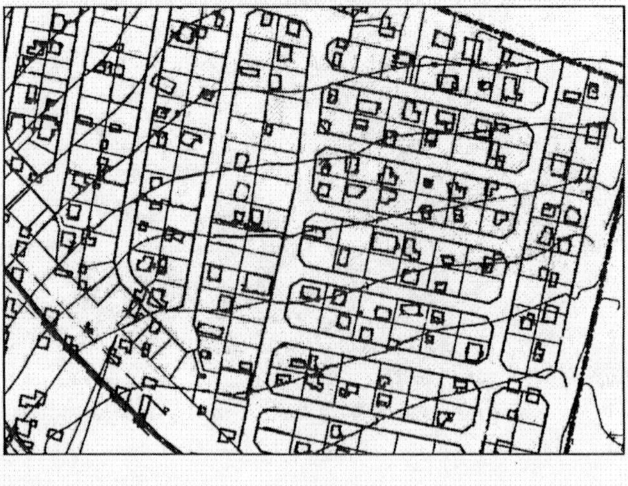

Figure 22: Kanana: standardised *in situ* layout based on the original invasion (source: Urban Dynamics).

Figure 23: Piesang River: high residential densities on a steep slope. Formally planned *in situ* layout as pegged (source: BESG/Pravin Amar Development Planners).

Figure 24: Pedestrian access to formally pegged sites at Piesang River.

Figure 25: Weiler's Farm: informal layout with plot sizes larger than $300m^2$ (source: EVN Consulting Engineers).

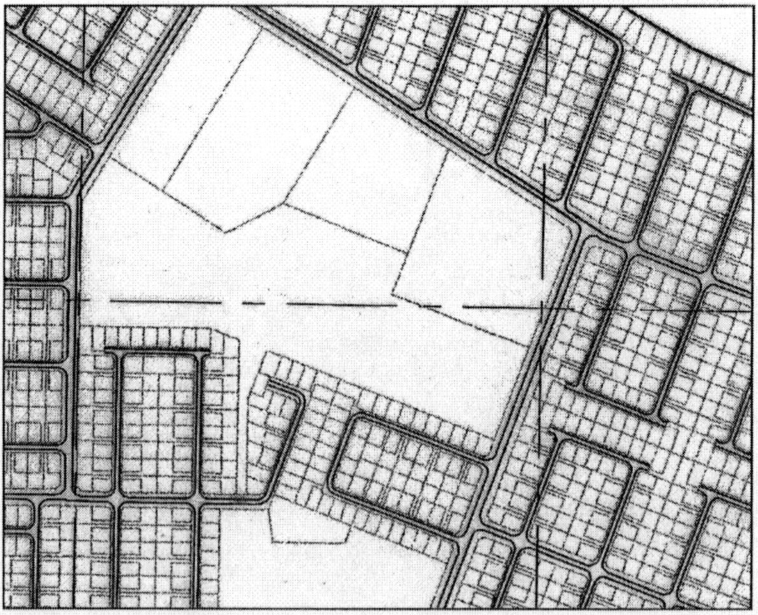

Figure 26: Weiler's Farm: planned layout with standardised plot sizes within the permissible $300m^2$ (source: EVN Consulting Engineers).

bias in the Gauteng Province towards large scale greenfield development by ensuring that some provincial housing subsidies were channelled into the development of land already informally occupied. The Weiler's Farm development formed one of its 11 pilot projects. Uniquely, however, the Weiler's Farm project application was not undertaken by the respective municipality. Due to lack of action on the side of the local authority, the Thuthuka Foundation applied directly to the provincial government, and was then appointed developer in the subsidy project. The remarkable pace at which the Weiler's Farm project progressed, caused much surprise to the provincial officials, who therefore recommended it to me for the purposes of this research.

Portioning the capital subsidy investment: collective versus individual assets

The individual capital subsidy is required to cover the three components of township establishment/land regularisation, infrastructure delivery and house construction. In the case of the Weiler's Farm development, the authorities made an up-front decision as to the portioning of the capital subsidy into the three components. In the case of Kanana, also in the Gauteng Province, this decision was made by the local authority through its external project design for the subsidy application. The community organisation at Kanana then strongly contested the portioning, and achieved a review in favour of greater spending on the individual house. In the case of Gunguluza, the Uitenhage Municipality set minimum standards for infrastructure, beyond which it allowed the residents to collectively weigh off higher levels of collective infrastructure against greater investment in the individual houses. As in the case of Kanana, the residents' decision was to maximise on the individual house. Below I return to the widespread quest for maximum house size, arguing that this reflects a major impact of the current intervention paradigm on the collective development strategies of informal settlement residents.

Piesang River is the only case study settlement that benefited from infrastructure development prior to the national housing policy and its subsidy system. Initial funding for Piesang River was secured in the early 1990s from the DFR-Forum.[27] This was in the form of a grant, in contrast to the individual capital subsidies released by the IDT at the time. The DFR-Forum grant funding then appeared to be more flexible than the household-based subsidy funding offered by the IDT. Indeed, an earlier application for upgrading at Piesang River had been turned down by the IDT, which required the identification of additional land for the 'de-densification' of the settlement. The DFR-Forum in turn approved of the project application without such additional land being identified.[28] However, in effect the DFR-Forum grant did not have particular benefits over IDT funding at the time. Unlike the flexible grant that allowed the early stages of the Besters Camp development to explore collective social facilities and social development programmes (as discussed in Chapter 6), the DFR-Forum grant was strictly assigned to the delivery of tenure, infrastructure and services, including individual toilet structures, as was the standard applying to IDT-funded projects at the time. According to the BESG project staff, the Piesang River residents rejected this principle, requesting houses rather than toilets. However, the civic organisation's acceptance of the funding is said to have been in full understanding of the attached conditions.

Intervention procedures: space for community-based approaches?

Infrastructure delivery through the capital subsidy in all four case studies was undertaken through conventional tender procedures and outside contractors, although residents were employed as temporary labourers by the contractors. Only the Uitenhage Town Council was exploring a concept of community-based contracting for infrastructure delivery. In the case of Gunguluza, community-based contractors had been trained and given the opportunity to tender in the reticulation of electricity in the settlement. It must be added, however, that electricity reticulation is funded through a separate grant, therefore not forming a component of the capital subsidy of the National Housing Ministry. It should further be pointed out, that the approach was one that ensured that community-based contractors could compete in a conventional contract procedure. Therefore, it was unlike the community contracting system in Sri Lanka discussed in Chapter 3, where the contracting procedure was specifically tailored to the realities of community-based initiatives.

Within the capital subsidy, it is the house-building component that may be implemented through community-based approaches. In Uitenhage, the Town Council has been strongly opposed to developer-driven mass-delivery of housing, instead favouring the People's Housing Process of the National Ministry of Housing.[29] Strong support for this position comes from the SANCO structures in Uitenhage (and to a lesser degree from individual councillors). In the Gunguluza settlement, a Housing Support Centre (see Figure 27) had been constructed through a grant from the People's Housing Process. Households were required to 'shift' their shacks to the back of their plots and to then build a formal house (either through self-construction or the employment of local builders) in the centre of the plot, according to approved building plans. The intention of the town council was to not tolerate informal building at Gunguluza, once all households had participated in the People's Housing Process. In reality, however, shacks at the back of the plots were not being demolished once formal houses were complete. It was suggested that extended family or second households were establishing themselves in these structures. Thus, while the town council had gone to great lengths to support a people-centred housing process, the conventional regulatory framework had not been adjusted. Again, this contrasts with the Sri Lankan experience discussed in Chapter 3, where the People's Housing Process is embedded in a responsive regulatory framework.

In the case of Piesang River, residents were eligible for the housing component of the capital subsidy, as the DFR-Forum grant had covered only the components of land and infrastructure. Homeless People's Federation members were able to access this portion of the individual subsidy through the uTshani Fund agreement, which the KwaZulu-Natal Provincial Government has entered into with the Homeless People's Federation/People's Dialogue alliance. Through this agreement, the Provincial Housing Board pays the eligible members' capital subsidy amount into the Federation's fund, allowing the Federation to oversee its implementation. At Piesang River and in the surrounding areas, such building was overseen through the Federation's BIT-Centre (see Figure 28).[30] At Kanana, likewise the locale of a regional BIT-Centre of the Federation (see Figure 29), individual residents had taken out housing loans from the Federation's collective savings fund. In the absence of an uTshani Fund agreement with the Gauteng Province, subsequent house construction was to take place through the People's Housing Process, to which the local authority (at the time of interviewing) had recently committed itself. At Weilers Farm, Thuthuka Foundation was considering various housing options including the People's Housing Process and, at the time of interviewing, it had not taken a decision.

7.6 Popular strategies for settlement improvement

Each of the four organised informal settlement communities in the case studies developed unique strategies for the improvement of living conditions. In some cases, initial strategies were articulated in the ignorance of a formal development framework, and not necessarily with the expectation of government support. In other cases, creative strategies were applied in order to access formal development. In all instances, community-based strategies had adjusted once the official development framework and its dictates became a reality. In all four case studies, the decision was to work within the prescribed approach, although community organisations have, to a varying extent, asserted their own development concepts. In the next section I examine the particular impact of the individual capital subsidy entitlement, and the associated development framework, on the strategies of the community organisations.

Weiler's Farm – a pragmatic pursuit of social and physical development

Turning first to those popular strategies that emerged without direct expectation of government assistance, I begin with the earlier stages of the Weiler's Farm settlement, after the abandoning of the land by its owner. With regards to infrastructure, the leadership had arranged a water supply system, using the farm boreholes (Black Sash, 1989:S5).[31] Despite transit camp status and pending relocation to Orange Farm, it appears that the vision of the leadership was focused on social development at Weiler's Farm. In 1987, a pre-school was established, catering for 150 children, and in 1988 a primary school, at one stage catering for over

Figure 27: The Gunguluza committee with the municipal housing coordinator, at the Housing Support Centre.

Figure 28: Savings and building activities at the Homeless People's Federation BIT-Centre at Piesang River.

Figure 29: The leadership of Kanana Phase 2, at the Homeless People's Federation BIT-Centre.

900 pupils (Mashabela, 1990:36). The primary school was operating from a prefabricated building secured through an educational NGO, and a clinic was arranged to operate from the former farmhouse. The government tactics to coerce residents to relocate included the removal of the prefabricated school building to Orange Farm, and the demolition of the farmhouse and clinic. In response, the leadership that was committed to opposing the relocation organised the collection of zinc plates and the building of a large shack for schooling. Four residents, including one of the leaders and now a director of the Thuthuka Foundation, volunteered to teach. The plight of the Weiler's Farm residents had aroused local as well as international sympathies. With various donations, two formal classrooms were later constructed (see Figure 30). Attempts were made to formalise the school, and outsider sympathies with the educational struggle at Weiler's Farm led to the temporary deployment of formally trained teachers in 1992.

I mentioned above that the civic organisation of Weiler's Farm had formed a Development Team, to investigate the formalisation of Weiler's Farm. The search for outside assistance in this endeavour met with closed doors in the early 1990s, but was not abandoned. Unaware of the official necessity to formalise the settlement layout and tenure prior to house construction, the Development Team pursued the residents' demand for formal house construction. A few individual households, with their own resources or with employers' assistance, were already constructing formal houses, while a shop owner had formally constructed a large store (see Figure 31). Concerned about the affordability of formal construction, and not aware of the housing policy negotiations which by then were clearly leading to an entitlement to a capital subsidy for the lowest income sector, the Development Team endeavoured to purchase a brick-making machine. With the commitment of one donation, and the hope of financial support from influential ANC personalities in the wake of the 1994 elections, they happened to make contact with the sympathetic ANC-aligned businessman mentioned earlier in this chapter. He then guided their development strategy towards more realistically engaging with the formal development framework, which indeed required first the approval of permanent residential development on the land, formalisation of the layout, reduction of plot sizes to the maximum of $300m^2$ and delivery of infrastructure, before house construction could take place. The unresponsiveness of this framework is illustrated by the fact that those houses previously constructed of permanent material, including the store, were (at the time of interviewing) to be demolished without compensation to the owners.

How then did the community leadership engage with this rigid framework? In the case of Weiler's Farm civic organisation and its Thuthuka Foundation, a remarkable degree of pragmatism was applied. The intention was to secure the best possible deal in terms of land, infrastructure and housing within the capital subsidy amount, and then to proceed with aspects of social development and income generation. Indeed, through the land agreement required for the capital

Figure 30: School buildings at Weiler's Farm.

Figure 31: Formally constructed store at Weiler's Farm, to be demolished with the settlement upgrading.

Figure 32: Food gardening on large informal residential plots at Weiler's Farm

subsidy intervention, adjacent land was secured for an agricultural project. Thus, while subsistence farming (see Figure 32) would be initially impeded through the reduction in individual plot sizes, commercial as well as subsistence farming was envisaged on the adjacent land in the longer term. Likewise, concrete plans and fundraising were underway (at the time of interviewing) for the development of commercial sites and sites reserved for social facilities. There is no doubt that the sympathetic businessman, first as a trusted outsider, and subsequently as one of the two directors of the Thuthuka Foundation, had an influence on the strategies of the community-based organisation. However, his consistent support strengthened the leadership's capacity to realise its original vision for social development. At the time of interviewing, requests were coming from other settlements, including Orange Farm, for guidance from the leadership at Weiler's Farm.

Gunguluza – from self-reliance to cooperation

The strategies of the leadership of the more recent Gunguluza settlement have been less dramatic, but nevertheless have made their mark. Not having experienced any supportive government intervention, Mrs Gunguluza and others had invaded the area with no direct expectation of government intervention. The orderliness of the site allocation, mirroring the adjacent layout, was said to have been for the sake of equity, rather than in the expectation of government funded upgrading. 'We were going to manage this ourselves', Mrs Gunguluza explained in an interview. The formalisation of the land occupation had then been initiated by SANCO, whose support Mrs Gunguluza had sought once eviction notices had been issued. A process of adjusting the informal settlement layout to the sites that were officially pegged on the ground, was driven by SANCO with support from the NGO Urban Services Group. Once existing pegs had been located, shacks were shifted accordingly and additional sites were allocated to residents of other informal settlements in KwaNobuhle that could not be formalised. A total of 745 sites was thereby reached. A team of Gunguluza residents was directly involved in the formalisation procedure, while Mrs Gunguluza is said to have kept detailed household records, not only in the formalisation but also during the initial invasion. She had followed up the credentials of those wishing to join the settlement, thus ensuring the exclusion of thugs or criminals. An official of the then KwaNobuhle Town Council acknowledged that Mrs Gunguluza ran 'a good administration, although informal … She made everything easy for the Council'. Her courage and initiative were also praised: 'It's not easy, sometimes, to help shack people, they talk a lot, they've a lot to say, some of them are very rude', but 'the community understood her, they worked hand-in-hand'.

After the initial ordering of the land occupation, the residents' first request to the town council (through their settlement committee) was for toilets and water. However, in line with the capital subsidy entitlement, they had been advised to apply not only for toilets and water, but for 'all of the things at the same time', including housing and individual freehold tenure. Ironically, at the time of interviewing, roads, underground services and electricity had been installed, housing was underway through the People's Housing Process (see Figures 33 and 34), yet formal access to toilets and water was still outstanding (see Figure 35). In the following section I return to this point, showing how knowledge of the capital subsidy entitlement shifted household priorities away from these 'basic needs'.

Kanana – respecting engineering dictates, yet challenging procedures

With the planned and orderly invasion of Kanana, the strategy appears initially to have been one of willingness to work hand-in-hand with the new government. The approach was to respect existing layout standards, as they were portrayed in the surrounding townships. An existing power line servitude, cutting through the invasion site, was likewise respected. Officials responded to the invasion by giving an eviction notice, not on the grounds of illegality of the invasion, but on grounds of health (there being no access to drinking water) (People's Dialogue, 1997). The organisers of the invasion, with financial contributions from the residents, then arranged the installation of 117 taps (*ibid.*). The laying of water pipes and the unauthorised connection to water mains were undertaken not with the intention of pirating water, but in full expectation that the authorities would respond by installing water meters and by charging for consumption. The officials in turn half-heartedly threatened legal action against the pirating of water, and then chose to ignore the settlement for the following two years (*ibid.*). People's Dialogue's documentation of the settlement process juxtaposes the 'people's development' with the 'formal development', showing how the community was 'pushed' by the officials 'to act autonomously' (*ibid.*:7). The resulting strategy of self-reliance was then strengthened through exposure to the Homeless People's Federation/People's Dialogue alliance, and the formation and growth of Federation structures in the settlement. With the creation of savings groups, a 'people-driven housing development process' was initiated (*ibid.*:10). A new dimension that the Federation enabled in the community's strategy was its lobbying with 'the highest level of government' (*ibid.*). In early 1995, the new Minister of Land Affairs visited the settlement and its BIT-Centre building, through which the Federation members demonstrated their self-construction and self-management skills. The Minister encouraged the Federation's endeavours and instructed the hitherto unwilling local government to apply for development funding from the Province for the formalisation of the settlement.

While the minister's visit to Kanana encouraged the auto-construction of houses through the Federation, it also triggered the imposition of the inflexible Urban Foundation-inspired model of informal settlement intervention. The experience at Kanana exposed the hostility of this development framework to community self-management and self-reliance. At the time of interviewing

Figure 33: Formal infrastructure at Gunguluza: gravel roads, electricity reticulation, high mast lighting and underground sewer and water reticulation.

Figure 34: House construction through the People's Housing Process at Gunguluza.

Figure 35: Continued use of pit latrines at Gunguluza, despite underground sewer reticulation.

in 1998, several Federation houses were to be demolished, as they violated the boundaries that had been pegged according to the approved layout plan (see Figure 36). It is relevant to note that the planners, on request from the Federation members, had been willing to adjust the layout plan to accommodate most of the existing buildings. However, the imposition of the rigid development framework had caused a seemingly irreconcilable divide within the settlement. The ward councillors, in support of the official orderly procedure, were said to have encouraged a portion of the residents to oppose the Federation, which was seen to be delaying the formal development. It was the opposing residents, then, who voted against having the layout plan adjusted to accommodate the houses of those that had violated the council's instruction not to build prior to the formal pegging and allocation of sites. The Federation members at Kanana in turn hold that this instruction had not been clearly made prior to construction.[32] Indeed, the various parties interviewed considered the communication between officials and the community-based structures throughout the project inadequate, the local government officials relying heavily on engineering and town planning consultants, rather than attending project meetings themselves.

Piesang River – from a submission to development dictates, to the exploration of alternatives

In the Piesang River settlement, despite a history that goes back to the 1960s, a consistent strategy for settlement improvement emerged only in the late 1980s with the formation of the civic organisation, which was then supported by the NGO BESG. Through this support, the strategy then was to engage in a formal

Figure 36: Homeless People's Federation house in conflict with the formal, approved layout for Kanana.

development project. As mentioned above, the funding framework at the time did not fulfil the wishes or meet the priorities of the residents. However, the civic organisation pragmatically agreed to the development approach. As mentioned above, the settlement, prior to the intervention, had been characterised by a high dwelling density. Individual shacks or wattle-and-daub structures were not fenced in (see Figures 14 and 15), and unbuilt space was used communally, accommodating residential, commercial and recreational activities. The official planning solution that was agreed to, in turn, was purely residential, with a highly individualised notion of a single dwelling centred on a well defined plot.[33]

I discussed with the former civic leader, then president of the Homeless People's Federation, the distance between plan and reality. With hindsight, after almost a decade of engagement in the radical development thinking of the Homeless People's Federation, he gave two reasons for the acceptance of the highly individualised proposal in the early 1990s. Firstly, crime levels had risen in the settlement with the introduction of official policing control through the 'Black Local Authority' in the second half of the 1980s. As the former community control over crime was undermined by ineffective official structures, 'the criminals got their space'. In this context, the notion of an individually fenced-in plot appealed, as it seemed defensible. Secondly, the development NGO is believed to have had an influence on the development thinking in the civic organisation. It is thought to have created a culture in which its professional technical advisors felt comfortable. A 'trench' was thus created, whereby the civic organisation had to adopt what the professionals had learnt. The NGO professionals were thereby defining a strategy for the community-based organisation. This contrasts with the role that the Homeless People's Federation/People's Dialogue alliance foresees for professionals, namely not to define a strategy, but to support and strengthen the existing strategies of community-based structures.

The emergence of the Homeless People's Federation at Piesang River, eventually leading to the withdrawal of the NGO BESG, may suggest that the NGO People's Dialogue influenced the strategising of a portion of the Piesang River leadership. However, it must be noted that the emergence of the Federation at Piesang River was itself part of the initial articulation of the Federation strategy in South Africa. In 1991, the Piesang River civic leader was invited (on nomination by BESG), alongside civic leaders from across the country, to a 'meeting on Land and Shelter', with delegates from neighbouring states, Europe and Asia (People's Dialogue, 1991). The civic leader recalled a revolutionary turn-about in the development thinking of many of the civic delegates. While they had each been using their political affiliation as a strategy, they now recognised that all the landless had something in common, irrespective of political affiliation, and that their concerns were the priority of no one but themselves. It was therefore recognised that networking among the poor might be an important strategy towards taking control of the situation. The civic leader from Piesang River was then invited to tour the country in the first networking exercise. Other early activities were attempts at negotiating, with the formal sector, means by which the lowest income sector could access credit. The disappointing outcome of these negotiations then led to a recognition that financial self-reliance was an important notion for the poor. A strategy of pooling savings and experience therefore emerged, Piesang River being the first settlement in South Africa to establish a savings group.

With the emergence of the Homeless People's Federation in Piesang River, it is understandable that those residents that agreed with the emerging Federation approach began to question the former strategy of the civic organisation, to which the NGO BESG was contractually bound. Indeed, the Federation leadership explained that 'a whole new culture developed ... the people were talking about a development revolution'. Piesang River, then, was the first venue for a 'Community-driven Shelter Training Programme' in South Africa (People's Dialogue, 1993), in which four Federation members had previously participated in India. The intention with this training programme at Piesang River was to mobilise women for the savings schemes, and to strengthen the formal development process by undertaking a physical survey and gathering household information (*ibid.*). An additional exercise was the building of cardboard models of the ideal house (*ibid.*). Implications of this training programme were twofold. On the one hand, individual priorities were focused on a complete, freestanding, four-roomed house, although the People's Dialogue (1993:17) documentation argues that participants 'knew that there was a long road ahead before they could live in houses like the ones they had modelled'. On the other hand, it was recognised that a development alternative to that of the formal infrastructure project underway in Piesang River did exist. However, neither house construction nor a more people-centred development could be realised through the existing development project. It is the housing aspect that the Federation at Piesang River then successfully pursued (see Figure 37). Below I discuss how the capital subsidy entitlement amplified the Federation's strong focus on the freestanding four-roomed house.

I mentioned above the distance between the actual residential density in sections of Piesang River and the official pegged layout that was developed through the project that BESG had managed. Official site allocation and relocation to other development areas to ensure that pegged sites were occupied by only one household (then able to build their freestanding house), was the task of the official council project that later picked up the loose ends of the abandoned project. At the time of interviewing, formal site allocation, partial relocation and the issuing of individual freehold titles was due to commence. In the interim, the Homeless People's Federation at Piesang River had established in a door-to-door survey that residents were not wishing to relocate (People's Dialogue 1998:6). The Federation, with People's Dialogue, had then explored a housing alternative that could accommodate higher densities at Piesang River (see Figure 38) and would therefore foreclose the need for relocation (see *ibid.*). According to the council's consultant, the demand for an alternative had not been communicated through the formal consultative channels that had been set up for the completion of the original project. The same applied to the Federation leadership's intention to hold the Piesang River land communally. Thus the legal procedures for the issuing of individual freehold titles had been set into motion. While a formal arrangement for group ownership of shared neighbouring plots had been made at the request of the Federation leadership, a considerable amount of relocation or 'de-densification' was nevertheless to occur.

The strategy of the People's Dialogue/Homeless People's Federation initiative of paralleling existing formal development with an exploration of alternative concepts did not significantly impact on the formal solution at the Piesang River settlement itself. However, People's Dialogue explained that such exploration of alternatives was important as a learning exercise for the Homeless People's Federation as a whole. The concepts of higher density housing and of communal land holding were being applied in some of the Federation's greenfield settlements elsewhere in the country. As argued by People's Dialogue, the Federation strategy is not primarily one of resolving development problems in any single settlement, but of increasing the capacity of the Federation country wide. The incompatibility between this strategy and the formal procedure into which most official role players are tied has caused much frustration, People's Dialogue therefore being perceived by officials and consultants as a disruptive and evasive initiative.

Figure 37: Homeless People's Federation members at Piesang River involved in the construction of their houses.

Figure 38: Semi-detached two-storeyed house piloted by the Homeless People's Federation/ People's Dialogue alliance as a solution to multiple site occupation at Piesang River.

7.7 The impact of the capital subsidy entitlement on popular and support-based strategies

summary

In Chapter 5, I demonstrated how the emergence of the post-1994 informal settlement intervention framework in South Africa was not through consideration of popular demand, but by placing faith in the proposals of the influential Urban Foundation, which represented the liberal demands of the private sector. In Chapter 6, I exposed flaws in the intellectual position that underpins the Urban Foundation model of informal settlement intervention. In the current chapter, I have positioned four informal settlements and their people-driven initiatives in relation to the official Urban Foundation-inspired intervention framework, showing how insensitive this has been to the informal settlement reality and to popular strategies for settlement improvement. I now examine the impact that the Urban Foundation-inspired model, and in particular the individual entitlement to a capital subsidy, has had on the strategies of the people-driven initiatives in the four case studies. I argue that the individual capital subsidy entitlement, and the associated distraction of collective attention into endeavours to seek the largest possible individual house, have prevented the people-driven informal settlement initiatives from initiating a fundamental review of the intervention framework.

Seeking the largest possible house

Informal settlement intervention post-1994 has been packaged as housing delivery, through the individual household-based capital subsidy which covers land regularisation, collective infrastructure and individual house construction. While originally intended by the Urban Foundation as a sites-and-services approach, the post-apartheid government amplified the capital subsidy to include a minimal top structure, henceforth terming it a 'housing subsidy'. Politically, focus has been placed on the individual entitlement to a freestanding house on an individual plot. Popular response to this entitlement has been to demand a house of adequate proportions. In most of the case study settlements, residents' concerns for a larger house appeared to be overriding any endeavours to address collective aspects of informal settlement improvement or social upliftment through the capital subsidy funding. As an individual entitlement, the subsidy in most cases was being considered a means of acquiring an individual household-based asset in the form of a house. An exception was the case of Weiler's Farm. There, the provincial government had defined the portion of the subsidy that was to go towards the top structure (or house), and the Thuthuka Foundation, on behalf of the residents, was intent on securing the best possible housing deal within this amount. At the same time, the Foundation had ensured that future social development was to be secured through the capital subsidy entitlement. As mentioned above, the land agreement included the acquisition of adjacent land for an agricultural project, while the layout plan ensured employment creation through commercial sites. At the time of interviewing, the Thuthuka Foundation, though managing the installation of infrastructure, was also pursuing means of realising the planned agricultural, commercial and social development.

I now turn to those cases where house size was the overriding concern. In the case of Gunguluza, an awareness of the capital subsidy entitlement had shifted the residents' priorities from the basic needs of water and toilets to the maximum size of the individual house. At the time of interviewing, the residents were content with not having access to the basic commodities (toilets and water) they had first demanded, although underground services had been laid. They had even turned down the local authority's offer of providing temporary toilets, which was to be financed through a separate grant and not subtracted from the individual subsidies. Being confronted with options in the development process, the residents had chosen, firstly, the lowest permissible standard of infrastructure, in order to maximise capital subsidy expenditure on the individual house. As a result, internal roads in the settlement were not tarred.[34] Secondly, they chose, not to have freestanding toilet structures installed with service provision (as was common practice with sites-and-services projects of the IDT), but to include toilets under the roof of the house. This saved building material costs, allowing the house size to be increased. Thirdly, residents had then chosen the People's Housing Process as a means of house construction, as it saved on profit making and labour, thus increasing the expenditure on building material and therefore house size. With household control over house construction through the People's Housing Process, some households had then gone as far as to exclude toilets from the house construction altogether, wishing instead to save on the plumbing and rather increase house size. In such cases the local authority was intervening, as the official building regulations applying to the capital subsidy intervention in that town stipulates that it is illegal to reside in a house without a toilet. The plastering of walls, likewise not a priority of the residents, was also a requirement for building approval. The final phase of the subsidy intervention, the issuing of freehold title, in turn could only be undertaken once the house construction was approved by the local authority.

At Piesang River there was likewise a shift away from the concern for basic needs of water and sanitation. Funding for the initial intervention that was managed by BESG and the development trust had required the installation of basic services, though allowing the residents a choice of service levels. The outcome of a participatory decision-making process through the block structures of the civic organisation had been a choice for conventional service levels: on-site water borne sanitation, individual yard taps and tarred roads. Although house construction was not a component of the BESG-managed project, towards the end of BESG's involvement formal house construction had become a reality. On the one hand, the national 'housing subsidy' policy had been launched. Piesang River residents, having already benefited from subsidised land regularisation and servicing, were still eligible for the housing portion of the individual subsidy. On the other hand, house construction was being explored through credit from the Homeless People's Federation's savings funds. Similar to the case of Gunguluza, the residents at Piesang River had then requested that the BESG-managed project postpone the construction of toilets until formal houses were being built, rather than constructing freestanding structures as with IDT sites-and-services projects. At the time of BESG's withdrawal, then, individual sites were not connected to the water and sewerage mains. However, the plan was still for conventional on-site access to water and sanitation.

Supporting individualisation: the Homeless People's Federation paradox

With the emergence of the People's Dialogue/Homeless People's Federation initiative and its training programme from India, it appears that a paradox emerged at Piesang River. On the one hand, members were encouraged to act collectively and to pool resources. A collective facility, the BIT-Centre and its fenced-in yard (see Figure 28) is the locale of a continuous buzz of collective activity, reminding some residents of the layers of collective activity that characterised the settlement prior to the BESG-managed project. On the other hand, as mentioned above, people's minds were focused on the ideal four-roomed house, within an individualised development model with on-site access to water and sanitation. I asked a Federation leader at Piesang River, what the Indian delegates had suggested with regards to access to services. Upon reflection, I was told that the Indians had pointed out the importance of communal water points, as places where women could meet and talk about the Federation. I was then told, that women in Piesang River had rejected the concept of communal facilities, their minds instead being set on individual yard taps. Accordingly then, the physical development model of the Federation has been one that mirrors conventional townships in all respects. Responding to this observation, People's Dialogue explained to me that: 'the Homeless People's Federation is not about getting rid of apartheid models (even national government has failed to do this, in fact they produce houses worse than the apartheid models). The Federation is about addressing the root of oppression through self-reliance'. They further explained that 'people start from where they are and development priorities they select reflect this. They begin with what they know and understand, and their knowledge builds on this point'. From this perspective, the individualised capital subsidy is considered part and parcel of what comprises the reality and knowledge of the poor, and is not challenged as such.

The impact of the capital subsidy on Federation thinking and action, however, appeared to be substantial, and not necessarily in the members' best interest. Through my conversations at Piesang River, it was evident that the Federation was actively comparing its houses with those built by developers. The Federation's negotiated access to the capital subsidy through the uTshani fund agreement in some provinces, enables it to compete directly with developer delivery. Indeed, the fact that the Federation is able to secure larger houses within the capital subsidy amount than those delivered by developers appeared to be a major draw card for Federation membership. People's Dialogue justifies the fixation on the house size by arguing that poor women universally prioritise houses. This, however, might be contradicted by some of my findings in non-Federation settlements. In the case of Weiler's Farm, it was on demand by the mothers that the leadership prioritised the organisation of a pre-school and primary school. In the case of Gunguluza, it was the demand for water and toilets that first took the representative leadership to the local authority. My finding, then, is that to a large extent it is the individual entitlement to the standardised capital subsidy that uniformly focuses priorities on the house, possibly at the cost of ignoring a complexity and diversity of actual needs.

Whereas the representative civic structure at Weiler's Farm is able to consider the development of collective facilities despite the capital subsidy entitlement, it appears that the membership-based structure of the Federation, in the context of an individual entitlement to a 'housing' subsidy, has led to a prioritisation of individual over collective needs. Indeed, the NGO People's Dialogue appears to stand back as Federation members stretch their resources to achieve their ideal township house. In Piesang River, house size was increased to the extent that members were required to pay for plumbing, plastering and other finishes themselves.[35] Thus, of many houses constructed through the Federation, only one was pointed out as 'already flushing'. People's Dialogue, aware of the problems brought about by the capital subsidy, have adopted the attitude that once the government subsidies run out, the Federation will explore alternative and possibly more collective models for development. They have therefore refrained from challenging as such the fundamentals underpinning the capital subsidy approach, although on a case-by-case basis, aspects of the Urban Foundation model have been confronted.

Limitations in challenging the Urban Foundation paradigm at settlement level

The settlement process at Kanana is an interesting case of the impact of the capital subsidy framework on popular strategies, exposing both conformity with, and opposition to, the official framework. As mentioned above, the initial informal layout conformed broadly with conventional engineering standards, as it was modelled on surrounding township layouts. The local authority's application to the provincial housing board, however, had foreseen an engineering layout that took no consideration of the existing layout of the settlement. The portion of the capital subsidy that was to be spent on layout and infrastructure was then budgeted according to the new design. The Kanana leadership, convinced not only of the adequacy of its own layout, but also of the people's ability to supply infrastructure at a lower cost, challenged the official plans. The intention thereby was to free a larger portion of the subsidy for individual house construction. This challenge took two forms. On the one hand, the leadership insisted that the planners and engineers consult an aerial photograph to see the conventionality of the layout. On the other hand, with their own resources, the residents then demonstrated a more affordable service reticulation in a portion of the settlement. In support of this endeavour, the NGO People's Dialogue arranged an exchange with the Orangi Pilot Project in Pakistan (People's Dialogue, 1997:13), where, as mentioned in Chapter 3, residents have been financing, planning and constructing their own sewerage reticulation. The achievement at Kanana was not an official acceptance of the self-constructed infrastructure, but instead a review of the layout plan and budgeting. The Kanana leadership then pragmatically agreed to an engineering design based on the existing settlement layout, and on a lower expenditure on the infrastructure component of the capital subsidy. The infrastructure was carried out through conventional contracting procedures, and not through the popular skills that were gained from exposure to the Orangi Pilot Project.

The process of official engagement with the existing layout had an interesting impact on the residents at Kanana. At seeing the informal layout on an aerial photograph, the engineers had been surprised by its resemblance of an engineering drawing, yet felt compelled to point out to the residents that inaccuracies existed in the layout. Some boundary lines were not straight, and plot sizes varied. Until this point, residents had been content with the informal layout, and were not aware of differences in plot sizes. The engineers' intervention then focused their minds on the entitlement to a maximum plot size of 300m^2 through the capital subsidy. According to the development consultant, the individual residents then insisted on the standardisation of the layout. In the process of formalising the layout, residents voted against accommodating those formal houses which Federation members had constructed prior to the formalisation of the layout, and which now violated the standardised and straightened boundary lines. It appears that the residents' consciousness of their individual entitlement turned their collective support away from the leadership that had selflessly arranged the invasion, secured a development commitment from government and was actively seeking the most advantageous deal within the capital subsidy amount. The majority of residents shifted their support to the official process to which they were entitled through the capital subsidy, and in which they were represented by their ward councillor. As mentioned earlier in this chapter, this then undermined Federation membership at Kanana, and caused a divide in the settlement.

A further impact of the capital subsidy is that it has discouraged the construction of permanent houses through community-based resources in informal settlements, prior to settlement formalisation through the official framework. It has therefore required provisional housing arrangements, with ongoing costs going towards the repair and upkeep of temporary shacks, rather than gradual investment in a permanent structure and asset, as in the case of the rapidly consolidating favelas in Brazilian cities. While the intention of state delivery of standardised housing may be commendable, the reality remains that only a small proportion of informal settlements were experiencing government intervention. The vast majority of informal settlement households in this country will be spending many more years awaiting their turn in the capital subsidy intervention process. In the case of Weiler's farm, early construction of permanent houses was being responded to with demolition without compensation. At Kanana, the pending demolition of a number of permanent houses unknowingly violating a planned provincial road reserve had resulted in an agreement that the individual households should be compensated. Responsibility for the compensation was being negotiated between the local authority, the Provincial Roads Department and the NGO People's Dialogue.[36] However, at the time of interviewing, a deadlock had been reached, with neither party admitting responsibility. On the part of the local authority, the resolution was not to set a precedent for compensation. Indeed, Kanana was not the only settlement in its jurisdiction where Federation building had violated official procedure.

Limitations in challenging the Urban Foundation paradigm at policy level

It may then be asked: Would a boldness in house construction prior to regularisation eventually lead to a review of the intervention framework? The housing right in South Africa has been interpreted popularly as a right to the standardised product attainable through the capital subsidy. If an increasing self-determination through, for instance, the Homeless People's Federation's credit mechanisms will lead to increasing house construction in informal settlements prior to formalisation, then the interpretation of the housing right may shift to a broad demand for the right to occupation, or to legalisation of permanent structures. In Chapter 3, I mentioned that this has been the case in Brazil, showing how the PROFAVELA law in Belo Horizonte represented an appropriate institutional response to the popular demand for the right to occupation. However, it must be noted that this demand in Belo Horizonte and elsewhere in Brazil was articulated through a strong popular movement of mobilised informal settlement residents, supported by sympathetic church leaders, professionals and politicians. Alternative proposals were articulated by this movement and brought to the attention of policy makers. In South Africa no such movement exists. The civic movement at national level, as mentioned in Chapter 5, has been plagued by internal inconsistencies, and does not primarily focus on the question of informal settlement. The Homeless People's Federation/People's Dialogue alliance likewise is not primarily concerned with the particular question of informal settlement. As a membership-based organisation, its concerns are to a large extent have been parochial. Many of its explorations of alternatives in the case study settlements were said to have benefited its members in greenfield development projects elsewhere. As suggested in the discussion above, the Federation's strategies in informal settlements appear to have been influenced by the individual entitlement to the 'housing' subsidy, which has tied informal settlement intervention into a framework of housing delivery. Finally, as discussed in Chapter 6, informal settlement research in South Africa has likewise been limited in supporting a popular challenge to the individualised intervention paradigm.

In closing, then, it appears that the community-based initiatives in informal settlements in South Africa, while exposing shortcomings in the formal intervention framework, have not been in a position to fundamentally challenge the dominant Urban Foundation inspired paradigm that I discussed in Chapter 6. The only underpinning of this paradigm that has been challenged on a case-by-case basis (as shown in the case studies in this chapter) is the flawed assumption that community-based organisations have no important role to play. However, this challenge has not been brought to higher levels of government, where informal settlement intervention policy is formulated. With regards to house construction, the Homeless People's Federation has challenged this aspect at provincial level. As a result, some provincial governments have entered into the uTshani agreement, thus allowing eligible Federation members' subsidies to be managed by the Federation. In a greenfield situation, this has enabled Federation control over all components of the subsidy (land, infrastructure and house construction). In informal settlements, however, Federation membership has never reached or maintained full coverage. As a result, Federation control over development has been restricted to individual house construction.

Turning to the other underpinnings of the Urban Foundation model, it is important to note that the Federation appears to question the relevance of individual freehold title, therefore the commodification of land. However, it is only in its greenfield settlements, where the Federation has full control over the capital subsidy intervention, that individual freehold title has been successfully challenged, and communal land holding has been explored. In the case of Piesang River, the Federation had requested communal ownership of the land. However, non-member households have the right to individual titles. The official solution was to offer group ownership in those instances where neighbouring Federation members wish to share their plots. At Kanana, the concept of individual freehold titles was not being questioned. The Federation then has an ambivalent position on the relevance of individualisation and commodification to the alleviation of poverty. I have mentioned above the paradox that on the one hand encourages communal means of combating poverty through pooling of savings, and on the other hand encourages individual households to stretch their resources to acquire the largest possible individual asset through the capital subsidy. It is the focus on the house, amplified by the capital subsidy entitlement, that has prevented the Federation from fundamentally challenging the Urban Foundation-inspired position that informal settlement intervention is simply a form of housing delivery.

7.8 Conclusion

Two of the support-based initiatives into which organised informal settlement communities in the case studies were able to tap, are modelled on international experience of responsive informal settlement intervention. The People's Housing Process, as mentioned in Chapter 3, is based on the support-based approach of the Sri Lankan housing policy. There, people-managed house construction, alongside community contracting and community action planning enable community management of the various components of informal settlement intervention. The Homeless People's Federation/People's Dialogue approach in turn is strongly inspired by the Indian National Slum Dwellers Federation and its supporting NGO SPARC (Society for the Promotion of Area Resource Centres), which explore responsive means of settlement improvement. The case study discussion in this chapter shows the extent to which initiatives in South Africa that are modelled on support-based approaches abroad, have been distorted by the entitlement to the standardised capital subsidy. Their focus has been distracted from the support of ongoing settlement-based processes of improvement, towards the once-off acquisition of a maximum sized house for individual households. Neither the People's Housing Process, nor the Homeless People's Federation/People's Dialogue alliance, have been able to place aspects of informal settlement improvement other than house construction into the control of organised informal settlement communities. Where the provincial government has, as an exception, placed control over the subsidy investment with a community-based developer (the Thuthuka Foundation in Weiler's Farm) the dictates of the capital subsidy framework defined the nature of the intervention product.

The informal settlement intervention framework in South Africa have thus required that priorities are externally defined through the capital subsidy components. These have then been realised through a once-off injection of development funding into an informal settlement. The efforts of residents, local government officials and professionals (even those of support-based initiatives) have gone towards the realisation of the best possible individual product within the capital subsidy amount. Indeed, this amount has been artificial, bearing no relevance to the ongoing resources of the poor or of local authorities. The combined development efforts have been towards an intervention that was never to be repeated in one settlement. While professional consultants and officials may have subsequently applied their skills in other capital subsidy projects, the settlement-based initiatives acquired skills that they were unlikely to use again. Even in the case of Kanana, where the Federation enables exchange with other settlements, the leadership that had actively engaged in the capital subsidy investment was frustrated with the skills it had developed and was unable to make use of again.

The case study discussion in this chapter consolidates the argument throughout this book that for informal settlement intervention in South Africa to be appropriate, it had to depart from the Urban Foundation-inspired paradigm. In the final chapter I will draw together the contributions of the comparison with Brazil, in enabling a more appropriate way of understanding and furthering the question of informal settlement intervention in South Africa.

Notes

1 This challenge is often interpreted as 'jumping the queue', as noted in Chapter 6.

2 Settlement visits and interviewing took place in November/December 1998. The interviewing was conducted in an informal conversational manner, with which the interviewees were most comfortable. Many indicated that they would not like the conversation to be tape-recorded, therefore I relied largely on hand-written notes taken during the conversations. These were later organised under headings broadly reflecting the questions which led the conversation and according to which the interview material was then analysed. Depending on the circumstances, interviewing within the settlements was conducted partly in groups and partly with individuals. As interviewing was mainly with prominent members of community-based organisations, it could be conducted in English and Afrikaans. Where residents were interviewed that were not fluent in either of these languages, other residents volunteered to act as translators.

3 While government officials tended not to comment and civics responded in broad agreement with my interpretation, rigorous critiques were received from the NGO People's Dialogue, clarifying aspects of their strategy and thinking that could not be accessed through the interviewing and the existing documentation. Each of the organisations in which I had interviewed then received a report on all four case studies, with a general discussion of the issues raised (see Huchzermeyer, 1999b).

4 'Piesang' is the Afrikaans word for Banana – the river is said to have once been lined with Banana trees.

5 Inkatha Freedom Party – see endnote 18 in Chapter 5.

6 With the capital subsidy intervention, the settlement was being renamed 'Kanana Park'. In order to avoid confusion with the other case study settlement named Kanana, I make use of the name 'Weiler's Farm' throughout this chapter.

7 The emergence of uncontrolled squatting in the district appears both to have been influenced by, and to have impacted on, the agricultural trends in the district. On the one hand, farming activities in the region were disrupted by the rezoning and expropriation of farmland for the establishment of coloured and Indian townships since the early 1970s (Crankshaw, 1993). With the cessation of agricultural activities, previous farm workers were displaced, while expropriated farms that were left unsupervised became subject to land invasion (*ibid.*). On the other hand, the abandoning of farms still zoned for agricultural land use, as in the case of Weiler's Farm, was itself a reaction to the growing fear of crime in the area, conservatively associated

with the phenomenon of squatting. According to an official document, farming in the area had virtually ceased by the mid-1990s, with 77 per cent of the landowners having abandoned their land due to crime (Department of Development Planning and Environment, 1995:7).

8 In townships, backyard shack tenants were expected to pay rents to occupants of township houses who themselves were boycotting rents charged by the council. Single-sex hostels (where occupants were increasingly joined by women and children) were in turn wrought with faction fighting and violence.

9 The fact that contemporary informal settlements in KwaNobuhle were named after prominent figures of the liberation struggle – Ramaphosa (120 households), Chris Hani (87 households), Joe Modise (130 households) (Uitenhage Town Secretary, 1995) – indicates the respect Mrs Gunguluza was afforded.

10 'Squatting' first emerged in KwaNobuhle in 1991, when the township is said to have been visibly bursting at its seems. There was then a general understanding within the municipality that the 'squatters' were not newcomers to the town. While merciless removals, from the 1940s township Langa (an ANC stronghold adjacent to the 'white' town), to KwaNobuhle township had led to the Uitenhage massacre in 1986, the official position in the early 1990s was one of tolerance. What had remained up to the time of interviewing (late 1998) was a high level of political consciousness among the KwaNobuhle residents, and with this a solidarity between those formally housed and those invading land. Informal settlement residents were making undisputed use of taps and toilets in surrounding serviced areas.

11 Uitenhage is an industrial town of approximately 300,000 people near Port Elizabeth in the Eastern Cape.

12 Although a strip of market garden had already been established as a buffer beyond the township.

13 The portions closer to the farmland were invaded in subsequent years and are officially referred to as Gunguluza Phase 2 and 3.

14 From the biblical 'Canaan', a name given to many informal settlements in South Africa.

15 Though having supported the protest action that led to the boycotting of rents for council houses, these subtenants were still being charged rent by the non-paying formal council tenants in whose yards they had constructed shacks and were living under severely overcrowded conditions.

16 This was by then affiliated to SANCO.

17 Such boldness was widespread and is reflected in the names of other informal settlements that sprung up in the surrounding, the most explicit being 'Election Park'.

18 The phenomenon of shacklordism or exploitative non-democratic leadership, which in the South African literature discussed in Chapter 6 is assumed to be widespread in informal settlements, was not investigated for the purposes of this chapter.

19 Since the early 1990s the ANC had built its own organisational network of local branches as a structure for mass-based support (Omer-Cooper, 1994:243).

20 This distinction was made explicit in an interview with the then BESG staff member and project leader at Piesang River, where the divergence between these two forms of organisation had particular implications for BESG's involvement in the project.

21 This is different in those cases where the Federation has secured vacant land and enables its active members from various areas to plan and construct a new settlement.

22 As the NGO was henceforth remunerated through the development funding, a stronger emphasis was placed on its professionalism, this causing an increased distance to the civic organisation.

23 The trust was to hold the ownership of the land until issuing of individual freehold titles, and to control the development funding.

24 Habitat for Humanity is an ecumenical self-help organisation based in the United States and operating on conventional principles of loan finance. The organisation offers an interest-free housing loan, though adjusted to inflation (BESG, 1998:28). The 47 creditworthy participants in the settlement were unable to access government housing subsidies at the time of the case study research, as their loans are from an international fund (this obstacle has since been resolved). Antagonisms therefore existed, as the Federation members were able to access capital subsidies through the uTshani Loan agreement.

25 At the time of interviewing, communication between the two housing initiatives had not taken place for several years.

26 Thuthuka meaning 'let's improve'.

27 The DFR (Durban Functional Region) Forum was a transitional non-statutory body that was given authority over the development capital of the Durban City Council, as the legitimacy of the latter had been challenged by the civic movement.

28 Arguably, this caused problems at a later stage, as the project design did rely on a degree of 'de-densification' and relocations. At the time of interviewing in 1998 this was yet to be resolved.

29 As discussed in Chapter 3, this approach was modelled on the Sri Lankan People's Housing Process, but is confined to the capital subsidy framework.

30 Building, Information and Training Centre – at the time of interviewing, the Federation was operating seven BIT-Centres in South Africa, each serving as a regional place of learning and administration.

31 Residents had constructed their own pit latrines, and plot sizes allowed refuse to be disposed of in pits on each plot.

32 Further demolition of Federation houses was pending due to a planned road servitude that bisects Phase 2 of the settlement, where the majority of Federation houses are concentrated. The plans for the road had also not been mentioned by officials in their early dealings with the settlement representatives.

33 It may be noted that the agreed minimum plot size of $150m^2$ at Piesang River, allowing for a buildable platform of $100m^2$ on sloped portions of the settlement, was considered unconventionally small, in comparison to the standard plot size of $250m^2$ that applied to IDT-funded projects at the time.

34 Dissatisfaction with the state of the roads was voiced in an interview with the settlement committee.

35 Here the local authority appeared not to be enforcing building regulations.

36 Surprisingly, national government which, through its ministerial visit to the settlement, encouraged the early house construction was not being called upon to compensate.

Chapter 8

Appropriate Informal Settlement Intervention: Prospects and Challenges for South Africa

8.1 Introduction

Informal settlement intervention, as has been practised through the national housing policy framework throughout the past decade in South Africa, has not been appropriate to the reality of informal settlement, as it has reduced this complex phenomenon to technocratic concerns around the delivery of standardised housing units. This book has critically explored this problem through a comparison with the way in which the informal settlement intervention question is treated in Brazil. I started this book by placing current practice in Brazil and South Africa in relation to shifts in international thinking, and in relation to the intervention approaches that have emerged internationally. I then compared how informal settlements emerged and were treated differently within the socio-political contexts of Brazil and South Africa, both by the state and by civil society. Through this comparison I have been able to critically examine the positions in the South African literature on informal settlement intervention, and the current South African practice.

What has this comparative research approach contributed to our understanding of informal settlement intervention in South Africa? On the one hand, it has confirmed that thinking on informal settlement intervention in South Africa stagnated around a powerful technocratic (product-driven) market-oriented approach. While there is evidence that this approach has not adequately addressed the reality of informal settlement, it remained largely unchallenged throughout the first decade of democracy. This lack of critical debate in South Africa has contrasted with a progressive debate in Brazil, emanating from a movement for urban reform, which is politically backed by the PT (Workers' Party). This movement, comprising academics, practitioners, politicians and organised residents, has challenged product-oriented market-driven informal settlement intervention, developing instead an approach based on the demands of mobilised informal settlement residents. The lack of critical debate on informal settlement intervention in South Africa also contrasts with the urban poverty debates conducted at the international level in the 1990s. These debates have challenged the technocratic market-oriented informal settlement intervention promoted internationally by the World Bank since the early 1970s.

On the other hand, this comparative approach has revealed distortions in the post-1994 South African informal settlement intervention framework. Here I have exposed an overemphasis on standardisation of the individual delivery product: the residential plot with freehold tenure, on-site services and a minimal house. As a result of this distortion, progressive process-oriented intervention, as promoted internationally by the debates on urban poverty, have been difficult to implement within the South African framework for informal settlement intervention. However, even technocratically driven *in situ* upgrading, as promoted by the World Bank in the early 1970s, which minimises physical disruption of the existing settlement, has been rendered impossible in South Africa. Instead, informal settlements have been remodelled according to standardised layouts. I have argued that the distorted delivery model in South Africa has been underpinned by the entitlement of most low-income households to a once-off product-linked capital subsidy. The inherent restrictions and rigid controls exercised through this model of intervention, while in conflict with the realities of the urban poor, have been legitimised due to the access that the capital subsidy entitlement promises to an individual asset, in the form of a house. I have shown that popular strategies have in turn been distorted by an endeavour to secure the largest possible individual house through the once-off capital subsidy entitlement.

Having confirmed that South African informal settlement intervention stagnated around a distorted model, the comparative research approach has enabled me to explore the reasons for this situation. By engaging with the international thinking and practice I have been able to view the South African intervention approach not simply as an inappropriate policy solution, but as the product of an entire paradigm of development. By examining the origins of the contrasting informal settlement intervention in Brazil and South Africa, I have been able to ask why this paradigm, with its distorted model of informal settlement intervention, could be entrenched in spite of the process of democratisation in South Africa. The comparison with Brazil, therefore, has not only exposed the shortcomings in the South African informal settlement intervention approach, but has exposed the socio-political conditions that allowed a particular development paradigm to gain dominance in South Africa. This understanding allows me to engage with the prospects in South Africa for a paradigm shift that would create the space for a more appropriate form of informal settlement intervention.

8.2 Shortcomings in the South African informal settlement intervention framework

What are the shortcomings in the South African informal settlement intervention repertoire of the past ten years that have been identified through this comparison with Brazil? Various forms of ***in situ*** intervention are practised in Brazil, ranging from comprehensive externally designed upgrading seeking minimal disruption of the physical environment, to support-based and community managed settlement improvement. In contrast, ***in situ*** upgrading in South Africa has come to mean the replacement of informal settlements with formal township layouts, standardised plots with freehold title, and formal housing. In South Africa, therefore, informal settlements have been regarded as temporary transit areas awaiting replacement by an individualised model of development. The inherent, though fragile, abilities of the informally established settlements to respond to the demands of urban poverty have been officially ignored. Likewise both the informal systems through which these settlements are managed and the community-based strategies through which they are improved have been ignored. Indeed, unofficial settlement improvement, particularly individual investment in permanent construction, has been discouraged due to the pending remodelling and standardisation of the settlement layout according to the norms and standards attached to the intervention funding. 'Shanty towns' or shack settlements have therefore been perpetuated until they are replaced through official intervention. This absence of consolidation applies even to recently established informal settlements, where organisers of the invasion have anticipated the standardised nature of formal intervention and have planned the layout accordingly. In a few exceptions, as in Kanana and Weiler's Farm (two of my case study settlements), individual households have mobilised resources and constructed permanent dwellings prior to formalisation and standardisation of the layout. However, such buildings have not been treated as permanent in the formal layout planning. The need for standardisation of the layout, resulting from the standardised capital subsidy entitlement, has overridden any consideration of early consolidations, or of settlement diversification through individual investment. Demolitions have been the rule.

A further shortcoming in South African informal settlement intervention that has been identified through this comparative study, is the absence in South Africa of any support-based approaches to informal settlement improvement. The only space which support-based approaches have been afforded in informal settlement intervention in South Africa is in the construction of houses once layouts have been standardised. While progressive approaches in Brazil have been developed and institutionalised in the PT municipalities, which allow for community-managed upgrading according to localised priorities, the national housing policy in South Africa has dictated a uniform product-driven treatment of informal settlements across all designated urban areas. Even in exceptional cases, such as Weiler's Farm (one of the case study settlements), where a community-based organisation was appointed as developer for the intervention, the dictates associated with the capital subsidy did not allow the community-based developer to define product and procedures. The same dictates have distorted the internationally-inspired support-based initiatives. Both the People's Housing Process of the national ministry of housing, and the independent Homeless People's Federation/People's Dialogue alliance, have become mechanisms for the production of the largest possible capital subsidy houses on standardised plots with freehold titles.

8.3 Exposing stagnation in the thinking on informal settlement intervention in South Africa

As mentioned above, this study has confirmed that both popular and scholarly thinking on informal settlement intervention in South Africa has largely been trapped in the product-oriented confines of the current intervention framework, and therefore stagnated. Widespread consensus on the entitlement of low-income households to a uniform product has stifled debate on intervention in existing irregular informal settlements. With regards to the limited challenge of popular initiatives to the official intervention framework, my finding has been that it is the individual household's awareness of its entitlement to the once-off capital subsidy that has resulted in relative complicity of community-based initiatives with the dictates of the formal development. Any substantial popular challenge to the national framework has been discouraged by the residents' prospects for an individual asset that was to be gained through the capital subsidy system. The South African informal settlement literature gives evidence of the failure of various aspects of the standardised capital subsidy approach to address the social and economic reality in informal settlements. However, the literature too has failed to substantially challenge the intervention framework. How then has the comparison in this book explained intellectual stagnation in South Africa, as opposed to the continuous search for more progressive informal settlement intervention in Brazil?

The socio-political causes of informal settlements in South Africa differ from those in Brazil. The diverging ways in which the exclusion of a substantial portion of society from formal housing was achieved in South Africa as opposed to Brazil resulted in diverging ways in which this ongoing exclusion has been interpreted and challenged. In Brazil, exclusion throughout the 20th century, was based primarily on class divisions, and was achieved through the unrestricted pursuit of economic interests. Brazilian cities were thus shaped, not by planning and regulation, but by processes of property speculation. Amongst the popular class and intellectuals, this fostered a consciousness of class divisions, and of the exploitative and exclusionary nature of market-oriented policies. An intellectual left in Brazil has critically engaged with informal settlements through the question of exclusion, and has aligned itself with popular movements, developing strategies to secure a physical and political stake for the working-class in the rapidly changing urban environment. Alternative approaches to informal settlement intervention emerged within this framework. Politically, these alternative approaches have been supported and promoted by the PT, which is home to social movements and to progressive academics and practitioners. The decentralisation of government and political power has then allowed the PT to institutionalise alternative approaches at municipal level. With successful political contestation, support for these alternative approaches could be institutionalised at state and eventually federal level. Political competition at all tiers of government, but particularly the municipal level in turn requires ongoing popular mobilisation around the realities of exclusion, and an ongoing search for more democratic government intervention, in order for the PT to contest conservative parties that promote a market-oriented and product-driven informal settlement intervention.

In contrast to the Brazilian situation, exclusion of a portion of the population from formal housing in South Africa was primarily the result of race-based control through rigid urban planning and regulation. This fostered a popular and intellectual consciousness primarily of race, although class has increasingly become a barrier to overcoming urban poverty and exclusion. The attempt in South Africa has been to redress such exclusion through the abolition of racially discriminatory legislation, though legitimising the continuation of the rigid urban controls that underpin the segregated urban land markets and perpetuate class-based spatial exclusion. It is the market-oriented considerations that have inspired the current individualised informal settlement intervention framework of the past ten years. Widespread consensus among the middle-class around the same neo-liberal considerations has then also prevented a substantial challenge to both the urban regulatory system and the framework for informal settlement intervention, and has discouraged the exploration of alternatives. More broadly, the neo-liberal consensus has discouraged class-based analysis, thus hiding the extent to which class is becoming an increasing barrier to inclusion. In addition, the centralised nature of urban policy in South Africa, in which local government acts largely as implementer, has discouraged the exploration of alternatives from within local government (though efforts at developing informal settlement upgrading programmes have emerged from local government in Durban and Cape Town, the main challenge having been how to draw resources from the capital subsidy system). In this context, the informal settlement question has not been politicised. A critical popular and intellectual consciousness of the flaws that underpin the market-oriented intervention framework has remained very weak.

8.4 Exposing the market-oriented paradigm in South Africa

The comparison with Brazil, in relation to international thinking, has then allowed me to associate the shortcomings in the South African informal settlement intervention framework, and the intellectual stagnation around this framework, with a particular market-oriented paradigm. This contrasts with the progressive paradigm of the pragmatic Brazilian left, which has pioneered democratic informal settlement intervention in close alliance with the favela movement. While the democratic approaches to informal settlement intervention practised in the PT municipalities in Brazil may have relevance to other contexts, the argument throughout this study is not for the direct transfer of more appropriate intervention approaches from Brazil to South Africa. The comparison between the two countries has revealed that not all aspects of the favela situation in Brazil have direct parallels to South Africa. Brazilian solutions are therefore not necessarily relevant to the South African informal settlement situation.

The question of tenure, as compared in this study, illustrates this divergence. In Brazil, the continuous displacement of favelas through processes of land speculation has triggered a popular demand for freehold title to the occupied land. As a result, progressive municipalities have taken on the legal challenge of delivering freehold title in favelas. In South Africa, the delivery of freehold title to informal settlement residents is not the progressive equivalent to that in Brazil. In contrast to the favela movement in Brazil, the civic movement in South Africa promoted a communal and de-commodified relationship to urban land, thereby responding to the realities of urban poverty and exclusion as they were being experienced in South African urban areas. Policy in South Africa did not respond to this approach, instead imposing freehold title within a neo-liberal or market-oriented paradigm. My examination of South African literature on informal settlements has confirmed that this neo-liberal drive for freehold title is underpinned by flawed arguments. Yet, the market-oriented framework remained largely unchallenged throughout the first decade of democracy in South Africa.

The argument in this book is for a significant paradigm shift in South Africa that would allow the development of progressive approaches to informal settlement intervention that respond, not primarily to business interests (as has been the case), but to informed and reflected demands from the informal settlement population and its organised initiatives.

8.5 Prospects for a paradigm shift in South Africa

What does the comparison with Brazil tell us about the prospects for such a real paradigm shift in South Africa? This book has compared the processes of gradual democratisation in Brazil and South Africa since the mid-1970s. Here a divergence between the two countries became evident at various levels. In Brazil, the socio-political conditions for a shift towards more responsive and democratic informal settlement intervention existed. Social movements such as those representing the favela population were articulating demands for favela legalisation and upgrading, and for a voice in urban policy-making. This position was consistently supported by the pragmatic intellectual left and politically promoted by the PT. A broad-based movement for urban reform then advanced this position. The challenge to exclusionary policies was successful, in part through the adoption of constitutional amendments and in part through democratic institutional mechanisms in those municipalities that are governed by the PT. More recently these have been incorporated into federal policy and are extended and given support by the newly elected PT government. As mentioned above, political contestation at local government level in Brazil requires ongoing conscientisation and politicisation around questions such as favela intervention. From this conscientised position, the Brazilian movement for urban reform has then also been able to critically engage with, and actively contribute to, the international debates on urban poverty.

In South Africa, the socio-political conditions for a challenge to unresponsive intervention did not exist. The closest equivalent in South Africa of the favela movement in Brazil was the civic movement, though representing not specifically the informal settlement population, but the African (black) urban population at large. As mentioned above, this movement articulated a development position of its own, based on the decommodification of land and other basic needs commodities. While extending this approach to informal settlements, thus eradicating the practice of tenancy, the civic movement was prevented from further articulating this development concept. Throughout most of the 1980s, the political struggle centred around the need to secure democratic non-racial government. Therefore, the primary focus of the civic movement was to protest against the imposition of illegitimate local government structures in urban townships. In response, the movement was violently repressed by the state. At the same time, the influential business-funded Urban Foundation was developing a market-oriented position on informal settlement intervention. In 1990, it published a benchmark proposal for a national housing policy in South Africa, articulating a market-oriented position on housing and informal settlement intervention. Policy-making in the early 1990s, in which both the fragile civic movement and the powerful Urban Foundation were represented, was then dominated by the market-oriented positions of the latter. The central ideas put forward by the Urban Foundation in the early 1990s were incorporated into the national housing policy after the 1994 elections. Through this policy, the once-off household-based capital subsidy has channelled housing intervention, be it on a greenfield site or in informal settlements, into the standardised delivery of plots with freehold title, on-site access to services and a minimal house.

In this study I have found that this intervention framework in itself was not likely to be challenged by its beneficiaries, as it promised an individual household-based asset in the form of a house. Thus, collective community-based strategies have tended to cooperate with the official framework, even if in disagreement with the imposed standards and procedures. While the South African literature has pointed to the insensitivity of the market-oriented intervention framework to the diverse reality of the urban poor, there has been no coordinated intellectual challenge to the Urban Foundation-inspired approach. Indeed, the intellectual left in South Africa has not rigorously and pragmatically engaged with the question of informal settlement intervention. Nor has it actively participated in the international debates on urban poverty. My sobering conclusion, therefore, was that the conditions have barely existed in South Africa for a paradigm shift towards more responsive informal settlement intervention driven from within society or by social movements, as has occurred in Brazil.

It must be noted that in the absence of policy guidance from national government for the first ten years after 1994, local governments in South Africa, particularly Durban and Cape Town in 2003, have begun looking to Brazil for inspiration. Past delegations to São Paulo (during the conservative term from 1992 to 2000) were shown the conservative Singapura Programme, which selected highly visible favelas for demolition and constructed blocks of flats in their place. However, in 2003, South African delegations to Brazil, whether visiting federal government in Brasilia or the municipality of São Paulo, were more likely to be received by progressive PT officials who speak about their engagement with social movements and their efforts at building citizenship and social inclusion through participatory governance. While these efforts to learn from Brazil may stimulate new thinking in South Africa, a deeper analysis needs to underpin a paradigm shift. This book hopes to make a contribution to this effect. This book goes to press following the subsequent announcement by the new Minister of Housing that a special policy mechanism will be introduced to enable the upgrading of informal settlements. The appropriate interpretation and implementation of this new policy, and its continuous refinement through 'learning by doing' will remain an ongoing challenge.

8.6 Challenges for South Africa

What concrete suggestions can this study then put forward for the shift to a more appropriate informal settlement intervention in South Africa? No doubt, the stagnation and distortion in South African practice must be redressed. Exposure to analyses of progressive practice such as that backed by the PT in Brazil, as well as to international debates on urban poverty, will increase awareness in South Africa of the distorted nature of the intervention framework of the past ten years. Such exposure should stimulate, not the direct transfer of approaches from abroad, but the search for appropriate means of intervention in South Africa.

However, the current intervention approach in South Africa has been entrenched through a rigorous framework, upon which local governments and practitioners have shaped their operations, and within which consultants and even development NGOs have found a secure niche. A substantial shift is therefore not likely to occur within these sectors of society. It may be noted that alternatives began to be explored in the area of tenure, with scholars searching for options to the imposition of freehold titles. However, the promotion of freehold title by the Urban Foundation is situated within a broader paradigm. It has promoted the product-oriented treatment of informal settlement intervention as a form of housing delivery, dismissed a role for community organisation in favour of a top-down engagement with the individual beneficiary, and primarily promoted stakes for the private sector, both in project implementation and through consumerism, encouraged through individualisation and commodification. This paradigm must be challenged as a whole.

For a true departure from the Urban Foundation inspired paradigm, a critical level of popular, intellectual and political consensus will be needed on the inappropriateness of its neo-liberal underpinnings to the reality of urban poverty as manifested in informal settlements. Only then may grant funded programmes in informal settlements in South Africa move away from the product-oriented nature of the once-off capital subsidy to the provision of support through flexible longer term support. Government subsidisation of informal settlement improvement should be designed for maximum impact in the form of direct poverty alleviation, and not as a means of building the urban economy by providing opportunities for the profit-making sector. With this orientation, unauthorised settlement improvement and consolidation through permanent building of houses, shops and social facilities should be encouraged, rather than the perpetuation of a transitional existence until the formal imposition of an individualised and standardised model of residential development. Such an orientation must likewise trust the poor in understanding their own situation, allowing the identification of improvement projects by community-based organisations themselves. It should then allow the release of government subsidisation for such projects, and their management and implementation by community groups. Ultimately, it should acknowledge the existence of community-based strategies for the upliftment of living conditions in informal settlements. These should be taken seriously, affording them space, rather than moulding them according to the role assigned to community organisation by the profit-making sector.

How then will a change in mindset and orientation be achieved in South Africa? I have argued that increased exposure among South African development professionals to progressive international insights, such as those gained through the debates and enquiries on urban poverty, might build professional awareness of the need for change. However, a coordinated shift from within this sector is unlikely to occur. The demand for alternative intervention might well have to be made from informal settlement residents themselves. In this regard, progressive long-term support for community organisations is required. Such support should encourage community groups to associate democracy with the right to demand government intervention which responds to the diverse dimensions of poverty as experienced in informal settlements, rather than the right to be at the receiving end of government delivery of a standardised product. Funding support for such a conscientisation might not be mobilised within South Africa. Here progressive international initiatives may have an important role to play in enabling the question of informal settlement intervention to enter popular and political debates. I have indicated in my introduction to this book that engagement with the Brazilian PT already exists in the civic and trade union movements in South African society. It is also emerging within the Homeless People's Federation, through the expansion of Slum Dwellers International (an international umbrella body for homeless people's movements) into Latin America. It is in this area, then, that a conscientisation of the way the informal settlement situation is treated within the framework of the PT may contribute to building critical demand from below.

In this book I have identified various gaps in our understanding of the informal settlement situation in South Africa. Many of these gaps would be addressed by conventional surveys gathering quantifiable data in areas hitherto ignored. However, I would argue that the fundamental intellectual challenge with regards to informal settlement intervention in South Africa lies not in filling these gaps, but in furthering a change of paradigm in our treatment of the informal settlement question. This requires an intellectual engagement with the current contours of social exclusion, including those created by the intervention paradigm of the past decade, and with the thinking of those collective initiatives within informal settlements that are committed to struggle for greater inclusion. It is in the relationship between intellectuals, progressive individuals based within government departments, and community-based organisations or social movements, that an analysis of four decades of Brazilian experience is of relevance to the struggle against exclusion and the search for more appropriate informal settlement intervention in South Africa.

References

Abbas, A. 1998. 'Down the drain'. In Anzorena, E. (ed.), *SELAVIP Newsletter, Journal of Low-Income Housing in Asia and the World*, April:109–18.

Abbott, J. 1996. *Sharing the City: Community Participation in Urban Management.* Earthscan, London.

Abbott, J. 2002a. 'A method-based planning framework for informal settlement upgrading'. *Habitat International*, 26(3):317–33.

Abbott, J. 2002b. 'An analysis of informal settlement upgrading and critique of existing methodological approaches'. *Habitat International*, 26(3):303–15.

Abbott, J. and Douglas, D. 1999. *Trends in Informal Settlement in the Cape Metropolitan Area.* Report prepared by the Urban GIS Group, Department of Civil Engineering, University of Cape Town, for the Directorate of Planning, Environment and Housing, Cape Metropolitan Council, Cape Town.

Abbott, J., Huchzermeyer, M. and Martinez, I. 1997. 'Methodologies for integrating GIS with social processes: the need for appropriate informal settlement intervention'. Paper presented at the *iKUSASA/CONSAS 97 international conference*, Durban, South Africa, 25 to 28 August 1997.

Abbott, J., Martinez, I. and Huchzermeyer, M. 2001. *An Analysis of Informal Settlements and Applicability of Visual Settlement Planning (ViSP) in South Africa.* WRC Report No. 786/1/01, Water Research Commission, Pretoria.

Abers, R. 1996. 'From ideas to practice: the Partido dos Trabalhadores and participatory governance in Brazil'. *Latin American Perspectives*, 91, 23(4):35–53.

Abers, R. 1998. 'Learning from democratic practice: distributing government resources through popular participation in Porto Alegre, Brazil'. In Douglass, M. and Friedmann, J. (eds.). *Cities for Citizens. Planning and the Rise of Civil Society in a Global Age.* John Wiley and Sons, Chichester, pp. 39–65.

Abrams, C. 1966. *Squatter Settlements, the Problem and the Opportunity.* Department of Housing and Urban Development, Washington DC.

Adler, J. 1994. 'Life in an informal settlement'. *Urban Forum*, 5(2):99–110.

Adler, T. and Oelofse, M. 1996. 'The housing subsidy scheme'. In Rust, K. and Rubenstein, S. (eds.). *A Mandate to Build*. Ravan Press, Johannesburg, pp. 109–37.

Afonso, M. and Azevedo, S. 1987. 'Cidade, poder público e movimento de favelados' (City, public authority and movement of favela residents). In Popemayer, M. (ed.). *Movimentos Sociais em Minas Gerais: Emergência e Perspectivas* (Social Movements in Minas Gerais: Emergence and Perspectives). Editoria UFMG (Universidade Federal de Minas Gerais), Belo Horizonte, pp. 109–39.

African National Congress. 1994. *Reconstruction and Development Programme: A Policy Framework*. African National Congress, Johannesburg.

Alsayyad, N. 1993. 'Squatting and culture: a comparative analysis of informal development in Latin America and the Middle East'. *Habitat International*, 17(1):33–44.

Alves, M. 1989. 'Interclass alliances in the opposition to the military in Brazil: consequences for the transition period'. In Eckstein, S. (ed.). *Power and popular Protest. Latin American Social Movements*. University of California Press, London, pp. 278–98.

Ambert, C. 2002. 'Privatising displaced urbanisation in Greater Nelspruit'. In Durand-Lasserve, A. and Royston, L. (eds.). *Holding their Ground: Secure Land Tenure for the Urban Poor in Developing Countries*. Earthscan, London, pp. 209–17.

Amis, P. 1984. 'Squatters or tenants: the commercialisation of unauthorised housing in Nairobi'. *World Development*, 121(1):87–96.

Amis, P. 1989. 'Key themes in contemporary African urbanisation'. In Amis, P. and Lloyd, P. (eds.). *Housing Africa's Urban Poor*. Manchester University Press, Manchester, pp. 2–31.

Amis, P. 1995. 'Making sense of urban poverty'. *Environment and Urbanisation*, 7(1):145–56.

Amis, P. 1996. 'Long-run trends in Nairobi's informal housing market'. *Third World Planning Review*, 18(3):271–85.

Anderson, A. and Pillay, G. 1997. 'The segregated spirit: The Pentecostals'. In Elphick, R. and Davenport, R. (eds.). *Christianity in South Africa: A Political, Social and Cultural History*. James Currey, Oxford, pp. 227–41.

Anzorena, J., Bolnick, J., Boonyabancha, S., Cabannes, Y., Hardoy, A., Hasan, A., Levy, C., Mitlin, D., Murphy, D., Patel, S., Saborido, M., Satterthwaite, D. and Stein, A. 1998. 'Reducing urban poverty; some lessons from experience'. *Environment and Urbanisation*, 10(1):167–86.

Ardington, E. 1992. *Buckpassing in Canaan: An Example of Authorities' Failure to Address the Needs of Informal Urban Dwellers*. Rural Urban Studies Working Paper no. 24, Centre for Social and Development Studies, University of Natal, Durban.

Arrigone, J. 1987. 'Low-cost housing in Latin America – models for South Africa'. *Unisa Latin American Report*, 3(1):4–19.

Arrigone, J. 1996. 'People's participation in low-income housing in Latin America: relevance to South Africa'. *Unisa Latin American Report*, 12(1):4–18.

Assies, W. 1993. 'Urban social movements and local democracy in Brazil'. *European Review of Latin American and Caribbean Studies*, 55:39–58.

Asthana, S. 1994. 'Integrated Slum Improvement in Visakhapatnam, India: problems and prospects'. *Habitat International*, 18(1):57–70.

Aubertin, C. 1992. 'Le droit au logement: enjeu démocratique ou instrument du clientélisme? L'example de Brasília – District fédéral' (The right to housing: democratic stakes or instrument of clientelism? The example of Brasilia – Federal District). *Cahiers des Sciences Humaines*, 28(3):461–79.

Awotona, A., Japha, D., Prinsloo, I., Le Grange, L., Huchzermeyer, M., Boberg, D. and Briggs, M. 1995. *Townships in Cape Town: Case Study Area Profiles*. The Integration and Urbanisation of Existing Townships in the Republic of South Africa – Working Paper No. 9, the Centre for Architectural Research and Development Overseas

(CARDO), University of Newcastle upon Tyne, UK, and the School of Architecture and Planning, University of Cape Town, South Africa.

Awotona, A., Huchzermeyer, M., Boberg, D., Japha, D., Le Grange, L., Prinsloo, I. and Higdon, D. 1996. *Townships in Cape Town: A Pilot Study of Nyanga, New Crossroads and KTC.* The Integration and Urbanisation of Existing Townships in the Republic of South Africa – Working Paper No.12, ODA Research Scheme Number R6266, Centre for Architectural Research and Development Overseas (CARDO), University of Newcastle upon Tyne, UK, and School of Architecture and Planning, University of Cape Town, South Africa.

Awotona, A., Higdon, D. and Huchzermeyer, M. 1997. *Nyanga Township: A Case Study of its People, Living Environment and Development Potentials.* The Integration and Urbanisation of Existing Townships in the Republic of South Africa – Working Paper No. 13, ODA Research Scheme Number R6266, Centre for Architectural Research and Development Overseas (CARDO), University of Newcastle upon Tyne, UK, and School of Architecture and Planning, University of Cape Town, South Africa.

Azevedo, S., 1998. 'Law and the future of urban management in the Third World metropolis'. In Fernandes, E. and Varley, A. (eds.). 1998. *Illegal Cities: Law and Urban Change in Developing Countries.* Zed Books, London and New York, pp. 258–73.

Badiane, A. 2003. 'From Habitat 1996 towards the World Urban Forum and the Millenium Development Goals: an African perspective'. Paper presented at the Gauteng Provincial Department of Housing conference *Urbanisation and Housing Challenges: Cities in Africa*, Johannesburg, 6 to 8 October 2003.

Baken, R. and van der Linden, J. 1993. '"Getting the incentives right": Banking on the formal private sector – a critique of current World Bank thinking on low-income housing delivery in Third World cities'. *Third World Planning Review*, 15(1):1–22.

Banck, G. and Doimo, A. 1988. 'Between utopia and strategy: a case study of a Brazilian urban social movement'. In Banck, G. and Koonings, K. (eds.). *Change in Contemporary Brazil.* CEDLA (Centre for Latin American Research and Documentation), Amsterdam., pp. 71–87.

Barbosa, R., Cabannes, Y. and Morães, L. 1997. '"Tenant today, *posseiro* tomorrow"'. *Environment and Urbanisation*, 9(2):17–41.

Barry, M., 1995. 'Conceptual design of a communal land registration system for South Africa'. *South African Journal of Surveying and Mapping*, 23(3):153–62.

Barry, M. 1998. 'Secure land tenure for informal settlement communities: the effectiveness of the cadastral system in Cape Town'. In Barry, M. (compiler). *Proceedings of the International Conference on Land Tenure in the Developing World, with a Focus on Southern Africa*, University of Cape Town, Cape Town, 27 to 29 January 1998.

Baumann, T. and Bolnick, J. 2001. 'Out of the frying pan into the fire: the limits of loan finance in a capital subsidy context'. *Environment and Urbanisation*, 13(2):103–15.

Beall, J. 1993. 'The Gender Dimensions of Urbanisation and Urban Poverty'. Development Planning Unit, University College London, Paper prepared for the Division for the Advancement of Women, United Nations Office at Vienna, *Seminar on Women in Urban Areas*, Vienna, 8 to 12 November 1993.

Beall, J., Crankshaw, O. and Parnell, S. 2002. 'Participatory Planning and Informal Settlement Upgrading in Diepsloot'. In Beall, J., Crankshaw, O. and Parnell, S.

(eds.). *Uniting a Divided City: Governance and Social Exclusion in Johannesburg.* Earthscan, London, pp. 129–50.

Beavon, K. 1992. 'The post-apartheid city: hopes, possibilities, and harsh realities'. In Smith, D. (ed.). *The Apartheid City and Beyond: Urbanisation and Social Change in South Africa.* Routledge/Witwatersrand University Press, Johannesburg, pp. 231–42.

Bénit, C. 2002. 'Rise and fall of the "community"? Post-apartheid housing policy in Diepsloot, Johannesburg'. *Urban Forum,* 13(2):47–66.

Berrisford, S. 1998. 'Law and urban change in the new South Africa'. In Fernandes, E. and Varley, A. (eds.). *Illegal Cities. Law and Urban Change in Developing Countries.* Zed Books, London, pp. 213–29.

BESG (Built Environment Support Group). 1998. *Assisted Mutual Help Housing Delivery in South Africa.* Report prepared by BESG for the Urban Sector Network.

Black Sash. 1989. *Nearly an A – Z Guide to Homelessness on the Witwatersrand.* Report compiled by the Black Sash Transvaal Region Urban Removals and Homelessness Group and Community Research and Information Network. Black Sash, Johannesburg.

Bolaffi, G. 1992. 'Urban planning in Brazil: past experience, current trends'. *Habitat International,* 16(2):99–111.

Bolnick, J. 1993. 'The People's Dialogue on Land and Shelter: community-driven networking in South Africa's informal settlements'. *Environment and Urbanisation,* 5(1):91–110.

Bolnick, J. 1996. 'uTshani Buyakhuluma (The grass speaks): People's Dialogue and the South African Homeless People's Federation (1994–6)'. *Environment and Urbanisation,* 8(2):153–70.

Bond, P. 1995. 'Urban social movements, the housing question and development discourse in South Africa'. In Moore, D. and Schmitz, G. (eds.). *Debating Development Discourses: International and Popular Perspectives.* Macmillan, Basingstoke and St Martin's Press, New York, pp. 149–77.

Bond, P. 1997. 'The housing question revisited. "Blacks like shacks", say SA's corporate liberal intelligentsia.' *Debate,* 3:98–117.

Bond, P. 2000. *Elite Transition: From Apartheid to Neoliberalism in South Africa.* Pluto Press, London.

Bond, P. and Mayekiso, M. 1998. 'Urban betrayal. The ANC in the townships'. *Southern African Report,* August, 4–8.

Bonduki, N. (ed.), 1993. '*Arquitetura & Habitação Social em São Paulo 1989–1992*' (Architecture and social housing in São Paulo 1989–1992), II Bienal International de Arquitetura de São Paulo, IAB – Instituto dos Arquitetos do Brazil/Fundação Bienal de São Paulo.

Bonduki, N. 1994. 'The housing crisis in the postwar years'. In Kowarick, L. (ed.). *Social Struggles and the City. The Case of São Paulo.* Monthly Review Press, New York, pp. 94–120.

Bonduki, N. (ed.). 1996. *Habitat: As Prácticas Bem-sucedidas em Habitação, Meio Ambiente e Gestão Urbana nas Cidades Brasileiras* (Habitat: The Best Practices in Habitation, Environment and Urban Management in the Brazilian Cities). Studio Nobel, São Paulo.

Bonner, P. 1990. 'The politics of black squatter movements on the Rand, 1944–1952'. *Radical History Review,* 46(7):89–115.

Boraine, A. 1988. '*Wham, Sham or Scam? – Security Management, Upgrading and Resistance in a South African Township*'. Paper presented at the Centre for African Studies, University of Cape Town, Cape Town.

Botes, L., Stewart, T. and Wessels, J. 1996. 'Conflict in development: Lessons from the housing initiatives in Freedom Square and Namibia Square'. *Development Southern Africa*, 13(3):453–67.

Bremner, L. 1994. 'Development and resistance: the lessons for the planners of Phola Park'. *Urban Forum*, 5(1):23–44.

Bretas, P. 1996. 'Participative budgeting in Belo Horizonte: democratization and citizenship'. *Environment and Urbanisation*, 8(1):213–22.

Buchanan, C. 1994. 'The government stance. The process of 'incrementalism' to solve the crisis'. *Planning*, 135: 74–5.

Budlender, G. 1990. 'Urban land issues in the 1980s: The view from Weiler's Farm'. In Murray, C. and O'Regan, C. (eds.). *No Place to Rest. Forced Removals and the Law in South Africa.* Oxford University Press, Oxford, pp. 68–85.

Burgess, J. 1977. 'Self-help housing: a new imperialist plot? A critique of the Turner School'. *Antipode*, 9(2):50–9.

Burgess, R. 1978. 'Petty commodity housing or dweller control? A critique of John Turner's views on housing policy'. *World Development*, 6:1105–33.

Burgess, R. 1982a. 'Self-help housing advocacy: a curious form of radicalism. A critique of the work of John F. C. Turner'. In Ward, P. (ed.). *Self-Help Housing. A Critique.* Mansell, Alexandrine Press, Oxford, pp. 55–97.

Burgess, R. 1982b. 'The politics of urban residence in Latin America'. *International Journal of Urban and Regional Research*, 6(4):465–80.

Burgess, R. 1985. 'The limits of State self-help housing programmes'. *Development and Change*, 16:271–312.

Burgess, R., Carmona, M. and Kolstee, T. (eds.). 1997. *The Challenge of Sustainable Cities. Neoliberalism and Urban Strategies in Developing Countries.* Zed Books, London.

Burns, E. 1970. *A History of Brazil.* Columbia University Press, New York and London.

Cabannes, Y. 1995a. 'Alternative municipal finance for home improvements in Brazil'. *Trialog*, 47:12–19.

Cabannes, Y. 1995b. 'Community-based housing finance. A step ahead ... who knows the direction? Lessons and limits learned from the experience'. *Trialog*, 47:54–8.

Cabannes, Y. 1997. 'From community development to housing finance: from *Mutiroes to Casa Melhor* in Fortaleza, Brazil'. *Environment and Urbanisation*, 9(1):31–58.

Cameron, R. 1996. 'The democratisation of South African local government'. *Local Government Studies*, 22(1):19–39.

Carneiro, S. 1996. 'The myth of racial democracy'. In Friedman, S. and Villiers, R. (eds.). *Comparing Brazil and South Africa. Two Transitional States in Political and Economic Perspective.* Centre for Policy Studies (CPS), Johannesburg, Foundation for Global Dialogue (FGD), Johannesburg, Instituto de Estudos Econômicos, Sociais e Políticos de São Paulo (Idesp.), São Paulo, pp. 176–91.

Castells, M. 1972. *The Urban Question: A Marxist Approach.* Edward Arnold, London.

Cearah Periferia. 1995. 'Well trained citizens exhibit higher participation in local affairs. A popular research and urban planning course'. *Trialog*, 46:30–3.

Chambers, R. 1995. 'Poverty and livelihoods: whose reality counts?' *Environment and Urbanisation*, 7(1):173–204.

Chipkin, I. 1997. 'Introduction'. In Chipkin, I. (ed.). *A Development Role for Local Government*, Centre for Policy Studies (CPS) Governance Programme, research commissioned by the Department of Constitutional Development for the Working Committee and the White Paper Political Committee, Pretoria, pp. 5–24.

Chossudovsky, M. 1997. *The Globalisation of Poverty: Impacts of the IMF and World Bank Reforms*. Zed Books, London.

Cities Alliance. 2002. *Cities Alliance/Cities without Slums*. http://www.citiesalliance.org.

Cohen, M. and Leitman, J. 1994. 'Will the World Bank's real "New Urban Policy" please stand up? Comment on 'The World Bank's "New" Urban Management Programme: paradigm shift or policy continuity?' by Gareth A. Jones and Peter M. Ward'. *Habitat International*, 18(4):117–26.

Cole, J. 1986. *Crossroads: The Politics of Reform and Repression 1976–86*. Ravan Press, Johannesburg.

Cole, J. 1989. 'State policies and urban struggles in the 1980s: a Western Cape perspective', Local Government and Planning Commission, Centre for Development Studies, University of the Western Cape, Cape Town. Paper prepared for the *Local Government and Planning Conference*, Harare, November 1989.

Cook, G. 1991. 'Cape Town'. In Lemon, A. (ed.). *Homes Apart: South Africa's Segregated Cities*. Indiana University Press, Bloomington, pp. 26–42.

Cooper, C., Shindler, J., McCaul, C., Brouard, P., Mareka, C., Seimon, J., Markovitz, M., Mashabela, H. and Pickard-Cambridge, C. 1987. *Race Relations Survey 1986 Part 1*. South African Institute of Race Relations, Johannesburg.

Corsalette, C and Lopes, M. 2001. 'PT diz que BID reprova o Projeito Cingapura' (Workers Party says that the Interamerican Development Bank disapproves of the Cingapura Programme), *O Estado de São Paulo*, 5 January, p.C2.

Crankshaw, O. 1993. 'Squatting, apartheid and urbanisation on the Southern Witwatersrand'. *African Affairs*, 92:31–51.

Crankshaw, O. 1996. 'Social differentiation, conflict and development in a South African township'. *Urban Forum*, 7(1):53–67.

Crankshaw, O. 1997. *Race, Class and the Changing Division of Labour under Apartheid*. LSE/Routledge, London.

Cross, C. 1994. 'Shack tenure in Durban'. In Hindson, D. and McCarthy, J. (eds.). *Here to Stay: Informal Settlements in KwaZulu-Natal*. Indicator Press, CSDS, University of Natal, Durban, pp. 177–90.

Cross, C. 1995. 'Shack tenure in the Durban area'. In Hemson, C. (compiler). *Land Use and Land Administration in the New South Africa*. Proceedings of a Winter School held at the University of Natal, Durban, July 1994, pp. 29–39.

Cross, C. 2002. 'Why the urban poor cannot secure tenure: South African tenure policy under pressure'. In Durand-Lasserve, A. and Royston, L. (eds.). *Holding their Ground: Secure Land Tenure for the Urban Poor in Developing Countries*. Earthscan, London, pp. 195–208.

Cross, C., Bekker, S. and Clark, C. 1994. 'Migration into DFR informal settlements: an overview of trends'. In Hindson, D. and McCarthy, J. (eds.). *Here to Stay: Informal*

Settlements in KwaZulu-Natal. Indicator Press, CSDS, University of Natal, Durban, pp. 83–98.

CSIR. 1999. *The State of Human Settlements South Africa, 1994–1998.* Report prepared by the CSIR for the Department of Housing, Pretoria.

DAG (Development Action Group). 1996. *Development Action Group, 1986–1996.* DAG, Cape Town.

Davenport, R. 1991. 'Historical background of the apartheid city to 1948'. In Swilling, M., Humphries, R. and Shubane, K. (eds.). *Apartheid City in Transition.* Oxford University Press, Cape Town, pp. 1–8.

Davies, R. 1991. 'Durban'. In Lemon, A. (ed.). *Homes Apart: South Africa's Segregated Cities.* Indiana University Press, Bloomington.

Davies, C. 1998. 'Land management in an informal settlement in East London'. Unpublished masters dissertation, Department of Surveying and Mapping, University of Natal, Durban.

Davies, C. and Fourie, C. 1998. 'A land management approach for informal settlement in South Africa'. *South African Journal of Surveying and Mapping,* 24 (5,6):239–46.

Davies, C. and Fourie, C. 2002. 'A land management approach for informal settlement in South Africa'. In Durand-Lasserve, A. and Royston, L. (eds.). *Holding their Ground: Secure Land Tenure for the Urban Poor in Developing Countries.* Earthscan, London, pp. 218–30.

De Grazia, G. 2002. 'Estatuto de Cidade: uma longa história com vitória e derrotas' (City Statute: a long history of victory and defeat). In Osorio, L. (ed.), *Estatuto da Cidade e Reforma Urbana: Novas Perspectivas para as Cidades Brasileiras* (City Statute and Urban Reform: New Perspectives for Brazilian Cities). Sergio Antonio Fabris Editor, Porto Alegre, pp. 15–37.

De Vos, P. 2001. 'Grootboom, the right to access to housing and substantive equality as contextual fairness'. *South African Journal on Human Rights,* 17(2):258–76.

Denaldi, R. 1995. 'Local government and community participation in Diadema'. *Trialog,* 44:26–9.

Denaldi, R. 1997. 'Viable self-management: the FUNACOM Housing Programme of the São Paulo municipality'. *Habitat International,* 21(2):213–27.

Denaldi, R., Bagnariolli, I. and Klink, J. 1997. 'Constructing an alternative housing policy at the local level. The case of Diadema, Greater São Paulo'. *Open House International,* 22(3):43–50.

Department of Constitutional Development and Planning. 1986. *White Paper on Urbanisation.* Department of Constitutional Development and Planning, Pretoria.

Department of Development Planning and Environment. 1995. 'Memorandum: Weiler's Farm Informal Settlement,' File Number GO 15/3/2–406. Department of Development Planning and Environment, Pretoria.

Department of Housing. 1994. 'White Paper on Housing. A new housing policy and strategy for South Africa,' *Government Gazette,* 354(16178), Notice 1376 of 1994, 23 December. Government Printer, Pretoria.

Department of Housing. 1995. *Implementation Manual. Housing Subsidy Scheme and other Housing Assistance Measures.* Department of Housing – Housing the Nation, Pretoria.

Department of Housing. 1997. *Urban Development Framework*. Department of Housing, Pretoria.

Desai, A. and Habib, A. 1994. 'Social movements in transitional societies: a case study of the Congress of South African Trade Unions'. *South African Sociological Review*, 6(2):86–8.

Development Works. 1998. 'Draft Report: Tenure Security in Urban South Africa,' report by development consultancy Development Works, Johannesburg, for IFAS (French Institute of South Africa).

Dewar, D. and Wolmarans, P. 1994. 'Responsive environments: a spatial analysis of five squatter settlements in the Western Cape'. Unpublished manuscript, School of Architecture and Planning, University of Cape Town, Cape Town.

Diaz, V. 1992. 'Landslides in the squatter settlements of Caracas: towards a better understanding of causative factors'. *Environment and Urbanisation*, 4(2):80–9.

Diniz, E. 1988. 'The political transition in Brazil: prospects for democracy'. In Banck, G. and Koonings, K. (eds.). *Social Change in Contemporary Brazil.* CEDLA (Centre for Latin American Research and Documentation), Amsterdam, pp. 9–22.

Douglass, M. 1992. 'The political economy of urban poverty and environmental management in Asia: access, empowerment and community based alternatives'. *Environment and Urbanisation*, 4(2):9–32.

Douglass, M. and Friedmann, J. (eds.), 1998. *Cities for Citizens: Planning and the Rise of Civil Society in a Global Age*. John Wiley and Sons, Chichester.

Drakakis-Smith, D. 1996. 'Third World cities: sustainable urban development II – population, labour and poverty'. *Urban Studies*, 33(4–5):673–701.

Drummond, D. 1981. *Architectes des Favelas* (Architects of the Favelas). Bordas, Paris.

Durand-Lasserve, A. 1998. 'Law and urban change in developing countries: trends and issues'. In Fernandes, E. and Varley, A. (eds.). *Illegal Cities: Law and Urban Change in Developing Countries*. Zed Books, London and New York, pp. 71–103.

Durand-Lasserve, A. and Pajoni, R. 1995. 'Synthesis of case studies: a seminar introduction'. In INTERURBA Groupement de Recherche, *Cities in Developing Countries, Integration of Irregular Settlements: Current Questions in Asia and Latin America.* Practiques Urbaines, 12, January, pp. 13–27.

Durand-Lasserve, A. and Royston, L. (eds.), 2002. *Holding their Ground: Secure Land Tenure for the Urban Poor in Developing Countries*. Earthscan, London.

Durand-Lasserve, A. and Tribillon, J. 1995. 'Synthesis of main findings', Abidjan Seminar – English draft manuscript of: Durand-Lasserve, A. and Tribillon, J. 'Une invitation au debat'. In 'Gestion foncfonciere urbaine, politiques de regularisation et developpement local en Afrique et dans les etats arabes,' Conclusions de l'etude et du seminaire, Abidjan, 21–24 March, 1995, CNUEH-Habitat, GTZ, UNCHS(Habitat), Serie gestion Fonciere No.5, Nairobi, pp. 14–34.

Ellis, G., Hendrie, D., Kooy, A. and Maree, J. 1977. *The Squatter Problem in the Western Cape, Some Cases and Remedies*. South African Institute of Race Relations, Johannesburg.

Emmett, T. 1992. 'Perceptions and conflicts associated with squatting'. In Emmett, T. (ed.). *Squatting in the Hottentots Holland Basin: Perspectives on a South African Social Issue*. Group: Social Dynamics, Human Sciences Research Council, Pretoria.

Environment and Urbanisation 1990. 'NGO Profile: SPARC: developing new NGO lines'. *Environment and Urbanisation*, 2(1):91–104.

Environment and Urbanisation 1995. 'NGO Profile: Orangi Pilot Project'. *Environment and Urbanisation*, 7(2):227–36.

Everatt, D., Rapholo, G., Davies, S., Adler, J., Mkhabela, I., Kholo, P. and Lengane, K. 1996. '*The South African Experience: Analysing Local-Level Governance in Tladi-Moletsane, Ivory Park and the Johannesburg Inner City*'. Volunteer Action and Local Democracy: A Partnership for a Better Urban Future, researched by CASE and ICDA for UNRISD, paper presented at the UNRISD/UNV International Meeting, Turkey, May 1996.

Fadare, W. and Mills-Tettey, R. 1992. 'Squatter settlement in Port Harcourt'. *Habitat International*, 16(1):71–81.

Fast, H. 1995. 'Pondoks, Houses and Hostels: a History of Nyanga 1946–1970, with Special Focus on Housing'. Thesis presented for the Degree of Doctor of Philosophy in the Department of History, University of Cape Town, Cape Town.

Federação Nacional dos Arquitetos e Urbanistas. 1996. *More Human Settlements, Assentamentos mais Humanos*. Brazilian Conference for Habitat II, Federação Nacional dos Arquitetos e Urbanistas, Rio de Janeiro, 9–12 May 1996.

Fernandes, E. 1993. 'The regularisation of favelas in Brazil – the case of Belo Horizonte'. *Social and Legal Studies*, 2:211–36.

Fernandes, E. 1996. 'Participatory budget: a new experience of democratic administration in Belo Horizonte, Brazil'. *Report*, 11:23–4.

Fernandes, E. 1998. 'The legal regularisation of favelas in Brazil'. Paper presented at the Workshop *Comparative Policy Perspectives on Urban Land Market Reform in Latin America, Southern Africa and Eastern Europe*, promoted by the Lincoln Institute of Land Policy in Cambridge, MA, July 1998.

Fernandes, E. 2001. 'New statute aims to make Brazilian cities inclusive'. *Habitat Debate*, 7(4):19.

Fernandes, E. and Rolnik, R. 1998. 'Law and urban change in Brazil'. In Fernandes, E. and Varley, A. (eds.). *Illegal Cities: Law and Urban Change in Developing Countries*. Zed Books, London, pp. 140–56.

França, E. 2000. *Recuperacão Urbana e Ambiental no Munićpio de São Paulo* (Urban and Environmental Recuperation in São Paulo). Marcos Carriho Arquitetos, São Paulo.

Friedman, S. 1996. 'South Africa's pacted transition'. In Friedman S. and de Villiers, R. (eds.). *Comparing Brazil and South Africa. Two Transitional States in Political and Economical Perspective*. Centre for Policy Studies (CPS), Foundation for Global Dialogue (FGD), and Instituto de Estudos Econômicos, Sociais e Polı́ticos de São Paulo (Idesp.), Cape Town.

Friedmann, J. 1998. 'The new political economy of planning: the rise of civil society'. In Douglass, M. and Friedmann, J. (eds.). *Cities for Citizens. Planning and the Rise of Civil Society in a Global Age*. John Wiley and Sons, Chichester, pp. 19–35.

Gardener, D. 1992. 'Planning the interface: approaches and mechanisms aimed at avoiding, resolving or minimising conflicts between residents of formal suburbs and new low-income settlements'. Unpublished report, Housing Policy Unit, The Urban Foundation, Johannesburg.

Gauteng Provincial Government. 1996. *Proposal: Informal Settlement Upgrading Programme.* Department of Land Affairs and Housing, Gauteng Province, Johannesburg.

Gauteng Provincial Government. 1997. *Water and Sanitation in Informal Settlements, April 1997.* Report prepared by Urban Dynamics for the Community Based Projects Department, Rand Water, Pretoria.

Gauteng Provincial Government. 1998. 'Report on Weilers Farm'. Unpublished manuscript in Weiler's Farm project file, Department of Land Affairs and Housing, Pretoria.

Gigaba, M. and Maharaj, B. 1996. 'Land invasions during political transition: The Wiggins saga in Cato Manor'. *Development Southern Africa,* 13(2):217–35.

Gilbert, A. 1994. *The Latin American City.* Latin American Bureau, London.

Gilbert, A. and Gugler, J. 1992. *Cities, Poverty and Development: Urbanisation in the Third World.* Oxford University Press, Oxford.

Grose, R. 1979. *Squatting and the Geography of Class Conflict: Limits to Housing Autonomy in Jamaica.* Programme on International Studies in Planning, New York.

Guillaume, P. and Houssay-Holzschuch, M. 2002. 'Territorial strategies of South African informal dwellers'. *Urban Forum,* 13(2):86–101.

Haferburg, C. 2002. 'The Informal settlement Phola Park in the context of Cape Town's plans for socio-spatial integration'. *Urban Forum,* 13(2):26–46.

Hardoy, J., Cairncross, S. and Satterthwaite, D. (eds.). 1990. *The Poor Die Young: Housing and Health in Third World Cities.* Earthscan, London.

Hardoy, A. and Hardoy, J., with Schusterman, R. 1991. 'Building community organisation: the history of a squatter settlement and its own organisations in Buenos Aires'. *Environment and Urbanisation,* 3(2):104–20.

Hardoy, J. and Satterthwaite, D. 1989. *Squatter Citizen: Life in the Urban Third World.* Earthscan, London.

Harms, H. 1982. 'Historical perspectives on the practice and purpose of self-help housing'. In Ward, P. (ed.). *Self-Help Housing. A Critique.* Mansell, Oxford.

Harrison, P. 1992. 'The policies and politics of informal settlement in South Africa: A historical perspective'. *Africa Insight,* 22(1):14–22.

Hart, T. 1992. 'Informal housing in South Africa: an overview'. In Verloren van Themaat Centre, *South Africa in Transition: Urban and Rural Perspectives on Squatting and Informal Settlement in Environmental Context.* Environmental Law Division, University of South Africa, Pretoria, pp. 19–35.

Hasan, A. and Vaidya, C. 1986. 'Two approaches to the improvement of low-income urban areas – Madras and Orangi'. *Habitat International,* 10(3):225–34.

Hattingh, P. and Horn, A. 1991. 'Pretoria'. In Lemon, A. (ed.). *Homes Apart: South Africa's Segregated Cities.* Indiana University Press, Bloomington, pp. 146–61.

Henessy, K. and Smit, W. 1994. *Squatter Settlements in Metropolitan Cape Town: Their Current Condition and Proposals for Their Future.* Division of Transport Technology, CSIR, Stellenbosch.

Hindson, D., Byerley, M. and Morris, M. 1994. 'From violence to reconstruction: the making, disintegration and remaking of the apartheid city'. *Antipode,* 26(4):323–50.

Hindson, D. and McCarthy, J. 1994. 'Defining and gauging the problem'. In Hindson, D. and McCarthy J. (eds.). *Here to Stay: Informal Settlements in KwaZulu-Natal.* Indicator Press, CSDS, University of Natal, Durban, pp. 1–28.

Holistic Settlements. 1996. 'iSLP Projects with the jurisdiction of the Central Substructure: status – August 1996'. Holistic Settlements (Project Coordinator, iSLP), Cape Town.

Housing by People in Asia 1998. 'Karachi mega sewerage plan checked: people's practical solutions show up "think-big" scheme ...'. *Housing by People in Asia*, Newsletter of the Asian Coalition for Housing Rights, No. 11 (April):15.

Housing in Southern Africa. 1998. 'Innovative planning approach to large scale in-situ upgrading'. *Housing in Southern Africa*, June:26–37.

Houssay-Holzschuch, M. 1999. 'Cape Town after Apartheid'. *Newtown Zebra* (IFAS-Research Supplement), 13:11.

Howe, G. 1982. *Squatter Crisis*. Occasional Paper No. 3, Centre for Intergroup Studies, Cape Town.

Huchzermeyer, M. 1999a. 'The Exploration of Informal Settlement Intervention in South Africa: Contributions from a Comparison with Brazil'. PhD thesis, Department of Sociology, University of Cape Town.

Huchzermeyer, M. 1999b. 'Current informal settlement intervention in South Africa: Four case studies of people-driven initiatives'. Department of Sociology, University of Cape Town, and Division of Building Technology (Boutek), Council for Scientific and Industrial Research (CSIR), Pretoria.

Huchzermeyer, M. 2001. 'Housing for the poor? Negotiated housing policy in South Africa'. *Habitat International*, 25(3):303–31.

Huchzermeyer, M. 2002. 'Land invasions, evictions and the law in South Africa'. Paper presented at the *9th Law and Urban Space Workshop*, International Research Group on Law and Urban Space, Porto Alegre, 17 to 19 July 2002.

Huchzermeyer, M. 2003. 'Housing rights in South Africa: invasions, evictions, the media and the courts in the cases of Grootboom, Alexandra and Bredell'. *Urban Forum*, 14(1):80–107.

Imparato, E. 1998. 'A regularização fundiára na cidade de São Paulo – a problemática da Zona Leste' (Land regularisation in the city of São Paulo – the problematic of the Eastern Zone), authors' manuscript. CEPAR (Center for Studies, Research, Assessment and Consulting on Urban Reform and Citizenship), Sao Paulo.

Imparato, E. 2002. 'Security of tenure in São Paulo'. In Durand-Lasserve, A. and Royston, L. (eds.). *Holding their Ground: Secure Land Tenure for the Urban Poor in Developing Countries*. Earthscan, London, pp. 127–37.

Instituto Pólis. 2002. *The Statute of the City: New Tools for Assuring the Right to the City in Brazil*. Instituto Pólis, São Paulo.

Jere, H. 1984. 'Lusaka: local participation in planning and decision-making'. In Payne, G. (ed.). *Low-Income Housing in the Third World: The Role of Sites and Services and Settlement Upgrading*. John Wiley and Sons, New York, pp. 55–69.

Jones, G. and Datta, K. 2000. 'Enabling markets to work? Housing policy in the "New" South Africa'. *International Planning Studies*, 5(3):393–416.

Jones, G. and Ward, P. 1994. 'The World Bank's "New" Urban Management Programme: paradigm shift or policy continuity?' *Habitat International*, 18(3):33–51.

Jornal da Tarde. 2002. 'Síndicas do Cingapura: desafio de adminstrar minicidades'. *Jornal da Tarde*, 25 September 2002.

Keck, M. 1992. *The Workers' Party and democratization in Brazil.* Yale university Press, New Haven.

Kowarick, L. 1979. *A Espoliação Urbana* (The Urban Spoliation). Paz e Terra, Rio de Janeiro.

Kowarick, L. 1985. 'The pathways to encounter: reflections on the social struggle in São Paulo'. In Slater, D. (ed.). *New Social Movements and the State in Latin America.* CEDLA (Centre for Latin American Research Documentation), Amsterdam, pp. 73–93.

Kowarick, L. 1997. 'Spoliation urbaine, luttes sociales et citoyenneté de notre récente histoire, (Urban spoliation, social struggles and citizenship of our recent history)' in CAHIERS Internationaux, *La Recherche sur la Ville au Brésil: Actes des Journées Franco-Brésiliennes du PIR Villes*, Programme interdisciplinaire de recherche sur la ville. CNRS, Paris, pp. 71–83.

Kowarick, L. 2000. *Escritos Urbanos: Espoliacão & Lutas Sociais & Cidadania* (Urban Writings: Spoliation & Social Struggles & Citizenship). Editora 34, São Paulo.

Kowarick, L. and Ant, C. 1994. 'One hundred years of overcrowding: slum tenements in the city'. In Kowarick, L. (ed.). *Social Struggles and the City. The Case of São Paulo.* Monthly Review Press, New York, pp. 60–76.

Kowarick, L. and Bonduki, N. 1994. 'Urban space and political space: from populism to redemocratization'. In Kowarick, L. (ed.). *Social Struggles and the City. The Case of São Paulo.* Monthly Review Press, New York, pp. 121–47.

Kowarick, L. and Singer, P. 1994. 'The Workers' Party in São Paulo'. In Kowarick, L. (ed.). *Social Struggles and the City: The Case of São Paulo*'. Monthly Review Press, New York, pp. 225–56.

Krige, S. 1991. 'Bloemfontein'. In Lemon, A. (ed.). *Homes Apart: South Africa's Segregated Cities.* Indiana University Press, Bloomington.

Kuhn, J. 1999. 'Customary tenure in South Africa: the final frontier'. Paper presented at the Workshop *Tenure Security Policies in South African, Brazilian, Indian and Sub-Saharan African Cities: A Comparative Analysis.* Johannesburg, 27 to 28 July 1999, Institut Francais d'Afrique du Sud, Development Works, Johannesburg, Lincoln Institute of Land Policies, Cambridge MA, Department of Land Affairs, Pretoria, Centre National de la Recherche Scientifique, CNRS, Paris.

Lago, L. 1992. 'Política urbana e a questão habitacional: novas tendências face à crise econômica brasileira'. Cadernos IPPUR/UFRJ, VI(1):41–7.

Lalloo, K. 1999. 'Arenas of contested citizenship: housing policy in South Africa'. *Habitat International*, 23(1):35–47.

Lankatilleke, L. 1990. 'Community action planning: a case study from Sri Lanka'. *Trialog*, 23/24:24–7.

Lawrence, A. 1994. 'Structure, identity and comparison: the ANC and the PT: a reply to Desai and Habib'. *South African Sociological Review*, 6(2):89–100.

Lee, B. 1994. Comment on 'The World Bank's "New" Urban Management Programme: paradigm shift or policy continuity?' by Gareth A. Jones and Peter M. Ward. *Habitat International*, 18(4):139–44.

Legal Resources Centre. 2002. *Annual Report for the Period 1 April 2000 to 31 March 2001.* Legal Resources Centre and Legal Resources Trust, Johannesburg.

Lemon, A. and Cook, G. 1994. 'South Africa,' in Tarver, J. (ed.). *Urbanisation in Africa: A Handbook.* Greenwood Press, London, pp. 315–41

Leon, F. 2000. '14 Cingapuras estão em area irregular' (14 Cingapuras are in unregulated areas). *Folha de São Paulo*, 29 December 2000.

Lester, A., Nel, E. and Bins, T. 2000. *South Africa, Past, Present, and Future: Gold at the End of the Rainbow?* Pearson Education, London.

Lohnert, B. 1997. 'From shacks to houses. Urban development in Cape Town/South Africa: the case of Marconi Beam'. In Aguiliar, A. (ed.). *Proceedings of the IGU Commission Meeting on Urban Development and Urban Life*, Mexico City, Mexico, pp. 1–6.

Lohnert, B. 1998. 'Rural-urban migration and land tenure: three case studies from Cape Town, South Africa'. In Barry, M. (compiler). *Proceedings of the International Conference on Land Tenure in the Developing World, with a Focus on Southern Africa*, University of Cape Town, 27 to 29 January 1998, pp. 380–89.

Lohnert, B. 2003. *Vom Hüttendorf zur Eigenheimsiedlung: Selbsthilfe im städtischen Wohnungsbau. Ist Kapstadt das Modell für das Neue Südafrika?* (From Shantytown to Homeownership Settlement: Self-help in the Urban Housing Construction. Is Cape Town the Model for the New South Africa?). Universitätsverlag Rasch, Osnabrück (Germany).

Lohnert, B., Oldfield, S., and Parnell, S. 1998. 'Post-apartheid social polarisation: The creation of sub-urban identities in Cape Town'. *South African Geographical Journal*, 80(2):86–92.

Lubisch, O., Brown, R. and Hart, A. (coordinators). 1996. 'Brazilian Housing "Lessons for South Africa"', Observations made by the B TECH class of 1995, Architectural Technology, Applied Design, School of Architecture and Building, Cape Technicon, Cape Town.

Lumby, A. 1983. 'Industrial development prior to the Second World War'. In Coleman, F. (ed.). *Economic History of South Africa.* HAUM Education Publishers, Pretoria.

Mabin, A. 1991. 'Is this our future? Learning from Sao Paulo, Brazil'. *Urban Forum*, 2(1):81–7.

Mabin, A. 1992. 'Changing patters of urban expansion in South Africa: some lessons from Sao Paulo'. *Planning*, 120:109–14.

Mabin, A. 1993. 'Between Zevenfontein and Hilbrow: alternatives for South African urban planning'. *Town and Regional Planning*, 34:10–19.

Machado, E. and Cardoso, F. 1995. 'Favelas da maré: ambiente, mobilidade e condição feminina na beira do mar' (Favelas of the tide: environment, mobility and conditions for women on the sea shore). In UNCHS (Habitat), *Challenge of the Informal Town: Routes Towards the Integration of Peri-urban Settlements*, International Seminar, Preparatory Event for the Habitat 2 Conference, Belo Horizonte, 11 to 15 September 1995, pp. 310–16

Mainwaring, S. 1984. 'The Catholic Church, popular education and political change in Brazil'. *Journal of Interamerican Studies*, 26(1):97–124.

Makhatini, M. 1994. 'Squatting as a process: the case of Cato Manor'. Paper presented at the *University of the Witwatersrand History Workshop*, Johannesburg, 13 to 15 July 1994.

Mamdani, M. 1996. *Citizen and Subject. Contemporary Africa and the Legacy of Late Colonization.* David Philip, Cape Town.

Mangin, W. 1967. 'Latin American squatter settlements: a problem and a solution'. *Latin American Research Review,* 2:67–98.

Mangurian, D. 1997. 'Nuevo futuro para favelas de Rio' (New future for favelas of Rio). *Bidextra,* Suplemento de EL BID, Publication of the Inter-American Development Bank, Washington DC.

Marais, H. 1998. *South Africa. Limits to Change. The Political Economy of Transformation.* Zed Books, London.

Marais, L. and Krige, S. 1997. 'The upgrading of Freedom Square informal settlement in Bloemfontein. Lessons for future low-income housing'. *Urban Forum,* 8(2):177–94.

Maricato, E. 1994. 'Reforma Urbana: limites e possibilidades. Uma trajectória incompleta (Urban Reform: limits and possibilities. An incomplete trajectory). In Ribeiro, L. and Santos Jr., O. (eds.), *Globalização, Fragmentação e Reforma Urbana: O Futuro das Cidades Brasileiras na Crise* (Globalisation, Fragmentation and Urban Reform: The Future of the Brazilian Cities in the Crisis). Civilização Brasileira, Rio de Janeiro, pp. 309–26.

Maricato, E. 1996. 'The Urban Reform, 33 years later'. In Federação Nacional dos Arquitetos e Urbanistas, *More Human Settlements, Assentamentos mais Humanos,* Brazilian Conference for Habitat 2, Federação Nacional dos Arquitetos e Urbanistas, Rio de Janeiro, 9–12 May 1996.

Maricato, E. 2000. 'A terra é um nó também nas cidades' ('Land is also a knot in the cities'). *Jornal dos Trabalhadores Rurais Sem Terra,* 18 (February):4–5.

Martin, R. 1987. 'Experiences with monitoring and evaluation in Lusaka'. In Skinner, R., Taylor, J. and Wegelin, E. (eds.), *Shelter Upgrading of the Urban Poor: Evaluation of Third World Experience.* Island Publishing House, with UNCHS (Habitat) and the Institute of Housing Studies (BIE), Manila, pp. 149–67.

Martin, R. and Ledogar, R. 1977. 'A squatter settlement in Lusaka, Zambia, "George Compound"'. Report submitted to the United Nations Centre for Housing, Building and Planning, Lusaka.

Marx, A. 1998. *Making Race and Nation. A comparison of South Africa, the United States, and Brazil.* Cambridge University Press, Cambridge.

Marx, C. 2003. 'Supporting informal settlements'. In Khan, F. and Thring, P. (eds). *Housing Policy and Practice in Post-Apartheid South Africa.* Heinemann, Johannesburg, pp. 299–320.

Mashabela, H. 1990. *Mekhukhu. Urban African Cities of the Future.* South African Institute of Race Relations, Johannesburg.

Mautner, Y. and Bueno, L. 1994. 'Urban Design, a social product of society'. Paper presented at the seminar *The Hidden Assignment – at Home in a City,* Rotterdam, Netherlands.

Mayekiso, Mzwanele. 1996. *Township Politics. Civic Struggles for a New South Africa.* Monthly Review Press, New York.

Mayekiso, Moss and Hanlon, J. 1994. *Making People-driven Development Work.* Report on Development Finance formed by the South African National Civic Organisation, submitted at the request of Jay Naidoo, convenor of the Reconstruction and Development Programme, 11 April 1994, Johannesburg.

Mazur, R. and Qangule, V. 1995. *Household Dynamics and Mobility of Africans in Cape Town: Appropriate Housing Responses.* Western Cape Community-based Housing Trust, Cape Town.

McCarthy, J. 1992. 'Local and regional government: from rigidity to crisis to flux'. In Smith, D. (ed.). *Apartheid City and Beyond: Urbanisation and Social Change in South Africa.* Witwatersrand University Press, Johannesburg, pp. 26–36.

McCarthy, J., Hindson, D. and Oelofse, M. 1995. *Evaluation of Informal Settlement Upgrading and Consolidation Projects.* Report to the National Business Initiative, Johannesburg.

Menezes, B. 1995. 'The challenge of the informal city'. Paper presented at the International Seminar: Challenges of the Informal Town, Belo Horizonte, Brazil, September 1995.

Merrifield, A., van Horen, B. and Taylor, R. 1993. 'The politics of public participation in informal settlement upgrading: a case study of Bester's Camp'. Proceedings of the *21st International Housing Association, World Housing Congress,* Cape Town, May 1993.

Ministry in the Office of the President, RDP. 1995. *Key Indicators of Poverty in South Africa.* Prepared for the Office of the Reconstruction and Development Programme (RDP) by the World Bank, based on the South African Living Standards and Development Survey, coordinated by the Southern Africa Labour Development Research Unit (SALDRU) at the University of Cape Town, Cape Town.

Ministry of Housing. 1997. *Housing the Nation: People's Housing Process.* Report prepared by the Ministry of Housing, Pretoria, 19 February 1997.

Mitlin, D. and Thompson, J. 1995. 'Participatory approaches in urban areas: strengthening civil society or reinforcing the status quo?' *Environment and Urbanisation,* 7(1):231–50.

Mngxitama, A. 2002. 'The landless have landed'. *Debate: Voices from the South African Left,* 8 (September):11–13.

Morris, M. 1992. 'Violence in squattercamps and shantytowns: power and the social relations governing everyday life'. In Verloren van Themaat Centre, *South Africa in Transition: Urban and rural perspectives on squatting and informal settlement in environmental context,* Environmental Law Division, University of South Africa, pp. 94–104.

Moser, C. 1995a. 'Women, gender and urban development policy: challenges for current and future research'. *Third World Planning Review,* 17(2):223–35.

Moser, C. 1995b. *Confronting Crisis: A Comparative Study of Household Responses to Poverty and Vulnerability in Four Poor Urban Communities.* Environmentally Sustainable Development Studies and Monographs Series No. 8, The World Bank, Washington DC.

Moser, C. 1995c. 'Urban social policy and poverty reduction'. *Environment and Urbanisation,* 7(1):159–71.

Moser, C. 1997. 'Urban social policy and poverty reduction'. In Burgess, R., Carmona, M. and Kolstee, T. (eds.). *The Challenge of Sustainable Cities. Neoliberalism and Urban Strategies in Developing Countries.* Zed Books, London, pp. 44–61.

N-AERUS. 1999. 'Press Release'. *International Workshop on Concepts and Paradigms of Urban Management in the Context of Developing Countries,* organised by the

European Science Foundation (ESF), the Network-Association of European Researchers on Urbanisation in the South (N-AERUS) and the Istituto Universitarion di Architettura di Venezia (IUAV), Venice, 11 to 12 March 1999.

Nathan, C. and Spindler, Z. 1993. 'Squatting as rent-seeking and pressure-group competition: a South African case study'. *Urban Studies,* 30(3):477–94.

National Housing Development Authority. 1988. *Community Land Regularisation and Blocking-out.* Ministry of Local Government Housing and Construction, Colombo, Sri Lanka.

National Housing Forum. Undated. 'The interface between high and low income settlements'. Status Report: 4.1.1.10, National Housing Forum, Pretoria.

National Ministry of Housing. 1998. *National Housing Policy: Supporting the People's Housing Process.* Department of Housing and the People's Housing Partnership Trust, Pretoria, March 1998.

Nientied, P. and van der Linden, J. 1988. 'Approaches to low income housing in the Third World'. In Gugler, J. (ed.). *The Urbanisation of the Third World.* Oxford University Press, New York, pp. 138–56.

Nuttall, J. 1997. *The First Five Years: The Story of the Independent Development Trust.* Independent Development Trust, Cape Town.

Oelofse, C. and Dodson, B. 1997. 'Community place and transformation: a perceptual analysis of residents' responses to an informal settlement in Hout Bay, South Africa'. *Geoforum,* 28(1):91–101.

Oestereich, J. 1996. 'From Habitat I to Habitat II – the way form Vancouver to Istanbul'. *Trialog,* 49:56–62.

Oldfield, S. 2002. 'Partial formalisation and its implications for community governance in an informal settlement'. *Urban Forum,* 13(2):102–15.

Oliveira, N. 1996. 'Favelas and ghettos. Race and class in Rio de Janeiro and New York City'. *Latin American Perspectives,* 91, 23(4):71–89.

Omer-Cooper, J. 1994. *History of Southern Africa,* 2nd edition. David Philip, James Currey, Heinemann, Cape Town.

Orkin, F. 1998. *The People of South Africa Population Census 1996. Census in Brief.* Statistics South Africa, Pretoria.

Pamuk, A. and Cavallieri, P. 1998. 'Alleviating urban poverty in a global city: new trends in upgrading Rio-de-Janeiro's favelas'. *Habitat International,* 22(4):449–62.

Parnell, S. 1992. 'State intervention in housing provision in the 1980s'. In Smith, D. (ed.). *Apartheid City and Beyond: Urbanisation and Social Change in South Africa.* Witwatersrand University Press, Johannesburg, pp. 53–64.

Parnell, S. and Hart, D. 1999. 'Self-help housing as a flexible instrument of state control in 20th-century South Africa'. *Housing Studies,* 14(3):367–86.

Parnell, S. and Pirie, G. 1991. 'Johannesburg'. In Lemon, A. (ed.). *Homes Apart: South Africa's Segregated Cities.* Indiana University Press, Bloomington, pp. 129–45.

Pasteur, D. 1979. *The Management of Squatter Upgrading. A Case Study of Organisation, Procedures and Participation.* Saxon House, Westmead.

Pathirana, V. and Sheng, Y. 1992. 'The community contract system in Sri-Lanka: an innovative approach for the delivery of basic services to the urban poor'. *Habitat International,* 16(4):3–14.

People's Dialogue. 1991. *The Southern African People's Dialogue on Land and Homelessness,* proceedings of the Broederstroom Meeting (a SACCAA Project), Cape Town, 17 to 21 March 1991.

People's Dialogue. 1993. *The First Community-based Shelter Training Programme in South Africa.* Part 2 of 'Regaining Knowledge – an Appeal to Abandon Illusions', The People's Dialogue Manual for Innovative, Community-based Shelter Training Programmes. People's Dialogue, Cape Town.

People's Dialogue. 1994. *Wat ons wil Hê! The Story of the People's Dialogue Housing Policy Conference and the Launch of the SA Homeless People's Federation.* People's Dialogue report, Cape Town, 21 to 25 March 1994.

People's Dialogue. 1995. *uTyani Luyathetha: a People's Dialogue newsletter.* People's Dialogue, Cape Town, September 1995.

People's Dialogue. 1997. *The Liberating Power of Self Reliance: People Centred Development in Kanana Settlement, Vaal Region, Gauteng Province,* Report compiled by People's Dialogue on behalf of the South African Homeless People's Federation. People's Dialogue, Cape Town.

People's Dialogue. 1998. 'From tall stories to double-storeys: Umfelandawonye tackles planners density problems in Piesang River'. *uTshani BuyaKhuluma, People's Dialogue Newsletter,* Cape Town, May, 9:6.

Petras, J. and Leiva, F., with Veltmeyer, H. 1994. *Democracy and Poverty in Chile. The Limits to Electoral Politics.* Westview Press, Oxford.

Phadu, T. 1997. 'Government support for a people-driven housing process'. *The African Communist,* Third Quarter:77–8.

Pickholz,. L. 1997. 'Managing politics and storytelling: meeting the challenge of upgrading informal housing in South Africa,' *Habitat Interantional,* 21(4):377–96.

Posel, D. 1991. 'Curbing African urbanization in the 1950s and 1960s'. In Swilling, M., Humphries, R. and Shubane, K. (eds.). *Apartheid City in Transition.* Oxford University Press, Cape Town, pp. 19–32.

Prefeitura Municipal de Belo Horizonte. 1985. *PROFAVELA: Belo Horizonte com novas Horizontes* (PROFAVELA: Belo Horizonte with new Horizons), 7 Plano Municipal de Habitação Popular II, Prefeitura Municipal de Belo Horizonte (7th Plan for Popular Municipal Habitation II, Municipality of Belo Horizonte), Belo Horizonte.

Prefeitura Municipal de Belo Horizonte. 1995. *Plano Diretor de Belo Horizonte, Lei de Uso e Ocupação do Solo – Estudos Básicos* (Guide Plan for Belo Horizonte, Law for Land Use and Land Occupation – Basic Studies), Prefeitura Municipal de Belo Horizonte (Municipality of Belo Horizonte), Belo Horizonte.

Pugh, C. 1995. 'The role of the World Bank in housing'. In Aldrich, B. and Sandhu, R. (eds.). *Housing the Urban Poor: Policy and Practice in Developing Countries.* Zed Books, London, pp. 34–92.

Rakodi, C. 1981. 'Participation in squatter upgrading in Lusaka, Zambia'. In Rakodi, C. and Schlyter, A. (eds.). *Upgrading in Lusaka: Participation and Physical Changes.* The National Swedish Institute for Building Research, Stockholm, pp. 55–80.

Rakodi, C. and Schlyter, A. 1981. *Upgrading in Lusaka: Participation and Physical Changes.* The National Swedish Institute for Building Research, Stockholm.

Ramphele, M. 1997. 'Foreword'. In Nuttall, J. *The First Five Years: The Story of the Independent Development Trust.* Independent Development Trust, Cape Town.

Rand Afrikaans University. 1997. 'Weilers Farm community analysis'. Unpublished manuscript, Department of Community Development, Johannesburg.

Reader's Digest. 1991. *Multi-Language Dictionary and Phrase Book.* Reader's Digest Association of South Africa, Cape Town.

Reichenheim, M. and Harpham, T. 1991. 'Maternal mental health in a squatter settlement in Rio de Janeiro'. *British Journal of Psychiatry,* 159:683–90.

Republic of South Africa. 1991. 'Less Formal Township Establishment Act, No. 113 of 1991', Government Gazette, 313(13359). Government Printer, Pretoria.

Republic of South Africa. 1996. *The Constitution of the Republic of South Africa,* Act No. 108 of 1996. Government Printer, Pretoria.

Ribeiro, F. 1994. 'Debates: Comparing Brazil and South Africa – a comment'. *South African Sociological Review,* 7(1):63–6.

Ross, F. 1993. 'Homes without doors: diffusing domesticity in Die Bos'. Unpublished masters dissertation, Department of Social Anthropology, University of Cape Town, Cape Town.

Ross, F. 1996. 'Diffusing domesticity: domestic fluidity in Die Bos'. *Social Dynamics,* 22(1):55–71.

Royston, L. 1993. *A Critical Study of Communities Involved in the Struggle for Access to the Witwatersrand Region, South Africa,* research report submitted to Habitat International Coalition and the International Development Research Centre, Planact, Johannesburg.

Royston, L. 2002. 'Security of urban tenure in South Africa: Overview of policy and practice'. In Durand-Lasserve, A. and Royston, L. (eds.). *Holding their Ground: Secure Land Tenure for the Urban Poor in Developing Countries.* Earthscan, London, pp. 165–81.

Sachs, C. 1981. 'Croissance urbaine et favelisation des métropoles. São Paulo et Rio de Janeiro (Urban growth and favelisation of the metropoles. São Paulo and Rio de Janeiro)'. *Economie Humanisme,* 260:13–25.

Sader, E. and Silverstein, K. 1991. '*Without Fear of Being Happy: Lula, the Workers' Party and Brazil*'. Verso, London and New York.

Saff, G. 1996. 'Claiming a space in a changing South Africa: the "squatters" of Marconi Beam, Cape Town'. *Annals of the Association of American Geographers,* 2:235–55.

Saff, G. 1999. *Changing Cape Town: Urban Dynamics, Policy and Planning during the Political Transition in South Africa.* University Press of America, Lanham.

Saff, G. 2001. 'Exclusionary discourse towards squatters in suburban Cape Town'. *Ecumene,* 8(1):87–107.

Sandercock, L. 1998. *Towards Cosmopolis: Planning for Multicultural Cities.* John Wiley and Sons, Chichester.

Sapire, H. 1990a. *Report on the Social and Political Ecology of Free-Standing Settlements on the PWV,* Urbanisation Unit/Centre for Policy Studies, The Urban Foundation, Johannesburg.

Sapire, H. 1990b. *The Reaction of Established White, African, Indian and "Coloured" Communities to Informal Settlement Nearby.* Urbanisation Unit/Centre for Policy Studies, The Urban Foundation, Johannesburg.

Saule Jr., N. 1998. 'Democratic and participative system of housing policy management – Brazilian experiences'. Paper presented at the International Conference *Law and Governance: New Trends in Urban-Environmental Management and the Reform of the*

Public Sector, Escola de Governo da Fundação Joâo Pinheiro, Belo Horizonte, 18 to 19 November 1998.

Schlyter, A. 1981. 'Upgraded George revisited'. In Rakodi, C. and Schlyter, A. (eds.). *Upgrading in Lusaka: Participation and Physical Changes.* The National Swedish Institute for Building Research, Stockholm, pp. 7–53.

Schlyter, A. 1987. 'Commercialization of housing in upgraded squatter areas. The case of George, Lusaka, Zambia'. *African Urban Quarterly,* 2(3):287–97.

Schmitter, P. 1996. 'South Africa and Brazil: a preliminary comparison'. In Friedman, S. and de Villiers, R. (eds.). *Comparing Brazil and South Africa. Two Transitional States in Political and Economic Perspective.* Centre for Policy Studies (CPS), Foundation for Global Dialogue (FGD) and Instituto de Estudos Econômicos, Sociais e Polÿticos de São Paulo (Idesp.), Cape Town, pp. 7–18.

Schusterman, R. and Hardoy, A. 1997. 'Reconstructing social capital in a poor urban settlement: the Integral Improvement Programme in Barrio San Jorge'. *Environment and Urbanisation,* 9(1):91–119.

Seekings, J. 1997. 'SANCO: strategic dilemmas in a democratic South Africa'. *Transformation,* 34:1–30.

Seekings, J. 1998. 'No home for revolutionaries? The structure and activities of the South African National Civic Organisation in Metropolitan Cape Town, 1996–97'. *Urban Forum,* 9(1):1–35.

Seethal, C. 1996. 'Reconstruction and postdevelopmentalism in South Africa: the case of an informal settlement in Pietermaritzburg-Msunduzi (1990–1995)'. *South African Geographical Journal,* 78(2):64–74.

Seidman, G. 1990a. 'Labour Movements in Newly-Industrialized Countries: South Africa and Brazil'. Dissertation submitted in partial satisfaction of the requirements of the Ph.D. degree in Sociology, Graduate Division, University of California, Berkeley, UMI Dissertation Services, Michigan.

Seidman, G. 1990b. 'The emergence of political unionism in Brazil and South Africa'. *South African Sociological Review,* 3(1):3–18.

Seidman, G. 1994. *Manufacturing Militance: Workers' Movements in Brazil and South Africa, 1970–1985.* University of California Press, London.

SELAVIP. 1981. 'Résumé of the document "Property and Use of Urban Land" in Brazil (Panel held during the XIX General Assembly of the Brazilian Episcopal Conference, which took place in Itaici, Sao Paulo, in February of 1981'. *SELAVIP (Latin American and Asian Low Income Housing Service) News,* IV(4):5–9.

Shakur, T. and Madden, M. 1991. 'Resettlement camps in Dhaka: a socio-economic profile of squatter settlements in Dhaka'. *Habitat International,* 15(4):65–83.

Shubane, K. 1991. 'Black local authorities, a contraption of control'. In Swilling, M., Humphries, R. and Shubane, K. (eds.). *Apartheid City in Transition.* Oxford University Press, Cape Town, pp. 64–77.

Silas, J. 1992. 'Government-community partnerships in kampung improvement programmes in Surabaya'. *Environment and Urbanisation,* 4(2):33–41.

Simpson, G. 1995. 'Informal housing and squatting on the Cape Flats: a comparative analysis between "black" and "coloured" areas'. Unpublished masters dissertation, Department of Geography and Environmental Studies, University of the Western Cape, Cape Town.

Singh, A. 1997. 'Residents' perception of informal settlement: the situation in Clare Estate'. In Singh, A., Thorold, A. and Vawda, S. (eds.). *Living on the Edge. Squatters in the Durban Area, South Africa.* Urban Research Working Papers, no. 43, Institute of Cultural Anthropology/Sociology of Development, Vrije Universiteit, Amsterdam, pp. 37–50.

Sirivardana, S. and Lankatilleke, L. 1988. *Some Key Issues in the Participatory Planning and Management of the Urban Low-income Housing Process.* National Housing Development Authority, Ministry of Local Government Housing and Construction, Colombo, Sri Lanka.

Sitas, A. 1998. 'South Africa in the 1990s: the logic of fragmentation and reconstruction'. *Transformation,* 36:37–50.

Smith, D. 1992. 'Conclusion'. In Smith, D. (ed.). *The Apartheid City and Beyond: Urbanisation and Social Change in South Africa.* Routledge, London, and Witwatersrand University Press, Johannesburg, pp. 314–17.

South African Institute of Race Relations. 1956. *Report on Nyanga.* South African Institute of Race Relations, Western Cape Region, Cape Town.

Souza, A. 1991. 'Invasões, intervenções e perspectivas. O caso da cidade do Salvador' (Invasions, interventions and perspectives. The case of the city of Salvador). *Cadernos de CEAS,* 136:65–78.

Souza, C. 1997. *Constitutional Engineering in Brazil: The Politics of Federalism and Decentralisation.* Macmillan Press, London and St. Martin's Press, New York.

Souza, M. 1993a. *Armut, Sozialräumliche Segregation und Sozialer Konflikt in der Metropolitanregion von Rio de Janeiro. Ein Beitrag zur Analyse der 'Stadtfrage' in Brasilien* (Poverty, Socio-spatial Segregation and Social Conflict in the Metropolitan Region of Rio de Janeiro. A Contribution to the Analysis of the 'Urban Question' in Brazil), Tübinger Geographische Studien, Heft 111, Tübinger Beiträge zur Geographischen Lateinamerika-Forschung, Heft 10, Geographisches Institut der Universität Tübingen.

Souza, M. 1993b. 'Reflexão sobre as limitações e potencialidades de uma reforma urbana no Brasil atual' (Reflections on the limitations and potentials of an urban reform in current Brazil). *Actas Latinoamericanas de Varsevia,* 15:207–28.

Souza, M. 1999. 'Urban planning and management as tools for social justice: some notes on recent Brazilian experiences'. Paper presented at the international conference *South to South: Urban Environmental Policies and Politics in Brazil and South Africa.* Institute of Commonwealth Studies, University of London, London, 25 to 26 March 1999.

Souza, M. 2003. 'Alternative urban planning and management in Brazil: instructive examples for other countries in the South?' In Harrison, P., Huchzermeyer, M., Mayekiso, M. (eds.). *Confronting Fragmentation: Housing and Urban Development in a Democratising Society.* University of Cape Town Press, Cape Town, pp. 190–208.

Sowman, M. and Gawith, M. 1994. 'Participation of disadvantaged communities in project planning and decision-making: a case-study of Hout Bay'. *Development Southern Africa,* 11(4):557–71.

Spiegel, A. 1999. 'The country in town: reconstitution of a discarded dichotomy?' Partially revised draft of a paper presented at the conference *Between Town and Country: Livelihoods, Settlement and Identity Formation in Sub-Saharan Africa,* Rhodes University, East London, June 1999.

Spiegel, A., Watson, V. and Wilkinson, P. 1994. 'Domestic fluidity and movement patterns among Cape Town's African population: some implications for housing policy'. Africa Seminar, Centre for African Studies, University of Cape Town, Cape Town, 11 October 1994.

Spiegel, A., Watson, V. and Wilkinson, P. 1996a. 'Devaluing diversity? National housing policy and African household dynamics in Cape Town'. *Urban Forum,* 7(1):1–30.

Spiegel, A., Watson, V. and Wilkinson, P. 1996b. 'Domestic diversity and fluidity among some African households in Greater Cape Town'. *Social Dynamics,* 22(1):7–30.

Spiegel, A., Watson, V. and Wilkinson, P. 1996c. 'Women, difference and urbanisation patterns in Cape Town, South Africa'. *African Urban Quarterly,* 11(1):11–21.

Spiegel, A., Watson, V. and Wilkinson, P. 1999. 'Housing and difference in Cape Town, South Africa: case studies and policy concerns'. In Awotona, A. (ed.). *Housing Provision and Bottom-up Approaches. Family Case Studies from Africa, Asia and South America.* Ashgate, Aldershot, pp. 145–60.

Stadler, A. 1979. 'Birds in the cornfield: squatter movements in Johannesburg, 1944–1947'. *Journal of Southern African Studies,* 6(1):93–123.

Swart-Kruger, J. 2002. 'Children in a South African squatter camp gain and lose a voice'. In Chawla, L. (ed.). *Growing up in an Urbanising World.* UNESCO Publications, Paris, and Earthscan, London, pp. 111–33.

Taschner, S. 1995. 'Squatter settlements and slums in Brazil: twenty years of research and policy'. In Aldrich, B. and Sandhu, R. (eds.). *Housing the Urban Poor: Policy and Practice in Developing Countries.* Zed Books, London, pp. 185–223

Taschner, S. 1997. 'Favelas e cortiços no Brasil: 20 anos de pesquisas e políticas' (Favelas and tenements in Brazil: 20 years of research and policies). *Cadernos de Pesquisa do LAP* 18, 2–79.

Teixeira, E. 1993. 'A emergência da sociedade civil no poder local' (The emergence of civil society in the local authority). *Cadernos do CEAS,* 144:48–58.

Telles, E. 1994. 'Segregação racial e crise urbana' (Racial segregation and urban crisis). In Ribeiro, L. and Santos Jr., O. (eds.). *Globalização, Fragmentação e Reforma Urbana: O Futuro das Cidades Brazilieiras na Crise* (Globalisation, Fragmentation and Urban Reform: The Future of Brazilian Cities in the Crisis). Civilização Brasileira, Rio de Janeiro, pp. 189–217.

Thomas, E. 2002. 'Local participation in development initiatives: The potential contribution of an understanding of social capital'. *Urban Forum,* 13(2):116–31.

Thomas, E. 2003. 'HIV/AIDS and development: Local level responses'. Paper presented at the Gauteng Department of Housing conference *Urbanisation and Housing Challenges: Cities in Africa,* Johannesburg, 6 to 8 October 2003.

Thorold, A. 1997. 'Methodological problems in the ethnography of a squatter camp'. In Singh, A., Thorold, A. and Vawda, S. (eds.). *Living on the Edge. Squatters in the Durban Area, South Africa.* Urban Research Working Papers 43, Department of Anthropology/Sociology of Development, Vrije Universiteit, Amsterdam, pp. 59–67.

Tipple, G. and Willis, K. 1991. 'Tenure choice in a West African city'. *Third World Planning Review,* 13(1):27–45.

Tomlinson, M. 1995a. *The First Million is the Hardest: Will the Consensus on Housing Endure?* Policy Review Series, Policy: Issues and Actors 8(8), Centre for Policy Studies, Johannesburg.

Tomlinson, M. 1995b. *From Policy to Practice: Implementers' Views on the New Housing Subsidy Scheme.* Research Report no. 44, Social Policy Series, Centre for Policy Studies, Johannesburg.

Tomlinson, M. 1995c. *Problems on the Ground? Developers' Perspectives on the Government's Housing Subsidy Scheme.* Research Report no. 46, Social Policy Series, Centre for Policy Studies, Johannesburg.

Tomlinson, M. 1996. *From Rejection to Resignation: Beneficiaries' Views on the Government's Housing Subsidy Scheme.* Research Report no. 49, Social Policy Series, Centre for Policy Studies, Johannesburg.

Tomlinson, M. 1997a. *Mortgage Bondage? Financial Institutions and Low-cost Housing Delivery.* Research Report no. 56, Social Policy Series, Centre for Policy Studies, Johannesburg.

Tomlinson, M. 1997b. *Watchdog or Lapdog? National and Provincial Legislators' Views of the New Housing Subsidy Scheme.* Research Report no. 59, Social Policy Series, Centre for Policy Studies, Johannesburg.

Tomlinson, M. 1998a. 'South Africa's new housing policy: an assessment of the first Two Years, 1994–96'. *International Journal of Urban and Regional Research*, 22(1):137–46.

Tomlinson, M. 1998b. *Looking at the Local: Local Governments and Low-cost Housing Delivery.* Research Report no. 63, Social Policy Series, Centre for Policy Studies, Johannesburg.

Tomlinson, M., with Bam, S. and Mathole, T., 1995. *More than Mealies and Marigolds. From Homeseekers to Citizens in Ivory Park.* Report by the Centre for Policy Studies for the Interfaith Community Development Agency, Johannesburg.

Tomlinson, R. 2001. 'Housing policy in a context of HIV/AIDS and globalisation'. *International Journal for Urban and Regional Research*, 25(3):649–57.

Tomlinson, R. 2003a. HIV/AIDS and urban disintegration in Johannesburg. In Harrison, P., Huchzermeyer, M. and Mayekiso, M. (eds.). *Confronting Fragmentation: Housing and Urban Development in a Democratising Society.* University of Cape Town Press, Cape Town, pp. 76–87.

Tomlinson, R. 2003b. An exploration of the shelter and services needs arising from HIV/AIDS? Paper presented at the Gauteng Department of Housing conference *Urbanisation and Housing Challenges: Cities in Africa*, Johannesburg, 6 to 8 October 2003.

Turan, M. 1987. 'Poverty, prudence, and place-making: strolling through Gecekondus'. *Habitat International*, 11(3):77–102.

Turner, J. 1968. 'The squatter settlement: architecture that works'. *Architectural Design*, 38:355–60.

Turner, J. 1976. *Housing by People: Towards Autonomy in Building Environments.* Marion Boyars, London.

Turner, J. and Fichter, R. (eds.). 1972. *Freedom to Build.* Collier-Macmillan, New York.

Uitenhage Town Secretary. 1995. *Uitenhage Squatter Policy '95 KwaNobuhle and Langa Squatter Project Report.* Report prepared by the Urban Services Group and Metroplan, Uitenhage.

UNCED. 1992. *Agenda 21.* The United Nations Conference on Environment and Development, Division for Sustainable Development, United Nations Department of Economic and Social Affairs: www.un.org.esa/sustdev/documents/agenda21/index.htm.

UNCHS (Habitat). 1991. *Global Strategy for Shelter to the Year 2000: Implementation of the First Phase*. United Nations Centre for Human Settlements (UNCHS), Nairobi.

UNCHS (Habitat). 1995. *Challenge of the Informal Town: Routes Towards the Integration of Peri-urban Settlements*. International Seminar, Preparatory Event for the Habitat 2 Conference, Belo Horizonte, 11 to 15 September 1995.

UNCHS (Habitat). 1996a. *The Human Settlement Conditions of the World's Urban Poor*. United Nations Centre for Human Settlements (Habitat), Nairobi.

UNCHS (Habitat). 1996b. *Urban Poverty: A World Challenge – The Recife Declaration, March 1996*. Habitat 2, Recife International Meeting on Urban Poverty, Recife, Brazil, 17 to 21 March 1996.

UNCHS (Habitat). 1996c. *The Habitat Agenda: Goals and Principles, Commitments and Global Plan for Action*. United Nations Conference on Human Settlements (Habitat 2), Istanbul, Turkey, 3 to 14 June 1996.

UNCHS (Habitat). 1996d. 'International Forum on Urban Poverty: Concept Paper'. Draft, 23 July. United Nations Centre for Human Settlements (UNCHS), Nairobi.

United Nations. 1999. *Statistical Yearbook, Forty-fourth Issue*. Department of Economic and Social Affairs, Statistical Division, United Nations, New York.

United Nations. 2000. United Nations Millenium Declaration. Resolution adopted by General Assembly, New York, 8 September 2000: www.un.org/millenium/declaration/ares552e.htm.

United Nations. 2002. *Key Outcomes of the Summit*. Johannesburg Summit 2002. World Summit on Sustainable Development, Johannesburg, 6 August to 24 September: www.johannesburgsummit.org/html/documents/summit_docs/2009_keyoutcomes_commitments.doc.

Urban Foundation. 1990. *Housing for All: Proposals for a National Urban Housing Policy*. Policies for a New Urban Future, Urban Debate 2010(9). The Urban Foundation, Johannesburg.

Urban Foundation 1991. *Informal Housing Part 1: Current Situation*. Policies for a New Urban Future, Urban Debate 2010(10). The Urban Foundation, Johannesburg.

Urban Foundation. 1994. *The Urban Foundation 1994 Annual Review*. The Urban Foundation, Johannesburg.

URBEL. 1996. 'URBEL 1993–1996: Habitação, Resgate da Cidadania', (URBEL 1993–1996: Housing/Habitation, Recovery of Citizenship). *Revista da URBEL*, Belo Horizonte.

Uys, E. 1986. *Brazil*. Pan Books, London.

Vaa, M. 1995. 'Issues and policies in the development of unauthorised settlements'. *Norsk geogr. Tidsskr.*, 49:187–95.

Valladares, L. 1978. *Passa-se uma Casa: Análise do Programa de Remoções de Favelas do Rio de Janeiro* (A House for Sale: Analysis of the Favela Removal Programme of Rio de Janeiro). Zahar, Rio de Janeiro.

Valladares, L. and Figueiredo, A. 1983. 'Housing in Brazil: an introduction to recent literature'. *Bulletin of Latin American Research*, 2(2):69–91.

Van der Linden, J. 1986. *The Sites and Services Approach Reviewed. Solution or Stopgap to the Third World Housing Shortage?* Grower, Aldershot.

Van Horen, B. 1996. 'Informal settlement in-situ upgrading in South Africa: the *de facto* rules'. Paper presented at the Association of Collegiate Schools of Planning

(ACSP)/Association of European Schools of Planning (AESOP), Joint International Congress, Toronto, Canada.

Van Horen, B. 1999. 'The *de facto* rules: The growth and change of an informal settlement in Durban, South Africa'. *Third World Planning Review,* 21(3):261–82.

Vink, N. 1985. 'Base communities and urban social movements: a case study of the metalworkers' strike 1980 – São Bernardo, Brazil'. In Slater, D. (ed.). *New Social Movements and the State in Latin America.* CEDLA (Centre for Latin American Research and Documentation), Amsterdam, pp. 95–125.

Volbeda, S. 1989. 'Housing and survival strategies of women in metropolitan slum areas in Brazil'. *Habitat International,* 13(3):157–71.

Von Broembsen, D. 1999. 'The National Urban Development Framework – South Africa's response to the Habitat Agenda'. Paper presented at the International Federation for Housing and Planning (IFHP) international conference *Urban Integration. Planning and Housing in the new South Africa,* Cape Town, 14 to 17 March 1999.

Walshe, P. 1997. 'Christianity and the anti-apartheid struggle: the prophetic voice within divided churches'. In Elphick, R. and Davenport, R. (eds.). *Christianity in South Africa: A Political, Social and Cultural History.* James Currey, Oxford, pp. 383–99.

Ward, P. 1982. 'Introduction and Purpose'. In Ward, P. (ed.). 1982. *Self-Help Housing. A Critique.* Mansell, Oxford, pp. 1–13.

Waring, M. and Allanic, B. 2001. 'South Africa's rural housing renaissance'. *Trialog,* 69:12–19.

Webb, A. 1983. 'Mining in South Africa'. In Coleman, F. (ed.). *Economic History of South Africa.* HAUM Educational Publishers, Pretoria, pp. 163–94.

Wegelin, A. and Borgman, K. 1995. 'Options for municipal intervention in urban poverty alleviation'. *Environment and Urbanisation,* 7(2):131–51.

Weichel, K., Smith, L. and Putterill, M. 1978. *Nyanga and Crossroads: Some Aspects of Social and Economic Activity.* Working Paper No. 2, Urban Problems Research Unit, University of Cape Town.

White, C. 1998. 'Democratic societies? Voluntary association and democratic culture in a South African township'. *Transformation,* 36:1–36.

Wilkinson, P. 1998. 'Housing policy in South Africa'. *Habitat International,* 22(3):215–29.

Wolf, M. 1994. '"Veränderungen von unten": PT und Basisbewegungen – Agenten der gesellschaftlichen transformation' ("Changes from below": PT and base movements – agents of societal transformation), *Lateinamerika-Studien* (Universität Erlangen – Nürnberg, Zentralinstitut (06), Sektion Lateinamerika), 33:339–57.

World Bank. 1991. *Urban Policy and Economic Development: an Agenda for the 1990s – A World Bank Policy Paper.* The World Bank, Washington, DC.

World Bank. 1994. *World Development Report.* Oxford University Press, New York.

World Bank. 1995. *Poverty and Vulnerability in Angyalföld, Hungary.* Urban Development Division, World Bank, Washington DC.

World Bank. 1997. *World Development Report.* Oxford University Press, New York.

Wratten, E. 1995. 'Conceptualising urban poverty'. *Environment and Urbanisation,* 7(1):11–36.

Yamazaki, D., França, E., Araújo, R. and Pini, P. 1996. 'Programa de saneamento ambiental da bacía do Guarapiranga em São Paulo' (Environmental sanitation programme in the Guarapiranga Basin). In Bonduki, N. (ed.). *Habitat. As Prácticas Bem-Sucedidas em Habitação, Meio Ambiente e Gestão Urbana nas Cidades Brasileiras* (Best Practices in Housing, Environment and Urban Management in the Cities of Brazil). Studio Nobel, São Paulo, pp. 116–25.

Yapi-Diahou, A. 1995. 'The Informal housing sector in Abidjan, Ivory Coast'. *Environment and Urbanisation,* 7(2):11–29.

Yose, C. 1999. 'From shacks to houses: space usage and social change in a Western Cape shanty town'. Unpublished masters dissertation, Department of Social Anthropology, University of Cape Town.

Zimmerman, C. 1998. 'Vom Paternalismus zur Partizipation: die Erfahrung der demokratischen Haushaltsplanung in Porto Alegre' (From paternalism to participation: the experience of democratic budgeting in Porto Alegre). *Trialog,* 59:11–14.

Zukin, S. 1980. 'The cutting edge. A decade of new urban sociology'. *Theory and Society,* 9(4):575–601.

List of Informants for the South African Case Studies

WEILER'S FARM (SOUTHERN JOHANNESBURG)

Government:

Dumisa Dlhamini: Assistant Director of Land Affairs and Housing, Gauteng Department of Land Affairs and Housing, 31.7.98, 23.11.98 and 12.1.99.

Johann Axel: Manager, Housing Projects, Southern Metropolitan Local Council, 3.12.98.

Thuthuka Foundation:

Wilson Bangisa: Director, Thuthuka Foundation, 26.11.98.

Steven Poullouras: Director, Thuthuka Foundation, 24.11.98.

Nomawethu Gwalempi: Secretary of the Allocation Committee, Thuthuka Foundation (also Secretary of the local ANC Women's League), 26.11.98.

Bethwell Dondashe: Chairman of Section Committee Forum, Thuthuka Foundation (also Chairman of Section B), 26.11.98.

Weiler's Farm Civic Organisation:

Randell Mjempu: Branch Secretary, SANCO (also Labour Officer of Thuthuka Foundation), 4.12.98.

Outside individuals:

Yvette Berkovits: Film producer and activist, 24.11.98.

Madelaine van der Steege: dispute resolution consultant (involved during the construction of the community hall), 27.11.98.

GUNGULUZA (UITENHAGE)

Local Government:

Roelf Basson: Town Secretary, Uitenhage Local Government, 11.11.98.

Tinus Blignaut: Senior Engineering Technician, Town Engineering Department, Uitenhage Local Government, 10.11.98.

Mr H. J. Botha, Senior Engineering Assistant, Town Engineers Department, Uitenhage Local Government, 10.11.98.

Anton Crause: Deputy Town Engineer, Uitenhage Local Government, 12.11.98.

Toni Ferreira: Chief Town Planner, Uitenhage Local Government, 12.11.98.

Johan Gerber: Building Control Officer, Uitenhage Local Government, 12.11.98.

Bidwell Mzwandile Made: Housing Co-ordinator, Uitenhage Local Government, 11.11.98, 13.11.98.

Councillor Mtana: Deputy Mayor of Uitenhage and Ward Councillor for Gunguluza and, Uitenhage Local Government, 11.11.98.

Philip Nel: Deputy Town Treasurer, and Zandra Cotzee: Accountant, Office of the Town Treasurer, Uitenhage Local Government, 11.11.98.

Peter Nielson: Assistant Electrical Engineer, Uitenhage Local Government, 12.11.98.

Gawie Rousseau: Assistant Town Secretary (Estates and Housing), Uitenhage Local Government, 11.11.98.

Housing support consultants:

Dorelle Sapere: formerly Housing Support Specialist with BOUTEK (CSIR), then with the People's Housing Partnership Trust, 21.7.98.

Tinus Kruger: Housing Support Specialist, BOUTEK (CSIR), 22.7.98.

Gunguluza Committee:

A group discussion was held with the following members of the Gunguluza Committee, 9.11.98:

Mrs Rosy N. Gunguluza, Malanga, Bertha Jobo, Peter, Thamsanqa Manana, Miriam Ndimba, Esther Stokwe, Thandeka Ramnewa (Acting secretary), Bertha Vuyelwa Jobo, Milton Nyiki, Zalisile Mana.

A written history of Gunguluza was also contributed by Mrs Rosy N. Gunguluza, 9.11.98 (translated from Xhosa by Patrick Mashiyi).

Civic organisation structure in KwaNobuhle:

Sipho Nyanga: Human Resources Executive, KwaNobuhle local Branch, SANCO, 12.11.98.

Bidwell Mzwandile Made: HOD Housing, Land and Services, KwaNobuhle local Branch, SANCO, 12.11.98.

NGO supporting the civic organisation:

Russel Alison: formerly with the NGO Urban Services Group, 13.11.98.

Person running a business in the Gunguluza settlement:

Mr M. G. Mqulwana: owner of a container shop in Gunguluza, former Township Manager for KwaNobuhle Town Council, 31.11.98.

PIESANG RIVER (DURBAN)

Local Government:

Nati Mdlala: Ward Councillor for Piesang River, member of the Homeless People's Federation, 19.11.98.

Consultant to Local Government:

Max Singh: project manager for current infrastructure and tenure investment, Pravin Amar Development Planners, 12.1.98.

Homeless People's Federation:

Patrick Hunsley Magebula: President of the Homeless People's Federation (national level), resident of Piesang River, 18.11.98.

Sam Mhlongo: Media Work and Communications, Homeless People's Federation (national level), resident of Piesang River, 16.11.98

Thembelihle Mkhize: Responsible for Enumeration, Homeless People's Federation (national level), and at Piesang River member of the Allocation Committee and responsible for building material ordering and deliveries (Homeless People's Federation), resident of Piesang River, 20.11.98.

Joyce Melwasi Makosi: Regional Convenor for house savings schemes, Homeless People's Federation, resident at Piesang River, 18.11.98.

Thandasile Spengani: Regional Convenor of the uTshani Fund of the Homeless People's Federation, resident at Piesang River, 20.11.98.

Constance Dwayisa: Bookkeeper for the region, Homeless People's Federation, 20.11.98.

People's Dialogue:

Joel Bolnick: People's Dialogue, Cape Town, 2.6.98.

Diana Mitlin: Consultant to People's Dialogue, Cape Town, 6.4.99.

Habitat for Humanity

Joyce Mkhize: Project coordinator, Habitat for Humanity, also resident at Piesang River, 18.11.98.

Residents of Piesang River:

Mr Mabusa: resident and shop owner in Piesang River, member of Homeless People's Federation, 19.11.98.

Majayiya Shaqa: elderly resident of Piesang River, member of Homeless People's Federation, 19.11.98.

Betina Mbambo: elderly resident of Piesang River, member of Homeless People's Federation, 19.11.98.

Juliet Gumede: elderly resident of Piesang River, member of Homeless People's Federation, 19.11.98.

Mr and Mrs Gumede: elderly residents of Piesang River, members of Homeless People's Federation, 19.11.98.

Built Environment Support Group (BESG)

Norah Walker: previously with the Built Environment Support Group (BESG), currently Director of DAG (Cape Town), 14.1.99.

Heather Maxwell: previously with the Built Environment Support Group (BESG), currently with the Cato Manor Development Association (CDMA), 20.11.98.

KANANA (SOUTHERN JOHANNESBURG)

Local Government:

Ace Mataung: Ward Councillor for Kanana Phase 2 (this was not a separate interview – he was present during the interview with the Independent People's Committee), 1.12.98.

Maretha Jordaan: Manager: Urbanisation and Development, Lekoa Vaal Metropolitan Council, 4.12.98.

Consultant to Local Government:

Bruce Welchman: Project Manager, Civemech, 4.1.99.

Jon Busser: Town Planner, Urban Dynamics, consultant for the Kanana housing subsidy investment (infrastructure and tenure), 12.1.99

People's Dialogue:

Vusi Ntuntsha: People's Dialogue Johannesburg, 30.7.98.

Joel Bolnick: People's Dialogue, Cape Town, 2.6.98.

Homeless People's Federation:

Agrenette Madwai: Regional Land Convenor, organiser and resident of the nearby land invasion Agrenette Hills (named after her), 2.12.98, 4.12.98.

A group interview has conducted with the following members of the Homeless People's Federation, 1.12.98:

Jacob Diamond: Regional Technician for the Homeless People's Federation (also secretary of the Independent People's Committee), resident of Kanana Phase 2.

Elizabeth Ramaesa: responsible for catering at the Kanana BIT-Centre.

Paulina Sikonjelo: Savings Scheme Collector.

Martha Molefi: Bookkeeper for the Kanana BIT-Centre.

Petrus Madona: Store Man/Caretaker of the Kanana BIT-Centre.

Agrenette Madwai: Regional Land Convenor, resident of the nearby informal settlement Agrenette Hills.

Rose Radebe: Regional Housing Schemes Convenor, resident of the nearby informal settlement Agrenette Hills.

Independent People's Committee:

Jan Maduna: Chairperson of the Independent People's Committee of Kanana Phase 2, and Community Liaison Officer for the housing subsidy investment project, 1.12.98.

Jacob Diamond: Secretary of the Independent People's Committee of Kanana Phase 2 (also regional technician of the Homeless People's Federation), 1.12.98.

Local ANC structures:

Daniel Mokoena: Secretary of the ANC Youth League, 4.12.98.

Esther Motloung: ANC Women's League – responsible for women's complaints (also a Homeless People's Federation member), 4.12.98.

Private developer:

The owner of Vusani Amadolopa Emerging Contractors (private developer with show house in Kanana Phase 1), 2.12.98.

Index

Alphabetical order is letter-by-letter. Page references in italic refer to illustrative material. SA refers to South Africa.